THOU SHALT KEEP THEM

Thou Shalt Keep Them

A Biblical Theology of the Perfect Preservation of Scripture

Kent Brandenburg, *Editor*

Pillar & Ground Publishing   El Sobrante, California

Thou Shalt Keep Them
Kent Brandenburg, *Editor*

Published by
Pillar & Ground Publishing
4905 Appian Way
El Sobrante, CA 94803
510-223-8721
www.pillarandground.org

Design and production
Dylan and Leah Saunders
Saberdesign
www.saberdesign.us
sales@saberdesign.us
Cover Illustration: Dylan Saunders

Copyright ©2003, 2007 Pillar & Ground Publishing

Notice of rights
All rights reserved. No part of this book may be reproduced, stored in a retrieval system, or transmitted in any form or by any means electronic, mechanical, photocopying, recording or otherwise, without the prior written permission of the publisher.

Library of Congress Control Number: 2003109684

International Standard Book Number (ISBN)
0-9743817-0-5

Printed in the United States of America
Revised Edition, 2007
1st Printing, 2003

Acknowledgements

The authors would like to thank Thomas Ross (B.A., University of California, Berkeley, English; M. A., Fairhaven Baptist College, Bible) for his assistance in editing the book, primarily in grammar and style, but also with a fine eye for logical consistency and exegetical accuracy. We also express our gratitude for some additional proofreading and other auxiliary work among the church members of our congregations. As you read this, you know who you are, and again we say thanks. Our churches enthusiastically encouraged us to use our time and energy until completion. We would also like to thank our wives and families for assisting us in a very personal way with their expressions of love and cooperation. Most of all we want to thank the God Who saved us, loves us, and enables us by His grace to serve Him.

Cover Image

This Hebrew text, dating from the 17th or 18th century, was scanned from a scroll that was found in a synagogue in Europe. It represents the kind of hand copying that had been done throughout the history of the Old Testament text, except that God's people also copied the text with the vowel points. This text was used for purely decorative purposes. Some texts in history were copied without the vowel points, but the position of Scripture and this book is that the Old Testament was originally written with consonants and vowels (the points).

Contents

Acknowledgments 5

Contents 6

Definitions and Abbreviations 9

Hebrew/Greek Transliteration Key 16

Preface 19
    Gary Webb

Introduction 21
    Kent Brandenburg

SECTION ONE – PASSAGES ON DIVINE PRESERVATION

Chapter One – The Permanent Preservation of God's Words, Psalm 12:6,7 29
    Thomas M. Strouse

Chapter Two – Every Word, Matthew 4:4 35
    Thomas M. Strouse

Chapter Three – Not One Jot or One Tittle, Matthew 5:17,18 41
    Gary Webb

Chapter Four – The Lord Jesus Christ and the Received Bible, John 17:8 51
    Thomas M. Strouse

Chapter Five – My Words Shall Not Pass Away, Matthew 24:35 59
    Kent Brandenburg

Chapter Six – Inspiration Implies Preservation, 2 Timothy 3:15-17 65
    Charles Nichols

Chapter Seven – God's Promise of Preservation as Seen in 1 Peter 1:23-25 69
    Gary La More

Chapter Eight – The Perfect Passive: "It is Written" 75
    David Sutton

SECTION TWO – PASSAGES ON AVAILABILITY

Chapter Nine – It Is Not Hidden, Neither Is It Far Off, ... 85
    Deuteronomy 30:11-14
    Kent Brandenburg

Chapter Ten – Be Mindful of the Words, 2 Peter 3:2 and Jude 17 91
    Gary La More

SECTION THREE – GOD'S METHOD OF PRESERVATION

Chapter Eleven – Israel, the Means of Preservation in the Old Testament: 97
Nâtsar (נָצַר) and Shâmar (שָׁמַר)
Kent Brandenburg

Chapter Twelve – Ekklāsia: The Congregation of the Lord in the 109
New Testament Tāreō (τηρέω)
Thomas M. Strouse

Chapter Thirteen – The Church's Part in Biblical Preservation, 1 Timothy 3:15 ... 117
Charles Nichols

Chapter Fourteen – Stewards of the Mysteries of God, 1 Corinthians 4:1,2 123
Gary La More

SECTION FOUR – PASSAGES ON THE REALITY OF TEXTUAL ATTACK

Chapter Fifteen – First Century Textual Attack, ... 131
2 Peter 3:15-17 and 2 Thessalonians 2:2
Kent Brandenburg

SECTION FIVE – THE STANDARD OF PERFECTION: SEVERAL PASSAGES AS EXAMPLES OF DOCTRINES CHANGED AND/OR PERVERTED BY TEXTUAL ALTERATIONS

Chapter Sixteen – Pure Words of God: Passages Which Manifest the 139
Standard of Perfect Purity for the Bible
Thomas Corkish

Chapter Seventeen – Old Testament Passages as Examples of 153
Doctrines Changed by Textual Alterations
Thomas M. Strouse

Chapter Eighteen – New Testament Passages as Examples of 165
Doctrines Changed by Textual Alterations
Gary Webb and David Sutton

SECTION SIX – OTHER PERTINENT EXEGESIS FOR EVERY WORD PRESERVATION

Chapter Nineteen – Test of Canonicity as Applied to Words 197
Kent Brandenburg

SECTION SEVEN – THE DOCTRINE OF PRESERVATION AS IT RELATES TO THE DOCTRINE OF SEPARATION

Chapter Twenty – Separation over the Veritable Words of God, ... 209
1 and 2 Timothy, with Special Attention Given to 2 Timothy 2:11-26
Thomas Corkish

Chapter Twenty-One – Who Is a Heretic over Preservation of Scripture? 221
Kent Brandenburg

ADDENDA

Addendum A – God's Providential Preservation of Scriptures 229
Gary La More

Addendum B – The Translation Model Predicted by Scripture 237
Thomas M. Strouse

Addendum C – The Superiority of the Fideistic Approach to 259
Preservation of Scripture
Kent Brandenburg

SELECT BIBLIOGRAPHY

Critical Text
Books 267
Articles 269

Majority Text
Books 270
Articles 270

Textus Receptus
Books 270
Articles 272
Commentaries, Grammars, and Other Resources 272

Scripture and Topical Index 276
Bio of Authors 313

Definitions and Abbreviations

Definitions

Active–the voice of a verb, either Hebrew, Greek, or English, which describes the subject as causing the action.
Agrapha–literally "not written"; writings not part of God's inspiration.
Aleph (א)–see *Sinaiticus*.
Alexandrian Text–the very few but old manuscripts of the Greek New Testament that originated in Alexandria, Egypt. They include *Codex Sinaiticus* (now in the British Library), *Codex Vaticanus* (now in the Vatican Library), and some papyri manuscripts. These copies essentially form the basis of what is known as the "Critical Text," the "Westcott and Hort Greek Text," or the "Nestle-Aland Greek Text" of the New Testament. There are over 5,000 differences (7% of the whole) between the Alexandrian Text and the *Textus Receptus* (However, there is no real unified Alexandrian Text, despite this terminology. Aleph and B differ in thousands of places. The Egyptian MSS do not form a unified text type as the *TR* MSS do.).
Aorist–the tense of a Greek verb expressing action as attained. In the indicative mood, the aorist also expresses completed action in past time.
Apographa–literally "from the written"; hand copies made of the original manuscripts and of the copies of those manuscripts.
Autographa–the original manuscripts of the Bible; the original Hebrew, Aramaic, and Greek manuscripts in the original handwriting of the human authors on the original materials.
B–see *Vaticanus*.
Biblical Criticism–a vain philosophy and methodology that approaches the Bible from a perspective of atheistic reasoning. This discipline was invented through the anti-supernaturalism of 19th century German Rationalism and includes textual criticism. As it relates to textual criticism, this rationalistic judgment of the Bible is ongoing as a means of determining which words are closest to those of the original manuscripts. The criteria for weighing the manuscripts are the same as those used in the criticism of ancient secular literature.
Byzantine Text–the manuscripts of the New Testament that multiplied in the area of the Eastern Roman or Byzantine Empire where the Apostle Paul started most of his churches. A majority of the manuscripts were found here because the churches of this area were keeping them. These manuscripts were disseminated, read, preached, and studied, so more copies were used, and they wore out faster. As a manuscript wore out, it was respectfully disposed of after being replaced by a newer copy, explaining why these copies are of a later date than the Alexandrian manuscripts. The *Textus Receptus* comes from the Byzantine Text.

Canonical–a book or letter that has passed the tests required for Israel and then the churches to have accepted it as a part of inspired Writ.

Church–a local, organized assembly of New Testament, immersed believers, with two offices, pastor and deacons, practicing baptism and the Lord's Table, and actively engaged in carrying out the Great Commission of the Lord Jesus Christ.

Codex–a manuscript that was sewn together into book form.

Critical Text–the Greek text of the New Testament that is the product of late 19th century textual criticism (a general description for everything from Westcott and Hort–1881 to the United Bible Society Fourth Edition); the New Testament text behind almost every modern Bible version.

Dynamic Equivalence–a translation philosophy that emphasizes the communication of the message or substance of the words of the original language rather than a literal word-for-word rendering.

Eclectic Text–a description of a text formed from varied manuscripts of potentially different text types that is based upon the choosing of a person or group in accordance with his or its subjective criteria.

Evangelical–a general term for those who preach salvation by grace through faith alone, primarily used, however, to describe the non-separatist variety of this persuasion. The broad use of the term includes people with wide and diverse definitions of grace and faith.

Fundamentalism–a continuing interdenominational movement which began in the early 20th century in the United States in response to growing institutional liberalism. It stressed the need for a literal understanding and practice of Scripture, including the doctrine of separation.

Future–the tense of a Greek verb expressing action in future time, usually aoristic or punctiliar action in the future.

Hapax Legomena–Latin for "only once said," referring to a word that is used only once in either the Old or New Testament text. Study of one of these words involves an examination of its usage in extra-Scriptural literature, earlier translations, such as the *LXX*, and to its immediate Biblical context.

Higher Criticism–a division of Biblical Criticism which draws conclusions about the date, place, authorship, and other facets of Scriptural books on the basis of humanistic, evolutionary theories.

Hiphil–a form of a Hebrew verb stem in the Old Testament that often communicates active cause.

Historical Criticism–the rationalistic science which attempts to determine the authorship, date, and history behind books of the Bible from atheistic presuppositions.

Hithpael–a form of a Hebrew verb stem in the Old Testament that often communicates an intensive reflexive.

Hophal–a form of a Hebrew verb stem in the Old Testament that often communicates passive cause.

Imperative–mood of a Greek verb that expresses action volitionally possible dependent upon the response of the recipient of the action; better known in English as a command.

Imperfect–Hebrew verb form expressing a state of unfinished action; including either incipient incomplete action or frequentative incomplete action. The Greek imperfect is the tense of a verb with continuous action in past time.

Indicative–mood of a Greek verb that expresses any real action.

Infallibility–the quality of not being capable of error; as applied to Scripture, it is to say that in teaching, authority, word order, the Bible is not capable of error.

Inerrancy–the quality of having no errors; usually applied to the original manuscripts of Scripture; however, based on Scriptural promises of preservation, it also characterizes the preserved text of Scripture.

Inspiration–the acts whereby God produced on earth without error every writing (letters, words, and order of letters and words) of Scripture by means of the Holy Spirit's movement upon human instruments.

Ipsissima Verba–Latin for the "very words" of Christ, which the Gospels record.

Ipsissima Vox–Latin for the "very voice" of Christ.

Itala Version–A version of the New Testament translated by Bible believing churches in the alpine valleys of Northern Italy from the *TR* by 157 A.D.

King James Only–a broad title for any individuals and institutions that read, study, preach, and use only the King James Version as an English translation. Some employ it to associate those who believe in the superiority of the KJV with supporters of double inspiration or English-only preservation.

Latin Vulgate–Jerome's Latin translation of the Bible, used by Roman Catholicism for most of its history (completed circa AD 400).

Locus Classicus–Latin for "classical source" or "classic location;" the passage that is most commonly cited to teach or defend a certain doctrine or position.

LXX (Septuagint)–translation of the Old Testament from Hebrew to Greek allegedly completed by seventy or seventy-two scholars, centuries before the life of Christ.

Majority Text–terminology generally synonymous with the Received Text in that a vast majority of extant manuscripts support the Received Text. Two modern published texts are also called The Majority Text, one edited by Arthur Farstad and Zane Hodges (1985) and the other by Maurice Robinson and William Pierpont (1991). These two published editions of the Greek New Testament result from the same rationalistic philosophy as the Critical Text, the premise that the Word of God has been lost, and, therefore, must be restored, in this case, by means of counting manuscripts.

Manuscripts–written texts, usually the original, but also, the portions of or full text copied by hand from either the original or from copies of the original. Manuscripts contrast with printed editions in that they are hand written.

Masoretic Text–the traditional Old Testament Hebrew text preserved by Old Testament Israel and copied by Jewish scribes until the invention of the printing press as a Divine means of preserving His Word; the Old Testament text behind the King James Version is the Ben Chayyim MT (1524, 52nd ed. of the Rabbinic Bible), the OT *Textus Receptus*, while modern versions use a different Ben Asher MT.

Middle–the voice of a Greek verb that describes the subject as participating in the results of the action.

Miniscule–a particular style of handwriting that used lower case letters, usually in a "cursive." Scribes began writing in this style just before the first millennium A.D. The extant *TR* manuscripts are mainly miniscule.

Modernism–a perspective of the Bible that subjects it to modern thought or newness, rejects a grammatical, historical explanation of Scripture, and rejects the major doctrines of the Bible, and supernaturalism in general. Most accept an early to middle 19th century origin for modernism, beginning in German Universities and then spreading to English and American higher education.

Mood–the expression of a Greek verb or verbal that is necessary to define its relation to reality.

Neo-evangelicalism–a continuing interdenominational movement which began in the middle of the 20th century in the United States and repudiated personal and ecclesiastical separation to cooperate with apostates and worldly professing believers.

Niphal–a form of a Hebrew verb stem in the Old Testament that often communicates a simple passive.

Number–in all languages, one of the determinations of the relation of the speaker to the assertion contained in the verb, the other being person. Singular–one; Plural–two or more.

Optative–mood of a Greek verb that expresses action subjectively possible.

Original Languages–the languages in which the Bible was originally written, that is, ancient Hebrew, Greek, and Aramaic.

Original Manuscripts–the writings and the materials, which God initially gave the Word of God to men, in contrast to copies.

Papyrus–a kind of reed in Egypt that was woven into a type of paper used to write ancient copies of Scripture.

Para-church–an organization outside of a New Testament church, such as a college, university, mission board, or publisher, that is not a ministry of or under the authority of a particular church.

Passive–the voice of a verb, either Hebrew, Greek, or English, which describes the subject as receiving the action.

Patristics–men from early Christendom whose writings have survived; usually divided into those who wrote before and after the Council of Nicea in AD 325. Most of the patristics believed in false doctrine, including baptismal regeneration. They cite the *TR* centuries before the composition of either *B* or א (Aleph).

Perfect–Hebrew verb form expressing a state of finished action. The Greek perfect is the tense of a verb which often expresses completed action of which the results continue into the present.

Person–in all languages, one of the determinations of the relation of the speaker to the assertion contained in the verb, the other being number. First Person–I, we, my, our; Second Person–you, thou, ye, thee, thy, thine, your; Third Person – he, she, it, its, they, her, hers, his, their, theirs.

Piel–a form of a Hebrew verb stem in the Old Testament that often communicates an intensive active.

Plenary–the whole, the sum total of the words of Scripture.

Present–the tense of a Greek verb with continuous, durative, or progressive action. In the indicative mood, the present also expresses continuous action in present time.

Preservation–complete, inerrant protection and general accessibility of every writing (vowels and consonants, words, the order of letters and words) of the Bible, the sixty-six books of the Old and New Testaments, for every generation of believers.

Preservationist–a New Testament church member who assists in the human side of preserving all of the Words of Scripture, both Old and New Testaments, which God has kept perfectly through and in OT Israel and NT churches since they were originally written.

Pual–a form of a Hebrew verb stem in the Old Testament that often communicates an intensive passive.

Qal–a form of a Hebrew verb stem in the Old Testament that often communicates a simple active.

Quelle–hypothetical "sayings" source higher critics have hypothesized to explain similarities in the Gospels.

Sinaiticus–(Aleph, א); an ancient manuscript of the New Testament found by Frederic Tischendorf in 1844 in a waste basket of the Greek Orthodox Convent of St. Catherine located at Mount Sinai, then published nearly 20 years later.

Static Equivalence–a translation philosophy that is concerned with a literal rendering of the Words of the original language of Scripture into a receptor language.

Subjunctive–mood of a Greek verb that expresses action objectively possible.

Syriac Peshitta–a translation of the New Testament into Syrian from the *TR* in 150 AD by the Bible-believing churches around Antioch where believers were first called Christians. *Peshitta* is a Syrian word meaning "common," a word parallel with the term "Received Text."

Tense–The aspect of a Greek verb which expresses kind and time of action, mainly kind.

Text Type–a categorization of manuscripts of Scripture by geography, history, time, and readings.

Textual Criticism–a division of Biblical criticism in which men judge extant copies of the text of Scripture and attempt to reconstruct the presumably lost readings of the original manuscripts.

Textus Receptus–Latin phrase meaning "Received Text," used to describe the Greek text of the New Testament received and preserved by the churches. The editions of Scrivener printed in 1881 and thereafter represent the exact Greek text underlying the King James Version of the Bible and the preserved *autographa*.

Traditional Text–the canonical Words that were received by the orthodox churches; another name for the Hebrew MT and the Greek *TR*.

Uncial–a particular style of handwriting in large, unconnected capital Greek letters which was used in a few hundred of the ancient manuscripts of the New Testament.

Variant Reading–a reading of Scripture that varies or differs from the text received and kept by OT Israel and NT churches.

Vaticanus–(*B*), an ancient manuscript of the New Testament in the Vatican library that was located and copied there by Frederic Tischendorf, then published in 1867.

Verbal–every word; the individual Words of the Bible.

Voice–property of a verb or verbal that indicates how the subject is related to the action.

Waldenses–Bible believing, separatist people of Northern Italy, southern France, and Switzerland who used translations of the Bible from the Received Text from the second century to the Reformation.

Abbreviations

1. General

1cp=first person common plural
3cp=third person common plural
1ms=first person masculine singular
2ms=second person masculine singular
3ms=third person masculine singular
1mp=first person masculine plural
2mp=second person masculine plural
3mp=third person masculine plural
2fs=second person feminine singular
3fs=third person feminine singular
Aleph=*Codex Sinaiticus* (א)
Adj.=adjective
Aor.=aorist tense
Aram.=Aramaic
cf.=confer; compare
CT=Critical Text
DSS=Dead Sea Scrolls
ff.=following
Fut.=future tense

Gr.=Greek
Heb.=Hebrew
Indic.=indicative mood
Imper.=imperative mood
Impf.=imperfect tense
LXX=Septuagint
MS(S)=Manuscript(s)
MT=Masoretic Text
NT=New Testament
Opt.=optative mood
OT=Old Testament
Part.=participle
Perf.=perfect tense
p.=page
pp.=pages
Pres.=present tense
Q=Quelle
Subj.=subjunctive mood
TR= Textus Receptus
vide="see"
v.=verse
vv.=verses

2. Translations

AV (KJB or KJV): Authorized Version, King James Version
ASV: American Standard Version
JB: Jerusalem Bible
KJB (AV or KJV): King James Bible
LB: Living Bible
NASV: New American Standard Version
NEB: New English Bible
NIV: New International Version
NKJV: New King James Version
RSV: Revised Standard Version
RV: Revised Version
TEV: Today's English Version

Hebrew/Greek Transliteration Key

English transliterations are provided in order to pronounce properly the Hebrew/Greek words. Various transliteration schemes exist, including certain standard methods. This plan intends to make the words the easiest to articulate. This key will help to get an exact pronunciation. At the far left is the Greek or Hebrew letter, then the transliteration in " " marks, followed by an example of how it sounds.

Greek

α – "a" in c<u>a</u>t
β – "b" in <u>b</u>at
γ – "g" in <u>g</u>ate
δ – "d" in <u>d</u>og
ε – "e" in <u>e</u>gg
ζ – "z" in <u>z</u>oo
η – "ā" in l<u>a</u>te
θ – "th" in <u>th</u>ree
ι – "i" in f<u>i</u>n
κ – "k" in <u>k</u>ill
λ – "l" in <u>l</u>ose
μ – "m" in <u>m</u>an
ν – "n" in <u>n</u>one
ξ – "x" in e<u>x</u>tra
ο – "o" in c<u>o</u>llar

π – "p" in <u>p</u>encil
ρ – "r" in <u>r</u>un
ῥ – "rh" sounding like <u>hr</u>
σ, ς – "s" in <u>s</u>it
τ – "t" in <u>t</u>ie
υ – "u" in d<u>u</u>de
αυ – "au" in cr<u>ow</u>d
ει – "ei" in bl<u>i</u>nd
ευ – "eu" in f<u>eu</u>d
ου – "ou" in f<u>oo</u>d
υι – "ui" in s<u>ui</u>te
φ – "f" in <u>f</u>ine
χ – "ch" in <u>ch</u>aracter
ω – "ō" in t<u>o</u>e
ʽ – "h" in <u>h</u>ello

Hebrew

Consonants
- א – " ' " (silent)
- בּ ב – "b" in <u>b</u>oy; "v" in <u>v</u>ery
- גּ ג – "g" in <u>g</u>o; "gh" in <u>gh</u>ost
- דּ ד – "d" in <u>d</u>ay; "th" in <u>th</u>em
- ה – "h" in <u>h</u>at
- ו – "w" in <u>w</u>ay
- ז – "z" in <u>z</u>eal
- ח – "ch" in <u>ch</u>aracter
- ט – "t" in <u>t</u>oy
- י – "y" in <u>y</u>et
- כּ כ – "k" in <u>k</u>eep
- ל – "l" in <u>l</u>et
- מ ם – "m" in <u>m</u>et
- נ ן – "n" in <u>n</u>et
- ס – "s" in <u>s</u>et
- ע – " ' " (silent)
- פּ פ – "p" in <u>p</u>et; "ph" in <u>ph</u>ilos
- צ ץ – "ts" in hi<u>ts</u>
- ק – "q" in oblique
- ר – "r" in <u>r</u>un
- שׂ – "s" in <u>s</u>o
- שׁ – "sh" in <u>sh</u>ell
- תּ ת – "t" in <u>t</u>oy; "th" in <u>th</u>ink

Vowels (called "points")
- ַ – "a" in h<u>a</u>t
- ָ – "â" in f<u>a</u>ther
- ֱ – "ĕ" in syst<u>e</u>m
- ֶ – "e" in m<u>e</u>t
- ֵ – "ā" in sw<u>ay</u>
- ֵי – "ē" s<u>ee</u>m
- ֶי – "ē" sc<u>e</u>ne
- ַי – "ā" in sw<u>ay</u>
- ָי – "â" in f<u>a</u>ther
- ִ – "ĭ" in p<u>i</u>n
- ֻ – "ū" in p<u>u</u>t
- ֹ – "ō" in r<u>o</u>ll
- וֹ – "ō" in r<u>o</u>ll
- וּ – "ū" in tr<u>u</u>e
- ְ ֱ ֲ ֳ – "ĕ" in governm<u>e</u>nt

Preface
Gary Webb

> "A Fundamentalist Maintains an
> Immovable Allegiance to the Inerrant,
> Infallible, and Verbally Inspired Bible.
> A Fundamentalist Believes that
> Whatever the Bible Says Is So.
> A Fundamentalist Judges All Things by the
> Bible and Is Judged Only by the Bible."[1]

A true fundamentalist is a Biblicist. When considering any matter he asks, "What does the Bible say?" When he finds the answer to that question through the study of Scripture, he considers the matter settled. No other authority can override the Bible for the Bible stands as the exact, verbal record of the mind and will of God. Therefore, an "immovable allegiance to the . . . Bible" defines and distinguishes the fundamentalist from all other divisions of professing Christianity.

Because Fundamentalism has this character, conflict has marked its entire history. Having arisen as a movement at the beginning of the twentieth century when Modernism and Liberalism denied the Divine nature of Biblical revelation and questioned its scientific and historical accuracy, fundamentalists met this challenge by expounding and demonstrating the doctrine of the inerrancy and infallibility of the Scriptures. Rather than retreat from the Scriptures or make appeals to human authorities, fundamentalists went to the Scriptures themselves to defend the Scriptures. When any new challenge or denial arose to the core or "fundamental" doctrines of the Christian faith, fundamentalists responded with "Thus saith the Lord," and therefore Fundamentalism kept its Biblical character.

The battle for the authority of Scripture continues today in the debate over the text of Scripture as it was given to man in the Hebrew, Aramaic, and Greek languages. Most Christian schools of higher learning have adopted the modern model of textual (lower) criticism that follows a rationalistic approach to determining the Words of Scripture. Rather than turning to the Scriptures to find a Biblical model, many fundamentalist colleges, universities, and seminaries have simply followed this same approach. They characteristically defend their allegiance to this method of textual criticism, not by expounding the Scriptures, but with textual "evidence" and with appeals to the statements of "respected" men of the past. Indeed, so committed are some to this approach

---

[1] These three statements are exact quotations from the "We Believe" Resolutions of the World Congress of Fundamentalists that met in Edinburgh, Scotland in 1976.

that they criticize those men who come to this issue with "theological presuppositions" derived from the Word of God.[2] This criticism springs from their pronounced belief that the Bible does not teach the perfect preservation of the text of Scripture, nor does it state how God expected to preserve His Words.[3]

The great need for Christians and Fundamentalists then is to once again ask the question, "What does the Bible say?" The teaching of the Bible must determine our approach to the textual issue and the debate over Bible versions. This book expounds Bible passages and clearly sets forth the Bible doctrine of the verbal preservation of Scripture. This doctrine leads men to adopt the "King James Only" position in the textual/version debate. In setting forth this doctrine, this book will also refute the denials of those who say that we have no Biblical statements on the preservation of the text of Scripture.

The Bible stands as the bedrock foundation for Christianity. We dare not have a Bible whose very Words are determined by men. God has spoken on this issue. Therefore this book will let Him speak by expositing His Word. May fundamentalists return to the position of judging all things by the Bible and of recognizing the Bible alone as the authoritative Judge of all things.

---

[2]Samuel Schnaiter, in critiquing *The Identity of the New Testament Text* by Wilbur Pickering, makes the following criticism of Pickering: "Finally, although Pickering has avoided an excessive reliance on theological presuppositions in his presentation, it is nevertheless clear that a theological presupposition essentially undergirds his entire purpose." This criticism is akin to criticizing the creation scientist for judging the fossil record on the basis of "theological presuppositions" derived from a study of Genesis. The *Biblical Viewpoint*, "Focus on Revelation", Vol. XVI, No. 1, April 1982, Bob Jones University, "Textual Criticism and the Modern English Version Controversy," pp. 68-74, quote from page 72.

[3]"Third, and most damaging, not only does no verse in Scripture explain how God will preserve His Word, but there is no statement in Scripture from which one can establish the doctrine of the preservation of the text of Scripture." W. E. Glenny, *The Bible Version Debate*, ed. Michael Grisanti (Minneapolis, MN: Central Baptist Theological Seminary, 1997) p. 95.

Introduction
Kent Brandenburg

"Have ye not read this Scripture?" The Lord Jesus Christ repeatedly asks this question or a similar one of the religious leaders of His day (Matthew 12:3,5; 19:4; 22:31; Mark 12:10, 26; Luke 6:3). The Lord almost exclusively quoted, read, and exposed Scripture as the basis of His authority on whatever doctrine or practice He was treating. Luke 24:27 is a wonderful example of this, when it says, "And beginning at Moses and all the prophets, he expounded unto them in all the scriptures the things concerning himself." Who would have known how to speak better from personal perspective on the subject of Himself, than the Lord Jesus Christ Himself? Yet He did not. Instead, He "expounded unto them in all the scriptures the things concerning himself." When the Lord did spiritual warfare directly with Satan in Matthew 4, He used Scripture alone to make His points against the prince of darkness. The Sermon on the Mount (Matthew 5-7) was a presentation that, in a major way, was intended to get the audience of the Lord's day back into the already revealed and written text of the Old Testament, and out of the fabrications and ruminations of the rabbis and rabbinical writing. This consistent manner of operation by the Lord was why the audience that heard Him said that "He taught as one having authority" (Matthew 7:29). When there is a conflict doctrinally or practically, the followers of the Lord will rely on His Word as the authority for the solution.

Much of the debate over the Bible texts and versions, from whatever position, has raged without authority. Using a modern colloquialism, this would be "Much heat with very little light." There can be no conclusion to a doctrinal controversy where opposing views utilize man's credentials, words, and reasoning as the basis for their arguments. These conflicts are reduced to a form of verbal mud wrestling. It might be entertaining to some, but much of what transpires is some slipping and sliding and getting dirty on both sides. Even though there have been books so far that have included and also depended on Scripture for conclusions on this issue, there are few or none that have relied exclusively upon the exposition of Scripture to arrive at their positions. This book, however, by God's grace, will do so.

Recently a pamphlet[4] was published which recorded selected excerpts from respected men of various denominations to support a position contrary to Scripture on the issue of the preservation of God's Word. These oracles of men were supposed to stand as weighty evidence for a less than Biblical view. 1 Peter 4:11 says, however, that "If any man speak, let him speak as the oracles of God . . . that God in all things may be glorified through Jesus Christ." Such oracles of men do not glorify God. God is glorified when men speak

---

[4]Mark Minnick "Trusted Voices On Translations" (Greenville: Mount Calvary Baptist Church, 2001).

as the oracles of God. The oracles of men only glorify men. Men become the standard for faith and practice. Many may participate in the praise of men, but this does not make it any less worthless. Those professing to be men of God, especially, should take seriously the proper use of a verbal giftedness. Without doing so, even the most Godly men can become nothing more than sounding brass and tinkling cymbals (1 Corinthians 13:1). On top of all this, authority shifts, sadly, from God to man. For anyone this is egregious; particularly when one does so in a position of leadership.

Little is gained through human documentation. Finding an old quotation from an out-of-print book is only authoritative insofar as it properly represents Scripture. So much of what functions as documentation also depends on craftily pulling a quotation from its context, either the context of the book itself or the context of history. In many cases, such non-contextual quotations are intended well, yet thoroughly skewed by the author's predisposition. These quotes are not inspired. None of them are dependable. All of them must be brought under the intense scrutiny of God's Word. At best, old printed material can stand as testimony of a historical theology. Even as that, it is still not entirely trustworthy. After all, God did not promise the preservation of man's words, only of His own.

The Lord's sheep hear His voice and follow Him (John 10:27). The sheep need the voice of the Lord for direction in every matter of life. The Bible is the only authority for faith and practice (2 Timothy 3:16,17). With this truth in mind, this book, through the combined expositions of many of the passages containing instruction concerning the preservation of Scripture, will yield God's mind on this issue. In so doing, the book will "speak with authority," the authority of God from His Word.

Technically, this whole book is a Biblical theology of the doctrine of preservation. Each author, using proper hermeneutics ("rightly dividing," 2 Timothy 2:15), will unleash the Bible to speak for itself on preservation, therefore having God Himself speak on this doctrine. For this to occur, each passage will be explained in its context. This means that pre, internal, and following context will be considered, as well as the context of the whole of each book. The meaning of the text in its context will always be given top priority. Full regard will be given to the meaning of the words, in both definition and usage. In so doing, each chapter will present how people would have understood the passages as they were given in their day. Parallel passages will be relied upon to shed further light, comparing Scripture with Scripture. When appropriate, the tense, mood, voice, person, and gender of verbs will be analyzed, along with the case usages of nouns and pronouns. All aspects of grammar and history will be examined in order to obtain the accurate interpretation, knowing that God has been clear in His Word.

Application and argument will only come after there is a proper understanding of the text. Extreme care will be given to ensure that conclusions will be drawn from

---

[5]"The preservation of the Word of God is perfectly accomplished by God in Heaven (Psm. 119:89). The preservation of God's Word on earth has been committed to people . . . God anticipated the possibility of failure on man's part in accurately preserving the autographs." Larry Oats, *Syllabus for Workshop IV*, "KJV Controversy: Let's Talk Portion. Presentations and Responses," *National Leadership Conference,*

within the parameters of the passage. With that prudence will also come boldness. All Scripture is profitable for doctrine (2 Timothy 3:16), so the authors will display what the Scriptures teach. God has not given the spirit of fear (2 Timothy 1:7) in the unashamed proclamation of His truth; what is worthy of belief is worthy of declaration. Scriptural exposition will unfold Scripture, but when properly applied, it will expose men as well. A Scriptural model of preaching and teaching does not veer from naming those that have publicly violated one of God's prescribed points of doctrine or behavior (cf. 1 Timothy 1:20; 2 Timothy 4:10).

Most professing Bible-believers express belief in the preservation of Scripture. However, a wide range of meanings are applied to the term "preservation." Some would say that all the Words are preserved perfectly in heaven alone.[5] Others profess that all the Words exist on earth, even if some of them are still buried near a future archaeological dig. Others would say that the Scriptures make no promise of the preservation of Words, only of the Word as a whole. Some would say that the doctrines are preserved, not the Words themselves. The position taken by the men writing this book is that Scripture teaches God has preserved every and all of His Words to the very letter, and these Words are available to every generation. This is verbal, plenary preservation. These Words are preserved in the Hebrew and Aramaic Old Testament and the Greek New Testament. The authors further contend that the only text that fulfills the Scriptural model is the one behind the King James Version of the Bible.

This basic position on preservation will essentially derive its authority from the passages in the first section of the book, the passages on preservation. These passages prove Divine, perfect preservation of the Bible. The doctrine of availability of Scripture will derive its authority from the passages of the second section. Availability is integral to a Scriptural position on preservation. Often in the preservation debate, those advocating unscriptural opinions will pronounce the unfounded declaration that "the Bible nowhere says how it would be preserved." This is not only untrue, but extraordinarily so. The Bible is the record of the stewardship of God's Words in His institution. The third section will exposit several passages that reveal how God would preserve every Word, that is, the method of preservation.

Vital in comprehending God's preservation is realizing the conflict with Satan over God's Word. The fourth segment will offer exposition of passages that predict the attack upon Scripture from the foundations of mankind and especially from the first century A. D. This point obliterates the "oldest is best" theory about superiority of manuscripts. The fifth section will illustrate the reality of this conflict by exposing the doctrines that are affected by an examination of the differences between the text behind the King James Version and that of the modern versions. This will unmask the "no doctrines are lost" falsehood. The sixth portion of the book will pick up other important and related

---

Calvary Baptist Church, Lansdale, PA, Feb. 27-Mar. 1, 1996. Larry Oats at the same *National Leadership Conference* said, "We know God could have preserved His Word, but history proved He did not." D. A. Waite, *Fundamentalist Distortions on Bible Versions* (Collingswood, NJ: The Bible For Today Press, 1999), p. 47. In the text Clinton Branine quotes Larry Oats.

teachings of Scripture that directly buttress the perfect preservation position. Passages on separation will be examined as applied to the Scriptural doctrine of preservation. Clear and accurate application will set forth God's will in the matter of separating over the preservation doctrine. Since the intention of the book is the exposition of Scripture, related material that is not clearly expositional will be included as a part of the addenda. These additional chapters are each vital for meeting the overall goal of the book.

The arena for truth in this age is the local church (1 Timothy 3:15). All of the resources given by God for the preservation of truth in our age were given to this institution. The authors all have their life's ministry in and through a church. All of them are pastors. God has promised to guard His teachings; however, those promises do not apply to para-church organizations. Those that would move truth outside of its God-ordained container do so at great peril. The authors of this volume come from varied educational backgrounds, but the years of weighing God's Words in the presence of the established witness of a New Testament congregation provide the common, uniting thread among them. In almost every instance, the stand on these truths brought a loss of sanction from the academic arenas from which they once came. The agreement among them on this doctrine does not come rubber-stamped by the sacral societies of this age.

After the Lord Jesus Christ asked the question, "Have ye not read this Scripture?" varied answers came from the religious leaders of His day. In Matthew 12, when He asked them twice, verse 14 reads, "Then the Pharisees went out, and held a council against him, how they might destroy him." This Pharisaic response to exposition of Scripture is not one to emulate. However, it is not unusual that one taking an unbiblical position would defend that position by attempting in some way to destroy the one that takes the authoritative viewpoint. Oftentimes today, this is accomplished through attacking the person rather than answering the argument (*ad hominem*). For someone who characteristically takes Scriptural stands, admitting that one's position has been unscriptural can be embarrassing. One might expect that someone of genuine faith would follow James' authoritative outline of the response to the presentation of the Word of God (James 1:19-21), " . . . swift to hear, slow to speak, slow to wrath." A proper reaction to God's Word is reception. True believers " . . . receive with meekness the engrafted word . . ." (James 1:21). It is not ironic that those that do not receive the Scriptural teaching on preservation are also not receptive to a perfect text of Scripture.

The issue of preservation is a Scriptural issue. It begins and ends with what the Bible says about it. This book will provide solid Biblical exposition for use in spiritual warfare. The truths of each text will hone the spiritual Sword for pulling down the strongholds in human reasoning. The expositions of Scripture will also be helpful for personal Bible study or devotional material. The design will make it unnecessary to finish the book in one sitting. Every chapter will stand on its own as a separate entity to be read in an available window of opportunity. For a pastor, it will be a valuable resource for study in preparation for sermons. For teachers, it will give additional aid in preparation for class. For anyone who confesses love for God and His Book, it will give ample evidence to defend the preservation of every Word that proceeds from the mouth of God (Matthew 4:4). After having read this book, the reader will be able to testify in answer to the Lord's question that began this introduction, "Yes, I have read the Scriptures."

SECTION ONE

Passages on Divine Preservation

CHAPTER ONE

The Permanent Preservation of God's Words
Psalm 12:6,7

Thomas M. Strouse

Introduction

Psalm 12 is a psalm of contrasts. It contrasts the Godly with the ungodly and the Words of the Lord with the words of men. The latter contrast provides the backdrop to one of the clearest promises in the OT of the preservation of God's Words. Although some dismiss or deny the declaration of the Lord that He will preserve His Words forever, a Hebrew exegesis of this Psalm will demonstrate unambiguously this proper understanding of verses 6-7 that God has indeed promised to preserve His Words (vv. 7-8 in Heb.) The KJB, in contradistinction to some modern versions,[6] gives this aforementioned rendering: "The words of the Lord are pure words: as silver tried in a furnace of earth, purified seven times. Thou shalt keep them, O Lord, thou shalt preserve them from this generation for ever."

Psalm 12

Title

The title[7] of this psalm reveals several important facts. The psalm was for the "choirmaster" (לַמְנַצֵּחַ, *laměnatstsāch*)[8] to be sung with the "eight stringed harps" (הַשְּׁמִינִית, *hashshěmēnēth*).[9] It was a "psalm" (מִזְמוֹר, *mizmōr*) that "David authored"

---

[6] For instance, the NIV reads "And the words of the Lord are flawless, like silver refined in a furnace of clay, purified seven times. O Lord, you will keep us safe and protect us from such people forever" (Psm. 12:6-7).

[7] The title of this psalm as well as others is part of the Masoretic text and should be considered part of the *autographa*.

[8] This word is found in the titles of fifty-five psalms as well as in Hab. 3:19.

[9] It may refer to the octave (cf. Psm. 6:1 [Heb.]).

(לְדָוִד, lĕthâwĕth).[10] David obviously lamented the evil words of his enemies, but the psalm's specific occasion is not revealed.

Structure

The structure of the psalm is asymmetric. This structure causes the focus to be on C., God's Promises (see box). David's lament carries the reader from the need for Divine help, because of the words of the ungodly, to a focus on the promises of God for deliverance, which include the permanent preservation of His Words, the antidote to the words of the ever-present wicked.

TITLE

A. The Recognition of the Need for Divine Help (v. 1)
B. The Threat of the Words of the Ungodly (v. 2-4)
C. God's Promises (v. 5)
B'. The Antidote of the Words of God (vv. 6-7)
A'. The Recognition of the Need for Divine Help (v. 8)

Summary of the Content of Psalm 12

A. The Recognition of the Need for Divine Help (v. 1)

David appealed to the Lord for "help" (הוֹשִׁיעָה, hōshē'âh),[11] fearing that the "godly man" (חָסִיד, kâsēth)[12] would come to an "end" (גָּמַר, gâmar) and "faithful men" (אֱמוּנִים, 'ĕmūnēm) would "vanish" (פַּסּוּ, phassū)[13] from mankind. The reference to the individual Godly man no doubt refers to David, and the "faithful men" refers to the larger community of believers, all of whom were on the brink of annihilation, or so the psalmist thought.[14] This apparent obliteration of the righteous was in contradistinction to the Lord's covenant promise for the remnant (cf. Gen. 12:1-3; Isa. 10:20).

B. The Threat of the Words of the Ungodly (vv. 2-4)

David acutely sensed the threat of the words of the ungodly around him. Using two different verbs יְדַבְּרוּ (yĕthabbĕrū, "they speak" [3x])[15] and אָמְרוּ ('âmĕrū, "said"), the wicked told "vanity" ("empty lies" שָׁוְא, shâwĕ')[16] with flattering lips (2x), a double heart, and a flattering tongue (2x). The psalmist recorded the claim of the wicked, who stated: "With our tongue will we prevail; our lips are our own: who is lord over us?" (v. 4). These wicked men asserted that they would "prevail" (גָּבַר, gâbbar)[17] and that they were autonomous. "Who is lord (אָדוֹן, 'thōn) over us?" suggests the rebellious attitude of those who said, "There is no God" (Psm. 14:1). The

---

[10]David is the predominant writer of the Psalter, having written at least seventy-three psalms (cf. Lk. 20:42).
[11]The verbal root יָשַׁע (yâsha) is behind the names Joshua, Jesus, and Hosanna.
[12]The consonants of this word relate to חֶסֶד (keseth) that refers to covenant love [of the Lord].
[13]This *hapax legomena* verb comes from פָּסַס (pâsas) and means to disappear.
[14]Elijah manifested this attitude of "solipsism" and was rebuked by the Lord (I Kings 19:14-18).
[15]This verb is translated "they speak"(2x) and "speaketh."
[16]This ms noun means worthless, empty speech.

"atheists" in this latter instance are those who rejected God's lordship (14:2, 4). David asserted or prayed that the Lord would "cut off" (יַכְרֵת, *yakĕrāth*) the braggarts he was facing. This Hiphil imperfect verb could be understood as an assertion "the Lord will cut off" or a prayer "may the Lord cut off."

C. God's Promises (v. 5)

The structure of the psalm focuses on the promises of God.[18] The Lord promised that, because "of the oppression of the poor," and "of the sighing of the needy," He would "arise and set him in safety from him that puffeth at him." Since the "poor" (עֲנִיִּים, *'ĕnĕyyēm*) were despoiled and the "needy" (אֶבְיוֹנִים, *'evyōnēm*) were groaning, the Lord made significant promises. "Now will I arise" (אָקוּם, *'âqūm*; cf. Isa. 33:10), the Lord promised, and set the psalmist "in safety" (בְּיֵשַׁע, *bĕyasha'*).[19] The Lord promised to arise (cf. Psm. 9:19) and intervene on the part of the faithful. His promise was to place him in safety, the very help for which the psalmist David asked (v. 1). The safety was physical deliverance from those that "puff at" (יָפִיחַ, *yâphēach*)[20] the author with manipulative and boastful words.

B'. The Antidote of God's Words (vv. 6-7)

The content of God's help was the assurance of His ever-present Words with promises of deliverance as an antidote to the words of the wicked. The psalmist reflected on the quality and endurance of the greatest tangible help that the Lord desires to give man – His perfect Words. The quality of the Lord's Words is likened to purified silver from a refining furnace. The result of the seven-fold refining process produced one hundred percent perfect silver in the ancient world, an apt illustration for the quality of the perfect Words of the Lord. Furthermore, David revealed the endurance of God's Words, indicating that they would be preserved from that generation forever.

A'. The Recognition of the Need for Divine Help (v. 8)

David concluded the psalm by recognizing his need for the Lord's help because the wicked were "all around" (סָבִיב, *sâvēv*) him. Their "vilest" (זֻלּוּת, *zūllūth*) nature was not only prevalent but "exalted" (רוּם, *rūm*)[21] among the "sons of man" (לִבְנֵי אָדָם, *livĕnā 'âthâm*). David recognized that the proud words of the wicked flatterers were a constant problem, but the perfect Words of God will always counter man's lies. Jeremiah expressed succinctly this tension between God's Words and man's words, stating "all the remnant of Judah . . . shall know whose words shall stand, mine, or theirs" (Jer. 44:28).

---

[17]The stem of this 1cp imperfect verb is *Hiphil*, suggesting the force of "we will cause to prevail." The root consonants are related to גָּבַר (*gever*), "strong man."

[18]Paul emphasized the importance of the promises of God to the believer, saying *"For all the promises of God in him are yea, and in him Amen, unto the glory of God by us"* (2 Cor. 1:20).

[19]This noun comes from יָשַׁע (*yâshă'*), which is the same root as "help" (v.1).

[20]The root of this *Hiphil* imperfect verb is פּוּחַ (*puak*) meaning to blow or breathe. The antidote to these man-breathed words are the God-breathed Words of the inspired and preserved Scripture (2 Tim. 3:16).

[21]The exaltation of the wicked parallels the vanishing of the godly in verse one.

Exegesis of vv. 6-7

This summary of Psalm 12 prepares for the careful exegesis of Psalm 12:6-7. The Masoretic text is exegeted as follows.

The psalmist recognized this tangible help God gives for the believer in the midst of the threats and claims of the wicked is His "Words" (אֲמָרוֹת, fp, *'ĭmĕrōth*). He likened the "pure Words" (אֲמָרוֹת, *'ĕmârōth*, fp, "words;" טְהֹרוֹת, *tĕhōrōth*, "pure") of the Lord to "silver" (כֶּסֶף, *kêseph*, "silver"). The verbs and pronominal suffixes of verse seven are critical. The LORD is addressed as the subject of the verbs "shall keep them" (תִּשְׁמְרֵם, *tĭshmĕrām*, Qal, imperfect, 2ms, with 3mp suffix) and "shall preserve them" (תִּצְּרֶנּוּ, *tĭtstsĕrennū*, Qal, imperfect, 2ms, with 3ms suffix). The object of the first verb (*tĭshmĕrām*, "shall keep them") must be the closest antecedent (*'ĭmĕrōth*, "words").[22] Although *'ĭmĕrōth* ("words") is fp and the suffix on the verb is אָם (*'ām*) and mp, this gender discordance is not unusual in other psalms dealing with God's Words. For instance, several examples are found in Psalm 119,[23] showing the psalmist's deliberate emphasis on masculinizing this extension (i.e., pure words) of the patriarchal God of Scripture. In Psalm 119:111 the Psalmist used the personal pronoun "they" (הֵמָּה, mp, *hāmmâh*, "they") to refer to the Lord's everlasting "testimonies" (עֵדוֹתֶיךָ, fp, *'āthĕwōthēkâ*, "thy testimonies"). Clearly the Lord's testimonies are what made the psalmist rejoice, and not the "wicked" (רְשָׁעִים, mp, *rĕshâ'ēm*, "wicked") of the previous verse (v. 110). Again, in Psalm 119:129, the Psalmist exalted the Lord's "testimonies" (עֵדוֹתֶיךָ, fp, *'āthĕwōthēkâ*, "thy testimonies") and referred to them with the verb "keep them" (נְצָרַתַם, mp suffix, *nĕsârâthām*, "keep them"). Psalm 119:152 continues to demonstrate the Biblically accepted gender discordance between the mp suffix and the fp antecedent. The psalmist knew of God's "testimonies" (עֵדוֹתֶיךָ, fp, *'āthĕwōthēkâ*, "thy testimonies") and that He "founded them" (יְסַדְתָּם, mp suffix, *yĕsathtâm*, "founded them"). Another example of accepted gender discordance is found in Psalm 119:167. The psalmist stated "I have guarded" the Lord's "testimonies" (עֵדוֹתֶיךָ, fp, *'āthōthekâ*, "thy testimonies") and that "I love them" (וָאֹהֲבֵם, mp suffix, *wâ'ōhĕvām*, "and I love them"). These examples show the importance of maintaining the Biblically accepted Hebrew grammar of closest antecedent and Biblically accepted gender discordance in exceptional cases for theological reasons.

The second verb תִּצְּרֶנּוּ (*tĭtstsĕrennū*, "thou shalt preserve them") has the pronominal suffix אֶנּוּ (3ms, *'ennū*, "him")[24] which refers to the individual Words. The pronominal suffix is not אָנוּ (1cp, "us")[25] and could not contextually be since the first

---

[22]The mp nouns עֲנִיִּים (*'ĕnēyyēm*, poor") and אֶבְיוֹנִים (*'evyōnēm*, "needy") cannot be the antecedents of the pronominal suffix אָם because they are not the closest antecedents and they violate the Biblically accepted gender discordance examples. Gesenius acknowledges this Hebrew phenomenon and states: "Through a weakening in the distinction of gender, which is noticeable elsewhere and which probably passed from the colloquial language into that of literature, masculine suffixes (especially in the plural) are not infrequently used to refer to feminine substantives." H. F. W. Gesenius, *Gesenius' Hebrew Grammar*, E. Kautzsch, ed., (Oxford: At the Clarendon Press, 1910), p. 440.

verb does not have אֹתָנוּ as its suffix. The first verb refers to all the Words the Lord preserved and the second to the very individual Words He preserved. The Lord promised to preserve every one and all of His Words for every generation, because every generation will be judged by the canonical Words (i.e., OT and NT) of the Lord Jesus Christ. The Lord stated this very truth, "He that rejecteth me, and receiveth not my words, hath one that judgeth him: the word that I have spoken, the same shall judge him in the last day" (Jn. 12:48).

Conclusion

The structure, context and exegesis of the Masoretic Hebrew Text of Psalm 12 all argue forcefully and irrefragably for the promise of the everlasting preservation of the perfect Words of the Lord. This is one of several clear passages in which the Lord promised to preserve His canonical Words for every generation. Man's pervasive words are lies; God's ever-present Words are Truth. This is the tangible help from the Lord that the righteous man has in every generation.

---

[23]Psalm 119 is the *locus classicus* on the complete and perfect Word of God.

[24]"Him" not "us" is the translation of the Hebrew in numerous passages including Psm. 5:12; 8:4; 21:3; 28:7; 34:19; 43:5, *et al.*

[25]The support for you shall keep "us" and preserve "us" (cf. the NIV) is found in the penultimate authorities of 11 Hebrew Mss. and the *LXX* (ἡμᾶς ... ἡμᾶς, hāmas ... hāmas).

CHAPTER TWO

Every Word
Matthew 4:4
Thomas M. Strouse

Introduction

Satan tempted the Lord Jesus Christ early in His ministry (Mt. 4:1-11).[26] The Lord answered the tempter with three references from Deuteronomy (8:3, 6:16, and 6:13, respectively). The first answer is significant. He stated, "It is written, Man shall not live by bread alone, but by every word that proceedeth out of the mouth of God" (v. 4, cited from Dt. 8:3).[27] This response summarizes the Lord's Bibliology.
1) He affirmed the doctrine of the verbal, plenary inspiration of the *autographa* by stating the source of Scripture – "proceedeth out of the mouth of God."
2) He affirmed the authority of the written Scripture, and consequently its infallibility and inerrancy, by upholding it as a standard by which "man shall . . . live."
3) He affirmed the availability of Scripture since He declared His personal access and implied mankind's general access to God's Words – "by every word."
4) He affirmed the doctrine of the verbal, plenary preservation of Scripture by the expression "It is written." The perfect tense, which He utilized, expresses a completed action with a resulting state of being. The result of the action continues from the past through the present and into the future. In effect, the Lord said "It was written and still is written."[28] The living Word (Christ) validated His written Words since He believed He had the verbal, plenary Old Testament (OT) Words intact in His day. The purpose of this chapter is to examine in detail the Lord's claims about the full and complete text of the Hebrew OT available in His day.

---

[26]Cf. Mk. 1:12-13 and Lk. 4:1-13.

[27]Although the Lord Jesus could have rebuked Satan with the power of His own personal authority (cf. Mt. 16:23), Christ submitted His personal authority to the written Scripture, and chose rather to rebuke His chief adversary with the highest authority – the written Words of God (Psm. 138:2).

[28]See Chapter Eight on the perfect passive, "It is written," by David Sutton.

Exegesis

Inspiration – "Proceedeth Out of the Mouth of God"

The verb behind "proceedeth" is ἐκπορεύομαι (*ekporeuomai*) and the infinitive means "to go out." The reference to the mouth (στόματος, *stomatos*) indicates that God, who is Spirit, nevertheless gave man Words that could be inscripturated. God, who was the Author of the original language (Gen. 1:3), and also of the various languages (Gen. 11:7), has revealed Himself through the medium of oral and written language (cf. Ex. 20:1 ff; Jer. 36:4).[29] The Lord God is the Source for the canonical *autographa* and decreed to put His self-revelation in the form of Words (2 Pet. 1:20-21). He gave His Divine Words through human language for the eternal benefit of mankind as Paul stated, "All scripture is given by inspiration of God, and is profitable for doctrine, for reproof, for correction, for instruction in righteousness: That the man of God may be perfect, throughly furnished unto all good works" (2 Tim. 3:16-17).

Authority – "Man Shall Live"

Israel needed to learn the wilderness lesson of hunger and that through her obedience the Lord would supply the nation's physical and spiritual food (Dt. 8:1-3). The Lord cited this passage to show how He has provided every daily need including not only manna for Israel but also His Words for all mankind.[30] The Bible is the rulebook[31] by which man should live and for which man will give an account to God. It tells how man may be justified before God, stating "Therefore being justified by faith, we have peace with God through our Lord Jesus Christ" (Rom. 5:1).[32] Since the Scripture "is profitable for doctrine, for reproof, for correction, for instruction in righteousness" (2 Tim. 3:16), it follows that man should live in light of Scriptures' injunctions. According to Psm. 119:98-100, God's Words make the believer wiser than his enemies, his teachers (even text critics), and the ancients. Scripture is necessary for salvation (1 Pet. 1:23-25) and sanctification (Jn. 17:17). The canonically inscripturated words of the Father and the Son constitute the standard by which man must live.

Availability – "By Every Word"

The Lord gave the *Torah* (5 books of the Law) to the Jewish nation through Moses so that she would be prepared to enter into Canaan (Dt. 1:1). Moses required the *Torah* to be placed in the Ark of the Covenant for future generations (Dt. 31:24-30). Centuries later Ezra read the *Torah* to the Jews in their new place of worship in Jerusalem (Neh. 8:1-9). There is no question that the Jewish scribes preserved the OT Scripture through God's ordained place of worship, either the Tabernacle or the Temple. God committed

---

[29]Since God spoke in words, the original Hebrew of the OT Scriptures must have had consonants and vowels (cf. Dt. 27:8). Consonants without vowels are not words and cannot be pronounced. Moses wrote the original words, including vowels (Dt. 31:24), apparently Ezra preserved the consonants and vowels (Neh. 8:8), and the Masoretes standardized the Hebrew OT text including the original consonants and vowel pointings.

[30]Jesus' food was obedience to God, as He stated, "My meat is to do the will of him that sent me and to

unto the Jews the oracles (τὰ λόγια, *ta logia*) of God as their blessed privilege (Rom. 3:1-2). That the Jews were the custodians of the inscripturated divine utterances in their place of worship is non-controversial. Scripture adduces that they preserved and dispersed the Lord's Words for general availability as well: "For Moses of old time hath in every city them that preach him, being read in the synagogues every Sabbath day" (Acts 15:21; cf. also Josh. 8:30-35).

The local New Testament (NT) church was and is the only custodian of the NT Canon and its Text. The Lord promised to use His people in His institution to preserve His Words, stating:

> Go ye therefore, and teach all nations, baptizing them in the name of the Father, and of the Son, and of the Holy Ghost: teaching them to observe all things whatsoever I have commanded you: and, lo, I am with you alway, even unto the end of the world. Amen. (Mt. 28:19-20)

The Lord Jesus Christ gave His Great Commission to His churches to disciple all nations, by going worldwide, and immersing and instructing believers. The Great Commission is the Divine mandate to plant immersionist churches worldwide. Furthermore, the leadership of the churches must teach the members to observe (τηρεῖν, *tārein*, literally "to guard") all things the Lord commanded (cf. Eph. 4:11-16). Ultimately, the "all things" would include the OT and NT Scriptures. Christ's Great Commission gives the sole responsibility of guarding the Bible Canon and its Words to the local NT church.[33] The NT Canon and the Words therein were written to local churches and local church members.

Paul confirmed that the local church has the sole responsibility to preserve the truth. He stated, "But if I tarry long, that thou mayest know how thou oughtest to behave thyself in the house of God, which is the church of the living God, the pillar and ground of the truth" (1 Tim. 3:15). The apostle identified the house of God as the church of the living God, the church that has bishops and deacons (vv. 1-13). Presumably, Paul alluded to the great Temple of Diana (cf. Acts 19:24 ff.), which had massive architectural pillars and foundations, to make his analogy with the local church at Ephesus. Just as the Temple of Diana was a physical depository for the wealth of the Artemesian cult, the Ephesian church was the depository for the Lord's spiritual wealth – the truth. The local churches initially and continually recognized and preserved the NT Canon and the Words of the NT Canon, which God originally determined. History has corroborated the Scriptural truth that God preserved His Words through the Lord's

---

finish his work" (Jn. 4:34).

[31]"Thy word is a lamp unto my feet, and a light unto my path" (Psm 119:105; cf. Prov. 6:23).

[32]Cf. Rom. 3:23-25; 5:9-10.

[33]This responsibility was not given to the Roman Catholic Church, Protestantism, Bible societies, or para-church organizations.

assemblies. The Lord Jesus preserved His Words which were manifested in the manuscripts and translations used by His churches, starting of course with the NT churches. The Apostolic churches used the Received Text (cf. Jn. 17:8 et al), which text the Syrian (1ˢᵗ century), Italic (2ⁿᵈ century), Gallic (2ⁿᵈ century), Celtic (3ʳᵈ century), Gothic (4ᵗʰ century), Waldensian (5ᵗʰ–16ᵗʰ centuries), Albigensian (13ᵗʰ century), Anabaptist (16ᵗʰ century) and Baptist (17ᵗʰ–21ˢᵗ centuries) churches preserved, either by translating or by promulgating the received translation over the past two thousand years.[34] The Lord God's institution of the local church has kept the Words of His Received Bible just as He promised and as history has corroborated.

Preservation – "It Is Written"

The passage at hand utilizes the expression "it is written" (Γέγραπται, *Gegraptai*) four times (vv. 4, 6, 7, 10).[35] The Lord submitted Himself to the written OT Scripture in response to Satan's temptations and claimed the preservation of three passages (Dt. 8:3, 6:16, and 6:13) for His defense (cf. Eph. 6:17). Satan was forced to submit himself to the written Scripture and even declared the preservation of Psm. 91:11-12 (v. 6) with "it is written." The Greek word Γέγραπται (*Gegraptai*) is the 3ms perfect indicative passive of γράφω (*graphō*) meaning "it was, still is and will continue to remain written."[36] Christ declared that the Hebrew text Dt. 8:3, לֹא עַל־הַלֶּחֶם לְבַדּוֹ יִחְיֶה הָאָדָם כִּי עַל־כָּל־מוֹצָא פִי־יְהוָה, ("not by bread alone shall man live, but by all [words] proceeding out of the mouth of Jehovah") was still intact, including the consonants and vowels, up to His day. There are at least three Biblical arguments that defend the position that the Lord always used the Hebrew text and not the Greek LXX.

1) The Lord referred to jots and tittles that make up the Hebrew language, not the Greek language (Mt. 5:17-18).

2) The Lord referred to the three-fold division of the *Tanak*, not the LXX, which included the *Torah* (law), the *Nabi'im* (prophets), and the *Kethubim* (writings), on several occasions (cf. Lk. 24:44).

3) The Lord referred to the first and last books of the *Tanak* (Lk. 11:50-51), describing the brutal deaths of the prophets from Abel (Gen. 4:8) to Zacharias (2 Chron. 24:20-22). Although the Lord cited precisely the Hebrew of Mt. 4:4, it is clear upon close examination of Dt. 8:3 that Christ did not quote the LXX, since at least two words are different.[37]

Not only did Matthew record Christ's temptation but Luke did also. Both writers record the Lord's inspired commentary on Dt. 8:3 with slightly different renderings. Several points must be considered.

---

[34] By faith one must believe that all legitimate extant manuscript readings and translations have been influenced by local NT churches. History cannot disprove this credo.

[35] It is used 67 times in the NT. In one case the word (*gegraptai*) refers to the words of John's Gospel (Jn. 20:31).

[36] The perfect tense is resultative in aspect and past with ongoing results in time (cf. Rom. 9:33).

1) The Lord had intact before Him the inspired and preserved Hebrew text of Dt. 8:3 (as well as the rest of Deuteronomy, and certainly verses 6:16 and 6:13).
2) Matthew cited Christ's inspired commentary on Dt. 8:3 verbatim, stressing the expression "that proceedeth out of the mouth" (ἐκπορευομένῳ διὰ στόματος Θεοῦ, *ekporeuomenō dia stomatos Theou*).
3) Luke selectively cited Christ's inspired commentary, omitting the aforementioned words found in Matthew's quote, and included the article ὁ (*ho*, "the") before "man." The inspired and preserved passage of Dt. 8:3 was intact in Christ's day, and the Biblical writers Matthew and Luke gave their inspired renderings of Christ's various inspired commentaries on Dt. 8:3.[38]

Conclusion

The Lord Jesus Christ's Bibliology is clear and consistent. He clearly stated His belief in the verbal, plenary inspiration of the Hebrew OT, since the Words proceeded from the mouth of God. He clearly stated His belief in the authority of Scripture, noting that it gave God's standard for how man shall live. The Lord clearly stated His belief in the availability of Scripture by assuming the accessibility of every Word. The Savior clearly stated His belief in the verbal, plenary preservation of God's Words since they had been and were still preserved intact in His day. The incarnate God in the person of Jesus Christ was consistent in His belief and practice since He submitted Himself to the perfectly preserved inscripturated Words He promised He would keep. It behooves Christians, including pastors, believers and scholars, to emulate Christ's teaching in their Bibliology, as the Father required: "This is my beloved Son, in whom I am well pleased; hear ye Him" (Mt. 17:5).

---

[37] The *LXX* adds ὁ (*ho*) and τo (*to*).

[38] The Gospel writers were not redactors (editors) in the sense of creating words supposedly stated by others as *redaktionsgeschichte* teaches. The Gospel writers gave the *ipsissimi verba* ("the very words") of Christ and not merely the *ipsissimi vox* ("the voice" or gist) of Christ's message.

CHAPTER THREE

Not One Jot or One Tittle
Matthew 5:17,18
Gary C. Webb

Introduction

The Lord Jesus Christ did not want His disciples to have concerns about the authority of the Scriptural record. In the Sermon on the Mount, the first sermon of Jesus chronicled by Matthew, He affirmed the absolute authority of the Word of God by making reference to the actual letters of the Hebrew text. From His statements one should derive a doctrine of textual integrity. The precise wording of the text of Scripture provides the authority of the inspired, inerrant Word of God. When one combines Jesus' promise that "one jot or one tittle shall in no wise pass from the law" with His assertion that spiritual greatness belongs to those who keep and teach the "least commandments," His statements demand a doctrine of verbal and plenary preservation of the text of Scripture. This passage considered in its context presents this doctrine, establishing for all generations the absolute authority of God's preserved Words.

The Interpretation of the Passage in its Context

The Purpose of the Sermon on the Mount

Although written for the spiritual profit of every believer, the Gospel of Matthew has qualities that indicate its particular relevance for a Jewish audience.[39] Matthew emphasizes Jesus' ministry to the Jews as opposed to the world at large.[40] Of course, Jesus delivered the Sermon on the Mount (Matthew 5-7) to a Jewish audience. As the first and longest of Jesus' sermons recorded by Matthew, it demonstrates the nature of the message Jesus intended to deliver to that nation. Israel, chosen of God for special

---

[39] Consider two simple examples of this emphasis: a) The reference to Hebrew letters in the text; b) The instruction given for Jews living in Palestine during the Tribulation Period when the largely Gentile population of the Church Age has departed in the Rapture (Matthew 24 and 25).

[40] Matthew 10:5-6, 15:21-24.

grace and privileges, had turned from Him to embrace outward ritual and empty religious works without true faith in or love for God. Therefore Jesus, like John the Baptist before Him, called the nation to repentance and condemned its religious hypocrisy.

Matthew gives a summary of Jesus' preaching (and therefore a summary of the message of the Sermon on the Mount) in Matthew 4:17: "From that time Jesus began to preach, and to say, Repent: for the kingdom of heaven is at hand." Matthew 4:23 adds, "And Jesus went about all Galilee, teaching in their synagogues, and preaching the gospel of the kingdom . . . .." Jesus wanted the Jews to see their sin, repent of their empty religion, and embrace a true faith in God, which would produce the inward transformation of salvation.

To get this message across Jesus first gave the Beatitudes (5:3-12) which teach the characteristics of true salvation: man sees his spiritual poverty (5:3), mourns over his sin (5:4), submits to God's will (5:5), begins to hunger and thirst for righteousness (5:6), exercises mercy because he will receive mercy at the Judgment (5:7), manifests purity from the heart (5:8), seeks to bring others to peace with God (5:9), and joyfully suffers persecution for his new righteousness (5:10-12). Jesus said that people who have experienced such a salvation act like salt to hold back the corruption of sin in the world and become light to a world covered in the darkness of unbelief (5:13-16). Israel had failed in this Divine purpose, providing little illuminating testimony to a pagan world and adding to the world's corruption with its own sin.

To make the Jews see more clearly their need of the repentance and faith that bring a soul into the Kingdom of God, Jesus then began to attack and correct their false understanding and applications of the teaching of the Old Testament. Six times Jesus referred to the false understanding common in that day, saying, "Ye have heard . . . ."[41] He corrected that false understanding with the true and complete understanding, "But I say . . . .."[42] His attack upon their religion continued in chapter six as He criticized the manner of their "alms"[43] (6:1-4), prayer (6:5-15), and fasting (6:16-18). Indeed Jesus condemned the very character of their society: their concern for earthly needs (6:19-33), their hypocritical judgment of others (7:1-6), and their failure to have faith in the benevolence of God (7:7-12). He admonished them to enter the narrow path of salvation (7:13-14). Then He concluded with a lengthy paragraph (7:15-27) that warned them of false teachers, warned them of the possibility of religious people being excluded from Heaven, and told them that only a life built upon His sayings would have a lasting foundation.

---

[41] Matthew 5:21,27,31,33,38,43. Verse 31 differs slightly; "It hath been said . . . ."
[42] Matthew 5:22,28,32,34,39,44.
[43] ἐλεημοσύνη (*eleāmosūnā*): acts of mercy.
[44] "Think" translates νομίσητε (*nomisāte*, aorist active subjunctive of νομίζω [*nomizō*]).
[45] "To destroy" translates the aorist active infinitive of καταλύω (*kataluō*), indicating purpose.
[46] "Verily" in verse 18 marks the first occurrence of ἀμήν (*amān*) in Matthew's gospel.
[47] "Jot" translates the Greek word ἰότα (*iota*), which English has adopted as the transliterated iota, still meaning something of minute size. The iota corresponds to our English letter I, and in the text refers to

Jesus sought to bring the Jews to repentance. The Sermon on the Mount is probably the greatest message ever delivered on that theme.

The Apologetic Assertion of Matthew 5:17-20

The Jews hearing Jesus deliver this sermon recognized the authority of Jesus' Words (7:28-29). He did not teach in the manner of the scribes (and of many professors in religious schools today) who frequently quoted the most respected scholars of their day to support their opinions. Instead, Jesus simply spoke, allowing the truth of His Words to demonstrate their authority. However, Jesus' pattern of correcting the commonly accepted understanding of Scripture by stating, "But I say . . ." left Him open to a serious criticism. His opponents might charge that Jesus intended to annul the teaching of the Old Testament and substitute His own teaching in its place. Some would welcome such an attempt, but that charge would turn most Jews against Jesus. Whatever the response, the charge was egregiously false, and Jesus spoke to set the matter to rest.

In the paragraph of Matthew 5:17-20, Jesus anticipated and confronted this criticism. He told them not to conclude[44] that He came to tear down[45] the Old Testament. Instead He came to "fulfil" the Law and the Prophets by demonstrating their full meaning. This Jesus did in His Person, providing a flesh and blood embodiment of the sketches of truth given by the Old Testament ceremonial laws. His life fulfilled the moral law in the accomplishment of comprehensive, perfect obedience, and fulfilled the preaching of the prophets by literal performance of their predictions. His teaching fulfilled the instruction of the Old Testament, opening its meaning so men could grasp the depth, spirit, and power of that record as none had ever done before Him. He did not come to destroy; He came to fulfill.

Jesus continued His defense with a solemn[46] statement of the plenary infallibility of the law. He indicated the authority of the smallest portion of the teaching of the Old Testament by referring to the smallest portions of the Hebrew text itself. The "jot" refers to the smallest Hebrew consonant.[47] Modern scholars normally define the "tittle" as only referring to a bend or point in the actual Hebrew letters themselves.[48] Jesus asserted that no portion of the teaching of the Old Testament would pass out of existence, lose its authority, or be annulled until every bit of it had its fulfillment. Indeed, he declared that such an occurrence is an absolute impossibility.[49]

Although Bible students accept this clear assertion of the Lord, this definition of the "tittle" needs clarification. The authority of the Old Testament depends upon the Words of the text. The Hebrew words depend (like English words) upon both

---

the Hebrew letter *yodh*. The Hebrew *yodh* is smaller than all the Hebrew consonants, being perched above the writing line, as seen in the word Israel יִשְׂרָאֵל.

[48]"Tittle" translates the Greek word κεραία (*keraiă*), meaning horn and referring partially to the parts of Hebrew letters that distinguish one from another as demonstrated by the difference between the Hebrew ד *D* and the Hebrew ר *R*.

[49]"Shall in no wise pass" translates οὐ μὴ παρέλθῃ (*ou mā pareltha*), combining the aorist active subjunctive of παρέρχομαι (*parerkomai*) with a double negative. The Greek subjunctive indicates possibility. Biblical Greek combines the subjunctive with a double negative to state an emphatic negation.

consonants and vowels. However, modern scholarship has excluded the vowels of the Hebrew text from the operation of Divine inspiration, stating that inspiration only gave the Hebrew consonants. This position which denies that "tittle" also refers to the vowel pointing of the Hebrew text completely undermines the Divine authority of the Hebrew Scriptures. If one accepts the assertion of Jesus in Matthew 5:18, he must understand that the term "tittle" also refers to the Hebrew vowels.[50]

When one considers the Hebrew consonants שער, what word do they represent? Depending on the points, one may form several different Hebrew words: שָׁעַר (shâ'ar) – to esteem; שַׁעַר (sha'ar) – a gate; שַׂעַר (sa'ar) – a disheveling; שָׂעַר (sâ'ar) – to shudder; שֵׂעָר (sĕ'âr) – the hair.[51] One may demonstrate the same thing with the English consonants F, R, and T. These letters combined with various vowels form the very different words fruit, fort, and fret. Scripture speaks of "words . . . which the Holy Ghost teacheth" (1 Corinthians 2:13), instructing us that God did not give an unintelligible grouping of consonants but breathed out whole words. Therefore, we understand from Jesus' statement in Matthew 5:18 that the Masoretes did not invent the vowel pointing but preserved the vowel pointing as it was given by God.

Jesus' assertion that a jot or tittle would in no wise pass away was a very strong defense of the plenary authority of the Old Testament. However it was still not strong enough for Him. In verse 19 He makes reference to the evaluation of individuals by God in the Day of Judgment, saying that anyone who disregarded the least commandment would cause God to regard him as the least in the Kingdom of Heaven. Although possibly referring particularly to religious teachers with the descriptive phrase "shall do and teach," Jesus may have simply indicated the teaching power or influence of our actions. Whatever His exact indication, He made the main point clear.

The assertion of verse 19 tied Jesus' defense of His teaching style back into the theme of His whole sermon. He had no criticism of God's Word, only of the Jews' interpretations and applications that allowed them to actually disobey the Lord's commandments. They had a false righteousness that had no real basis in the law of God. He drove this point home in verse 20 with a reference to the scribes and Pharisees. The scribes copied, studied, and taught the Bible. The Pharisees had a reputation as the most devout religious sect in Jewish society, zealously keeping an elaborate code of man-made, religious rituals. Jesus chose these two groups because the Jews regarded them as the most righteous. However, Jesus proclaimed that no one would enter Heaven if His righteousness did not exceed the righteousness of the scribes and Pharisees.[52] They needed a

---

[50] One may find a defense of this definition in John Owen's *Biblical Theology* (Morgan, PA: Soli Deo Gloria Publications, 1996 rpt.), pp. 495-533. For an article that defends this position and demonstrates that early Christians held it until infidel scholarship rejected it, consider George Sayles Bishop's (1836-1914) article "The Inspiration of the Hebrew Letters and Vowel-Points," *in Plains Baptist Challenger*, ed. E. L. Bynum (Lubbock, TX, July 1991), pp. 3-8. Bishop asserts, "The constant, uniform tradition of the Jews, affirming that the points came down from Moses, and the giving of the Law, was a tradition unbroken down to the year 1538, twenty-one years after Luther had nailed up his Theses." See footnote #135 in chapter nine by Kent Brandenburg on Deuteronomy 30:11-14.

[51] Bishop, p. 3.

true righteousness based upon the teaching of God's Word that condemns man's sin and points him to the Savior as his only hope of righteousness in the eyes of God.

Jesus ably defended His manner of teaching from a false accusation. He had no intention to loose anyone from the authority of even the least commandment of God's Word. Instead, He established the Bible as the authority that would rule creation as long as it lasted. True righteousness is presented in the full teaching of the law, and spiritual greatness belonged to those who do and teach it all.

The Application of the Passage to the Textual Debate

The Demand for the Verbal Preservation of the Text of Scripture

Jesus established the plenary authority of the Old Testament teaching in this passage. He did this with the intention that the Jews (and indeed all men) might see their need of repentance and of a Divinely provided Savior who could fulfill the righteousness of the law. All men fall hopelessly short of that righteousness. Jesus perfectly lived out that righteousness in man's place and also fulfilled the demands of its condemnation of mankind by shedding His blood and dying as a substitute upon Calvary's cross. Any individual may obtain the righteousness of God by faith in the Person and Work of Jesus Christ.

Those who obtain such righteousness by faith also begin to "hunger and thirst after righteousness" (5:6). This hunger drives them to do and to teach the least of God's commands (5:19). Because of their gratitude to their Savior and their great love for Him they want to be called "great" in the Kingdom of Heaven. They, therefore, diligently study to show themselves approved of God as workmen who have no reason for shame (2 Timothy 2:15). They give their greatest emphasis to the weightier matters of the law, but they do not leave the lesser matters undone (Matthew 23:23), knowing that those who are faithful in the least matters will prove faithful also in the greatest (Luke 16:10).

One must ask how a man can prove faithful in those commandments if he does not have an exact record of them. Could the changing of one letter in the Hebrew or Greek text change a word and thereby affect the meaning of a command or doctrine? Certainly it could and usually does.[53] What if a Christian, facing severe repercussions,

---

[52]"Ye shall in no case enter" once again utilizes the combination of the Greek subjunctive with a double negative.

[53]Commentators recognize this point in this passage. Albert Barnes says: "The Hebrew letters were written with small points or apices, as in the letter Schin שׁ or Sin שׂ, which serve to distinguish one letter from another. To change a small point of one letter, therefore, might vary the meaning of a word, and destroy the sense . . . Hence the Jews were exceedingly cautious in writing these letters, and considered the smallest change or omission a reason for destroying the whole manuscript when they were transcribing the Old Testament. The expression, 'one jot or tittle,' became proverbial, and means that the smallest part of the law should not be destroyed."

struggles with the issue of complete honesty in a certain situation? The day of importance arrives, and he rises early to meet with his God. His soul agonizes as he opens his New American Standard Version of the Bible to the seventh chapter of John's Gospel, the place assigned by his daily reading schedule. In that passage he reads that Jesus lied to his brothers, saying that he would not go to the feast in verse 8, when in fact verse 10 says He did go up later.[54] Surprised to read this about Jesus, he nevertheless believes he has his answer from God. A "proper" interpretation of that text tells him he can lie in some circumstances. That "proper" interpretation would also nullify the sinlessness of Christ and render Him incapable of accomplishing our redemption.

This example demonstrates that the integrity of the text plays a major role in the believer's ability to do and teach the least of God's commandments.[55] Does Jesus' statement in Matthew 5:18, where He mentions "one jot or one tittle," have any reference to the integrity of the text? If it does not, then His statement in verse 19 loses its authority. A simple and unbiased consideration of this passage produces a doctrine of Divine, verbal preservation of the Hebrew and (by extension to the complete Scriptural record) the Greek texts.

Why did Jesus make reference to the Hebrew letters in verse 18? Did He just utilize a phrase in common use among the Jews, or did He intend to put emphasis upon the actual Hebrew text?[56] Certainly those who believe in the verbal inspiration of the Scriptures have no doubt that Jesus chose His Words purposefully. He could have made the same point about the teaching of the Scriptures without ever referring to letters. Yet the Lord did refer to them and said that the letters would not pass away until all of the law was fulfilled.

Some have argued that the Lord clearly did not refer to the Hebrew text but only to the prophetic fulfillment of what the Old Testament taught.[57] That argument especially fails with verse 19 in the immediate context. But, as the Lord indicated, the authority and validity of the least command or any command in Scripture depends upon the exact wording of that command in the Scriptural text. For example, did Paul rightly base his argument in Galatians 3:16[58] upon a Hebrew plural or did he have a Hebrew

---

[54] The NASV follows the Critical Text in verse 8, omitting the small Greek word οὔπω (yet) found in the AV/TR and inserting οὐκ (ouk, not), a small change that replaces one Greek letter with two others.

[55] See the chapter on doctrinal changes in the Old Testament by Thomas Strouse and those in the New Testament by Gary Webb and David Sutton.

[56] Although Alford [Henry Alford, *Alford's Greek Testament*, (1844; repr. Grand Rapids: Baker Book House, 1980), 1:43] gives "jot and tittle" as a proverbial saying, it did not apply in general to small matters but to the actual Hebrew text: "The rabbinical writings have many sayings similar in sentiment to this, but spoken of the *literal* written law (See Lightfoot, Hor. Heb. In loc.)." For actual examples, see John Gill's commentary on Matthew 5:18, *John Gill's Expositor*. In *Online Bible Millennium Edition*. Version 1.03.02. (Winterbourne, Ontario, Canada: Timnathserah, Inc, Sept. 2001).

[57] Glenny makes this argument, p. 87: "The point of this verse is that Jesus did not come to destroy (or to perpetuate for that matter) the OT Law. He is the one to whom all the OT points (Luke 24:25-27, 44-46) and He came to fulfill all that was prophesied about Him in it . . . . This passage is not speaking about the preservation of the exact words found in the *autographa*; it is declaring that all the prophecies in the OT which pointed to Christ will be fulfilled down to the smallest detail."

manuscript containing an erroneous variant reading made by a copyist? The necessity of the integrity of the Hebrew text becomes obvious. Jesus promised here that "one jot or one tittle shall in no wise pass from the law, till all be fulfilled." That could not mean only that the teaching would maintain its authority until all is fulfilled because Jesus immediately states man's obligation to obey and teach all the commands, even the least of them, which demands that we must have the very jots and tittles that express those commands.

Some scholars and textual critics mock this clear, unbiased, derived doctrine of verbal preservation, claiming that the "evidence" of copies containing errors refutes the Bible doctrine.[59] The Bible gives the answer to this criticism in Romans 3:3-4: "For what if some did not believe? shall their unbelief make the faith of God without effect? God forbid: yea, let God be true, but every man a liar; as it is written, That thou mightest be justified in thy sayings, and mightest overcome when thou art judged." The "evidence" claimed by evolutionists does not cause the believer to give up the Bible doctrine of creation. Why? Because he knows that the evolutionist's humanistic presuppositions have caused him to view and judge the "evidence" wrongly. Likewise, the scholar who follows the humanistic precepts of modern textual criticism makes the same type of error, judging the evidence with rationalistic presuppositions rather than by those in Scripture.

Some will note the previous use of the phrase "derived doctrine of verbal preservation" and claim that Matthew 5:18-19 does not explicitly say that God will preserve every jot and tittle of the Hebrew text nor does He tell us how He will do it. Yet verse 18 does say God will preserve the jot and tittle and verse 19 demands that this preservation includes the text God has given to man. But if the doctrine is "derived" by combining these two verses, does that lessen the fact or the authority of the doctrine? If one removes the text of I John 5:7 from Scripture (as the Critical Text and the modern versions do), the doctrine of the Trinity becomes a "derived doctrine." The Bible makes no other direct statement of this doctrine, but we derive it from such passages as Matthew 3:16-17 and 28:19. Does one therefore discount or deny the doctrine of

---

[58]"Now to Abraham and his seed were the promises made. He saith not, And to seeds, as of many; but as of one, And to thy seed, which is Christ."

[59]Consider the words of Samuel Schnaiter, "Textual Criticism and the Modern English Version Controversy" in *Biblical Viewpoint*, Vol. XVI, No. 1, ed. Stewart Custer (Greenville, SC: Bob Jones University Press, 1982), pp. 72-73: "Pickering shows that he has fallen into the error of equating inspiration with preservation as described above. He also demonstrates that his view of the authority of God's Word depends on the recovery of the original wording of the New Testament text. And if it is true that his concept of authority is dependent on the preservation of precise wordings, then it is scarcely conceivable that even such a scholar as he has arrived at his conclusions from the evidence as much as from his predisposition. Knowledge that Pickering's concept of authority depends upon preservation of precise wordings brings into question his entire procedure."

How could a Christian who professes to believe in verbal inspiration make such statement? Verbal inspiration guarantees "precise wordings," which are the basis for every Christian doctrine. If we do not have "precise wordings," we do not have "the faith which was once delivered unto the saints" (Jude 3). For the Christian the "predisposition" of a preserved text of Scripture which provides "precise wordings" should underlie our conclusions on the textual debate just as it does our conclusions on every other issue of faith and practice.

the Trinity? No; indeed one brands all that deny this doctrine "false teachers" or even "unbelievers" because of the essential nature of this doctrine. Where does that leave those who deny a doctrine as fundamental as the verbal preservation of Scripture?[60]

Some claim that those who support the King James Version (and other language translations based upon the Hebrew Masoretic Text and the Greek Received Text) have made up the doctrine of verbal preservation of the autographs in order to support their position. However Matthew 5:18-19 demands this doctrine. As such, those who have faith in the Lord Jesus Christ must give this passage its proper authority in the textual or Bible version debate.

The Invalidity of the Principles Which Produced the Critical Text

The most basic premise of modern textual criticism is that man does not have a verbally preserved text of Scripture in either the Old or New Testaments. Modern textual criticism seeks to restore or recover the original wording while plainly admitting it cannot accomplish such a goal and, in many cases, has no desire to do so.[61] In 1882 when Westcott and Hort published their *The New Testament in the Original Greek*, in which they set forth the procedures for modern textual criticism, they repeatedly stated that textual critics cannot recover the actual text of the New Testament.[62]

These admissions reveal that their procedure rests upon a foundation of unbelief: they did not believe God had preserved His written Words. Therefore, although the textual critical procedure used to produce the Greek and Hebrew texts behind the modern versions may have some merit for restoring secular texts, it has no merit for authoritatively establishing preserved Scripture. Bible versions such as the New International Version and the New American Standard Version, though perhaps translated by conservative, evangelical scholars, have the corrupting flaw of utilizing Hebrew and Greek texts produced by this unbelieving textual criticism. The same rationalistic unbelief that shaped higher criticism [which edits the content of Scripture] also underlies and has shaped lower (textual) criticism [that edits the text of Scripture]. This realization coincides with the fact that most textual critics today do not have saving faith.[63] Indeed, neither Westcott nor Hort believed in the inerrancy of the original

---

[60]Glenny, p. 99, says that he believes in the preservation of God's Word. However, he does not base his belief in preservation upon the teaching of Scripture but on the evidence of history: "It is obvious from the evidence of history that God has providentially preserved His Word for the present generation. However, it is also obvious from the evidence of history that God has not miraculously and perfectly preserved His Word in any one manuscript or group of manuscripts, *or in all the manuscripts*" [emphasis added]. This is rank unbelief and heresy.

[61]The most respected textual critics today have no connection with genuine Christianity. Eldon Jay Epp, speaking at Southeastern Baptist Theological Seminary on April 7, 2000, insisted that no variants are spurious but all are important because they give us a "living text": "The greater the ambiguity in a particular passage, the more we have the original reading . . .. Textual criticism is diminished when its purpose is only to recover the original wording." [Taken from personal notes]

[62]Consider two examples: 1) "Every transcription of any kind of writing involves the chance of introduction of some errors: and even if the transcript is revised by comparison with its exemplar or

manuscripts,[64] a position that denies the doctrine of inspiration.

The teaching of Matthew 5:18-19 also directly confronts a key issue in the criticism of the Old Testament text. That issue concerns the use of the Septuagint (*LXX*, a Greek translation) in determining the text when variant readings exist in Old Testament Hebrew manuscripts. Many textual critics today put great weight upon readings found in the *LXX* that differ from the Hebrew Masoretic text because scholars assert that Jesus and the early church used the *LXX* as their Bible. However, in Matthew 5:18 Jesus clearly refers to the Hebrew text, since "jots" and "tittles" are found in Hebrew, not Greek. Furthermore, in Luke 11:50-51 Jesus said "From the blood of Abel unto the blood of Zacharias," again referencing the Hebrew, and not the Greek Old Testament. The Hebrew book order has Genesis first (from which Jesus referred to Abel) and 2 Chronicles last (from which He referred to Zacharias) while the *LXX* ends with Malachi. In Luke 24:44 Jesus also referred to the threefold order of the Hebrew text ("in the Law of Moses, and in the prophets, and in the psalms" = Torah, Prophets, and Writings), an order not followed by the *LXX*.[65] These definite Biblical references to the Hebrew text should settle the question concerning the authority of the Hebrew Masoretic text and overrule the preference that textual critics give to the readings of the *LXX*.

The comparison of these few but fundamental principles of modern textual criticism with Matthew 5:18-19 demonstrates that they contradict the teaching of the Bible about the preservation of its text. However, these principles have received widespread acceptance in conservative and fundamental colleges and seminaries. If Christians apply the teaching of Jesus in this passage to textual criticism, they will reject the modern method that has produced the critical texts of the Hebrew Old Testament and the Greek New Testament.

---

immediate original, there is no absolute security that all the errors will be corrected (page 5, paragraph 7). 2) "The gain or loss to the intrinsic purity of texts from mixture with other texts is from the nature of the case indeterminable," [Westcott, Brooke Foss, and Fenton John Anthony Hort, *The New Testament in the Original Greek*, (1882; repr. Collinswood, NJ: The Bible For Today, 1985) pp. 5, 8].

[63]None of the editors of the *United Bible Societies Third Edition* (Kurt Aland, Matthew Black, Carlo Martini, Bruce Metzger, and Allen Wikgren) professes to have evangelical faith.

[64]"Little is gained by speculating as to the precise point at which such corruptions came in [to the Bible]. They may be due to the original writer, or to his amanuensis if he wrote from dictation, or they may be due to one of the earliest transcribers." [Westcott, Foss, and Hort, *The New Testament in the Original Greek*, pp. 280-281]

[65]These references to the book order of the Hebrew text are particularly significant because they appear in the gospel written by Luke, the only Gentile writer of any New Testament book.

Conclusion

In defending Himself against the possible criticism that He came to "destroy" the teaching of the Old Testament, Jesus gave Christians an absolute assurance in Matthew 5:18-19 of the verbal and plenary preservation of the text of Scripture. His Words demand that Christians concerned about textual criticism return to a position of faith, a position that builds its textual method on the teaching of the Bible. Modern textual criticism does not do this but ignores or discounts Jesus' exact assurance.

Whom then should Christians believe? Did God leave the preservation of the texts of the Old and New Testaments to fallible copyists? Do Christians have only the evidence of history to support the doctrine of preservation? Should believers put their faith in Bibles put together by unbelieving textual critics? Or did Jesus mean what He taught when He said, "For verily I say unto you, Till heaven and earth pass, one jot or one tittle shall in no wise pass from the law, till all be fulfilled"? Jesus taught that the authority of God's Word rested upon the Divine preservation of the text. Belief in this doctrine leads men today to reject modern textual criticism with its invalid texts and to accept the texts (and the methods that produced them) behind the King James Version of the Bible.

CHAPTER FOUR

The Lord Jesus Christ and the Received Bible
John 17:8
Thomas M. Strouse

Introduction

Around AD 96, Clement of Rome wrote *1 Clement,* an epistle to the Corinthians, encouraging them to be united as Paul advised them in I Corinthians. Although some may consider Clement's effort to write extra-biblical writings commendable, this early tendency among the patristics to produce penultimate authorities for Christianity is the quintessence of the extra-biblical authoritarianism of Roman Catholicism. The apostle Paul had already written, under the process of inspiration, the inspired and canonical book of 1 Corinthians.[66] The Corinthian Church, and all churches struggling for unity, need to heed the *autographa*, and not some non-authoritative, non-canonical epistle of a proto-Roman Catholic bishop. This tendency to look for penultimate authorities to settle matters of truth is prevalent today within Christianity. Theologians want to bolster their arguments with quotes from John Calvin, C. H. Spurgeon, D. A. Carson, etc. Even in the arena of Bibliology, fundamentalists are looking for the ultimate, final quote or statement that will resolve all issues. Some look to B. F. Westcott and F. H. A. Hort, or Bruce Metzger, or to Daniel Wallace for the final, authoritative answer to the supposed complex issue about which text/translation

---

[66]Paul knew his oral teachings which were inscripturated were inspired, stating "Which things also we speak, not in the words which man's wisdom teacheth, but which the Holy Ghost teacheth; comparing spiritual things with spiritual "(1 Cor. 2:13). Also, Peter knew Paul's writings were inspired, saying "As also in all his epistles, speaking in them of these things; in which are some things hard to be understood, which they that are unlearned and unstable wrest, as they do also the other scriptures, unto their own destruction" (2 Pet. 3:16). The fact that John attached a colophon to the Apocalypse (Rev. 22:18-19) indicates that he recognized that any change in the Words of the Book of Revelation (whole Bible?) would result in a change of the message of Scripture.

is the best.⁶⁷ Those who look lightly at the great Bibliological truths of Scripture concerning inspiration and preservation in theology look strongly at extra-biblical authorities in practice.

The Bible, however, attests to its own inspiration, preservation, and authority. Furthermore, the author of Scripture, the Lord Jesus Christ, spoke clearly about the doctrines of perfect inspiration, perfect preservation and their resultant text and translations. The Bibliologist does not need to listen to secondary authorities since the Ultimate Authority on Scripture has spoken. This essay will demonstrate, by exegeting John 17:8 in the context of Christ's great intercessory prayer for unity, that the Lord Jesus Christ is the Author of the received Bible mindset and expects His followers to be united around the received Bible movement throughout history.

Exegesis of John 17:8

Background

John recorded the Lord's "high-priestly" prayer following His farewell discourse (Jn. 13-16). The prayer naturally divides into three parts; He prayed for Himself (vv. 1-5), for His immediate audience of apostles and disciples (vv. 6-19), and for future generations of believers (vv. 20-26).⁶⁸ Christ recognized the culmination of His redemptive purpose in the incarnation (cf. Jn. 2:4; 7:6, 8, 30; 8:20; 12:23, 27-28, 31-32; 13:1, 31) and prayed. The Lord's prayer for Himself included His desire for mutual glorification of the Son and the Father, His acknowledgment of the scope of the Son's redemptive purpose to give eternal life to those given Him (cf. Jn. 3:15-16; 6:37, 44; 10:28-30), His assertion that He had finished God's redemptive plan (cf. Jn. 19:30), and His request to return to His previous glory shared with the Father (cf. Jn. 10:30).⁶⁹

The Son's prayer for His apostles and disciples is longer than His prayer for Himself.⁷⁰ The Lord interceded for them that they would be kept (vv. 11, 15) and would fulfill their ministry of the Word (vv. 8, 17). Christ was confident that the Father would hear His intercession because the disciples had been given to Him by the Father (vv. 6-7, 9-12), they had been obedient (v. 8), and the Lord Jesus had kept them. (v.

---

⁶⁷Some even maintain that a textual "savior" will come along and save the day for text criticism as J. Whitcomb and H. Morris (*The Genesis Flood: The Biblical Record and Its Scientific Implications*, [Philadelphia: The Presbyterian and Reformed Publ. Co., 1961]) supposedly did for Biblical creationism.

⁶⁸There may be a parallel with the high priest who offered sacrifices for himself, his family, and the nation on the Day of Atonement (cf. Lev. 16:1-34).

⁶⁹Certainly the Lord Jesus Christ's request to return to mutual glory with the Father bespeaks of His pre-existence and deity (cf. Phil. 2:5-11).

⁷⁰These disciples, although they had limitations, were obedient to Christ (cf. Jn. 2:22; Mt. 16:22-23).

⁷¹Apostates manifest the world's hatred for the Words of God through higher and lower criticism. Their efforts to analyze and evaluate the Bible from the anti-supernatural, rationalist approach eviscerate the Words of the Bible and the character of its Author. The liberal and modernistic approach is to "minister questions, rather than godly

12). The Son interceded for His apostles because He had given them the Father's Words to minister in the world (vv. 8, 20), which would hate them (vv. 14-19).[71]

The Lord Jesus' prayer extended to future believers as well, who would unite with Christ through the apostles' ministry of the Word (v. 20). He prayed that His disciples would be one in relationship with God (as the Son was in the Father) and that relationship would be manifested with love based the apostles' ministry of the Word (vv. 20, 23, 24, 26). As the Son of God had a spiritual relationship with God the Father (vv. 21-23), so Christ prayed for spiritual unity among His disciples (vv. 11, 21-22), who were in the heritage of the Apostles, who received the Lord Jesus Christ's Words which He in turn received from the Father (vv. 8, 17, 20).

Context

The Received Bible

> For I have given unto them the words which thou gavest me: and they have received them, and have known surely that I came out from thee, and they have believed that thou didst send me (John 17:8).

God the Father gave Words (ῥήματα, *rhāmata*) to God the Son (cf. also Jn. 12:49; 14:10). Presumably these Words would be the "all Scripture" (πᾶσα γραφὴ, *pasa graphā*,) of the Bible canon (2 Tim. 3:16). These Words are the ones Christ promised would not pass away (Mt. 24:35). The Lord's canonical Words would be available for every generation, He declared, because His canonical Words, and not His *agrapha* (not written), will be the judge of every man. The views that not all of the Lord's spoken Words have been written down and consequently His promise in Mt. 24:35 is for prophecy only[72] or is hyperbole,[73] are certainly wrongheaded and refuted by Christ's claim that "He that rejecteth me, and receiveth not my words, hath one that judgeth him: the word that I have spoken, the same shall judge him in the last day" (Jn. 12:48). Mankind will not be judged by all of Christ's spoken words since many were not canonical. God is just in His judgment (Jn. 5:30; cf. Rom. 2:2) and will judge man on the basis of His ever available, perfectly preserved, inscripturated Words.

---

edifying which is in faith" (1 Tim. 1:4). Questions such as who wrote the Pentateuch or what was the ultimate source for Mark's Gospel or does the *pericope de adultera* (John 8:1-11) belong in Scripture ring of "Yea, hath God said" (Gen. 3:1). This man-centered "wisdom descendeth not from above, but is earthly, sensual, devilish" (Jam. 3:15).

[72]Daniel Wallace argues that Christ must be referring to "His prophecies" because in John 21, "Everything that Jesus did and said, the whole libraries of the world could not contain. Obviously not all the words of Jesus are written down. So what happened to the preservation of those words? It doesn't mean that. It means . . . prophecy," The John Ankerberg Show Transcript. "Which English Translation of the Bible is Best for the Christian to Use Today" (Chattanooga, TN: The Ankerberg Theological Research Institute, 1995), pp. 44,46.

[73]"Matthew 24:35 uses the same hyperbolic language as Matthew 5:18." William W. Combs, "The Preservation of Scripture," *Detroit Baptist Seminary Journal* (Detroit: Detroit Baptist Theological Seminary, 2000), Vol. 5, p. 24.

The process, to which the Lord alluded (in Jn. 17:8), was the process of inspiration, wherein the Father breathed out His Words[74] to the Lord Jesus Christ (Jn. 8:28), who in turn breathed out these inerrant and authoritative Words to His Biblical writers. The Lord's Biblical writers in His immediate audience, such as Matthew, John, Peter and others, received the Words and ultimately inscripturated them in their canonical writings which were passed on to future generations through those who would believe on the Lord Jesus Christ through Apostles' respective Scriptures (cf. v. 20).[75]

The Lord's disciples "have received (ἔλαβον, *elabon*)[76] them," unlike the unbelieving Jews who "receive not" (οὐ λαμβάνετε, *ou lambanete*) the Lord's spoken words (Jn. 3:11).[77] Those that had received (ἔλαβον, *elabon*) the Lord Jesus Christ in salvation (Jn. 1:12) readily received His Words for sanctification (Jn. 17:20), John averred. Upon receiving the Lord's Words (Jn. 17:8), these ministers of God's Words acknowledged (ἔγνωκαν, *egnōkan*; cf. Jn.16:30) and believed (ἐπίστευσαν, *episteusan*; cf. 3:16-17) that the Father sent the Son (cf. Jn. 5:36-37). The Lord Jesus Christ required His original audience to receive His Words and guard them (cf. Mt. 28:20; "to observe" [τηρεῖν, *tārein*]) them.[78] This "received text" or "received Bible" mindset originated with the Lord Jesus Christ, not with Erasmus, Beza, or the KJB translators.[79] Believers of every generation have expected to receive God's preserved Words. The requirement for and the expectation of the Lord's received Bible has had a theological and historical continuity which shall not be broken, according to Scripture (cf. 1 Tim. 3:15). The fact that believers in the first century, in the seventeenth century, and in the twenty-first century, have had a "received Bible" mindset is built upon Scriptural teaching, not historical necessity.

The "received Bible" mindset of the first century Christians is corroborated by the practice of the first century churches. These NT churches and the members thereof received the oral apostolic teaching which ultimately became the inscripturated Words of God. These inscripturated Words in the form of Gospels and Epistles became the NT Canonical Words which the churches were charged to guard (Mt. 28:19-20; 1 Tim. 3:15; Rev. 22:18-19). Several examples of this "received Bible" mindset in the practice of the NT churches follow.

Peter preached his great Pentecost sermon from within the Jerusalem assembly to hostile Jews. When many of these Christ-rejecting Jews heard the preaching of Peter

---

[74]These canonical Words were no doubt the archetypal Words to which the Psalmist referred when stating "For ever, O Lord, thy word is settled in heaven" (Psm. 119:89). Combs, like many others, rejects "the idea of an archetypal Bible in heaven," (p. 17), but is rebutted by Scripture. Daniel was informed of the same heavenly Bible that contained the prophesied history of the nations and leaders relative to Israel's future. The informing angel stated, "But I will shew thee that which is noted in the scripture of truth . . . and now will I shew thee the truth . . . "(Dan. 10:21-11:45; cf. Isa. 65:6).

[75]Doubtless the Holy Spirit has used Paul's Epistle to the Romans, for example, as the means to justify multitudes of repentant sinners through the ages for the Lord's glory.

[76]This word is a 3rd person, plural, 2nd Aorist, active, indicative verb from *lambano* (λαμβάνω) and means "to take" or "to receive."

[77]The Person of the Lord Jesus Christ and His Words are inextricably united so that rejection of one

about repentance and remission of sins, they received (ἀποδεξάμενοι, *apodexamenoi*)[80] his authoritative Words, as Luke recorded; "Then they that gladly received his word were baptized: and the same day there were added unto them about three thousand souls" (Acts 2:41). They realized their responsibility before God and received the oral tradition that ultimately became the inscripturated Words of truth.

Not only were Jews saved when they fulfilled their responsibility before God and received His preached revelation, but so were the Samaritans. Luke stated, "Now when the apostles which were at Jerusalem heard that Samaria had received the word of God, they sent unto them Peter and John" (Acts 8:14). The church in Samaria was established because Samaritans, or half-Jews, had received (δέδεκται, *dedektai*) the Words of God preached by a Jew named Philip.

Luke recorded that Jews and Samaritans entered into the Christian life with the "received Bible" mindset. Next, he stated concerning the Gentiles, "And the apostles and brethren that were in Judaea heard that the Gentiles had also received the word of God" (Acts 11:1). These Gentiles received (ἐδέξαντο, *edexanto*), along with Jews and Samaritans, the Lord's revealed truth in preached form. Thus mankind has the responsibility to receive God's revelation by faith and some have exercised this "received Bible" mindset.

The Jewish Bereans "received (ἐδέξαντο, *edexanto*) the word with all readiness of mind" (Acts 17:11) and compared Paul's apostolic preaching with the OT Scriptures. They had already received the OT Scriptures as authoritative revelation, and now practiced this "received Bible" mindset with the oral tradition.

The Apostle Paul identified his preached Word and the Words of God in his ministry at Thessalonica. He stated,

> And ye became followers of us, and of the Lord, having received the word in much affliction, with joy of the Holy Ghost . . . For this cause also thank we God without ceasing, because, when ye received the word of God which ye heard of us, ye received it not as the word of men, but as it is in truth, the word of God, which effectually worketh also in you that believe (1 Thess. 1:6; 2:13).

---

leads to the rejection of the other. Did not Christ warn the Jews, "For had ye believed Moses, ye would have believed me: for he wrote of me. But if ye believe not his writings, how shall ye believe my words?" The field of Biblical Criticism, of which Text Criticism is one facet, is a system of unbelief originated and promoted by apostates. Why are professing fundamentalists attracted to and entertained by any facet of this anti-supernatural movement?

[78]Christ commended the members of the church of Philadelphia because they had guarded or "kept" (ἐτήρησας, *etārasas*) His word for perhaps some forty years (Rev. 3:8, 10).

[79]That believers coined the term "received text" (*textus receptus*) in 1633 and have remained comfortable with the term to this very day demonstrate historically this heritage of the "received Bible" mindset which originated with Christ.

[80]The root behind this Aorist participle is *dechomai* (δέχομαι) which means "to take" or "to embrace."

The apostle commended the Thessalonians since they received his preached Word as God's Words and not as man's words. Eventually Paul's canonical preached Words became inscripturated in Acts and the Pauline Epistles. The Thessalonians are another testimony to the fact that first centuries churches maintained a "received Bible" mindset.[81]

In summary, the Lord Jesus Christ gave perfectly in inspiration and preservation the heavenly Words of the Father to His disciples. They in turn received these perfect Words and obediently kept them for future generations. That the early NT churches did this is incontestable. The Lord prophesied the means of His inspiration and preservation and fulfilled His bibliological work through His NT churches. The NT declares that the movement of the "received Bible" mindset originated with and is perpetuated by the Lord Jesus Christ through the instrumentality of His NT churches.

The Unity of Immersed Believers

The Savior prayed for the unity of those that the Father had given the Son. He stated, "Holy Father, keep through thine own name those whom thou hast given me, that they may be one, as we are" (Jn. 17:11). The foundation of this unity ("one"ἕν, *hen*) is built on the indwelling (ἐν, *en*) relationship of Christ with the believer and is likened to the Father and Son's indwelling relationship with each other (cf. v. 21).[82] As the believer receives the Lord through His Words (Jn. 1:12; 17:20) in salvation and receives the Lord's Words as truth in sanctification (Jn. 17:17-19), he continues to believe and obey God's revelation.[83]

Those that receive the revelation of truth believe and obey the Lord. The Lord Jesus Christ required early on that those who received Him as Messiah needed to obey Him by publicly identifying with Him through John's baptism (Mt. 3:6-17; 21:25-27).[84] This baptism pictured the death, burial and resurrection of Jesus Christ (cf. Rom. 6:1-4).[85] John's baptism became the baptism of the Great Commission (Mt. 28:19-20)[86] and was consistently practiced by the NT churches throughout the book of Acts (2:41-47; 8:12; 9:18; 10:47-48; 16:33; 18:8 *et al*).

Christ prayed for the unity of those the Father gave Him, who in turn received the Lord and His Words, and believed and obeyed Christ by identifying with Him through believers' baptism.[87] Paul recognized the answer to the Lord's prayer in part in Galatia. The Apostle addressed the churches of Galatia (Gal. 1:2) and stated, "For as many of

---

[81]All saints enter into salvation in Christ with the "received Bible" mindset. It is only after some believers are indoctrinated contrary to this Biblical mindset and embrace the "restored Bible" mindset do denials of truth unfold.

[82]Cf. Jn. 10:30; "I and my Father are one."

[83]The Lord Jesus said, "If a man love me, he will keep my words . . . " (Jn. 14:23; cf. vv. 21 and 24; *vide* 1 Jn. 5:2-3).

[84]Almost all Protestant denominations as well as the Roman Catholic Church and the Eastern Orthodox Church recognize and practice baptism as the entrance requirement for church membership. These groups usually undermine the NT doctrine of believers' immersion.

[85]The meaning of *baptizein* (βαπτίζειν) is "to immerse" and the mode is immersion, according to the NT (cf. Mt. 3:16; Acts 8:37-39; Col. 2:12). Nowhere in the NT are the words for "sprinkle" or "pour"

you as have been baptized into Christ have put on Christ. There is neither Jew nor Greek, there is neither bond nor free, there is neither male nor female: for ye are all one in Christ Jesus" (Gal. 3:27-28). The immersionist churches of Galatia manifested the "received Bible" mindset (Gal. 1:9) and were united in doctrine and practice. Based on contextual exegesis and grammar, the Lord Jesus Christ's prayer for unity was a prayer for those immersionists who have the "received Bible" mindset to be united around the Lord Jesus Christ. For one to reject Biblically this interpretation one would have to prove from Scripture that faithful followers of the Lord do not need to be baptized, that NT baptism is not believers' immersion, that the Lord Jesus would entrust His Words to disobedient believers, that believers' baptism is not the entrance into the local church, that Christ did not give His Great Commission to the local church, that believers did not have the responsibility or mindset to receive Christ's Words and that they did not have the responsibility to keep His Words.[88]

Conclusion

The Lord prayed for the unity of "the pillar and ground of the truth" movement (cf. 1 Tim. 3:15). He gave His inspired and preserved Words to His initial churches of the first century for safekeeping. These apostolic churches had the expectation to receive His preserved Words and keep them for every generation. He wants His immersionist assemblies that have received His Words to be united in truth as is He with His Father. The received Savior with His received Words becomes foundational to the unity He wants for His institution of the immersionist assembly, as this Divinely ordained and preserved institution preserves the Scriptures for every generation. The Lord Jesus Christ's preserved churches should be united in Him as they preserve His Words.

---

ever used for the ordinance of baptism.

[86] Baptized believers must recognize that they have the responsibility to guard the Lord's Words in their respective churches, according to Christ's Great Mandate.

[87] This does not mean that immersion is necessary for salvation, because it clearly is not. However, the Lord's whole prayer was concerned with those who receive, believe, and obey. Where do the un-immersed disobedient ones fit in relative to this prayer? Rather, why not ask why don't or won't the disobedient obey? The disobedient, and not theologians, create problems like this.

[88] It is apparent as one looks upon the landscape of fundamental Christianity that those on the forefront of the preservation/text/translation issue are the pastors and church members of received text/Bible, Baptist churches who are rightly battling the leaders and scholars of denominations, conventions, fellowships, para-church ministries, Bible colleges, and seminaries.

CHAPTER FIVE

My Words Shall Not Pass Away
Matthew 24:35
Kent Brandenburg

Introduction

In Matthew 24:35, the Lord Jesus Christ makes the significant prophecy, "Heaven and earth shall pass away, but my words shall not pass away." Although in its context the prophecy relates to His Second Coming, it also directly concerns the future of heaven and earth and God's Words.

The Context of Matthew 24:35 as a Whole

The Lord in His mercy has established His own credibility by means of prophetic Scripture. There is no one that would expect one hundred per cent consistency if someone made predictions of solely human origin. Because God alone can be expected to be perfectly consistent, only the Bible has truly prophetic material. Titus 1:2 says that " . . . God . . . cannot lie . . . . " The Bible is full of prophecy and fulfilled prophecy in which God establishes the veracity of Scripture. In Isaiah 42:9 He says, "Behold, the former things are come to pass, and new things do I declare: before they spring forth I tell you of them." Then in Isaiah 48:3-5, the Lord repeats, "I have declared the former things from the beginning; and they went forth out of my mouth, and I shewed them; I did them suddenly, and they came to pass. Because I knew that thou art obstinate, and thy neck is an iron sinew, and thy brow brass; I have even from the beginning declared it to thee; before it came to pass I shewed it thee: lest thou shouldest say, Mine idol hath done them, and my graven image, and my molten image, hath commanded them." The uniqueness of Biblical prophecy testifies to its authority and perfection.

Matthew 24 and 25 stand as one of the great prophetic passages, of the Gospels especially, but also the New Testament and the whole Bible. The Lord Jesus Christ is God, so He can speak prophetically, and He does so in this text. Since He says that the events prophesied in these two chapters are going to occur, one can count on them occurring. The Lord gives the religious leadership of Israel a last opportunity in Matthew 22 and 23. In Matthew 23, He tells them that Israel was facing considerable, but not total destruction. The question would arise, "What then is the future for Israel and the world?" Before the Lord dies, is buried, rises, and ascends to heaven, He teaches what will happen in Matthew 24 and 25.

The Immediately Preceding Context of Matthew 24:35

This discourse to the disciples on the Mount of Olives starts with their questions in Matthew 24:3, "When shall these things be? And what shall be the sign of thy coming, and of the end of the world?" Matthew 24:4-31 answers the second question of v. 3. Verses 32-35 partially answer the first question that they asked in v. 3. The Lord's answer, as recorded here, reveals the truth of the inevitability of His return.

This small section (vv. 32-35) starts with a parable. Parables would conceal truth from an unbeliever (Matthew 13:13,15), or reveal truth to a believer (Matthew 13:10,11,13,16). The Lord gives this parable of the fig tree to His disciples to help them understand His teaching about His Second Coming. The parable is not some complicated allegory, but a simple analogy. Palestine had an abundance of fig trees, which were not only grown commercially, but were also found in many family yards for the sake of the delicious fruit and the provided shade. Few figures would have been as familiar to the disciples of Christ as that of a fig tree, which the Lord Himself used on numerous other occasions as a teaching aid. The verses following this parable relate to it, so it is imperative to know why He is using it.

The Lord Jesus Christ commands the disciples to "learn" this parable (v. 32). "Learning it" would be to receive it as true and to apply it to one's life, to genuinely understand it and to accept its teaching. He next reminds them of what was commonly known already about the fig tree. When the sap begins to flow into its branches, making them tender, and new leaves appear on those branches, then summer is near. The budding fig tree meant that it was spring and that summer would soon follow when the ripened figs would be harvested.

The ripening of the fig tree is the harvest time. The harvest is a figure of judgment, a time of separating unbelievers from the believers, and of condemning the unbelievers (Mt. 3:12; 9:37,38). The Second Coming of Christ will be a time of judgment and destruction for those who have not received Christ. In this parable of the fig tree, the Lord Jesus Christ was illustrating that, when the signs that He had just been describing (vv. 16-28) begin to transpire, the time of His return will be very near. They will come one on top of another. The coming of Christ will follow these signs like the ripening of the figs follows the budding of the fig tree, and like the harvest follows the ripening of the figs. Verse 33 makes this application clear. When Israel will see "these things" (that is, the birth pangs of vv. 4-14, the abomination of desolation of v. 15, the need to flee because of impending peril of vv. 16-28, and the catastrophic upheaval of the universe of v. 29), then the Second Coming of Christ will be near, even as the budding of the fig tree indicated that summer was near. When the given signs occur, the Lord Jesus Christ will be right at the door, knocking, ready to come in.

Giving further application in v. 34, the Lord says that the generation that sees the budding of the fig tree (the commencement of these signs) will not pass until all of them have been fulfilled. The span of time in which all of the end time events recorded in Matthew 24 will occur will be less than one generation. The generation that witnesses the previously described signs will live to see the coming of the Lord Jesus Christ. This is the answer to the disciples' question concerning the "when" of His coming in v. 3. The generation of people that will see these signs is the generation that will enter the tribulation period unsaved, but many Jews will be saved during the tribulation period (Revelation 7).

This material is timed information. The people to whom it is most applicable will be people who are living in the tribulation period. At the time of these sign events, there will be incredible and dramatic changes in the topography of the earth. Revelation 6:14 says, "And the heaven departed as a scroll when it is rolled together, and every mountain and island were moved out of their places." The things, on which the people of this world depend, the *terra firma*, are passing away. One can count on the destruction of the earth, and one can count on the things of the world passing away (1 Cor. 7:31; 1 Jn. 2:15). This also includes the ultimate destruction of heaven and earth (2 Peter 3:10). So, the things that people depend on the most in space and time cannot be counted upon.

The Text of Matthew 24:35 and the Following Context

Most people think that such predictions as the Lord is making could not be credible or valid. Prophecies can easily be doubted. They seem impossible. They actually would be impossible to trust, except that the supreme, all-knowing, all-powerful God Who created this universe has given them. The Words of the Lord can be trusted more than even heaven and earth, because His Words will not pass away.

During the tribulation period, someone may buy an island to survive, to get himself out of the mainstream. Someone else may dig out a tunnel or a bomb shelter. There may be a person who will get into a spaceship to escape to outer space. Others may seek to survive through such means as rubber gloves, the sterilization of everything, breathing masks, or even through self-defense skills such as martial arts. However, none of these men will be able to elude the judgments of the tribulation period and the Second Coming of Christ. One can expect that the Lord's Words will continue, and everyone will be without excuse, because His warning will stand.

The Lord's Words here in His Olivet Discourse should be relied upon because His Words in general will not pass away. His Words by nature do not pass away. The generation that will see these signs, and will be here for the Second Coming of Christ, will still have available the Words of the Lord. That generation is still in the future, so today one should surely trust, based upon this prophecy of the Lord Jesus Christ, that His Words today are extant and available. The instruction of this passage, word for word, will exist in the day of that generation because the Lord promises preservation of every Word. People hearing this in the time the Lord taught this would have known of the promises of preservation of the Words of God already,[89] so this would have been no new doctrine. However, it would have been another reinforcement of that particular promise of the Lord in Scripture (cf. Isaiah 40:8; 59:21).

All of the portions of Scripture that contain unfulfilled prophecy are passages that are necessary for generations of people that are yet future. For instance, the detailed prophecy of the millennial temple in Ezekiel 40-48 does not wholly apply to any generation until the millennial kingdom arrives. Then these Scriptures will provide a handbook for worship. In this same way, these Scriptures on the Second Coming signs will give the greatest help to generations that are still in the future. If professing believers of the present-day generation are not willing to believe in the preservation of God's Words, what hope would the generation have that will most need them? This, however, is not something about which one is to be apprehensive as a believer. One would assume that believers would trust the Lord when He says that His Words will not pass away.

Some might say that v. 35 is about the authority of the Word of God. This is true. This is not all that this text teaches, however, or even what it mainly teaches. It also says that the very Words of the Lord will still be around when the Second Coming generation is alive, even when heaven and earth will pass away. Every generation that ever lives will

---

[89]Johannes Schneider in the *Theological Dictionary of the New Testament*, Vol. 2, ed. Gerhard Kittel (Grand Rapids, MI: Wm. B. Eerdmans Publishing Company, 1964) on p. 682 cites H.L. Strack and P. Billerbeck, *Kommentar zum NT aus Talmud und Midrasch*, p. 1922ff, "What Jesus says of His Word the Rabbis maintain of the Torah, namely, that it will last forever."

[90]James A. Borland in his Spring 1999 article in *The Master's Seminary Journal*, "The Preservation of the New Testament Text," p. 41, wrote, "The concept is that God's words, and hence His promises, will never fail to be performed." However, *epangelia* (ἐπαγγελία, Gal. 3:16; Rom. 9:4; 2 Cor. 1:20; Heb. 11:33) and *epangelma* (ἐπάγγελμα, 2 Peter 1:4; 3:13) are nouns used with the understanding of "promise(s)" in addition to the Greek verb *epangello* (ἐπαγγέλλω) being used in the middle (Acts 7:5; Rom. 4:21) and passive (Tit. 1:2; Heb. 6:13; 10:23; 11:11; 12:26) voice as "to promise," so God could have used that word if He so desired. Since He specifically used "words" when He had another choice, it seems obvious that Borland is straining to redefine a clear term in order to fit his predisposed theological (perhaps better, historical) position. Borland clearly reveals the basis for his eisegesis of "words" when he comments on Matthew 5:17,18, p. 42, "In fact, not only jots and tittles, but also entire words and even larger chunks of material have accidentally been omitted during the copying of individual manuscripts. The preservation of the New Testament text is not to be founded upon a glib quotation of these or other such verses." Borland depicts perfect preservationists as "glibly" (superficially, insincerely) quoting Scripture in their defense of this doctrine (*ad hominem* argument). This argument (the glib quotation argument) is inherently weak.

[91]There are four points from the Greek text that illuminate further the understanding of this verse of Scripture.

be able to count on these same Words. It does not just teach their existence, but clearly implies their availability. The purpose of the Words is to warn of the timing of the Lord's coming. Those who should be warned will be able to access the Words for the purpose of that warning. This does not at all concur with the view that the Words are in heaven only, in museums, or buried somewhere in the Middle East or Egypt. For the Words to fulfill their clearly implied and prophesied purpose would require them to be available to those alive for the Second Coming and for succeeding generations as well.

Does the text say that all of God's Words will be available even after heaven and earth pass away? The use of the plural "Words" (*logoi*, λόγοι) communicates an emphasis on the individual Words themselves, not just the Word of God in general.[90] All of the specific Words of God will continue to be available. Since the text does not say "some of the words" or in some other way restrict this aspect of this promise, the clear conclusion should be that every single word and all of the Words of God's inspired originals (*autographa*) exist and are available for believers. For this text to teach something else would require some kind of qualifier, at least. The absence of a qualifier and faith in the Lord's prophecy, and, therefore, in the veracity of the Lord Jesus Christ as the Divine Truth-Teller, necessitate belief in perfect and available preservation of Scripture.[91]

The following context does not take away from this meaning and application toward perfect and available preservation of every Word. Verses 32-35 make the point of inevitability of His return. Beginning in verse 36 the Lord teaches the unexpectedness of His return, despite its inevitability. People will be able to count on the return of the Lord Jesus Christ, whether they are expecting it or not, because His Words can be trusted. A contrast exists between the expectation of preserved Words and the expectation of the Lord's return. People should be expecting the coming of the Lord because of the trustworthy Words of God. The following context reveals that most men in the

---

First, there is the use of the Greek double negative regarding the "words not passing away." The double negative makes this prediction even more emphatic, that is, that the Words certainly will not pass away. A second point is the use of the noun *logoi* (λόγοι) as opposed to *rhāmata* (ῥήματα) for "words." The use of *rhāma* occurs when there is a reference not to the whole Bible, but to the individual Scripture or phrase of Scripture. If the Lord Jesus Christ was referring to just the Olivet Discourse, He likely would have used *rhāma*, but He uses *logoi*. *Logoi* would do more to ensure that the Lord's prediction refers to all of His Words, not just some of the Words, or a particular passage. The third observation relates to the verb *parerchomai* (παρέρχομαι, "shall pass away"). There is a temporal aspect to this verb. Heaven and earth will have time run its course. The Lord's Words are eternal, so will not have time outlast them. His Words are not bound by time. The same word is used in 2 Peter 3:10 and Revelation 21:1 to describe what will befall the old heavens and earth. God's first created heaven and earth are time-sensitive. His Words do not have this limitation. They will continue to be available on into eternity. Fourth, there is the tense and mood of the verb *parerchomai* (παρέρχομμαι). In the first half of the verse, "shall pass away" is a future indicative. In the second half of the verse, it is an aorist subjunctive. The future indicative says that heaven and earth will really pass away in the future. The aorist subjunctive says that it is definitely not possible that His Words will ever have a point where they will pass away. The contrast between the tense and mood of the same root word in the two parts of this verse make the preservation of His Words that much more emphatic. Analysis of the usage of this verb demonstrates that its normal meaning denotes the mortality of a thing or period (2 Cor. 5:17; James 1:10; 1 Peter 4:3), and, with the negative, it clearly communicates the immortality of a thing or period. Together, these four Greek points indicate that all of the Words of the Lord will emphatically not pass away, even after heaven ("the heaven") and earth ("the earth") [individually] pass away.

tribulation will not trust God's Words, and will, therefore, not trust in His return. This lack of trust in the perfect preservation of God's Words is directly related to the lack of expectation for the Lord's Second Coming.[92]

Conclusion

With all of this in mind, the text in its context very clearly supports the doctrine of the preservation of God's Words. Matthew 24:35 teaches that every one of God's Words, as He gave them of old to holy men of God, are extant and available for every generation. To not believe this is to deny or reject this verse of Scripture in its context.

---

[92] 2 Peter also clearly makes this point (2 Peter 1:16-21; 3:1-10). People who attack the expectancy of the Lord's return strongly impugn the veracity of Scripture. Attacking preservation will cast doubt on the trustworthiness of God's prophecies of Christ's Rapture and Second Coming.

CHAPTER SIX

Inspiration Implies Preservation
2 Timothy 3:15-17
Charles Nichols

Introduction

In recent days the charge has been made by some that it is dishonest to draw support for verbal preservation from passages where that is not the main point in the context. This is absurd. The supporting truths in a particular text undergird the main message declared. One cannot obtain a clear understanding of the primary theme of any passage without understanding the meaning of the terms used in presenting it. Invariably, the force of the main point of any passage is dependent upon the implied truths used to convey it. Word studies and consideration of word associations are vital to proper Biblical interpretation for all who have an honest appreciation for Biblical inspiration and preservation.

Biblical preservation is not the major thrust of 2 Timothy 3:15-17. Paul, who has little hope of surviving his second Roman imprisonment, is passing a mantle of ministry to Timothy in this epistle for the continuation of the faith. In the context of this chapter, Paul guarantees a perfect and authoritative Bible to supply sufficiently the man of God in the midst of false teachers and their corrupt doctrine. Terms and combination of terms in this passage demonstrate the preservation of the Words of Scripture. The role of the pastor in leading a local church to keep the Words of God (1:13,14) combines with the doctrine of the perfect inspiration of those Words (3:15-17) to provide the clear and dynamic teaching of the perfect preservation of Scripture.

The Text of 2 Timothy 3:15-17

In 2 Timothy 3:15 the word "holy" is used as an adjective describing the Scriptures. Paul utilizes this term (ιερός, *hieros*) to describe that which is sacred, unadulterated, and pure from defilement. W. E. Vine's *Expository Dictionary of New Testament Words* declares the Greek term used in 1 Timothy 3:15 is synonymous with the Greek term ἅγιος (*hagios*), employed in conjunction with God, the Father, Son, and Holy Spirit (Revelation 4:8).[93] In utilizing this adjective to describe the Old Testament Scriptures available to Timothy, the writer implies that they had been preserved unadulterated into the first century A. D. They were holy, so necessarily perfect.

The expressed definite article ("*the* Holy Scriptures") further contributes to this implication that Timothy had come to know the very perfectly preserved Words of God.[94] The word "Scriptures" is γράμματα (*grammata*). Even though "the Holy Scriptures" is an idiom for the Old Testament,[95] the primary meaning of γράμματα is "letters." Letters constitute written words. A single letter can easily make the difference between one word and another.[96] This expression also implies the availability of the letters of the Old Testament to Timothy. Only available letters could make someone wise unto salvation. He knew and continued to know (*oida*, οἶδα[97]) these letters, which were the basis of his salvation.

The clear declaration of the inspiration of Scripture is itself another strand of evidence for verbal preservation. The adjective "all," as translated in the King James Version, is a term W. E. Vine says "radically means 'all' (πᾶς, *pas*)" and when used without the article, signifies "every."[98] Even when translated as "all" without the article *pas* has the understanding of "every," as in "every kind."[99] This term would then dictate the inspiration of each part of Scripture, necessitating the inspiration of the whole. This coincides with Christ's words recorded in Matthew 4:4, ". . . man shall not live by bread alone but by every word that proceedeth out of the mouth of God." The word "Scripture" in v. 16 is γραφὴ (*graphā*), a term that refers to that which was written, the letters and Words, not just ideas. God's inspiring every writing implies that He would use Divine means for its preservation. What value is an inspired Scripture for extended generations of human beings if it is not preserved in that inspired form? Timothy did not have the original manuscripts of the Old Testament. Verse 16 implies that the Old Testament copies that made Timothy wise unto salvation were the preserved equivalent to inspiration. What God inspired is perfect. Therefore, the Old Testament was perfectly preserved to Timothy's day.

---

[93]W. E. Vine, *Expository Dictionary of New Testament Words*, Vol. 2 (Old Tappan, NJ: Fleming H. Revell Company, 1966), p. 313. The use of the word *hieros* instead of *hagios* is telltale, however. *Hieros* is related to the worship of God through His institution in the Old Testament. The related words (*hieron* – temple; *hiereus* – priest) associate with the edifice and office of Old Testament worship. This was a unique term that distinguished this book as the holy Old Testament.

[94]The CT removes the definite article, leaving a much weaker statement on the sufficiency and authority of the Bible.

[95]The Greek speaking Jews of the day used these three words ("the Holy Scriptures") as their common designation for the Old Testament.

[96]See chapter three on Matthew 5:17 by Gary Webb, where the OT letters include the Hebrew vowels.

[97]Οἶδα is a progressive perfect verb, meaning that he knew as a child and continued knowing until this very time as an adult.

[98]Vine, p. 46.

[99]Used in Ephesians 1:3, the KJB translates *pas* (πᾶς) "all," as in "all spiritual blessings," but the understanding can be "every spiritual blessing." In Ephesians 2:21, "all the building" can be conceived as

All Scripture, not the Old Testament alone, is inspired.[100] Sufficiency depends on every writing God breathed. Every Scripture is necessary to overcome the deceivers and avoid being deceived (1 Timothy 3:14), and to render the man of God complete ("perfect") and fully fitted ("throughly furnished") for doctrine (his beliefs), reproof (his error illuminated), correction (his error repaired), and instruction in righteousness (his ability to do right in the future). Since every writing of God is necessary to equip sufficiently the man of God, the availability of every writing is an obvious ramification of "all Scripture is profitable."

God is just and no respecter of persons. John 12:48 declares that each individual will be ultimately judged according to the Word of God.[101] Since God does not respect persons and He will justly judge each one of every generation, the natural implication is that all Scripture inspired of God must of necessity be preserved for every generation of mankind. The many benefits listed in 2 Timothy 3:16-17, obtainable from the detailed entirety of inspired Scripture, imply that a just God, Who views all men equally, must provide every generation of mankind with the very Words He breathed out. Inspiration of Scripture without preservation of the God-breathed Words would be profitable only for the generations alive at the time the original manuscripts of Scripture were available. Since total, generational apostasy is impossible (Matthew 16:18; 28:19-20; 1 Timothy 3:15), one can be assured that men of God have lived in every generation up to and including today. The "man of God" of v. 17 is generic, so the truth of vv. 16, 17 is axiomatic.[102] The unlikely alternative is the extinction of the man of God after the death of Timothy. All of this says that every Word of God must be perfectly preserved for every generation.

Inspiration without preservation undermines the revealed character of God. Every God-breathed writing is said to be sufficient to make one wise unto salvation, teach, reprove, correct, and completely furnish. To argue that God only provided those Words to those who received the original manuscripts calls into question His goodness and fairness.

"every building," and in Acts 2:36, "all the house" could be translated as "every house." From the usage, this is not a hard and fast rule that *pas* without the article is always understood as "every." However, without the article as an adjective with a noun, *pas* normally should be understood as "every."

[100] 1 Timothy 5:18 calls Luke 10:7 "Scripture." 2 Timothy 3:16 included not just the Old Testament, but the sections of the New Testament, like Matthew and Luke, already given by inspiration as well.

[101] The Lord Jesus Christ declares the "Words" of God to be the standard of judgment for unbelievers in that last day. The Lord clearly implies that believers receive His Words. Response to His Words adjudicates between salvation and condemnation. Every man of every generation is, therefore, responsible for all the Words God has revealed up to that time. Based on verses such as John 12:48 and 17:8, the Christian has Biblical authorization for expecting to have all of the Words of Christ.

[102] The singular noun could only be particular or generic. Since Timothy is not the only man of God, it must be a generic usage of the singular noun. A Platonic understanding might make "the man of God" the universal, invisible man of God (a non-grammatical usage), but the obvious understanding is the generic man of God, representative of the class of men of God.

Conclusion

The Spirit of God in this passage used the term "holy" to describe the Scriptures that Timothy had come to know intimately. This clearly implies that the unadulterated Words, recorded up to or more than a thousand years earlier, were available to Timothy in the first century. Furthermore, the emphasis on the inspiration of the available letters and writings assumes their perfection. The necessity of Scripture for the perfect preparation of the man of God also demands the preservation of every Word of God for every man of God in every generation. To deny the benefits of vv. 16, 17 to men of God of succeeding generations by rejecting perfect preservation taints God's attributes of goodness and justice. 2 Timothy 3:15-17 strongly suggests perfect, available, verbal, and plenary preservation of Scripture just as it establishes God's inerrant, verbal, plenary inspiration. Perfect inspiration without perfect preservation would leave inspiration a worthless Biblical doctrine.[103]

---

[103]The CT position means that no verbally, plenarily inspired Bible is available today, only an errant one.

CHAPTER SEVEN

Words Which Abide Forever
1 Peter 1:23-25
Gary La More

Context for 1 Peter 1:23-25

As the reader comes to 1 Peter 1, he discovers an overview of some glorious facts concerning salvation. What are these facts? In 1 Peter 1:1-9 Peter presents the source (vv. 1,2), the guarantee (vv. 3-5), and the joy (vv. 6-9) of one's salvation. This salvation fulfilled prophecy (vv. 10-12a) and is that which angels have desired to investigate (v. 12b). The salvation these angels witness should look like the God, the Lord Jesus Christ, Whom they know, and vv. 13-17 says that the saved life is holy even as He is holy. In vv. 18-19 Peter talks about the cost of one's salvation, and then manifests the Person of salvation in vv. 20-21. Peter comes to the vehicle of one's salvation in vv. 22-25. In vv. 22-23a, Peter presents the fact that one must experience regeneration in order to be saved. How does this come about? According to 1 Peter 1:23b-25, God's Word brings this about.[104]

Salvation produces the ability to stand faithful in the midst of pressure from this world system.[105] Strangers and pilgrims (1:1; 2:11) gain strength internally from their position in Christ. The salvation described in 1:1-12, when possessed, enables imperatives for a child of God. God commands believers to continue hoping (1:13), become holy (1:15), live in fear of God (1:17), love one another (1:22), and desire the sincere milk of the Word (2:2) because saved people have the ability to practice each one of these.[106] Their behavior sets believers apart from those whose home is this world. The Word of God supplies the faith and power for obeying these commands.

Within this theme of salvation and its enabled practices, 1:23-25 draw attention to a particularly important truth. What is the truth found in 1 Peter 1:23-25? The truth is

---

[104]Harold L. Willmington, *The Outline Bible* (Wheaton, IL: Tyndale House Publishers, Inc., 1999), pp. 733-734.

[105]The theme of 1 Peter as a whole is steadfastness for God despite severe opposition from the world system.

God's promise of preservation. Why the promise of preservation? Why is this promise so important to a believer? This chapter will answer these two questions.

Historic Baptists have always believed in the perpetuity of the Lord's true churches. An accompanying belief in the perfect preservation of God's Words comes from clear promises of Scripture.[107] 1 Peter 1:23-25 demonstrates the truth of preservation.

The Text of 1 Peter 1:23-25

Verses 23-25 of 1 Peter 1 reveal to the reader that God has provided for him the vehicle for his salvation. The purifying of the soul in v. 22 that results in the holiness of vv. 15,16 comes because of the regeneration experience that is described in v. 23 as: "Being born again, not of (ἐκ, *ek*, "out of," "from") corruptible seed, but[108] of incorruptible,[109] by (διά, *dia*, "through," "by means of") the word of God, which liveth[110] and abideth[111] forever." So, how does this regeneration come about? It comes about by the Divine Word.[112] The Divine Word is the incorruptible seed which liveth and abideth forever.[113] This Divine Word is the means God uses to impart new life in an unbeliever (cf. Rom. 10:17; Jas. 1:18). Moreover, Peter's emphasis on the fact that the

---

[106]The backbone of 1 Peter 1:12-2:3 is these five Greek imperatives.

[107]Based upon the latter part of 1 Timothy 3:15, God's true churches have been given the responsibility of preserving His Word from century to century. They have fulfilled this responsibility to this day. See chapter thirteen on 1 Timothy 3:15 by Charles Nichols.

[108]The word for "but" in 1 Peter 1:23 is ἀλλά (*alla*). This is the strongest contrasting conjunction in the Greek language.

[109]The seed of man is corruptible, it passes away, but the Word of God is incorruptible. It will not change. It will not pass away. It will not decay. That is Bible preservation. D.A. Waite, *First Peter Preaching Verse by Verse* (Collingswood, NJ: The Bible For Today Press, 2001), p. 29.

[110]ζῶντος (*zōntos*) is a present active participle, genitive singular masculine from ζάω (*zaō*). The present communicates continuous action.

[111]μένοντος (*menontos*), is a present active participle, genitive, singular, masculine from μένω.

[112]λόγου . . . Θεοῦ (*logou . . . Theou*).

[113]ζῶντος καὶ μένοντος (*zōntos kai menontos*) – both participles are adjectival, in the predicate position, restrictive and are in agreement with λόγου (*logou*) [See footnotes 5, 6, and 7 above], which is a genitive of agent, used with the preposition ἐκ (*ek*). Θεου (*Theou*) is a genitive of description. What then is living and abiding forever? God's written Word, as given in the Bible, is living and abiding forever. Why? Because God has promised to preserve His Word to all generations. "Peter's point [here] is to emphasize the permanency of God's [W]ord. How does Peter do this? Peter does this by putting his emphasis on the '[incorruptible]' and 'abiding' nature of God's [W]ord." Wayne A. Grudem, *The First Epistle of Peter*, (Grand Rapids, MI.: William B. Eerdmans Publishing Company, 1988), pp. 90-91. The following context (vv. 24, 25) proves that "liveth" and "abideth" refer to the Word and not God. Since the participles here indicate durative action, Peter indicates, by using the present active form of the participle, that the Word of God is living and abiding forever. Preservation of God's Word is indicated with the present tense of the participles and the final idiomatic phrase, εἰσ τον αἰῶνα (*eis ton aiōna*, "into the age," that is, "forever"). An attack on the doctrine of preservation exists in the omission of this last phrase in the CT.

[114]Grudem, p. 91.

Word of God is living (cf. Heb. 4:12) suggests its power – unlike that of any merely human words – to generate new life in Christ. And the fact that it is abiding (cf. Mk. 13:31) reinforces the idea of the permanence of the new life generated by it.[114]

Therefore, in order to be regenerated, a man must have a Divine Word that is living and abiding forever.[115] Without a living and abiding Word being preserved continuously by God, the believer would not have what he needs to be born again. God has promised perpetuity to His Word because He knows that without it there would be no hope of eternal salvation. An eternal God has given an eternal Word that results in an eternal salvation. For the God of Psalm 90:2 to do any less would go contrary to His unchanging character.

In verses 24 and 25, God refers to Isaiah 40:6-8 and contrasts the perishable nature of the flesh with the eternal viability of the Word of God.[116] The saints, with all of the blessings of verses 3 through 13, are born from above of imperishable seed (verse 23). All else, all unregenerate flesh on earth, however affluent and currently powerful and prestigious, is like the grass – perishable. The flower that stems from it is destined to fade and fall.

Corruptible[117] seed, standing in sharp contrast with incorruptible, must exist somewhere. The words of men are corrupt and corruptible seed, including words of men posing as words of God. This passage explicitly teaches that Scripture is categorically incorruptible seed.[118] Belief in possible errors in actual Scripture runs contrary to

---

[115]There is enough of God's Word (at least 93%) in the CT that a person could be born again by means of that text. However, the dependence of salvation upon the Word of God indicates the danger of corruption. We are saved by means of incorruptible seed, not the corruptible. An application could and should be made that the corrupted text will be less effective or powerful because of its level of corruption. As strong as this text is in relating salvation to the purity of the Bible, it does not go so far as to teach that conversion can only occur by means of the King James Version. However, it is clear enough for legitimate fear of preaching from a tampered text. What are thought to be advantages for evangelism using the modern translations (from the CT) are actually severe disadvantages in light of the importance of purity. Ironically, this very point can be made in this very text. The CT omits διὰ πνεύματος (*dia pneumatos*) in v. 22. The important truth that obedience to the gospel, that is, salvation, is a work of the Holy Spirit is thus removed. The CT also excludes καθαπᾶς (*kathapas*). The necessity of regeneration and the receipt of a new heart, as well as the necessity of being right with God for acceptable worship and service, are now erased from this passage. In the following context, the CT pins εἰς σωτηρίαν (*eis sōtārian*, "into salvation") on the end of 2:2. This tends toward teaching salvation by works. 2:3 makes it clear that the growth of 2:2 is post-justification. The "therefore" of 2:1 makes the assumption that the new birth has occurred before all that Peter discusses in 2:1-3.

[116]"The voice said, Cry. And he said, What shall I cry? All flesh *is* grass, and all the goodliness thereof *is* as the flower of the field: The grass withereth, the flower fadeth: because the spirit of the LORD blowethe upon it: surely the people *is* grass. The grass withereth, the flower fadeth: but the word of our God shall stand for ever." In this last verse, we have a promise of preservation. "The word of our God shall stand for ever." What more evidence is needed? God has said it; what more proof does one need than this? The true believer in Christ is to accept by faith what God has said in His Word.

[117]This word "corruptible" appears elsewhere in the NT in Rom. 1:23; 1 Cor. 9:25; 15:53,54; 1 Pet. 1:18.

[118]The *TR* is the only text that is even asserted to be incorruptible, "pure," "unadulterated," and without error. Neither the advocates of the CT or of the Hodges-Farstad text even assert this for their text. This verse indicates the *TR* is the preserved Word of God.

what is taught here and what ought to be expected, since this is God's Word.

In contrast to the corruptible seed, the Word of God, which gives life to the believer, is eternal. The "but" of verse 25 is adversative.[119] Without a doubt, earthly glory fades (see verse 24) but the Word of God abides forever (v. 25).[120] This Word of the Lord is that which had been preached to them.[121] Thus Peter shows that the good news, by which God gave them their eternal inheritance, is eternal (1 Peter 1:4).[122] All of this is in heavenly contrast to the shabby, temporal and non-viable society of the world all about them. Once one realizes the riches of the eternal inheritance which has been given to him by the birth from above, he will see the necessity and great wisdom of growing in grace until he can take full advantage of it.[123]

When He was on earth, Jesus constantly affirmed that His message was eternal, that the very Words which He spoke had been given to Him by God the Father before the creation of the world (John 12:49-50). In His "High-Priestly" prayer Jesus also states emphatically that the Words that He had spoken to His Apostles had been given to Him in eternity by God the Father. "For I have given unto them the words which thou gavest me" (John 17:8). The Scriptures, therefore, are eternal. God gave to Jesus Christ His Son "the words of eternal life" (John 6:68). These are the Words that Christ brought down from heaven for the salvation of His people, and now remain inscribed in holy Writ. Therefore, Peter, being true to His Lord and Saviour, Jesus Christ, the founder of His *ekklāsia* (Matt. 16:18), testifies to the eternality of God's Word in 1 Peter 1:23-25. Peter recognized that the Sovereign God of the universe is eternal and he promised the eternality of His Word.

The gospel message proclaimed was preached using His Word (ῥῆμα, *rhāma*). The Word that abides forever in v. 23 is (present tense) the Word (the Gospel text) that is preached (v. 25), equating the two (*logos* in v. 23 and *rhāma* in v. 25). The Old Testament was used, for the Gospel was "according to the Scriptures" (1 Corinthians 15:2,3), so this passage does apply to the written Word (and not merely the oral Word).[124] Since this Word was the text of the Old Testament, no Old Testament passages were lost at the time of 1 Peter. The teaching here is that the Word that believers preach on earth is eternal. Believers preach the whole counsel of God's Word (Acts 20:27), therefore, every Word must be available.

---

[119] δέ (*de*)

[120] The Greek word translated "abideth" is μένει (*menei*), again a present active indicative verb, and so communicates durative action, but the word itself is the one usually used to describe the abiding of God or the things of God, making these things eternal. It distinctly differentiates God from the transitory things of this earth. The sense of the word is that of something "taking up residence." Other places to consider this usage are John 15:4-7; 1 John 2:14, 24, 27; and 3:15, 17, 24.

[121] Two Greek words are used in 1 Peter 1:23 and 1:25, namely, λόγος (*logos*) and ῥῆμα (*rhāma*). The significance of *rhāma* (as distinct from *logos*) is exemplified in the injunction to take "the sword of the Spirit, which is the Word of God," Eph. 6:17; here the reference is not to the whole Bible as such, but to the individual Scripture, which the Spirit brings to one's remembrance for use in time of need,

Conclusions

1 Peter 1:23-25 powerfully concludes what Peter has said in the first 22 verses of the first chapter of his epistle. The source of one's salvation, the guarantee of one's salvation, the joy of one's salvation, the response of one's salvation, and the cost of one's salvation depends on the eternality of the Word of God. How is one saved? He is saved by the Word of God which liveth and abideth forever. Without a doubt, Peter's message in verses 23 through 25 demands the preservation of God's Word.

---

a prerequisite being the regular storing of the mind with Scripture. W.E. Vine, Merrill F. Unger, William White, Jr., *Vine's Complete Expository Dictionary of Old and New Testament Words* (Nashville, TN: Thomas Nelson Publishers, 1985), p. 683. The use of the word *rhāma* says that incorruptible seed is not the Word in general, but specific passages. This takes away the argument that it is the "Word as a whole that is preserved, but not the Words."

[122]1 Peter 1:4, "To an inheritance incorruptible, and undefiled, and that fadeth not away, reserved in heaven for you."

[123]Yeager, *The Renaissance New Testament*, Volume 17, p. 85.

[124]Further evidence that this Word is the inscripturated Word is found in 2:2.

CHAPTER EIGHT

The Perfect Passive: "It is Written"
David Sutton

Introduction

The New Testament declares the doctrine of preservation when it employs the phrase "it is written." When quoting passages in the Old Testament, this phrase translates the perfect passive verb *gegraptai* (γέγραπται) and succinctly states that the verse at hand was written in the past and the results continue to be written down. Believers, unbelievers, the Lord Jesus Christ, and even Satan evidence the reality of preservation by using *gegraptai*. If the nature of this perfect passive *gegraptai* means that particular verses from the Old Testament are preserved just as they were written, then one should conclude that *gegraptai* implies that all the Old Testament and all the New Testament are preserved just as they were written.

The Meaning of the Perfect Passive

The Perfect Tense

God, the author of language, has the ability to reveal His message to people. God is omniscient and perfect; therefore, when God communicated His truth to mankind, He only used language that conveyed His meaning. For example, when the Holy Spirit authored an aorist tense verb, He did so with a full understanding that He might have chosen the imperfect tense instead. When God authored a perfect tense verb, He employed it over other tenses because the perfect tense expresses the unique idea that an event was accomplished in the past and the results continue in the present.[125]

The perfect tense is different from other tenses. In the indicative mood, the aorist and perfect tenses both depict activity in the past. While the aorist tense views the

---

[125] For a definition of the perfect tense, see Daniel B. Wallace, *Greek Grammar beyond the Basics* (Grand Rapids, MI: Zondervan Publishing House, 1996), pp. 572, 573.

past event as a whole, the perfect tense shows completed past action with the results of that action continuing to the present. The perfect tense is different from the present tense, which, generally, is present, ongoing action. The perfect tense also must not be confused with the pluperfect (past perfect) tense, for the pluperfect tense views the action, along with its results, as terminating in the past.

The Passive Voice

The passive voice shows that the action of the verb is being done to the subject by someone. In the passive, the subject is not doing the action to something (active voice) or to itself (middle voice); something or someone acts upon the subject.[126]

The Perfect Passive

Combining the perfect tense with the passive voice shows the action of the verb completed in the past by an agent other than the subject of the verb with the results of the action continuing to the present. The perfect tense, and the perfect passive in particular, is often used in Scripture to teach doctrine and illustrate preservation of truth.

The Doctrine from the Perfect Passive

The Perfect Tense

Since the man of God is to divide rightly the Word of truth, he must objectively recognize, learn, believe, explain, and practice the significance of the Words of Scripture in their grammatical and historical context. If he does not, he fails to obey the command of God, fails to receive the Word of God, and fails to feed the flock of God. Since the Bible is where believers receive their doctrine, the very Words of Scripture teach doctrine. Much doctrine is bolstered by the perfect passive. Before one contemplates the perfect passive, he should consider the implications of the perfect tense on its own.

When John introduced the Son of God to his worldwide audience in the first chapter of his gospel, he introduced Him as Creator: "All things were made by him; and without him was not any thing made that was made" (1:3). The first two verbs in the verse ("were made" and "was made") are the aorist tense of *ginomai* (εγενετο, *egeneto*). Thus, Jesus Christ, in six literal days, created all things. The last "was made" (γέγονεν, *gegonen*) is the perfect tense form of the same verb. In other words, the results of what Jesus Christ created have continued. For instance, the trees that grow today are not the trees of some 6,000 years ago, but they are the offspring of those that were created. The perfect tense teaches that results of creation continue from what Christ created.

A few verses later the evangelist states, "No man hath seen God at any time" (1:18).

---

[126]In the writing of Scripture, man was the human instrument, but God the Divine author. Consequently, one could say that the Scriptures were written by man and were written by God (cf. 2 Pet. 1:21).

The verb "hath seen" (ἑώρακε, *heōrake*) is in the perfect tense. No one in the past had ever seen God (cf. Ex. 33:20), and that reality continued to the time of the writing of the Fourth Gospel. To this day, no man has seen God at any time.

On the road to Damascus, Saul of Tarsus was persuaded that Jesus of Nazareth was the Messiah and believed on Him (cf. Acts 9:6). Near the end of his life, Paul testified to Timothy: ". . . for I know whom I have believed, and am persuaded that he is able to keep that which I have committed unto him against that day" (2 Tim. 1:12). When Paul wrote the verbs translated "have believed" and "am persuaded," he used the perfect tense (πεπίστευκα, *pepisteuka*, and πέπεισμαι, *pepeismai*, respectively). Paul professed that in the past he began believing on the Son and was convinced that Christ was able to keep that which he had committed to Him. Both his belief and his conviction continued to persist even to the point of his writing the epistle. Very clearly, the perfect tense establishes actions as being completed in the past with the results continuing to the present.

The Perfect Passive

Having hung on the cross for six hours and having suffered the brutality of crucifixion, the Lord Jesus Christ said, "It is finished" (Jn. 19:30). *Tetelestai* (Τετέλεσαι) is a perfect passive and can also be understood as "It has been finished." God's plan to offer His only begotten Son as the sacrifice for man's sins and Christ's suffering for them was complete for all of time, yet the results of Christ's offering would continue. The death of the Testator brought about the terms of the New Covenant and forever satisfied God's demands for justice (cf. Heb. 9:17). The perfect passive *tetelestai* teaches the eternal sufficiency of Christ's bloody death on the cross.

Not only did Christ die, but also He was buried, and He rose again the third day according to the Scriptures (1 Cor. 15:3,4). The perfect passive verb ἐγήγερται (*egāgertai*) that Paul used for the resurrection of Christ signifies that Christ was raised[127] at a moment in the past and the results of His resurrection continue. Hebrews 2:16[128] and 10:12 corroborate that Jesus Christ rose bodily and continues in such a state. The perfect passive teaches that the results of the bodily resurrection of Jesus Christ continue.

When a sinner believes on the Lord Jesus Christ, he has eternal life. The eternal security of the believer appears in the perfect passive participle in Ephesians 2:8: "For by grace are ye saved through faith." This classic verse on salvation gleans its eternal security teaching from the construction of the linking verb "are" (ἐστε, *este*) and the perfect passive participle "saved" (σεσωσμένοι, *sesōsmenoi*). God is teaching believers that they are always in the state of having been saved by God. In the past salvation came to the lost soul, and from that time on, he is always saved. The perfect passive clearly teaches the present results of past salvation.

---

[127] All three members of the Godhead were active in the resurrection of Christ (cf. John 2:18-22; Rom. 10:9; 14:9; 1 Pet. 3:18).

[128] Cf. the present tense of the Greek word behind "took" (ἐπιλαμβάνεται, *epilambanetai*).

These verses inarguably verify the doctrinal significance of the perfect passive, which has action completed in the past by someone with the results of that action continuing to the present. Knowing this pattern influences one's understanding of the perfect passive "it is written."

The Preservation in the Perfect Passive

Sixty-three times in the NT the exact phrase "it is written" occurs. The perfect passive verb *gegraptai* underlies fifty-nine of these references, while the other four occasions represent the perfect passive participle *gegramenon* (γεγράμενον). Following the custom of grammar, one would understand this phrase as "it has been and still is written." In other words, in the past someone wrote something, and that writing continues written down.[129]

One must not confuse the aorist tense with the perfect passive, for the aorist verb *egrapsa* (ἔγραψα) is used differently from the perfect passive *gegraptai*. In the NT the aorist is consistently used to describe the composition of a personal letter (cf. Acts 15:23; I Cor. 7:1), the OT Law (cf. Jn. 5:46), or a NT epistle (cf. Eph. 3:3; Philm. 21). Punctiliar action appropriately denotes the writing process, because the author at a point in time penned words on some medium. However, *gegraptai* does not encompass the process of writing the message alone, but affirms the continuation of the written message. God carefully distinguished among the forms of *graphō* (γράφω); consequently, the occurrences of the perfect passive inform the reader of a significant reference to Scripture that enables or bolsters some particular belief or practice.[130]

Particular Words made up of distinguishable letters were deliberately written. Therefore, one should conclude that when God gave man the text of the Bible, He gave specific Words and not general thoughts. One should also conclude that if Words are preserved, then the letters forming those Words are also preserved.

The first instance of the perfect passive "it is written" is in Matthew 2:5. Herod had asked the chief priests and scribes where Christ should be born. Without hesitation these religious scholars referenced the OT and gave a confident answer, which relied on the precise prophecy of Micah, the prophet. Their ability to identify the Messiah was based on the preserved prophecy of Christ's birthplace, which Divinely narrowed the possible candidates for Messiah. Since Micah 5:2 was preserved, as testified by *gegraptai*, the pinpoint knowledge of Messiah was preserved.

Many times the Lord Jesus connected prophecy to Himself. When He used *gegraptai*, He implied that those prophecies were sustained through time. Prophecies

---

[129]*Gegraptai* should be interpreted as an intensive perfect because of its emphasis on the results of the action. Thus, the strong durative quality to this verb provides the basis for its translation as a present state.

[130]The initial meaning of *graphō* (γράφω) was likely "to carve" or "to engrave," for Homer used it to describe a lance tearing flesh and to describe engraving on a table. Kittel, ed., *Theological Dictionary of the New Testament*, Vol. I, p. 742. This understanding associates the verb with the letters used to write given words.

of Messiah's forerunner were preserved, and Jesus refers to one, Malachi 3:1, when speaking of John the Baptist (Mt. 11:10). Because John had the preserved Scriptures, he could study the prophecies pertaining to himself and know his role and activity as forerunner (cf. Mk. 1:2). The Jews were looking for a conquering Messiah, but the Scriptures foretold a suffering Servant. Mark recorded the Lord's words in 9:12, which referred back to the OT to disclose His suffering.[131] Christ said, according to Hebrews 10:7, that He came to do God's will, just as "it is written" in the volume of the book. The heavenly roll never changes, and the Lord Jesus simply obeyed what continues to be written down in heaven. This text in Hebrews teaches that earthly preservation of Scripture is identical with heavenly preservation of Scripture. The Lord Jesus often referenced or quoted OT prophecies regarding His suffering (cf. Mt. 26:24,31 with Zech 13:7). When He did, He said that they had been written and continued to be written down. Before His crucifixion, Christ recognized that the message of Zechariah 9:9, which predicted that He would ride into Jerusalem on a donkey's colt (cf. Jn. 12:14), was still written down some five hundred years after its utterance.

The perfect passive maintains the integrity of other prophecies and statements about Christ. For example, Christ reminded His disciples of His prophesied suffering and resurrection from the dead on the third day (Lk. 24:46). The Lord Himself stated here once more that the Scriptures were written in the past and continued written down. Paul said that Christ at the resurrection was made a quickening spirit in contradistinction to Adam, who was made a living soul (I Cor. 15:45). This commentary about the first man is extremely familiar, for it continues to be found in Genesis 2:7. Because prophecies and statements about Christ are declared to be preserved with the phrase "it is written," the reader of Scripture can have certainty about the Scriptures' fulfillment and continuation.

The Lord Jesus Christ demonstrated His belief in preservation again when He quoted the OT to defeat Satan. The tempter's insidious solution, given to the Holy One of Israel after forty days and nights of fasting, was to satisfy His hungering stomach, proving His power to turn the stones into bread (Mt. 4:4; Lk. 4:4). The Master relied upon Scripture and indicated its preservation with the verb *gegraptai*. Citing Deuteronomy 8:3, Christ used the verse in its context to defeat the tempter. Two other times the Lord used *gegraptai* and then relied upon Scripture's authority by quoting the inscripturated Word to battle temptation (Mt. 4:7,10; Lk. 4:8). It is interesting that Satan understands Scripture's preservation, for he too recognized that the Words of God were written in the past and continue to abide (Mt. 4:6; Lk. 4:10). In the Lukan account of Christ's temptation, Jesus made an association between God's spoken Words and written Words by saying "It is said" (4:12). God has said (εἴρηται, perfect tense) His Words and their preservation continues in written form.

---

[131] *Graphō* consistently occurs in the NT with reference to writing words made with letters. For instance, Zacharius wrote words on a tablet (Lk. 1:63), Pilate authorized the superscription on the Lord's cross (Jn. 19:21,22), Paul wrote words in the epistle sent to Galatia (Gal. 1:20), and John wrote words in a book (Rev. 1:3,11; 14:13). Words consisting of letters are written on the Lord's vesture and on His thigh (Rev. 19:16).

The doctrine of salvation is dependent upon preservation: if there were no preserved Words, then there would be no preached Word, and man could not believe on Jesus Christ; for "faith cometh by hearing, and hearing by the Word of God." Paul explained in Romans 1:17 that in the gospel of Christ the righteousness of God is revealed. He quoted Habakkuk. 2:4, "As it is written, 'The just shall live by faith'" to show the association between the gospel and living by faith. Those who live by faith fully depend on God in contrast to those upon whom the wrath of God is revealed (1:18). Believers live by faith because of having received the gospel, and the gospel is according to the Scriptures (cf. I Cor. 15:3,4). Paul also used *gegraptai* to prove his treatise that both Jew and Gentile are under sin when in Romans 3:10-12 he referred to Psalm 14:1-3 and 53:1-3 to prove the total depravity of man. The apostle testified to the fact that the writings of David continued to exist for reference when he wrote Romans. Paul appealed to the authority of preserved Scripture to make his point: man is wicked because God has said so.

The NT exhorts Christ-like living based on declarations of the preserved OT. In Romans 15:3,4 Paul used two different tenses when communicating the believer's duty to live selflessly. In verse three, when the apostle explained how Christ pleased not Himself, He employed *gegraptai* to introduce Psalm 69:9. In the ensuing explanation Paul wrote the aorist *proegraphā* (προεγράφη)[132] to explain that the OT Scriptures were written "for our learning, that we through patience and comfort of the scriptures might have hope." If Christians are to live like Christ by learning from the Scriptures, God will ensure that they have every Word of Scripture available (cf. Mt. 4:4). Peter commanded his audience to become holy in every aspect of conduct, and his basis for this exhortation was the nature of God recorded in the law (I Pet. 1:15,16). The Holy Spirit guided Peter to establish his injunction from Leviticus 11:44, as witnessed by his use of *gegraptai*. The apostle to the Jews testified to the Scripture's preservation when he commanded saints to become presently holy.

Since God preserved His Word, man has sure footing on prophecy and its fulfillment. Without the perfect preservation of Scripture, prophecies of Christ would be obscure and even lost, and salvation by grace through faith would be impossible.

---

[131]Christ's decision to suffer for the sins of the world antecedes His incarnation in that prophecy and the rest of Scripture are timeless (cf. Ps. 119:89,152).

Conclusion

The grammar of the perfect passive teaches that someone caused an event in the past and the results of that action continue to the present. Much doctrine that the believer holds is established in the perfect passive. Consistency demands that the perfect passive *gegraptai* means that the Scriptures were written in the past and they continue written down in the present. Based on their inspired use of the perfect passive *gegraptai*, the writers of Scripture believed in perfect preservation. Likewise, believers today should believe in the perfect preservation of Scripture, because "It is written."

---

[132] The literal meaning of προεγράφη (*proegraphā*) is "to write before." Coupled with its punctiliar tense, the verb in 15:4 refers to the *autographa* penned by inspiration. One must see the significance of the two verbs and their tenses. In the latter verse Paul speaks of the OT Scriptures at their writing, and in the former verse he speaks of those Scriptures continuing in written form.

SECTION TWO

*Passages
On
Availability*

CHAPTER NINE

It Is Not Hidden, Neither Is It Far Off
Deuteronomy 30:11-14

Kent Brandenburg

Introduction

The people of Israel, to whom God had given many and significant privileges, could still be tempted to excuse themselves from responding to a call to salvation by faith, reasoning that they had not had the Words of God sufficiently accessible to clearly know and understand this message. The Words written by Moses under God's inspiration in Deuteronomy 30:11-14 reveal that this was absolutely not the case: "For this commandment which I command thee this day, it is not hidden from thee, neither is it far off. It is not in heaven, that thou shouldest say, Who shall go up for us to heaven, and bring it unto us, that we may hear it, and do it? Neither is it beyond the sea, that thou shouldest say, Who shall go over the sea for us, and bring it unto us, that we may hear it, and do it? But the word is very nigh unto thee, in thy mouth, and in thy heart, that thou mayest do it." These Words, in their context, teach the doctrine of the general availability of all the Words of Scripture for every generation.

Context of the Whole Book

The original recipients of Deuteronomy, both in its verbal and written presentations, were the second generation of the nation Israel subsequent to Mt. Sinai. The original Hebrew title of Deuteronomy is translated "These Be the Words," from the first two Hebrew words of the book (*'ālleh haddĕvârēm* – אֵלֶּה הַדְּבָרִים). Moses, who would not enter the land with the nation, but was preparing to die, gave this group a review or explanation of these Words of God which made up the Law of God. The title of Deuteronomy itself says that the Words themselves were available to the people of God's ordained institution (Israel in the Old Testament, the church in the New

Testament). Every generation of Israel needed the Words for the purpose of reviewing, remembering, believing, and practicing them. In Deuteronomy, they were told to remember them fourteen times, and ordered not to forget His Words nine times. Much of the Bible carries on this theme of being reminded of or remembering God's Words (cf. 2 Peter 1:12-21), which, of course, implies that those Words would be preserved and available for review.

The layout of Deuteronomy resembles the ancient suzerain treaty form with which Israel would have been familiar.[133] Practically, this treaty says: God deserves surrender, the believer will surrender, will obey His Laws in manifestation of that surrender, and blessing and/or cursing is dependent upon whether one of or all of Israel does surrender to what God has said. The Lord was the Suzerain and Israel the vassal. Israel was to surrender to the Lord, especially since He had delivered, protected, and provided for her. The conditions to be met by Israel to fulfill the covenant were more than just lists of legal stipulations. There was a heart condition that God expected first. This condition was for the individual Israelite and it was by means of this fundamental, internal surrender to God that each person was saved (Genesis 15:6; Deuteronomy 5:29; 6:4,5; 30:1-14). Without someone surrendering his person to God first, conformity to particular regulations would be vain and futile. Not to be missed, however, is that the one who would believe in the Lord for salvation knew that salvation included an agreement to obey all of the Words of God in His law. Deuteronomy integrates seamlessly surrender to God from the heart and detailed adherence to His stipulations.

Context of the Chapter

The heart surrender, repentance, or saving faith of the individual Israelite or Israel as a whole is revealed in the thirtieth chapter of Deuteronomy. Within the whole book, this chapter stands as an invitation for Israel to receive salvation. This point is further substantiated by the use of this text in the New Testament in this same way (Romans 10:1-10). The blessings and the curses are elaborated in the previous few chapters (27-29), and here the choice of blessing is clearly revealed. Moses draws the curtain on Israel's future to exhibit the Lord's plan for her. There is hope for her to impact her own outcome, based on her response to what God has said.

---

[133]Some believe that God purposefully laid out Deuteronomy as one of these treaties in order to help Israel understand her responsibility to God. Others believe that any resemblance to this treaty would at best be coincidental. This writer takes the former view. The Omniscient Jehovah used this treaty form in order to communicate mercifully His will to His people (like the Lord Jesus Christ did in the New Testament with illustrations and illusions that people would understand). The suzerain treaty was the surrender of a weaker nation (the vassal) to the stronger (the suzerain). These treaties include an introduction of the suzerain author, the past benefactions made by the more powerful suzerain, which led to the gratitude and obedience of the weaker vassal, the basic and detailed obligations that were laid down for the vassal by the suzerain, the making public of the general and specific conditions of surrender, the inclusion of witnesses, and then

The first nine verses of chapter thirty display the future humbling (v. 1), repentance (v. 2), blessing (vv. 3-5), transformation (v. 6), protection (v. 7), lifestyle (v. 8), and abundance (v. 9) of the Israelite. The Lord had benevolent preparations for each one who would concede to His covenant. Verse ten states the condition necessary to receive the blessings synthesized in verses one through nine; they would materialize for each who would meet the condition of salvation in verse ten. It is essentially one requirement, to take what God says seriously and turn to Him with heart and soul. Innate to meeting this condition is respect for and willingness to obey everything God has written in His Book.

Setting for 30:11-14

The plan of salvation is simple, but there are still arguments made against it that are sufficient to keep the majority of men from receiving it. A fundamental argument made by the unsaved person (in this case, the unbelieving Jew) to attack the authority of God's message is that God's Words are not available. The Bible intimates this argument or excuse elsewhere.[134] People can feel justified in their rebellion by convincing themselves that they could not be responsible for believing or obeying something that they were not sure was available. Knowing the deceived nature of man, the Lord erases this argument against availability in verses eleven through fourteen of chapter thirty of Deuteronomy. No one would be excused from doing God's will because the Words expressing His will were not available. These verses clearly delineate the accessibility of God's Words, even explaining how extremely available they were.

The previous verse (v. 10) establishes that this availability was for the Lord's commandments and statutes. The clear implication is that since the command to surrender was an order to acquiesce to all of the commandments and statutes, all of them would also need to be available. The plural form of "commandments" and "statutes" rules out the idea that only the concepts, thoughts, or doctrines were available; "commandments" and "statutes" imply Words. This is buttressed in the context with earlier verses such as Deuteronomy 29:9, "Keep therefore the words of this covenant, and do them, that ye may prosper in all that ye do."

---

the curses and blessings that are tied into either resisting or receiving this treaty. One can find these parts in Deuteronomy; yet even if the book was not in the form of one of these treaties, the message would be the same.

[134]One form of the argument is that God has not been clear. People excuse themselves by saying that the Bible is not something that they can understand. Another form of it is that 'there are millions who could not have had access to it,' giving everyone an excuse for not receiving God's Words. Romans 1:18-21 dispels this when it establishes the sufficiency of general revelation to justify the wrath of God. Satan deceived Eve in part by confusing her about whether she knew exactly what God had said. By the time he was done, she was not sure what He had commanded (Gen. 3:1-8).

Text of 30:11-14

When this passage is quoted by the Apostle Paul in Romans 10:8, "word" (*dâvâr* – דָּבָר) is translated *rhāma* (ῥῆμα) which is the specific term in the Greek that is used to speak of a particular group of Words. The exact written text that is necessary for a person to fulfill God's covenant was and is available. The revelation necessary to be saved is not a single word, but the series of Words that are necessary for the knowledge that produces saving faith (Romans 10:17; 1 Peter 1:23-25; 2 Peter 1:2,3; etc.). In this context, it goes further. A person is agreeing to keep all of the statutes, commandments, and Words of God (29:9; 30:10). Even when it is used singularly, within this context *dâvâr* (דָּבָר) essentially means "what God says or said." "What God said" is what is available. It expresses the revelatory work of the Lord, what God revealed. Throughout God's Law and the rest of the Old Testament, the Divine revelation that God has written is called "the word of the Lord" (*děvâr Yěhōwâh* – יְהוָה דְּבַר).[135] When this says that the Word was very near, it is talking about all of the Words because it is referring to the statutes and commandments of God.

The excuse or argument intimated is that the Words are not available. That excuse or argument is deflated perhaps even in advance of it being made with the Words of this text. To ensure that every angle of availability is covered, the text verges on hyperbole to meet its goal. Accessibility is communicated negatively and then positively.

Negatively, the commandment is not hidden, nor is it far off. The Hebrew words translated "not hidden" appear in many different ways in the KJB,[136] but together they

---

[135] Deuteronomy 5:5, "(I stood between the LORD and you at that time, to shew you <u>the Word of the LORD</u>: for ye were afraid by reason of the fire, and went not up into the mount;), saying . . . ." The preservation of Hebrew Words includes the vowel points (see chapter three on Matthew 5:17,18 by Gary Webb). Nevertheless, not adding the vowel points, as in the name of God *Yehōwâh*–יְהוָה, does not assume the consonants are pronounced without vowels. The assumption should be that the preserved vowel points represent God's preserved Words. In addition to Matthew 5:18, several other Old Testament verses relate to the originality and inspiration of the vowel points (Dt. 4:2; 17:18-20; 31:9-12; Josh. 8:31-35; 24:25-27; 2 Kings 22:8-13; Is. 59:21; Jer. 36:6,8,10,11,13,16,17-18,27-28, 32). The "constant, uniform tradition of the Jews, affirming that the points came down from Moses, and the giving of the Law, was a tradition unbroken down to the year 1538, twenty-one years after Luther had nailed up his Theses" (p. 44, *The Doctrines of Grace and Kindred Theme*, George Sayles Bishop, New York: Gospel Publishing House, 1919, in the chapter "The Inspiration of the Hebrew Letters and Vowel Points."). In the Reformation era Protestants contended for the inspiration of the points against Popery, rationalism, and those under their baneful influence; the Reformed (i. e., Francis Turretin [1623-1687], *Institutes of Eclectic Theology*, Vol. 1. trans. George M. Giger, ed. James T. Dennison, Jr., Phillipsburg, NJ: P & R Publishing, 1992, pp. 55-167, esp. 106-123), also Geradus, Junius, Gomarus, Polanus, Whitaker, Buxtorf Sr. and Jr., Ussher, Rainolds, Voetius, Deodatus, Lightfoot, and Heidegger, etc. (pp. 55-56, "The Debate over the Vowel Points and the Crisis in Orthodox Hermeneutics," Richard A. Muller, *The Journal of Medieval and Renaissance Studies*, 10 [1980] 1), Lutherans (i. e., Flaccius and Gerhard, p. 55, Muller), English men of God such as John Owen (1616-1683) ("Digression on the Origin of the Hebrew Vowel-Points," pp. 495-533 of *Biblical Theology: The History of Theology from Adam to Christ*, Morgan, PA: Soli Deo Gloria, 1994 trans. from Latin by Stephen P. Westcott, orig. pub. in 1661), and others, such as Broughton, Piscator, Joseph Cooper, Samuel Clark, and Whitfield (pp. 51, 59, "Life of Elias Levita," in *The Library of Biblical Studies*, ed. Harry M. Orlinsky, *Jacob Ben Chajim Ibn Adonijah's Introduction to the Rabbinic Bible and The Massoreth*

essentially mean "accessible," hence, knowable. Words that are hidden might be in a library or buried in some ruin or desert. These qualities ("not hidden," "nor far off") certainly give a tangible quality to the commandment, written down and available in writing. Words far off could be those for which there is no available copy. They could be confined in a museum in a display box in one location where the only people who could see it would have to travel a great distance to do so. They could also just reside in heaven, which the text goes on to dismiss as a valid possibility. God-guaranteed access to the Words would not require passing over a sea. The negative section of vv. 11-13 overrules unavailability. Since hearing and doing is dependent on accessibility, the text promises that these Words will not be inaccessible.

Positively, the Word is nigh.[137] It is close. The sufficient proximity of people to the Word is revealed by the further description of " . . . in thy mouth, and in thy heart . . . " in v. 14. This promise is repeated in the New Testament passage mentioned earlier (cf. Romans 10:6-8). "Mouth" and "heart" express the closest proximity. They express intimacy. They leave no room for an argument against the truth of the availability of God's Words as a possible excuse for unbelief and disobedience.[138]

The Lord in His Omniscience offers in advance the argument that this passage dispels (v. 13b). The promise of accessibility eliminates the excuse that accompanies lack of access. Lack of access is also advanced against the righteousness of God's wrath in Romans 1, where it rejected in much the same manner as here. God has revealed the knowledge necessary for salvation, so all are without excuse (Romans 1:19,20), but instead of glorifying God and thanking Him after they knew Him, they did just the opposite (Rom. 1:21).

Ha-Massoreth of Elias Levita, trans. and notes by C. D. Ginsburg, 2nd ed., New York: KTAV, 1968) contended for them; the inspiration of the points was affirmed in the Reformed confession the *Formula Consensus Helvetica* of 1675 (trans. Martin I. Klauber, Trinity Journal 11 [1990]: pp. 103-123). The Masoretic Text underlying the King James Bible, the 1524-1525 Rabbinic Bible edited by Jacob Ben Chayyim, "accepted as the authoritative text (*textus receptus*) for four hundred years or more . . . [and which] fixed the vowel-lettters, the vowel points, and the accents as well" (pp. ix, xi-xii, "Prologemon," Ginsburg), contained an introduction by Ben Chayyim that assumed that the vowel points were given by inspiration to Moses at Sinai (pp. 36-57, *Introduction to the Rabbinic Bible,* Jacob Ben Chayyim, in Orlinsky), as well as a Jewish treatise that took the same view (pp. 123,124, *Massoreth, Ha-Massoreth,* Levita, with p. 7, *Introduction to the Rabbinic Bible,* both in Orlinsky). The classic expositions of evidence for the antiquity of the points are Buxtorf Sr.'s 1620 *Commentary on the Massorah* and Buxtorf Jr.'s 1648 *A Treatise on the Origin, Antiquity, and Authority of the Vowel Points and Accents in the Hebrew Scriptures of the Old Testament, against Lewis Cappellus' Mystery of the Points Unveiled,* arguing against Levita and Cappellus, respectively.

[136] The root meaning of *pâlâ'* (hidden – פָּלָא) is "marvelous or wonderful," and in this context with the negative, the sense is that the Words of God are not too wonderful that a person could not have access to them. The Words were not for marveling, but for understanding and obeying.

[137] When *qârōv* ("nigh" – קָרוֹב) is used as an adjective it shows closeness with reference to distance or proximity (Gen. 19:20), and is often used with "far" to show the whole range of distance, as in "far and near" (I Kings 8:46; Isaiah 33:13; Ezekiel 22:5). The word is also translated "neighbor." In this case, the nearness is emphatic with the addition of the adverb "very" (מְאֹד, *mĕ'ōth*).

[138] When individual Israelite fathers are commanded to believe, practice, and teach all God's Words, one should assume that all of those Words would be available (Deuteronomy 6:1-10).

The reason for the availability or accessibility is so that one " . . . may hear it, and do it" (vv. 12c, 13c), or that one " . . . mayest do it" (v. 14b). The words here do not just assume that what God wants people to do; He would also first give them the opportunity to know. The point is clearly stated here.

The seriousness of availability follows in Deuteronomy 30:15-20. Life, good, and ability to please God are dependent upon it. The potential consequences of unavailability, cursing and loss of blessing, stress the necessity of availability. The expression of the punishment adds to the guarantee that His Words will be accessible. God is holy and just. He is merciful. There is a clear intimation in the blessings and curses that a holy, just, and merciful God will make sure that, with so much dependent on the accessibility of His Words, He will make sure that they are available.

Logic

From this, at least one logical syllogism surfaces. *Major Premise:* If it is necessary that His Words be available to every generation,[139] then a holy and just God will ensure their availability. *Minor Premise:* It is necessary. *Conclusion:* God's Words are available to every generation.

Conclusion

The powerful Suzerain (the Lord Himself) made a covenant with His weak and dependent vassal, Israel, in Deuteronomy. The terms of the covenant are in Words. These Words are the Word of the Lord. The Suzerain agreed to fulfill promises to those who agree to obey His Words. He guaranteed that these Words would be available to those who desired to have them. The Word of God on salvation is accessible. Salvation involves agreeing with God about obeying all of His Words. By saying that His Word is available, the context clearly implies that every one of His Words is also accessible. That guarantee continues to apply to this present age, since it is repeated in Romans 10:6-8.[140] Since God guarantees the accessibility of all the Words of both the Old and New Testament, believers should conclude that they will be available to every generation.

---

[139]Deuteronomy repeatedly implies the preservation of God's Words for generations forever into the future (Deuteronomy 5:29; 7:9; 12:28; 19:9; 23:3; 29:29).

[140]Romans 10:6-8 provides conclusive evidence that the promise of accessibility applies to more than just the book of Deuteronomy or even the entire Old Testament. The fashion in which Paul uses this text in Romans 10 assumes that one was to have known that this teaching in Deuteronomy 30:11-14 applied to all of God's Words. In the context of Romans 10, vv. 9,10 are also characterized as the word "nigh thee, even in thy mouth, and in thy heart." The Gospel Words of chapter ten are not only a quotation from the Old Testament. They are new inspiration to which this Deuterononomy 30:11-14 promise of availability is extended. The two passages (Dt. 30:11-14; Rom. 10:6-8) combined produce the teaching of availability for all of Scripture. Belief in Christ assumes reception of all God's Words as much as the belief of Deuteronomy 30:11-14 assumed the reception of all God's Laws (cf. John 17:8).

CHAPTER TEN

Be Mindful of the Words
2 Peter 3:2 and Jude 17
Gary La More

The Petrine Authorship of 2 Peter

For someone with the correct presuppositions about Scripture, 2 Peter 1:1 is sufficient as a basis for concluding Peter wrote this epistle. Peter clearly states that he is the human author.[141]

The Context of 2 Peter 3:2 and Jude 17

Peter admonishes his readers to remember the great truths spoken by the Old Testament prophets (3:2a),[142] the New Testament apostles (3:2c), and the Saviour Himself (3:2b).[143] Remembering these preserved Words would prepare these believers for the attacks of the false teachers described in 2 Peter 2. These apostates had belligerently called the Word of God "cunningly devised fables" (2 Peter 1:16), so Peter

---

[141]In answering the question of who wrote 2 Peter, another has said, "The writer leaves us in no doubt on the matter. He says he is 'Simon Peter, a servant and [an] apostle of Jesus Christ' (1:1). He was on the mount of Transfiguration with Jesus (1:16-18) where only Peter, James and John were with him (Mk. 9:2-12). He had written on a previous occasion to the recipients of this letter (3:1) and is on familiar terms with them (3:1, 8, 14, 17). Furthermore, he calls Paul 'our [beloved] brother' (3:15), and at the time of writing he was expecting to die quite soon (1:14). There is no evidence to suggest that any of these facts were later inserted into the letter to make people accept it . . .." G.J. Wenham, ed., *New Bible Commentary 21st Century Edition* (Leicester, England: Inter-Varsity Press, 1994), p. 1386.

[142]One other fact in these first two verses is the unity of Scripture. The prophets of the Old Testament, the Words of Jesus Christ, and the preaching and teaching of the apostles are all tied together and put on an equal footing. They were all considered to be authoritative, to be the Word of God. Paul's writings were also considered to be Scripture by Peter when he was writing this letter (3:15-16). Paul's writings were already considered to be the very Word of God to men. Therefore, without a doubt, the early apostles studied the prophets and the Words of Jesus. Thus they studied the Scriptures that were available to them. *The Preacher's Outline & Sermon Bible*, Volume 12 (Chattanooga, TN: Leadership Ministries Worldwide, 1991), pp. 190-191.

[143]Harold L. Willmington, *The Outline Bible* (Wheaton, IL: Tyndale House Publishers, Inc., 1999), p. 741.

ensured its trustworthiness (2 Peter 1:17-21). Jude exclusively deals with defectors from the faith. Believers are exhorted to contend with them for the faith (3, 4), especially in light of their end (5-7) and their vile qualities (8-16). Jude 17-19 outline the characteristics of apostasy, their scoffing and divisiveness, and the apostates own evil instincts, which are totally devoid of God,[144] as the apostles had warned (2 Peter 2:1-3:4; 1 John 2:18; 2 John 7-11).

The Exegesis of 2 Peter 3:2 and Jude 17

2 Peter 3:2

Obviously Peter would not have given an aimless reminder.[145] Intent on promoting the welfare of his readers, Peter's desire is "that [they] may be mindful of the words which were spoken before by the holy prophets, and of the commandment of . . . the apostles of the Lord and Saviour." "'That ye may be mindful' renders an aorist infinitive (μνησθῆναι, *mnāsthānai*) expressing purpose, and restates the actual result he hopes to achieve in giving this reminder. Peter especially desires for these believers to keep their first beliefs in view of the new false teaching."[146] He wants them to remember the Old Testament Prophets and the revelation of the New Testament Apostles. The Words spoken (τῶν προειρημένων ῥημάτων, *tōn proeirāmenōn rhāmatōn*) were the prophetic declarations made in the former dispensation. The perfect tense (*proeirāmenōn*) underlines the permanence of these prophetic utterances.[147] The Words were spoken in the past and continued into Peter's day, available for Peter and the audience of his epistles. The "words" in particular are the prophetic announcements of the Messiah's coming.[148] "By the holy prophets" (ὑπὸ τῶν ἁγίων προφητῶν, *hupo tōn hagion prophātōn*) presents Old Testament human authors as the agents God used to declare His message. Peter characterizes them as "holy" so that when the false teachers deny the truth of their prophetic utterances, they become guilty of blasphemy.[149] The term "holy" is the same one used as an attribute of God (Revelation 4:8), and in so using this term, Peter emphasizes the purity of the Words they wrote as well.

---

[144]Ibid, pp. 751-752.

[145]Peter's reminder here is that although there are false teachers among them who also claim to be representing God, believers must recognize, accept, and obey only the true Word of God as found in the Old Testament (the holy prophets) and in the preaching of the apostles (meaning, of course, himself and the other apostles). All that has been said in this section of 2 Peter speaks of the availability of the Word of God, then and now. *King James Bible Commentary* (Nashville, TN: Thomas Nelson Publishers, 1999), p. 1749.

[146]D. Edmond Hiebert, *Second Peter and Jude* (Greenville, SC: Unusual Publications, 1989), p. 139.

[147]Ibid.

[148]Ibid.

[149]Hiebert, op. cit., pp. 139-140.

[150]This double possessive genitive attributes the "commandment" first to the Lord Jesus Christ, then to the apostles.

Peter is also challenging his readers here to remember "the commandment of . . . the apostles of the Lord and Saviour" (τῆς τῶν ἀποστόλων ἡμῶν ἐντολῆς τοῦ Κυρίου καὶ σωτῆρος, *tās tōn apostolōn hāmōn entolās tou kuriou kai sōtāros*).[150] He, along with the other Apostles, recognized that they were building a New Testament superstructure upon an Old Testament foundation. All of both the Old and New Testaments is the inspired Word of God (2 Peter 1:21; 2 Tim. 3:16). Therefore, both the foundation and the superstructure are on the same level of authority and dignity. To denigrate one to exalt the other is to be out of harmony with apostolic thought (2 Tim. 2:15). For most of the first half of the first century the Christians had only the Old Testament to read.[151] When 2 Peter was written, they had much of the New Testament as well.[152] Both the Old and New Testaments taught the bodily Second Coming of Christ. This point alone sufficiently contradicted the scoffing and corrupt instruction of the false teachers. Later in 2 Peter 3, Peter gives more arguments against the "scoffers" of the Second Coming.

What did Peter want his readers to adhere to and remember? Peter wanted the believers obediently to remember and to adhere to the Word of God as written and spoken by both the prophets and the apostles.[153] The call to remembrance assumes the availability of the Old Testament and what was completed of the New Testament.

Jude 17

"The words of the Apostles, spoken before Jude wrote, are now a part of the written record."[154] Peter has already written that the apostles and the Old Testament prophets warned of false teachers earlier.[155] As in 2 Peter, "were spoken" translates a perfect passive participle indicating the completion of the speaking of these Words with the results continuing into the present. Earlier Jude speaks of these Words as "the faith once (ἅπαξ, *hapax*, "once and for all") delivered unto the saints" (v. 3). Oral tradition was not completed and continuing into the present.[156] Neither was it delivered once and for all. These qualities only characterize the special revelation of God's Words.[157] The whole purpose of Jude's letter is to remind them that the Word of God was given once and for all by the apostles.[158] God through Jude clearly extends this teaching to not

---

[151] Yeager, Ibid. Galatians and James were two books, at least, that were available before AD 50.

[152] Much of the New Testament was completed before 2 Peter and Jude (AD 67-68). Matthew, Mark, Luke, Acts, Romans, 1 & 2 Corinthians, Galatians, and more were all already available.

[153] Albert Garner, *1 Peter 2 Peter*, New Testament Commentary, Volume XIII (Lakeland, FL: The Blessed Hope Foundation, 1975), p. 123.

[154] Yeager, Ibid, p. 477.

[155] Ibid, p. 477.

[156] Three places mention apostolic "tradition" (παράδοσις, *paradosis*), and in each case this noun is joined by an aorist verb (1 Corinthians 11:2; 2 Thessalonians 2:15; 3:6). These traditions were not intended to continue into the present, as only God's Words hold that promise with the use of the perfect.

[157] See chapter eight on the perfect passive, "It Is Written," by David Sutton.

[158] *King James Bible Commentary*, Ibid, p. 1772.

just the "Word of God" (the Word in general), but to the "words (ῥημάτων, *rhāmatōn* which were spoken" (the specific Words and passages). This not only strongly implies that Jude had the Words of the apostles (the New Testament writings completed at that point in time), but also unequivocally states that the believers to which he writes also had these Words available. There is no reason for anyone to believe that these Words were anything but all the Words available at that time. Without an implication of perfection in the Words, this passage would also play right into the hands of the apostates about whom it warns.

Conclusions

False teachers go out into the world seeking to destroy men with their false messages and false hopes. These corruptors of God's Word follow the example and work of their father, the devil. They further Satan's agenda by leading believers astray from the truth of Scripture. An important aspect of their strategy is to cast doubt on the validity of Scripture. To combat this, both Peter and Jude call on the saints to remember the Words of the Old and New Testaments, Words available to them.

The apostles, in quoting from the Old Testament, never questioned whether they had available the true Word of God. The apostles acknowledged that what others had written in the New Testament was also God's Word. At the time of 2 Peter and Jude, the New Testament authors were not looking to verify what they had of the Old Testament as the true Word of God. Like all believers, they gladly received it. They were not looking for a lost Bible. God in His providence had seen to it that His Word was passed on from one generation to the next. The apostles received as authentic what they read and quoted from the Old Testament prophets as it had been passed on to them. True believers today should do the same thing. The correct and obvious interpretation of these texts and the implied belief of the apostles was that they had every Word of God preserved and available to them. Based upon legitimate application of this text, the Lord's true churches today have available to them not only the Words of the Old Testament prophets but also the Words of the New Testament apostles and other New Testament writers. The teaching of the availability of every Word of Scripture has been and continues to be a strong basis for opposing the attacks on the teaching of Scripture by the apostates.

SECTION THREE

God's Method of Preservation

CHAPTER ELEVEN

Israel, the Means of Preservation in the Old Testament:
Nâtsar (נָצַר) and *Shâmar* (שָׁמַר)

Kent Brandenburg

Introduction

The Bible not only explains how preservation is to and will occur, but it also represents the act of preservation as a major theme. This doctrine of the means of preservation begins in the Old Testament. The Old Testament is the history of the nation Israel, but it is also the history of Israel's part in the keeping of God's Words.

Man's Part in Preservation

Inspiration is a miracle of God in which He supernaturally delivers every one and all of His Words to men (2 Timothy 3:16; 2 Peter 1:20,21). Preservation is a miracle of God in which He supernaturally keeps every one and all of His Words for every generation of men (Psalm 12:6,7; Matthew 24:35).

A common argument against inspiration is that the words were "written by men." A common argument against preservation is that the Bible does not say "how it will be preserved."[159] Neo-orthodoxy assumes that men could not write down words perfectly,

---

[159] Glenny writes (p. 79), "... the Bible nowhere tells us how God will preserve His Word" (repeated on pp. 94 & 95). Rod Bell, longtime president of the Fundamental Baptist Fellowship, recently wrote in *Frontline*, "We believe in the preservation of Scripture because it is a Bible doctrine. We have no right to dictate to others how God did it when He didn't tell us. No one has that right. This Fellowship, as long as I am going to be in it, is not going to become a battleground for the textual issue. We'll not do it. When you elevate your opinions and your theories above or equal to the clear teachings of the Scriptures, that's heresy, and you know it. That's dangerous – you're guilty of adding to the Scriptures. This Fellowship is meant to be a fellowship, not a platform for unnecessary conflict." (Rod Bell, A Note from the President: "Charting the Course: The Fellowship Principle" *Frontline*, Sept.-Oct. 2002, Vol 12, No. 5).

despite the doctrine of inspiration. That assumption would seem reasonable if God had not said that man did write down Words perfectly (2 Timothy 3:16). An even larger group of professing believers suppose that men could not keep God's Words perfectly, despite the doctrine of preservation. That assumption would seem reasonable if God had not made the promise of perfect preservation, and had not said that He would use men to affect that preservation.

Like many other doctrines, what God has promised to do, He has accomplished by the means of men. This is another example of the razor-edge balance between the truths of human responsibility and Divine sovereignty. There are many verses that establish the truth of Divine preservation, but there are even more verses that establish the truth of human responsibility in preservation.

The Two Words

Large portions of Scripture communicate what God expects men to do with reference to the preservation of His Words. This chapter, however, will deal specifically with what God said in the Old Testament in this regard. Most of the verses in the Old Testament that reveal the "how" of preservation do so with the use of two Hebrew words, *nâtsar* (נָצַר) and *shâmar* (שָׁמַר). The two Hebrew words, *nâtsar*, used 60 times in the Old Testament, and, *shâmar*, used 420 times in the Old Testament, are both primarily translated "to keep."

Nâtsar (נָצַר) has the understanding of "protect, maintain, obey, and preserve."[160] Proverbs 27:18 clearly uses it in the sense of protecting or preserving an item of agriculture, saying, "Whoso keepeth the fig tree shall eat the fruit thereof: so he that waiteth on his master shall be honoured." *Nâtsar* was used to communicate the function of protecting military or agricultural properties (Job 27:18; Nahum 2:2), and those employed in this activity were called watchmen (Jer. 31:6; 2 Kings 17:9; 18:8). In Psalm 141:3 ("Set a watch, O LORD, before my mouth; keep the door of my lips.") *nâtsar* describes the ethical maintenance of one's mouth or vocal mechanism (cf. Prov. 13:3). This same use of *nâtsar* relates to the preservation of one's heart (Proverbs 4:23), tongue (Psalm 34:14), and path of life (Proverbs 16:17).

Shâmar (שָׁמַר) is used with the meaning of "to hedge about, guard, protect, attend to, or exercise great care over." *Shâmar* appears in Genesis 3:24[161] as the activity of the Cherubim in protecting or guarding the Garden of Eden after God had evicted Adam and Eve. Other locations give this same sense of guarding against intruders with reference to gatekeepers (Isa. 21:11) or to watchmen (Song of Solomon 5:7). In Genesis 2:15[162] *shâmar* is used for Adam's activity of taking care of or tending to the things of

---

[160] As derived from its usage in the Old Testament.

[161] "So he drove out the man; and he placed at the east of the garden of Eden Cherubims, and a flaming sword which turned every way, to keep the way of the tree of life."

[162] "And the LORD God took the man, and put him into the garden of Eden to dress it and to keep it."

the Garden of Eden. In this way it is also used for the keeping of a flock (Genesis 30:31) or a house (2 Samuel 15:16). In Proverbs 6:24, *shâmar* characterizes the guardianship of a young man from the strange woman, in essence, the instruction of a parent protecting his moral purity. Cain in Genesis 4:9 asked, "Am I my brother's keeper?" This use of *shâmar* applies to the defending or attending to someone for his safekeeping.

Both of these words, as witnessed in their usage, contain the strong sense of "guarding, protecting, tending, preserving, or maintaining." Any object toward which these two verbs might direct their action would receive this same essential thrust. How these verbs are used with objects other than "words" or some synonym of "words" should be applied to their understanding when they are used with "words" or some synonym of "words." Understanding the meaning of the words is vital to a grammatical-historical interpretation from which comes the doctrine of Scripture. *Nâtsar* and *shâmar* should be understood based on their uses in Scripture. Their usage implies preservation.

The Activity of Men with Reference to the Words of God

In the Old Testament, many terms are employed as an expression of God's Word. The terms utilized in Psalm 119 provide a good sampling of the various ones used: Law (Psalm 119:1; *Tōrâh*, תּוֹרָה), Testimonies (Psalm 119:2, '*Āthâthâ*, עֵדָתָי), Precepts (Psalm 119:4, *Pĭqqūthēm*, פְּקֻדִים), Statutes (Psalm 119:5, *Chūqqēm*, חֻקִּים), Commandments (Psalm 119:7, *Mitswōth*, מִצְוֹת), Judgments (Psalm 119:7, *Mishpĕtâh*, מִשְׁפָּטֵי), Word (Psalm 119:9, *Dâvâr*, דָּבָר), and Word or Promise (Psalm 119:11, '*Imrâh*, אִמְרָה). The term "Law" is used in the Old Testament as a single command or the whole body of the law, especially the Pentateuch, but also, ultimately, of the Scriptures as a whole. "Precept" points to a particular instruction of the Lord, as He is One Who cares about detail. "Statutes" communicates the binding nature or permanence of Scripture. "Commandments" emphasizes the authority of what is spoken, and that God has the right to have done what He says. *Dâvâr* ("word") is the most general term, embracing all of God's truth, and '*Imrâh* is a noun that comes from the verb form "to say," '*Imrâh* ("word" or "promise") being, therefore, what God said. Whenever any of these terms is the object of *nâtsar* or *shâmar*, they are referring to God's Word or Words, and most of the time, referring to all of God's Word or every one of God's Words.

In Psalm 12:7 both *shâmar* and *nâtsar* are used in revealing God's work in preservation. "Them" of v. 7 has the antecedent "words" in v. 6, which states, "Thou shalt keep them, O LORD, thou shalt preserve them."[163] "Keep" is *shâmar* and "preserve"

---

[163] "Words" is feminine and "them" is masculine, but this is a recurring feature in the Hebrew. "Them" and "words" are both plural, therefore matching in number. Proximity takes precedence over gender accord. Gender discord is purposeful in order to attach the Divine Person to the Words of God. This same discord is found in Psalm 119:129, 152, 169, documenting this usage in the Old Testament. See chapter one on Psalm 12:6,7 by Thomas Strouse.

is *nâtsar*. Psalm 146:5, 6 reiterate the truth of Divine preservation, saying, " . . . the LORD his God . . . Which made heaven, and earth, the sea, and all that therein is: which keepeth truth forever." "Keepeth" here is *shâmar*. The Lord does this keeping of His Words, that is, He guards, protects, and preserves His Truth, His Words. God has His part in the preservation of Scripture, and ensures it.

However, like so many activities of God, He intends the cooperation of believing men. What God is keeping, He wants men keeping. God ensures keeping, but He uses men to do it. No one should doubt that God will keep His Words, but this does not take away from the responsibility that man has in preservation. Repeatedly, God instructs man to keep His Words.

> Exodus 15:26, "And said, If thou wilt diligently hearken to the voice of the LORD thy God, and wilt do that which is right in his sight, and wilt give ear to his commandments, and <u>keep all his statutes</u>, I will put none of these diseases upon thee, which I have brought upon the Egyptians: for I *am* the LORD that healeth thee." ("keep"=*shâmar*)
>
> Exodus 20:5, 6, "Thou shalt not bow down thyself to them, nor serve them: for I the LORD thy God *am* a jealous God, visiting the iniquity of the fathers upon the children unto the third and fourth *generation* of them that hate me; And shewing mercy unto thousands of them that love me, and <u>keep my commandments</u>." ("keep"=*shâmar*)
>
> Leviticus 18:4,5, "Ye shall do my judgments, and <u>keep mine ordinances</u>, to walk therein: I *am* the LORD your God. Ye shall therefore <u>keep my statutes</u>, and my judgments: which if a man do, he shall live in them: I *am* the LORD." ("keep"=*shâmar*)
>
> Deuteronomy 4:2, "Ye shall not add unto the word which I command you, neither shall ye diminish *ought* from it, that ye may <u>keep the commandments</u> of the LORD your God which I command you." ("keep"=*shâmar*)
>
> Deuteronomy 11:22, "For if ye shall diligently <u>keep all these commandments</u> which I command you, to do them, to love the LORD your God, to walk in all his ways, and to cleave unto him;" ("keep"=*shâmar*)
>
> Deuteronomy 29:9, "<u>Keep</u> therefore the words of this covenant, and do them, that ye may prosper in all that ye do." ("keep"=*shâmar*)
>
> Joshua 22:5, "But take diligent heed to do the commandment and the law, which Moses the servant of the LORD charged you, to love

the LORD your God, and to walk in all his ways, and to <u>keep his commandments</u>, and to cleave unto him, and to serve him with all your heart and with all your soul." ("keep"=*shâmar*)

1 Kings 2:3, "And keep the charge of the LORD thy God, to walk in his ways, to <u>keep his statutes</u>, and his commandments, and his judgments, and his testimonies, as it is written in the law of Moses, that thou mayest prosper in all that thou doest, and whithersoever thou turnest thyself:" ("keep"=*shâmar*)

2 Kings 17:13, "Yet the LORD testified against Israel, and against Judah, by all the prophets, *and by* all the seers, saying, Turn ye from your evil ways, and <u>keep my commandments *and* my statutes, according to all the law which I commanded your fathers</u>, and which I sent to you by my servants the prophets." ("keep"=*shâmar*)

1 Chronicles 29:19, "And give unto Solomon my son a perfect heart, <u>to keep thy commandments, thy testimonies, and thy statutes</u>, and to do all *these things*, and to build the palace, *for* the which I have made provision." ("keep"=*shâmar*)

2 Chronicles 34:31, "And the king stood in his place, and made a covenant before the LORD, to walk after the LORD, and <u>to keep his commandments, and his testimonies, and his statutes</u>, with all his heart, and with all his soul, to perform the words of the covenant which are written in this book." ("keep"=*shâmar*)

Nehemiah 1:9, "But *if* ye turn unto me, and <u>keep my commandments</u>, and do them; though there were of you cast out unto the uttermost part of the heaven, *yet* will I gather them from thence, and will bring them unto the place that I have chosen to set my name there." ("keep"=*shâmar*)

Psalm 78:7, "That they might set their hope in God, and not forget the works of God, but <u>keep his commandments</u>:" ("keep"=*shâmar*)

Ecclesiastes 12:13, "Let us hear the conclusion of the whole matter: Fear God, and <u>keep his commandments</u>: for this *is* the whole *duty* of man." ("keep"=*shâmar*)

Ezekiel 11:20, "That they may walk in my statutes, and <u>keep mine ordinances</u>, and do them: and they shall be my people, and I will be their God." ("keep"=*shâmar*)

Daniel 9:4, "And I prayed unto the LORD my God, and made my confession, and said, O Lord, the great and dreadful God, keeping the covenant and mercy to them that love him, and to them that <u>keep his commandments</u>;" ("keep"=*shâmar*)

These examples indicate that this responsibility continues through the entire history of Israel in the Old Testament.

Psalm 119, the preeminent chapter in the Old Testament on the Word of God, communicates this responsibility repeatedly (all *shâmar*, unless otherwise noted) – Psalm 119:2 (*nâtsar*), 4, 5, 8, 17, 22 (*nâtsar*), 33 (*nâtsar*), 34 (*nâtsar*), 55, 56 (*nâtsar*), 57, 60, 63, 67, 69 (*nâtsar*), 88, 100 (*nâtsar*), 101, 106, 115 (*nâtsar*), 129 (*nâtsar*), 134, 136, 145 (*nâtsar*), 146, 158, 167, 168.

The "keeping" is the responsibility of the corporate and of the individual believer. This is manifested by the use of both the singular and plural personal pronouns with "to keep." The individual believer is responsible for the preservation of Scripture. Psalm 119:17, "Deal bountifully with thy servant, *that* <u>I</u> may live, and <u>keep</u> thy word." The congregation of the righteous, God's people, is responsible for the preservation of Scripture. Leviticus 26:3, "If <u>ye</u> walk in my statutes, and <u>keep</u> my commandments, and do them." The prophet Daniel was specifically commanded to do the keeping, with the assumption that those after him would continue this task of guarding God's Word. In Daniel 12:4, the Lord told Daniel to "shut up the words" and "seal" the book that he had written. Later, in Daniel 12:9, the Lord confirms that "the words are closed up and sealed till the time of the end." The command (v. 4) is explicit regarding man's responsibility in preservation, while the confirmation of the Lord (v. 9) clearly states the truth of God's sovereignty in preservation.

Some might argue that the word "keep" is essentially a synonym for "do" or "obey." There are several reasons why this is not true. The first is the meaning or usage of *nâtsar* and *shâmar*. These words do not mean "do" or "obey." They do mean "keep, protect, preserve, or guard." Second, there are Hebrew words for "do" and "obey." Deuteronomy 12:1 uses "do" (*âsâh*, עָשׂה) with reference to God's Word when it says, "These *are* <u>the statutes and judgments, which ye shall observe to do</u> ("to do," *'âsâh*) in the land, which the LORD God of thy fathers giveth thee to possess it, all the days that ye live upon the earth." Deuteronomy 11:27 used "obey" (*shâma'*, שָׁמַע)[164] with reference to God's Word when it says, "A blessing, if ye <u>obey the commandments</u> of the LORD your God, which I command you this day." The words "do" or "obey" could have been used with reference to Words if the concept of "do" or "obey" was the idea that God wanted communicated, but He did not. There is more to *nâtsar* and *shâmar* than "doing" or "obeying." A third reason why "keep" is not a synonym for "do" or "obey" is that there are several verses that show a differentiation between "keep" and "do" or "obey" right in the verse itself.

---

[164] "Obey" is just one possible translation of this Hebrew word, that has a root meaning of "to hear," but in its usage is an effective hearing that would result in obeying or doing. The King James translators knew this when they translated the word "obey" as it related to God's Word.

Leviticus 25:18, "Wherefore ye shall do my statutes, and <u>keep</u> my judgments, and <u>do</u> them; and ye shall dwell in the land in safety." ("keep"=*shâmar*; "do"= *'âsâh*)

Deuteronomy 13:4, "Ye shall walk after the LORD your God, and fear him, and <u>keep</u> his commandments, and <u>obey</u> his voice, and ye shall serve him, and cleave unto him." ("keep"=*shâmar*; "obey"= *shâma'*)

Ezekiel 36:27, "And I will put my spirit within you, and cause you to walk in my statutes, and ye shall <u>keep</u> my judgments, and <u>do</u> them." ("keep"= *shâmar*; "do"= *'âsâh*)

Ezekiel 37:24, "And David my servant shall be king over them; and they all shall have one shepherd: they shall also walk in my judgments, and <u>observe</u> my statutes, and <u>do</u> them." ("observe" = *shâmar*; "do"= *'âsâh*)

The word "keep" (*nâtsar* or *shâmar*) is not used as a synonym for "do" or "obey." Instead, it has its own distinct meaning that was used to distinguish a particular activity with reference to His Words.

God's Words, all and each of them, are kept by more than just doing or obeying them. "Keep" elevates the task beyond solely "obeying" or "doing." God's Words are preserved by His people through their believing, preaching, teaching, practicing, and defending them. Every one of these tasks is taught in God's Word and they are all interrelated. Belief leads to teaching and practice. Teaching leads to belief and practice. Practice leads to belief and teaching. If Scripture is lost because it is not defended, then it cannot be believed, taught, or practiced. God's Word is defended by believing, teaching, and practicing it. Wrong belief leads to wrong teaching and practice. Wrong teaching leads to wrong belief and practice. Wrong practice leads to wrong belief and teaching. Therefore, when one does not teach correctly, the Scriptures are not defended. When Scripture becomes less valued or important because of wrong belief, teaching, and practice, then Scripture will be ignored and lost by the ones responsible for keeping it. Vigilance in keeping (*nâtsar* and *shâmar*) requires more than just doing or obeying; it involves all the activities that will allow God's Word to be passed down from one generation to the next for the glory of the Lord.[165]

---

[165]This can be directly applied to the preservation issue as a whole. People may value inspiration, but wrong teaching on preservation will affect teaching on inspiration which in turn affects many other doctrines.

The Institution for Preservation in the Old Testament

The individual man of God in the Old Testament, predominately the Jew, was responsible for keeping God's Words. Even more, God established a corporate responsibility. Preservation was not primarily unilateral because God gave that responsibility to an institution He founded. The "ye" of preservation in the Old Testament was Israel, which was essentially local and visible. The nation Israel was God's congregation in the Old Testament.[166] God gave the Old Testament to the congregation of Israel as His means of preservation. This history starts with the covenant of God that Israel was to keep, beginning with Abraham. Genesis 17:9,10, "And God said unto Abraham, Thou shalt <u>keep</u> my covenant therefore, thou, and thy seed after thee in their generations. This *is* my covenant, which ye shall <u>keep</u>, between me and you and thy seed after thee; Every man child among you shall be circumcised." The commandments given to Moses on Mt. Sinai were to be kept by Israel. Exodus 20:6, "And shewing mercy unto thousands of them that love me, and <u>keep</u> my commandments." When Moses repeated God's Words in Deuteronomy, Israel again was responsible to keep what God said (19:9, "If thou shalt <u>keep</u> all these commandments to do them, which I command thee this day, to love the LORD thy God, and to walk ever in his ways; then shalt thou add three cities more for thee, beside these three:"). This is further and explicitly stated by the prophecy in Isaiah 26:2, "Open ye the gates, that the righteous nation which <u>keepeth</u> the truth may enter in."

God gave responsibility for preservation of the Old Testament to Israel. These three examples verify Israel as the recipient for this stewardship of Words.

> Acts 7:38, "This is he, that was in the church in the wilderness with the angel which spake to him in the mount Sina, and *with* <u>our fathers: who received the lively oracles to give unto us</u>:"
>
> Romans 3:1,2, "What advantage then hath the Jew? or what profit *is there* of circumcision? Much every way: chiefly, because that <u>unto them were committed the oracles of God</u>."
>
> Romans 9:3-5, "For I could wish that myself were accursed from Christ for my brethren, my kinsmen according to the flesh: Who are Israelites; to whom *pertaineth* the adoption, and the glory, and

---

[166]Israel is referred to as "the congregation of Israel," "of God," or "of the Lord" at least sixty-four times. Forty-five times, Israel is referred to as the assembly, God's assembly. "House" is a visible and local metaphor. At least one hundred ninety-three times Israel is called "the house," either of Israel or of Judah.

[167]The Old Testament says "saith the LORD" to leaders of Israel eight hundred forty-one times. Two hundred forty-eight times "the word of the LORD" or "of God" came unto, was spoken unto, or commanded unto God's leadership or prophet in Israel or Judah. Twenty-eight times the Old Testament says "the Lord said unto me" to the Lord's prophets (mainly Moses). Ten times "God said unto"

the covenants, and the giving of the law, and the service *of God*, and the promises; Whose *are* the fathers, and of whom as concerning the flesh Christ *came*, who is over all, God blessed for ever."

God spoke to mankind in the Old Testament through the leadership of Israel.[167] From the New Testament, there is the clear sense that the Jews considered the Law and the Prophets to be given to them for the keeping.[168] Israel was God's depository and repository for His Words in the Old Testament.

The Old Testament surely exhorts Israel toward vigilance in keeping God's Word. Just like it is impossible for believers to keep saved (1 Peter 1:5, "kept by the power of God"), it was not possible without God for Israel to keep His Word. It is obvious that Israel only succeeded at preservation by means of the grace of God. God chose to use Israel at times even without her cooperation. First, it is explicitly stated that Israel had her difficult periods in this regard. Amos 2:4 explains not keeping God's Word as the reason for the captivity of Judah when it says, "Thus saith the LORD; For three transgressions of Judah, and for four, I will not turn away *the punishment* thereof; because they have despised the law of the LORD, and have not kept (*shâmar*) his commandments, and their lies caused them to err, after the which their fathers have walked." Malachi echoes this sad refrain in Malachi 3:7a, "Even from the days of your fathers ye are gone away from mine ordinances, and have not kept (*shâmar*) *them*." Second, there are examples of the leadership of Israel rebelling against the preservation of God's Word. There was a lengthy period in Israel's history when the leadership of Israel chose not to keep God's Word. The success or failure of various kings was evaluated in a major way upon whether or not they kept the Word of God. God's Word was dishonored by Israel publically from Manasseh until Josiah, when Hilkiah retrieved the Book of the Law from the house of the LORD (2 Kings 22:8-20). Concerning the retrieval, King Josiah says in 2 Chronicles 34:21, "Go, enquire of the LORD for me, and for them that are left in Israel and in Judah, concerning the words of the book that is found: for great *is* the wrath of the LORD that is poured out upon us, because our fathers have not kept (*shâmar*) the word of the LORD, to do after all that is written in this book." During the times of terrible and yet not total apostasy, priests had apparently in some way ensured the preservation of God's Word in the temple. Poor conditions in Israel were directly tied to their performance in the keeping of God's Word (even as prophesied in Dt. 28,29).

Further instruction in the Old Testament to Israel regards carefulness with the stewardship of His Word. Deuteronomy 4:2 and 12:32 both admonish the nation

---

Abraham, Isaac, or Jacob. One hundred eight times "God said unto" Moses. Twelve times "God said unto" Joshua or Samuel. Three times "God said unto" David. Four times the "word of the Lord came to" the prophet. The point here is that God gave His Word(s) to Israel for keeping.

[168]John 1:45, "Philip findeth Nathanael, and saith unto him, We have found him, of whom Moses in the law, and the prophets, did write, Jesus of Nazareth, the son of Joseph." Acts 24:14, "But this I confess unto thee, that after the way which they call heresy, so worship I the God of my fathers, believing all things which are written in the law and in the prophets:"

to neither add to nor take away from God's Word.[169] Satan had already established this type of perversion of God's Word in the Garden of Eden with his addition (Genesis 3:1, "Ye shall not eat of every tree of the garden.") and with his subtraction (Genesis 3:4, "Ye shall not surely die"). This admonition "not to add or subtract" strongly affirms the place of Israel in the keeping of God's Word.

The Means of Preservation within the Nation

Part of the continuation of any aspect of Israel's worship was dependent on the practice of individual families as led by their fathers. Worship at the temple only continued when fathers persevered in bringing their animals to that location for sacrificial offerings. Passing down God's Word relied upon the diligent transfer to the children. As the nation was God's preserving institution, the family accomplished this task on the most foundational level. This is clearly laid out by God for Israel in Deuteronomy 6:6-9, "And these words, which I command thee this day, shall be in thine heart: And thou shalt teach them diligently unto thy children, and shalt talk of them when thou sittest in thine house, and when thou walkest by the way, and when thou liest down, and when thou risest up; And thou shalt bind them for a sign upon thine hand, and they shall be as frontlets between thine eyes. And thou shalt write them upon the posts of thy house, and on thy gates." The same message is read in Deuteronomy 11:18-21, "Therefore shall ye lay up these my words in your heart and in your soul, and bind them for a sign upon your hand, that they may be as frontlets between your eyes. And ye shall teach them your children, speaking of them when thou sittest in thine house, and when thou walkest by the way, when thou liest down, and when thou risest up. And thou shalt write them upon the door posts of thine house, and upon thy gates: That your days may be multiplied, and the days of your children." When parents keep God's Words themselves, and pass them down to their children, then nations also keep and pass them on.

God specially chose men within Israel as a whole to spearhead the stewardship of the Words of God. These unique individuals were the scribes. The scribe functioned within the nation Israel much like the pastor leading the local congregation in keeping God's Words. Ezra 7:10, 11 says, "For Ezra had prepared his heart to seek the law of the LORD, and to do *it*, and to teach in Israel statutes and judgments . . . Ezra the priest, the scribe, *even* a scribe of the words of the commandments of the LORD, and of his statutes to Israel." Nehemiah 8 manifests some of what it was to be a scribe for Ezra at the time of the rebuilding of the walls in Jerusalem. Verses five, eight, and nine of this chapter record, "And Ezra opened the book in the sight of all the people; (for he was above all the people;) and when he opened it, all the people stood up: So they read in the book in the law of God distinctly, and gave the sense, and caused *them* to understand the reading . . . and Ezra the priest the scribe, and the Levites that taught the people, said unto all the people, This day *is* holy unto the LORD your God; mourn not, nor weep. For all the people wept, when they heard the words of the law." From these two passages, within the nation the man in the office of the scribe took the responsibility of keeping God's Words. The scribe would copy, read, and teach God's Words.

Conclusion

The position that God does not explain how He will preserve His Word is Scripturally untenable when one considers the evidence in the Old Testament. God delivered His Words to Israel, then told her to keep them. When Israel failed to keep His Words, God turned that responsibility over to another institution, the church (Matthew 16:18,19). Not only does God reveal how His Words will be preserved in the Old Testament, but how they are preserved might be its major theme. Living the truth and passing it down to the next generation within and through God's ordained institution underlies every aspect of the Old Testament. God gave His Words to Israel's leadership. The leadership wrote His Words down. Israel's leaders gave God's Words to the people. The people kept God's Words by means of their families and their scribes. In the Old Testament God clearly revealed the means by which He would preserve His Words.

---

[169]Deut. 4:2, "Ye shall not add unto the word which I command you, neither shall ye diminish *ought* from it, that ye may <u>keep</u> the commandments of the LORD your God which I command you." Deut. 12:32, "What thing soever I command you, observe to do it: thou shalt not add thereto, nor diminish from it."

CHAPTER TWELVE

Ekklāsia: The Congregation of The Lord In The New Testament: *Tāreō* (τηρέω)

Thomas M. Strouse

Introduction

Contrary to the sentiments of many Bibliologists, the Bible gives the precise means for its own preservation. Most scholars are quick to dismiss the Biblical evidence for the Divine means of preservation. In fact, they must dismiss it because it is cumbersome to their non-biblical theories.[170] However, the Biblical writers clearly delineated the means for the preservation of God's OT and NT words in Scripture. That the Lord used His NT congregation, as He did His OT saints, to be the agency through which His Words were preserved is irrefragable. This essay will set forth the case that the Scriptural means through which the Lord Jehovah preserved His Words was the OT and NT saints in their respective places of worship. He gave His revelation to His people with the stern warning that His believers should recognize, receive, guard, and make available each and every one of His Words in written form. The Lord's church (ἐκκλησία, *ekklāsia*) was the means God used to preserve (τηρεῖν, *tārein*) His inspired OT and NT Words initially in the first century and continues to use until the end of the church age.

---

[170] It is apparent that many CT Bibliologists focus their efforts on extra-biblical argumentation. Cf. the pamphlet by Mark Minnick "Trusted Voices On Translations." Quite often their exegesis, if any, of pertinent Scripture is characterized by brevity, denial, and unproved assumptions.

The Divine Means for Preserving God's Words

For the OT Scriptures[171]

The Lord promised to preserve every one of His Words for every succeeding generation (Psm. 12:6-7).[172] He used human instrumentality to preserve His Words. For instance, the Lord commanded Daniel to shut up and seal the inspired Words he wrote (Dan. 12:4). The Lord nevertheless guaranteed that He would indeed shut up and seal until the end of time these very Words inscripturated by Daniel (v. 9). God used the Jewish nation to be the instrument through which His OT revelation came. Paul affirmed this truth when he stated, "What advantage then hath the Jew? Or what profit is there of circumcision? Much every way: chiefly, because that unto them were committed the oracles of God" (Rom. 3:1-2). The Hebrew OT Scripture was available for personal and public study in the first century. Timothy, along with his grandmother and mother, studied the OT Scriptures from his youth (2 Tim. 3:15). All around Judea Jews studied publicly the Words of Moses in the Torah, as Luke states, "For Moses of old time hath in every city them that preach him, being read in the synagogues every sabbath day" (Acts 15:21).

Case Study: Joshua (Joshua 1:7-8)

Joshua was the Divinely appointed replacement for Moses (Num. 27:18-19) and Jehovah instructed him to continue to be faithful to the Scripture. The Lord's will had not changed with this new leader but remained the same with respect to the land promise (cf. Gen. 12:1-3). The Torah was still the written law for the Jews in the land of Canaan. The Lord commanded Joshua to be strong and very courageous (vv. 6, 7, and 9). According to the Divine instruction, Joshua was to meditate (הָגָה, *hâghâh*)[173] on the Words of the Torah so that he and the Jews would consequently obey it. They were not to deviate from the written law to the right or the left. If Joshua would observe or guard (שָׁמַר, *shâmar*) the Words of the Torah, the Lord would prosper him as the leader of Israel. Joshua and Israel had the responsibility to guard the very Words of the Torah, to not allow any deviations (cf. Dt. 4:2; 12:32), and practice it faithfully for His blessings. Examples of the obedience of Joshua and the Israelites include the circumcision of all males in preparation for the Passover (Josh. 5:2-5; 7-12; cf. Ex. 12:43-45) and the removal of the king's carcass before sundown (Josh. 8:29; cf. Dt. 21:22-23). The Case Study of Joshua is one Biblical example of innumerable occasions of God's expectation for Israel's leaders to preserve His Words. That the Lord expected His people to preserve His Words intact and that He used them to that end is without controversy.

---

[171] See chapter eleven entitled "Israel, The Means of Preservation in the Old Testament: *Nâtsar* and *Shâmar* by Kent Brandenburg."

[172] See this author's chapter (one) entitled "Psalm 12:6-7."

[173] The word conveys the idea of private and vocal recitation.

[174] See chapter eight by David Sutton.

[175] Although the DSS do support many readings in the MT, these scrolls are nevertheless penultimate authorities.

Christ's Imprimatur on the Received Hebrew OT

The Lord Jesus Christ put His Divine imprimatur upon the received Hebrew Old Testament text. He stated that the Hebrew Scriptures were perfectly preserved and intact in His day when He stated "It is written" (γέγραπται, *gegraptai*) in responding to the Devil's temptation (Mt. 4:4).[174] He referred to the Hebrew Scriptures received by the Jews of His day, and not to the enigmatical *LXX* or to the perverted texts of the cultic Qumran sect as manifested in the Dead Sea Scrolls (DSS).[175] There is no Biblical evidence that Christ or the apostles ever cited the *LXX*. There is overwhelming evidence that the Lord held in His hands the Hebrew OT because He referred to its jots and tittles (Mt. 5:18), its three-fold division (*Torah, Nebi'im,* and *Kethubim*) in Lk. 24:27 and 44, and its canonical order of Genesis to 2 Chronicles (Lk. 11:50-51). The received Hebrew text, upon which the Lord Jesus put His Divine imprimatur, became the OT Scriptures for the first century churches to preserve along with the canonical NT Scriptures.

For the NT Scriptures

The Ekklāsia and the Great Commission

The Lord used the OT saints to write and preserve His Words in relation to His designated place of worship, the Tabernacle or Temple. Similarly, He used His church, the *ekklāsia*,[176] as the custodian of the NT Scriptures. The Gospel of Matthew records the Lord's establishment of this new institution, the Book of Acts shows its early progress, the Epistles reveal the theology and polity of the *ekklāsia*, and the Book of Revelation unveils His future for mankind to seven local churches. The Lord Jesus Christ established His *ekklāsia* and promised to edify it (Mt. 16:18).[177] He built up His church with church discipline (Mt. 18:17-18), the Lord's Supper (Mt. 26:24 ff.), the Great Commission (Mt. 28:19-20), Holy Spirit empowerment and accreditation (Acts 2:1 ff.), and deacons (Acts 6:2-8).[178]

In His post-resurrection appearance to the disciples, the Lord Jesus Christ gave His *ekkāsia* the Great Commission (Mt. 28:19-20). This commission, which the Lord had already practiced,[179] was the command to continue to establish NT immersionist churches until the end of the age. The Great Commission can be divided into three main parts of speech that give the thrust of it. The controlling verb is the imperative "teach" (μαθητεύσατε, *mathāteusate*) with three participles, "go" (πορευθέντες, *poreuthentes*), "baptizing" (βαπτίζοντες, *baptizontes*) and "teach" (διδάσκοντες, *didaskontes*) and the infinitive "to observe" (τηρεῖν, *tārein*). The full expression of the

---

[176]The word *ekklāsia* is found 115 times in the *TR*. For the etymological and contextual meaning of a local, visible assembly or congregation, see Acts 19:32-41.

[177]The future verb *oikodomāsō* does not mean "I will originate, create, or start." A careful study of the NT reveals that the best etymological and contextual understanding is "I will edify."

[178]Cf. Thomas M. Strouse, *I Will Build My Church: The Doctrine and History of Baptist Churches* (Newington, CT: Emmanuel Baptist Theological Press, 2000), pp. 28-37.

[179]Christ required His disciples to identify with Him through John's immersion (Mt. 3:1 ff.) and to obey His continued instruction (Jn. 13:34-35). He had a flock over the which He was the shepherd or pastor (Jn. 10:14).

Great Commission is to make disciples of all nations, subsequently baptizing them in the name of the persons of the Trinity, and teaching them to keep Christ's canonical Words (OT and NT) for all subsequent generations until His return. The Lord gave local NT church pastors and members several responsibilities.

1) All NT immersionist churches have the responsibility to recognize and receive Christ's canonical Words.[180]

2) All NT immersionist churches have the responsibility to preserve Christ's Received Words for all generations.

3) All NT immersionist churches have the responsibility to guard Christ's Words against heresy. This movement of local, NT immersionist churches, which had bishops and deacons (1 Tim. 3:1, 8), is what Paul called "the pillar and ground of the truth" (1 Tim. 3:15).

Recognize and Receive Christ's Words

The Lord Jesus Christ gave the Father's Words, which were "forever settled in heaven" (Psm. 119:89), to His disciples and apostles. The Lord expected His disciples to recognize these Words (Jn. 10:27) and receive them (Jn. 17:8). They in turn were to write them down as the Holy Ghost brought the Lord's Words to their remembrance (Jn. 14:26; 16:13). Throughout the NT, and especially in Acts, the Lord's disciples and apostles maintained this "received Bible" mindset relative to the OT and NT canonical Words of Christ.[181]

Preserve Christ's Received Words For All Generations

As the infinitive "to keep" (*tārein*) unfolds in the NT relative to Bibliology, it becomes apparent that the word indicates that the early Christians had the responsibility to observe, keep, guard and preserve the Words that the Lord gave them. Throughout His earthly life, the Lord prepared His followers for the ministry of preserving His Words. He enjoined the young man seeking eternal life about the sober responsibility of keeping the commandments (Mt. 19:17). He stressed the importance of keeping His Word to the Jews who were resisting Him as the fulfillment of Scripture about the Christ (Jn. 8:51-55). In the Lord's last discourse, He gave a series of admonitions to keep His commandments. He said, "If ye love me, keep (τηρήσατε, *tārāsate*) my commandments" (Jn. 14:15). He said, "He that hath my commandments, and keepeth (τηρῶν, *tārōn*) them, he it is that loveth me . . . " (Jn. 14:21). The Lord continued saying, "If a man love me, he will keep (τηρήσει, *tārāsei*) my words . . . He that loveth me not keepeth not my sayings: and the word which ye hear is not mine, but the Father's which sent me" (Jn. 14:23-24). He promised, "If ye keep (τηρήσητε, *tārāsete*) my commandments, ye shall abide in my love; even as I have kept (τετήρηκα, *tetārāka*)[182] my Father's commandments, and abide in his love" (Jn. 15:10). He warned concerning the world, "Remember the word that I said unto you, The servant is not greater than his lord. If they have

---

[180]Mankind will be judged on the basis of Christ's canonical, inscripturated Words (Jn. 12:48), and not on His *agrapha* as many unbiblically suppose.

persecuted me, they will also persecute you; if they have kept (ἐτήρησαν, *etārāsan*) my saying, they will keep yours also" (Jn. 15:20). Keeping Christ's commandments included receiving them, guarding them intact for obedience, and obeying them.

The Lord prepared the early Christians with the theme of receiving, guarding, and obeying His commandments even after His earthly ministry. He said through James, "For whosoever shall keep (τηρήσει, *tārāsei*) the whole law, and yet offend in one point, he is guilty of all" (Jam. 2:10). Paul reminded the Corinthian church members, saying, "Circumcision is nothing, and uncircumcision is nothing, but the keeping (τήρησις, *tārāsis*) of the commandments of God" (1 Cor. 7:19). The Apostle John repeatedly encouraged believers concerning their responsibility to preserve the Lord's Words, stating "And hereby we do know that we know him, if we keep (*tāromen*) his commandments. He that saith, I know him, and keepeth (τερῶν, *terōn*) not his commandments, is a liar, and the truth is not in him. But whoso keepeth (τηρῇ, *tārā*) his word, in him verily is the love of God perfected: hereby know we that we are in him" (1 Jn. 2:3-5). Also, John said, "And whatsoever we ask, we receive of him, because we keep (τηροῦμεν, *tāroumen*) his commandments, and do those things that are pleasing in his sight . . . and he that keepeth (τηρῶν, *tārōn*) his commandments dwelleth in him and he in him. And hereby we know that he abideth in us, by the Spirit which he hath given us" (1 Jn. 3:22,24).

These aforementioned passages prepare the Bible reader for the culminating truth concerning the need to receive, guard, keep, and obey God's revelation. The Lord Jesus Christ clearly instructed the church members of the seven churches about their Great Commission responsibility (cf. Mt. 28:19-20). He gave a beatitude, saying, "Blessed is he that readeth, and they that hear the words of this prophecy, and keep (τηροῦντες, *tārountes*) those things which are written therein: for the time is at hand" (Rev. 1:3). He promised the church in Philadelphia that "Because thou hast kept (ἐτήρησας, *etārāsas*) the word of my patience, I also will keep thee from the hour of temptation, which shall come upon all the world, to try them that dwell upon the earth" (Rev. 3:10). The practice of keeping God's revelation will continue in the Tribulation, as John states, "And the dragon was wroth with the woman, and went to make war with the remnant of her seed, which keep (τηρούντων, *tārountōn*) the commandments of God, and have the testimony of Jesus Christ" (Rev. 12:17). Likewise, John assured the reader concerning the Tribulation saints, saying, "Here is the patience of the saints: here are they that keep (τηροῦντες, *tārountes*) the commandments of God, and the faith of Jesus" (Rev. 14:12). Finally, an angel of God gave John a beatitude, stating, "Behold, I come quickly: blessed is he that keepeth (τηρῶν, *tāron*) the sayings of the prophecy of this book . . . See thou do it not: for I am thy fellowservant and of thy brethren the prophets, and of them which keep (τηρούντων, *tārountōn*) the sayings of this book: worship God" (Rev. 22:7, 9). These various passages echo the truth of the Great Commission that requires all believers to receive, preserve and obey God's oral and written revelation.

---

[181] Cf. my chapter entitled "The Lord Jesus Christ and the Received Bible."
[182] Having received the Fathers' Words perfectly intact, the Son of God guarded and practiced them perfectly.

Guard Christ's Words against Heresy

New Testament immersionist churches, having recognized, received, and preserved Christ's Words, also have and do guard, *ipso facto*, these Words against heretical attacks. Bibliological heresy was foisted upon NT churches in the first century and these churches recognized the heresy and dealt with it. Peter recognized that Paul's letters were wrested (στρεβλοῦσοιν, *streblousin*, literally "twisted") by church heretics as other Scriptures were and warned his audience (2 Pet. 3:15-16). Paul realized some heretic in the Thessalonian church had forged a letter in his name and was teaching some sort of heretical Post-Tribulation Rapture position (2 Thess. 2:2). The NT warns about heretics in the churches and gives instruction on dealing with them (Tit. 3:10;[183] cf. also 2 Tim. 2:24-26).

The apostles recognized that the local churches, and not they as individuals, were the Lord's institutions to preserve His truth. When the heresy of "another gospel" (ἕτερον εὐαγγέλιον, *heteron euangelion*) arose in the Galatian churches, Paul quickly asserted "that the truth of the gospel might continue with you" (Gal. 2:5). The Greek word translated "might continue" is the *aorist* active subjunctive *diameinā*, (διαμείνῃ) meaning "to continue permanently." Coupled with the expression "with you" (πρὸς ὑμᾶς, *pros humas*), this verb indicates that the Lord's truth would be passed on permanently through local churches such as the Galatian churches. The Lord's assemblies have had the responsibility to preserve the truth of His Words and purge heretical attacks against them.

Case Study: the church of Colosse (Col. 4:16)

The Case Study of the Colossian church corroborates the truth that local church members have had the responsibility to receive, preserve and obey the Lord's revelation. Paul stated to the Colossians that " . . . when this epistle is read among you, cause that it be read also in the church of the Laodiceans; and that ye likewise read the epistle from Laodicea" (Col. 4:16). As soon as the church of Colosse received the Epistle of Paul to the Colossians, they were to read it in their services (cf. 1 Tim. 4:13). This public reading would help insure public reception, preservation, and obedience. Furthermore, this assembly at Colosse was to receive, preserve and obey the Epistle from Laodicea (Philemon; cf. Col. 4:17 with Phile. 1:1-2). That these Colossian church members received and preserved intact Paul's canonical letters is irrefragable. What other option did they have in light of the numerous passages demanding of believers the intact

---

[183]Cf. Kent Brandenburg's chapter (twenty-one) on Titus 3:10, "Who Is a Heretic on the Preservation of Scripture?"

[184]In Romans 5:1, Wallace posits the fallacious notion that Tertius misspelled *echomen* (ἔχομεν), changing Paul's indicative "we have" to the subjunctive "let us have." Supposedly Paul caught the mistake and made a correction in the original Epistle to the Romans so that the recipient audience would not know which reading was correct and which was erroneous. Daniel Wallace, "Do Christians Have Peace with God? A Brief Examination of the Textual Problem in Romans 5:1." http://www.bible.org/docs/soapbox/rom5-1.htm, 2/10/2002. This scholarly nonsense is easily refuted by passages such Jer. 36:4 which teaches that God's Words were inscripturated perfectly by the scribe (i.e., Baruch) in the inspiration/preservation process.

reception and preservation of the Lord's revelation? These immersed believers would have known if the Colossian Epistle was forged (cf. 2 Thess. 2:2) or tampered with (cf. 2 Pet. 3:16-17). When they made copies of the Epistle to the Colossians they would have copied them perfectly in keeping with the ongoing requirement to preserve God's Words perfectly (Dt. 4:2; Mt. 28:19-20). And of course these copies would be copied and copied perfectly intact throughout the church age, except when heretics tampered with and changed the Words. The Colossian church is a Biblical example of a local church that recognized, received, and preserved perfectly the Words of God.

Case Study: the churches of Asia Minor (Rev. 2-3)

The Ephesian church members received the Apocalypse from the Apostle John (Rev. 1:11; 2:1). They were encouraged to preserve it (Rev. 1:3) and warned not to allow any deviations (Rev. 22:18-19). At some point, the Ephesian church needed to send the book of Revelation on to the church of Smyrna, some 35 miles away. They probably kept the original and sent an accurate copy. How accurate would their copy be? Word perfect![184] This process of perfect Words preservation would have continued as the church of Smyrna sent a perfect copy to the church of Pergamos which sent a perfect copy to the church of Thyatira which sent a perfect copy to the church of Sardis which sent a perfect copy to the church of Philadelphia which sent a perfect copy to the church of Laodicea. This process of perfect Words preservation was demanded by the Lord Jesus Christ in numerous verses (Rev. 1:3; 22:7, 9) and fulfilled by church members since textual deviations were not an option (Rev. 22:18-19). Heretics produced the deviations and for centuries Christianity did not countenance their efforts (cf. the late interest [19th century] in Aleph and B).[185] The preservation of God's Words was the sole responsibility of local immersionist churches such as these seven and has continued on for generation after generation up until this very moment. This human responsibility in the Divine preservation of God's Words was demanded and guaranteed by the Lord Jesus Christ in and through His local churches. The preservation process is not the responsibility of para-church scholars,[186] but of local NT church members who have the spiritual capacity (Jn. 10:27; I Jn 2:27; Rom 8:16) and mental acumen (Col. 3:15-16; Rev. 22:7) to fulfill the Great Commission. The seven churches in Asia Minor received the Book of Revelation and preserved it verbally intact to pass on to succeeding generations of local churches that have continued the preservation process into the twenty-first century.

---

[185] *Codex Sinaiticus* includes two non-canonical books (the Epistle of Barnabas and the Shepherd of Hermes) in its NT canon and both *Codex Sinaiticus* and *Codex Vaticanus* disagree with each other in thousands of places.

[186] None of these scholars has Biblical authority and many do not have the spiritual requirement of regeneration to engage in Christ-honoring Biblical studies.

Conclusion

The Bible gives the means for the Lord's preservation process in spite of the darkened counsel of text critical scholars.[187] He used His OT believers in their place of worship to preserve the Hebrew text and He has used and continues to use NT saints in their place of worship, which is the institution of the local church, to preserve Christ's Hebrew, Aramaic and Greek Words in accurate translations. The Lord gave His assemblies the Great Commission that includes the responsibility to preserve His Words for all generations and against heretical attacks. Local NT churches as God's permanent institution, and not apostles, could and did recognize, receive, preserve, and keep the canonical Words of the Lord Jesus Christ through the centuries. That the Lord chose His immersionist assemblies to preserve perfectly all of His Words for all generations is without controversy among those who recieve the Bible. After all, Paul affirmed that "the house of God, which is the church of the living God, [is] the pillar and ground of the truth" (I Tim. 3:15).

---

[187]The text criticism these critics practice is a humanistic and hopeless effort to restore God's Words. If ever "achieved," how would one know except by faith that it was restored, since no original exemplar exists?

CHAPTER THIRTEEN

The Church, the Pillar and Ground of the Truth
1 Timothy 3:15

Charles Nichols

Introduction

One of the questions posed concerning Biblical preservation of the inspired texts is, "By what means did God preserve it?" It is obvious that the Bible has not been preserved by way of the original documents. Therefore, those original texts, since they have been preserved as God has promised, have been preserved by way of accurate copies. The questions then arise: What channel did God use to provide His people with accurate copies? Is there any Scriptural indication concerning whom God has appointed to guard His holy Word?

God's Guardian of Old Testament Scripture

Recognition of the many variations in available ancient manuscripts of the Scriptures leads to an obvious question: Has God left believers with no means to determine where to look for intact accurate copies of the Scriptures? Regarding the Old Testament, the Lord recorded in Romans 3:2 by the pen of the apostle Paul, "...unto them [the Jews] were committed [entrusted] the oracles of God." God preserved the Old Testament through the nation of Israel's meticulous and laborious copying of the Word of God.[188]

---

[188] In his book, *Defending the King James Bible*, (Collingswood, NJ: The Bible for Today Press, [N.d.]), pp. 24-26, D. A. Waite quotes from H.S. Miller, who lists the rules for copying the Hebrew synagogue rolls of the Old Testament Scriptures. "The parchment must be made from the skin of clean animals, must be prepared by a Jew only, and the skins must be fastened together by strings taken from clean animals. Each column must have no less than 48 or more than 60 lines . . . The ink must be of no other color than black, and it must be prepared according to a special recipe. No word or letter could be written from memory, the scribe must have an authentic copy before him, and he must read and pronounce aloud each word before writing it. [For instance "In the beginning God created the heaven and the earth." One

These methods of copying the Holy Scripture hardly leave room for anyone to say:

> . . . the copyists (scribes) made every conceivable error, as well as at times intentionally altering (probably with the idea of 'correcting') the text. Such errors and alterations survived in various ways, with a basic tendency to accumulate (scribes seldom left anything out, lest they omit something inspired).[189]

Christ and the New Testament writers quoted the Old Testament copies of Scripture as though they were the preserved, inspired Word of God centuries after the original manuscripts were written. In His use of Deuteronomy 8:3 in Matthew 4:4, Christ demonstrated His belief in the preservation and absolute authority of the Scriptures available in His day. It may also be noted in Christ's usage of this passage that His appreciation is evident for the verbal inspiration and verbal preservation of that Old Testament Scripture that had been originally written over fourteen hundred years earlier.[190]

The Guardian of New Testament Times

Just as God singled out Old Testament Israel as guardian of the Old Testament Scriptures in the Old Testament period, He singled out the church of Jesus Christ to guard the New Testament.[191] One could hardly conceive that the copyists of the Scriptures within those first Biblical New Testament churches would be unaware of the rules for Old Testament copyists. That they would have been any less meticulous in copying Scripture than their Old Testament predecessors is a false presumption. Those early New Testament saints were certainly not unaware of the realities before them. Their own faith, as well as the New Testament faith for which they were hazarding their lives, was dependent upon an authoritative, accurate copy of the words they were copying. 1 Timothy 3:15 reads, "But if I tarry long, that thou mayest know how thou

---

has to pronounce the word "in the beginning" in Hebrew, (*bĕrā'shēth*); "God," ('*Elōhēm*); "created," (*bârâ*'); "the heavens" ('*āth hashshâmayēm*); "and the earth" (*wĕ'āth hâ'ârets*). He had to pronounce every word before he wrote it down, with an authentic copy before him. He had to pronounce it aloud, not just see it in his mind. This was to avoid any errors, duplications, omissions, etc.] He must reverently wipe his pen each time before writing the word for "God" [which is '*Elōhēm*] and he must wash his whole body before writing the name "Jehovah" lest the Holy Name be contaminated. Strict rules were given concerning forms of the letters, spaces between letters, words, and sections, the use of the pen, the color of the parchment, etc. The revision of a roll must be made within 30 days after the work was finished; otherwise it was worthless. One mistake on a sheet condemned the sheet; if three mistakes were found on any page, the entire manuscript was condemned. [*Author note:* What if the man got from Genesis all the way through to Malachi, so to speak, and found three mistakes? He would have to start from Genesis and go all the way to Malachi again. One sees the meticulousness with which the Jews were ordered to guard the Words of God. Those men believed that the Words they were copying were God's holy Words. Because of this, they guarded them, unlike men today who add, subtract, and change at will such has been done in the NKJV, NASV, NIV, and in other new versions. To that extent, they are perversions

oughtest to behave thyself in the house of God, which is the church of the living God, the pillar (στύλος, *stulos*) and ground of the truth." When Paul declared the church the pillar of the truth, he taught that God entrusted the church[192] with the responsibility of preserving the truth (God's Word, John 17:17) in this needy world. By declaring it to be the ground (ἑδραίωμα, *hedraiōma*) of the truth, the Lord committed to her the responsibility of being a bulwark and protectorate of truth in this corrupting world.

This epistle is addressed to Timothy, the pastor of the church at Ephesus where the famed temple to Diana was located. In this setting the allusion to a "pillar" and "ground" would have had a clear significance to this first recipient of this epistle. The temple of Diana was securely founded on a platform 239 feet wide and 418 feet long. Upon this huge base 117 sixty foot high columns or pillars, each measuring six feet in diameter, stood to support the magnificent 180 feet wide by 377 feet long edifice.[193] The pillars held up the structure, and the ground was the foundation on which the entire structure rested. In this text the pillar and ground combine to uphold and protect the truth, which is actually the Bible itself. The church performs like those two features of a temple, having been given that responsibility and authority from God.

Though the meaning of this allusion to the church as "the pillar and ground of the truth" hardly needed reinforcement to the early church of Ephesus, Jude 1:3 reinforces the responsibility described in I Timothy 3:15 for all by using an intensified present infinitive form of the word "contend." Jude thereby asserts that "the faith once delivered," while apparently still existing, must continue to earnestly be guarded and preserved.

Further support for this responsibility of true New Testament churches to keep and guard closely the Word of God is seen in such passages as Revelation 3:8 and 10,[194] where the aorist active form of the Greek verb τηρέω (*tāreō*) is rendered "hast kept." This Greek word means "to keep, to watch over, to preserve." The New Testament church at Philadelphia is commended for its faithfulness in preserving the Word of God and is assured that it would be kept (future active form of the same verb) from the hour of temptation to come. A great deal of the confusion and conflict that has arisen over the centuries regarding textual issues has arisen from acceptance of textual vari-

---

of truth and Scriptures. Every word and every letter was counted. The exactness was staggering. Yet, that was the method God used to preserve the Old Testament.] If a letter were omitted, an extra letter inserted, or if one letter touched another, the manuscript was condemned and destroyed at once." [Miller, op. cit., pp. 184-185.].

[189] Douglas R. McLachlan, *The Bible Version Debate*, p. 3.

[190] See chapter two by Thomas Strouse on Matthew 4:4.

[191] In this dispensation, God uses the church to preserve the Old Testament as well.

[192] Only a local church would have a pastor (bishop, 1 Timothy 3).

[193] D.G. Hogarth, *The Biblical World, A Dictionary of Biblical Archeology* (Grand Rapids: Baker Book House, 1966), p. 229.

[194] From examining Revelation 3:10, keeping His Word has the same sense of "preserve" as Christ's keeping the Philadelphian church from the hour of temptation. Like this church preserved His Word, He would preserve it from the hour. One should also note 3:3, which contains a present imperative form of the same verb. See chapter twelve, *Ekklāsia*: The Congregation of the Lord in the New Testament: *Tāreō* (ητηέω), by Thomas Strouse.

ants that came from spurious sources, that is, from places other than that specifically designated by God in His Holy Word.

New Testament Local Churches Behave Themselves

Much perplexity has arisen through both a failure to accept only the Scriptures as perpetuated through the church of Jesus Christ, and a lack of discernment in what constitutes a true church of Jesus Christ. If all the copies of Scripture that have come by way of some other channel than the true church were discarded, most, if not all, of the Scriptural text problems would be dissolved.

The word, "oughtest," used in 1 Timothy 3:15, does not leave room for ungodly, carnal behavior in the church of the living God. It is translated from the Greek word δεῖ (*dei*). This term appears in the Greek New Testament approximately 105 times. In the King James Version it is translated 58 times as "must," 31 times as "aught," 5 times as "must needs," 4 times as "should," and 7 times in other ways.[195] In the Greek lexicons, is consistently described as a word that denotes a necessary or required action, or a compulsion of any kind. It appears in 1 Timothy 3:2 to stipulate the necessity of the listed qualifications for those who would occupy the office of a pastor. 1 Timothy 3:2 ff. does not leave room for many who are occupying pastorates today, and 1 Timothy 3:15 does not allow the ungodly music and lifestyles that many are allowing into their assemblies. The extent that a local church behaves Scripturally is directly related to her function as protector and propagator of the truth. Assemblies demonstrating such prevailing disregard for the dictates of Scripture stand suspect as to their ability to fulfill this God-ordained function of "pillar and ground."

When one recognizes that the Lord did not designate some individual, a religious denomination, or some institution that simply chooses to call itself a church of Christ, the guardian of truth, one can then recognize that the whole textual issue is greatly dependent upon what one accepts as a church. There are some obvious basic ingredients the Word of God reveals for an organization to be duly constituted as a church of the living God. The first three chapters of the book of Revelation provide the seeking soul a great deal of insight into this issue. Although each of these seven churches was distinctively different in numerous ways, they all had some things in common. It is evident that all of these were churches of the living God, since the apostle John (Rev. 1:4) and the Lord Himself addresses them as such (Rev. 2, 3).[196] Recognition of common elements in these churches helps one to recognize what constitutes a New Testament church. There are at least four qualities common to all seven of these assemblies:

---

[195]Jacob Brubaker Smith, *Greek English Concordance* (Scottdale: Herald Press, 1995), p. 77.

1. All seven of these churches are autonomous local assemblies, each operated as a church and each was addressed independently as a church. No universal visible or invisible body is designated a "church" in this passage. No inter-church or denominational organization fits in this context, nor, it may be added, any other New Testament context.
2. All seven of these churches had Christ in their midst (1:13, cf. Matt. 18:20). Spirit-filled Christians invariably are able to sense a lack of the Divine presence in assemblies that are no longer, or possibly never were, churches of Jesus Christ.
3. All seven of these churches have an angel [messenger] being held in the right hand of the Lord Jesus Christ (1:16, 20). Those seven stars (angels/messengers) are seen in chapters 2 and 3 as divided among the seven churches, each church having its own angel/messenger. Most students of the Bible recognize the angel/messenger as the pastor of the church. In 1:16 they are found in the right hand of the Lord, which clearly signifies being owned and controlled by Him.
4. All seven of these churches are individually responsible to hear and respond to the Divine message given by the Divinely owned and controlled messenger (2:5, 11, 16, 29; 3:6, 13, 22). The Word of God was not entrusted to apostate assemblies to perpetuate. It was not entrusted to a school, an individual, a denomination, a society (i.e., the Evangelical Theological Society), or a movement (i.e., "fundamentalism"). The Word of God in this age has been committed to local, autonomous churches that refuse to give up their autonomy, refuse to call or retain a pastor who does not consistently evidence that he is owned and controlled by the Lord, and refuse to divorce themselves from their responsibility to hear and respond to the Divine message, dictates, and warnings given them. Only assemblies such as these remain churches of the Lord, pillars and bulwarks of the truth.

One who sees unscriptural behavior in a particular assembly that calls itself a "Christian" church should employ these Biblical principles (at least) to determine if it truly qualifies as a genuine church of Jesus Christ.

Conclusion

As the Lord appointed Israel to guard His Word in Old Testament times, so He has appointed faithful, New Testament churches as guardians of His Word in the present dispensation. Details that God has indeed provided to guide men in their search for the preserved Word must not be ignored. The trail of truth travels in and through the local

---

[196]Revelation 2 and 3 are the most comprehensive teaching of the Lord Jesus Christ Himself on the nature and function of the church. A vast majority of His usage of *ekklāsia* is found in these two chapters.

church.[10] The *TR* has been accepted by the churches and the *TR* text type was used by the churches from the first century. All others must be rejected as spurious. If this were done, all such original-language texts and their resulting translations would be rejected, the modern-day textual issue would evaporate, and the battles over the preservation of Scripture would never have arisen. To accept spurious texts may be eclectically and intellectually inviting, but it is surely Biblically unacceptable. Those who have been snared by the eclectic manuscript mania which prompts the acceptance of spurious texts and translations need to recognize that the variant readings of the texts that underly all of these modern-day versions did not arise through faithful, New Testament churches. It behooves all discerning believers in these perilous times to receive only the text that has been protected and passed down by New Testament local churches, the Scriptural channel that God has chosen for the presentation and the preservation of His Holy Word.

---

[10]David Otis Fuller in his book, *Which Bible?* (Grand Rapids: Kregel, 1970), pp. 174-378, proves demonstrably that the Waldenses and other historic New Testament churches received the *TR* and rejected the CT.

CHAPTER FOURTEEN

Stewards of the Mysteries of God
1 Corinthians 4:1,2
Gary La More

Introduction

Stewardship over the goods and house of the master by a devoted servant was part of ancient Biblical culture (Gen. 15:2; 43:19; 44:4; 1 Chron. 28:1). Jesus Christ used this analogy to depict proper Christian service and responsibility (Matt. 20:8; Luke 12:42; 16:1-8). Paul now identified the minister in this fashion (1 Cor. 4:1-5).[197]

An Exposition of 1 Corinthians 4:1-2

Verses 1 and 2 of 1 Corinthians 4 give the characteristics of a steward.[198] First of all, in the light of the foolishness of worldly wisdom, Paul wanted his missionary companions, the church at Corinth, and him to be recognized as "ministers of Christ."[199] He includes his audience, the church, with the use of the plural pronoun ("us," ἡμας, *hāmas*). This attitude identifies Paul, his church-planting associates, and the Corinthian church as men of humility and dedication to Jesus Christ – not ones who strive for position and power.[200] Paul, in 1 Corinthians 4:1, does not use the typical word for minister (*diakonos*, διάκονος), but rather employs the word *hupāretas* (ὑπηρέτας),[201] which

---

[197]Robert G. Gromacki, *Called To Be Saints, An Exposition Of I Corinthians* (Grand Rapids, MI.: Baker Book House, 1977), p. 51.
[198]Ibid.
[199]Ibid. "The word "minister" is not merely a name given to a preacher. It is a designation of *rank* and a delegation of *work*. It describes the position of service . . . ." Roy L. Laurin, *First Corinthians Where Life Matures* (Grand Rapids, MI.: Kregel Publications, 1987), p. 89.
[200]Ibid.
[201]This term, *hupāretas* (ὑπηρέτας), is used only here in Paul's epistles. It differs from the word translated "ministers" in 3:5 in that it has the idea of an attendant or helper that assists a master. The apostle or minister of Christ then is simply an underling, or an attendant of Christ. He takes orders and executes them. *King James Bible Commentary* (Nashville, TN: Thomas Nelson Publishers, 1999), p. 1465.

literally means an "under-rower."²⁰² Paul did not see himself as a man of high spiritual status, but as Christ's assistant,²⁰³ a helper willing to do the lowest task.²⁰⁴ Under rowing in the galley of a ship took no special talent or ability, just vigilance and persistence.

Secondly, Paul wanted the Corinthian church to see himself and themselves as "stewards (*oikonomos*, οἰκόνομος) of the mysteries of God."²⁰⁵ The word "steward" carries with it the idea of "custodian" of the mysteries of God.²⁰⁶ A steward was an administrator, a trustee, or an overseer of an estate. He was under the owner and over others within the house. Both Paul and Peter (1 Peter 4:10) knew that God had assigned to them an awesome responsibility over the assembly and the revealed truths of the New Testament. As ministers, both Paul and Peter were to serve and to do; as stewards, they were to protect and to guide.²⁰⁷

The word "steward" can also signify "overseer," "superintendent," or "distributor." The apostles and comrades were responsible to God since they were charged with the task of disseminating the Divine message found in the Word of God. The message therefore is not of apostolic origin, but has God as its source. The Apostles were not responsible for the ultimate truth of it, but only for the fidelity with which they conveyed it.²⁰⁸

The "mysteries of God" and the Word of God are synonymous. The root word for "mystery" is μύειν (*muein*), meaning "to close" (the mouth, the lips). When a mystery is made known, instead of the mouth staying closed, it is now opened. What was not known is now known and what was not revealed is now revealed. Mysteries of God are known by special revelation. The Divine plan of salvation from creation to glorification is removed from the grasp of worldly wisdom and only spiritually discerned (1 Corinthians 2:14). The revelation and the mystery are inextricably connected. The mystery is disclosed by revelation, so that making it known is revelation. For this reason, mystery is very often used with terms for revelation (Romans 16:25,26; 1 Corinthians 2:10; Ephesisans 1:9; 3:3, 5, 8; 6:19; Colossians 1:26,27; 4:4).

---

²⁰²Gromacki, loc. cit. This word was used of the slave who rowed in the lower bank of oars on a large ancient ship. Subsequently, it came to refer to any subordinate – usually an assistant, a helper, or a synagogue attendant (Luke 4:20). It was used of John Mark (Acts 13:5), of gospel preachers (Luke 1:2), and of Paul himself (Acts 26:16). Gromacki, Ibid. The minister, as an under-rower, is under orders from a higher authority. Laurin, ibid.

²⁰³An "attendant" or "assistant" is someone who takes orders from another, simply put, one who is in the *service* of God. Jay E. Adams, *The Christian Counselor's Commentary, I Corinthians, 2 Corinthians* (Hackettstown, NJ: Timeless Texts, 1994), p. 28.

²⁰⁴Gromacki, loc. cit.

²⁰⁵Ibid, p. 52. The οἰκονόμος (*oikonomos*) is held to strict account. The Lord of the steward is the auditor, and the judgment is made on the Lord's standards, not on the standards of the world. What is the steward's stock in trade? They are Divine mysteries. Therefore the question to be answered is, "Has the steward faithfully conveyed the essence of the message given to him?" If he has, he is faithful. Christ will say, "Well done, thou good and faithful servant." (Mt. 25:21). Yeager, op. cit., pp. 382-383.

²⁰⁶Ernest R. Campbell, *First Corinthians* (Silverton, OR: Canyonview Press, 1989), p. 67. In addition,

Paul committed to Timothy and the Ephesian church the stewardship of the Words that God had given him (1 Tim. 1:11, 18-20; 4:6-16). He designated the house of God, the church, as the pillar and ground of these mysteries ("the truth;" 1 Tim. 3:15). In 1 Timothy 3:9, Paul refers to God's message as the "mystery of the faith." He asked the Colossian church to pray that God would open a door "to speak the mystery of Christ" (Colossians 4:3). In Ephesians 3:3 Paul explains "how that by revelation [the Lord Jesus Christ] made known unto [him] the mystery of Christ." Believers put on "the armor of God" and "pray always" "that [Paul] may open [his] mouth boldly to make known the mystery of the gospel" (Eph. 6:10-19). Paul calls those houses of God in which stewards faithfully kept the truth "the fellowship of the mystery" (Eph. 3:9). The mystery kept and spoken by the churches is the Word of God.

In 1 Corinthians 4:1 the word "mystery" is plural (μυστηρίων, *mustāriōn*). The plural intimates the Words or passages of Scripture, the various special revelations of God. Each mystery is important, and the faithful steward will put forth due diligence to lose none of them, but to faithfully keep them within the house given the authority by his Master to do so. The Master is the Lord Jesus Christ, the Head of the church, the house in which the stewards labor in keeping the mysteries.

Finally, Paul wanted to be known as a faithful man.[209] Having designated himself as a steward of the mysteries of God in the preceding verse, Paul now sets forth the primary requisite for a steward – he must be "faithful" (πίστος, *pistos*), true and worthy of trust and confidence (1 Tim. 1:12).[210] Since his stewardship involved the mysteries of God, he accurately and aggressively proclaimed these truths.[211]

Faithfulness involves doing all that the master has commanded, executing it according to the master's method, and finishing it in the assigned time. The quality of the stewardship may vary, but the sphere of stewardship never does, for Luke 12:48 says, "But he that knew not, and did commit things worthy of stripes, shall be beaten with few *stripes*. For unto whomsoever much is given, of him shall be much required: and to whom men have committed much, of him they will ask the more." Associated

---

Gromacki says that the word for *steward* has a root meaning of "house law." Ibid. Garner also says that *oikonomous* refers to the church of Jesus Christ, as found in 1 Tim. 3:15. The "house" metaphor is one commonly applied in the New Testament to the church (1 Corinthians 3:5-17; 2 Timothy 2:19-21). In light of this, the house in which the steward of Christ keeps His ministries could only be understood as the local church. Garner, loc. cit. According to Roy L. Laurin, a steward was a manager entrusted with the management of his master's affairs. In the case of the Christian steward, his was the administration of Divine truths as found in the Word of God, the wise employment of Divine power, and the faithful propagation of God's message entrusted to his care. Laurin, loc. cit.

[207] Gromacki, loc. cit.
[208] Yeager, ibid.
[209] Gromacki, loc. cit.
[210] It is not required that Christian stewards be found popular or successful in a world-wise way. It is rather required that they be found faithful in relation to the substance and the service entrusted to their management. Laurin, loc. cit.
[211] Campbell, loc. cit.
[212] *King James Bible Commentary*, loc. cit.

with the idea of stewardship is a particular stress on accountability.[212] As what would characterize the writing of Paul, in verse 2 he moves from the plural to the singular ("stewards"–"a man"). He moves from the principle to the particular; it is sought for in all stewards, that each one be found reliable and trustworthy.[213]

"Ministers of Christ" have a sense of personal responsibility to the Lord in Whose service His minister is engaged. The phrase, "stewards of the mysteries of God," refers to the lynchpin activity of the crucial servant in a household who had the task of transferring the resources of the owner to the members of his household according to their needs. As one of these stewards, Paul had been entrusted with the wisdom of God, and so was a transferer of truth.[214]

Conclusions

Since the philosophy of heaven, the message for which the steward is held responsible, is nonsense to the unsaved world (1 Cor. 1:18), he should not be interested in trying to please it. In fact, he must not concern himself in the least with what the world thinks of his stewardship. The faithful steward must please his Owner, God.[215] Strong temptation exists for the steward, especially today and particularly on the issue of perfect preservation of God's Words, to please the academic crowd, which is most likely to reward his subjugation with a false label of scholarship. The seduction is a self-serving lure of intellectual pride.

Paul was to transfer to everyone "the mysteries of God" given him by God and found in the Scriptures which Paul already possessed. He was obedient to the One who had called him. He did not doubt that he had what God wanted him to transfer to the household of faith in Corinth; obviously Paul accepted this trust as the very Words of God. He was not looking for a lost Bible.

God was looking for a steward, a man who would be faithful to pass on to the generations to come what the Lord had given to him. Paul was that man. Unlike many of the academics of today, he was not concerned about intellectualism and the acceptance of his contemporary world. He sought only to obey God and pass on what He had entrusted to him, namely, His Words. By including the church at Corinth along with himself in this task, he fulfilled this duty.

God did not commit this stewardship to textual critics. He works the best through stewards in His church who are faithful to His Word and its message. Paul knew that God had preserved His Word; otherwise he would not have written 1 Corinthians 4:1-2. The faithful members of the church today, like those members of the Corinthian church, are given the stewardship of the Words of God. This is the

---

[213]Ibid.
[214]G.J. Wenham, ed., *New Bible Commentary 21ˢᵗ Century Edition* (Leicester, England: Inter-Varsity Press, 1994), p. 1167.
[215]Yeager, op. cit., p. 383.

message of the Apostle Paul in this text. These members receive the Words, guard the Words, and pass on those very Words to the next generation of local church members. God is under no obligation to give His message to one He knows will not faithfully receive the Words steadfastly conveyed from one generation of local churches to the next. Implied in faithful stewardship is faithful reception, an implication that disqualifies modern lower critics.

A man must proclaim his Biblical faith, like Paul and Peter of old, through God's perfectly preserved Words, and ignore the foolish opinions of the world. Those opinions are really quite absurd to God and He does not abide such silliness. The world of modern Biblical scholarship dismisses the true Biblical Christian for holding that every Word of God is has been perfectly preserved in one edition.[216] Satan has used a coterie of worldly-wise scholars to write many trranslations. If the true Biblical Christian is a fool then he is a fool for Jesus' sake. If God is for him, who then can be against him? The faithful steward will stand for the only preserved Word of God as a trustworthy custodian of these, the mysteries of God.

---

[216]The King James Version is God's perfect Word accurately translated into the English language. See *Addendum* B by Thomas Strouse on how the King James Version fulfills the model of Scriptural preservation.

SECTION FOUR

Passages on the Reality of Textual Attack

CHAPTER FIFTEEN

First Century Textual Attack 2 Peter 3:15-17 and 2 Thessalonians 2:2
Kent Brandenburg

Introduction

Those who dispute the preservation of Scripture often use words or phrases such as "the most reliable manuscripts" or the "best texts." Upon closer examination, those using this terminology generally mean "the earliest or oldest manuscripts."[217] To them, the best texts are the oldest ones. Those who weigh manuscripts using criteria such as age believe that people, even today, should labor at restoring the text of the New Testament to a condition closer to that of the originals. This ongoing process of textual criticism does not represent the Biblical doctrine of the perfect preservation of Scripture. The contention that the "oldest is best" is at best rationalistic speculation. It theorizes that more recent copies have had more time to accumulate errors that were introduced incrementally into each preceding generation. However, to understand Scriptural behavior, the Bible itself must be the authority. The Bible contains no verses espousing the "oldest is best" criterion. Instead, it teaches early and often that textual attack will come from Satan and his human instruments (Genesis 3:1-6; Matthew 4:1-11).

Bible believers maintain a distinctive bias toward what Scripture teaches. Scripture says God will preserve every Word. Scripture declares God will use His ordained institution, Israel in the Old Testament[218] and churches in the New Testament, to preserve every Word. Knowing that God says this, believers assume that He will do what He says. They trust Scriptural criteria and not human reasoning. It might make sense in

---

[217]In *From the Mind of God to the Mind of Man,* ed. James B. Williams (Greenville, SC: Ambassador-Emerald International, 1999), p. 198, J. Drew Conley writes concerning the *Revised Standard Version*: "Thirty-two scholars with an advisory board of fifty representatives from a variety of denominations worked on the project, convinced that the older manuscripts provided a far more reliable text basis (that is, readings closer to what the original documents contained) than did the few manuscripts available to the King James translators."

[218]See chapter eleven, Israel, the Means of Preservation in the Old Testament: *Nâtsar* (נָצַר) and *Shâmar* (שָׁמַר), also by Kent Brandenburg.

man's thinking that old, rarely used manuscripts are superior to newer, often-used ones. However, guided by the Holy Spirit, churches not only can but also will reject corruptions in manuscripts. Before the printing press, believers received the unadulterated Scriptures,[219] made copies of them (Colossians 4:16), used them (2 Timothy 2:15), and taught them (Matthew 28:20; 2 Timothy 2:2). When their copy or copies wore out, they made sure to preserve what they had by making new copies.[220] Believers, who had a conviction about the preservation of Scripture, were very careful to make their copies as accurately as possible from other ones that were used by the churches. This process resulted in numerous copies of Scripture being made by the churches that existed in the early centuries after Christ ascended into heaven.

What did believers do with corrupted manuscripts? Churches did not characteristically receive the contamination of Scripture. Pure manuscripts and readings were embraced while the others were rejected. This behavior stemmed from authoritative warnings concerning tampering with Scripture. The Bible establishes clearly that there were corruptions of first century manuscripts by means of purposeful textual attack, a truth firmly demonstrated in 2 Thessalonians 2:2 and 2 Peter 3:15-17.[221] History testifies that these were not copies the churches used or accepted. These two passages, among others, establish that New Testament local churches were to reject texts intentionally corrupted and by implication receive and carefully preserve the Words that were genuinely from God.

2 Thessalonians 2:2

The Context of 2 Thessalonians 2:2

The epistles of 1 and 2 Thessalonians are generally regarded as some of Paul's earliest writings (A.D. 51-52).[222] Paul left the church at Thessalonica after only approximately three weeks (Acts 17:1-10), and the letters he sent back to this church gave them inspired apostolic commendation and correction. False teaching about the Rapture ("gathering together unto him" 2 Thess. 2:1) had deluged the church at Thessalonica. The Apostle Paul specifically corrected their confusion about its timing,

---

[219]See chapter four, The Lord Jesus Christ and the Received Text, John 17:8, by Thomas Strouse.

[220]See chapter twelve, *Ekklāsia*: The Congregation of The Lord In The New Testament: *Tāreō* (τηρέω), by Thomas Strouse.

[221]Daniel B. Wallace (Associate Professor of New Testament Studies from Dallas Theological Seminary) on p. 2 of an article entitled *Mark 1:2 and New Testament Textual Criticism* ([N.p.]: Biblical Studies Press, available at http://www.bible.org, 1997) enumerates three humanistic arguments against a position of purposeful corruption of the Scriptural text (what Wallace calls the theory of "conspiracy" regarding corruption of the text). However, he completely ignores the authoritative and vastly superior Biblical evidence of these two passages that describe this very conspiracy, as well as the related passages on this specific strategy of Satan as chronicled in the Bible (Gen. 3, Mt. 4). One would think that a seminary level professor of New Testament Studies might go to the New Testament to accredit a particular line of thinking. Instead, he highlights the often repeated reliance by defenders of a non-perfect preservation view

for some of the believers there thought it had already occurred and they had been left behind. Several points made in chapter two debunk this false teaching. 2 Thessalonians ends with extensive teaching in 3:6-15 on separation from those who would adulterate Scripture in their belief or practice.

The Teaching of 2 Thessalonians 2:2

The false teachers shook and troubled the Thessalonians believers through three different means, swaying the beliefs of church members and then affecting them emotionally. Firstly, deception came by means of "spirit," supposed prophetic revelation or supernatural communications that were concocted by the deceivers. Secondly, distortion of Scriptural truth came by "word," probably sermons they preached which contained their false teaching. Lastly, deceiving counterfeiters of the Apostle Paul penned bogus letters in his name.

The Evidence of First Century Textual Attack in Second Thessalonians 2:2

When 2 Thessalonians was written in the middle of the first century, Satan already was using men to purposefully attack Scripture.[223] Certainly this particular attack altered the text even more than changes made to single paragraphs, sentences, or words, by adding to Scripture an entire epistle. However, it does reveal the existence of textual variants in the first century. Forgers who would add an entire epistle would not scruple to make smaller changes within canonical books.

2 Peter 3:15-17

The Context of 2 Peter 3:15-17

Peter wrote 2 Peter shortly before he died at the hands of the Roman emperor Nero (A.D. 67-68)[224] to the general audience of Jewish believers to whom he had written the first epistle.[225] Since 1 Peter, the apostle had become concerned about false teachers

---

on corrupt logic that arises from a fallacious major premise (correction of Scripture is necessary in all manuscripts if it is necessary in the oldest ones) culled from either revisionist history or Freudian analysis of human behavior.

[222]Since these letters came from Corinth (Acts 18:5), and since Gallio's pronconsulship of Achaia recorded in Acts 18:12ff would have been from AD 51 to 52, 1 Thessalonians was likely written in the summer of AD 51 and 2 Thessalonians in the fall or early winter of AD 51.

[223] A major variation such as the addition of an entire epistle was obviously very damaging to the eschatological belief of the church at Thessalonica. The variations of 1 Thessalonians in the CT continue to significantly affect eschatology (1:10; 2:11, 12, 15; 3:2; 4:8, 13; 5:27). Those changes alter eschatological understanding even before 2 Thessalonians.

[224]2 Peter 1:14.
[225]2 Peter 3:1.

that had infected the churches of his original audience, so he wrote to expose, thwart, and defeat them. These false teachers primarily maligned the doctrine of the Second Coming of the Lord Jesus Christ (2 Peter 3:3,4). In so doing, they cast doubt upon God's Word, essentially denying the reliability of God's promise of His coming.

To combat this false teaching Peter repeatedly taught the believers to remember the will of God as revealed in His Word. He put them in remembrance of the saving and sanctifying knowledge of the Lord Jesus Christ (2 Peter 1:1-15). The false teachers sought to reduce inspired Scripture to something that was no different than anything authored by men. However, believers knew they could fully trust the truths of which they were reminded because of the surety of the Word of God (2 Peter 1:16-21).[226] In chapter two, Peter instructed these believers to reject the false teachers because of their doctrine (2:1-3a), their doom (2:3b-9), their depravity (2:10-17), and because of the type and the tragedy of their deceptions (2:18-22). He devastates their best arguments against the reality of the Second Coming in the first ten verses of chapter three (3:1-10).[227] Peter ends the epistle with specific behavior that results from the proper belief in the Lord's return (3:11-18). The doctrine of Christ's Second Coming results in expectation, peace, purity, increased evangelism, and growth in the knowledge and adoration of the Lord (3:11-15a, 18). The life changed by the truth of the Second Coming stands in direct contrast to the corrupt life of the scorner (2:2,3; 3:3b).

The Teaching of 2 Peter 3:15-17

The closer the world gets to the judgment of the Lord Jesus Christ, the more desperate Satan becomes in deceiving people about His Second Coming. Satan wants to lead men into error and sway believers away from a usable condition for their Lord (3:17). The inspired prophetic writings of Peter (3:15b – "even as . . . also") and the Apostle Paul contain passages less than easy to understand. Sincere believers will interpret them accurately, but those characteristically unbelieving will not. Since saved people know the tendency of the "unlearned" (i.e., ignorant, those without enough information) and

---

[226]God's writings are not like something made up by men, but are more sure than even genuine Divinely produced experiences such as Peter encountered on the Mount of Transfiguration. The inspiration of the Scriptures assumes their perfection. The original manuscripts with the prophecies of the Old Testament are not available, but these writings as preserved in the copies can be trusted because they are clear ("of no private interpretation"), and they come directly from God. This is also explicitly stated in the present tense ("have") in 2 Peter 1:19, "We have also a more sure word of prophecy; . . ." The saints to whom Peter wrote could trust their copies of Scripture as though they were the autographs.

[227]One argument against the scorners is the Old (3:2a) and New (3:2b) Testaments. The Bible is characterized as "words" which were spoken, not as ideas or concepts. Confidence in the Bible is confidence that the Words of the Bible are the Words of God.

[228]"Wrest," in a literal sense, means to put a body on a rack, to torture, rack, and wrench it – and these men so "wrest," that is, torture the truth. One should note that these false teachers wrest the actual writings, and not just their teachings. Some might say that wresting "scriptures" assumes teachings, but since the word "scriptures" is chosen, corruption of the text of the Bible is at least included.

[229]These writings must be God's Word if any distortion of them leads to destruction (Rev. 22:18,19). God severely warns people that add or take away from the Words of Scripture. The way that 3:16b ties into Revelation 22:18,19 both in activity and result teach that no Scripture should receive any additions or subtractions. No man should assume that God does not refer here to all and each of His Words.

"unstable" (i.e., vacillating in their character) in wresting these and all the other writings of God's Word, they must beware.[228] These false teachers, and those that join them in the perversion of Scripture, do so to their own destruction (3:16b).[229] Discernment concerning distortion of Scripture is another result of the believer's anticipation of the Second Coming of Christ. This text, and the rest of 2 Peter, imply that the church members will reject the false manuscripts about which they are being warned and then separate from those who are perverting Scripture.

The Evidence of Textual Attack in the First Century in 2 Peter 3:15-17

Second Peter was written in the first century, just like 2 Thessalonians, and it provides further evidence that men were purposefully attacking and twisting the text of Scripture.[230] They distorted all of the teachings that did not fit in with their unstable character. Note that Peter called what Paul had written "Scripture." The first half of verse sixteen says the false teachers distort the prophetic passages of the inspired writ of Peter and Paul, and the second half of verse sixteen declares they alter all the other inspired writings as well. The actual writings themselves were being changed to fit the doctrine and practice of the false teachers.[231] This again evidences textual attack in the first century.

Conclusion

Biblical principles and promises are the basis of a Scriptural Bibliology. No verses in Scripture teach a theory that the oldest manuscripts are the best, but these two references in the New Testament among others,[232] reveal intentional corruption of the New Testament text in the first century. The Scriptures themselves denounce the theory of

---

[230]The scoffing and lust of these false teachers (2 Pet. 3:3,4) reveal their intentional attacks on the Words and their doctrine. These attacks result from ignorance and instability, but they are intentional nonetheless.

[231]Most anti-Trinitarian apologists use the Critical Text as the basis of their false doctrine. The internet is presently filled with apologists of the Jehovah's Witnesses, Moslems, religious Jewry, Christadelphians, The Way International, Restoration Fellowship, etc. who use the CT to attack the Deity of Christ. One example is the recent book by Anthony Buzzard and Charles Hunting, entitled *The Doctrine of the Trinity: Christianity's Self-Inflicted Wound* ([N.p.: International Scholar's Press, 1998). Buzzard teaches at Atlanta Bible College and is the head of the Restoration Fellowship. Their view is that the early manuscripts were better because they leave out the Trinity doctrine. Included in their documentation are attacks on 1 John 5:7,8 by such men as Daniel B. Wallace (http://reslight.addr.com/1john5-7.html, 2002). These anti-Trinitarians argue that the Trinity was not a doctrine until the fourth and fifth centuries AD, just like 1 John 5:7,8 (in their opinion) was not introduced into Scripture until that time.

[232]E.g. 2 Corinthians 2:17, "For we are not as many, which corrupt the word of God." For anyone who wished to explain away 2 Thessalonians 2:2 and 2 Peter 3:15-17, perhaps claiming that one or both do not deal with textual variants, this verse proves men were altering the text from the originals in the first century. A whole chapter could have been written on this verse also.

"oldest is best."[233] These passages all indicate that the Bible was intentionally changed in the first century. Scripture does not teach the theory that mistakes stayed in the Bible that had gradually come into the text by means of scribal blunders, but affirms that the errors were introduced by Satanic instigation.[234] Instead of receiving a text based on human rationalism, the believer will receive the text that has been preserved and agreed upon by the churches and so authorized by God as His Word.

---

[233] Examination of the oldest manuscripts has revealed intentional altering. David Cloud in his *Myths about the Modern Bible Versions* (Oak Harbor, WA: Way of Life Literature, 1999), p. 193, quotes Frederick Henry Scrivener's *A Full Collation of the Codex Sinaiticus* (original publisher unknown, 1864), N.p., "The *Codex* (*Sinaiticus*, Aleph) is covered with alterations of an obviously correctional character – brought in by at least ten different revisers, some of them systematically spread over every page, others occasional, or limited to separate portions of the Ms., many of these being contemporaneous with the first writer, but for the greater part belonging to the sixth or seventh century."

There are good reasons to believe in the later received manuscripts and reject some of the oldest existing texts. The following is a reasonable alternative to "oldest is best." Few of the same type of manuscripts as the corrupt oldest ones survived because the churches rejected these and their type. These few oldest manuscripts endured due to lack of use. Churches rejected them because of their error, and false teachers did not use them because they were not interested in the truth. The copies (exemplars) from which copies were made were either worn out from use or destroyed because of their wear, leaving only the later manuscripts. Multitudes of later manuscripts remain because they represent the kind preserved by the churches. Few of the type of the oldest exist because the churches never had an interest in copying them.

[234] There were major variants of Scripture due to intentional corruption in the first century. After corrupting the text in the first century, those perverted copies could initiate a multitude of future corrupted copies. There are few copies, however, in the family of corrupted copies. They did not last because God used the churches to reject them. Only relatively recently have some texts that were formerly discarded by the churches been given prominence by "freelance scholars."

SECTION FIVE

The Standard of Perfection: Several Passages as Examples of Doctrines Changed and/or Perverted by Textual Alterations

CHAPTER SIXTEEN

Pure Words of God: Passages Which Teach the Perfect Purity of the Bible
Thomas Corkish

Any philosophy, speculation, theory, approach, practice, or prediction that is without an authoritative base can bring no conviction. There is no certainty, credibility, nor confidence without substantiality, foundation, evidence, data, verification or documentation. Faith, however, is "substance" and "evidence" (Heb. 11:1). It does not need to see and examine in a scientific way, but finds a conviction of things not seen. Jesus mentioned this concept to Thomas when He said: ". . .Thomas, because thou hast seen me, thou hast believed: blessed are they that have not seen, and yet have believed" (John 20:29).

When there was no written revelation, God provided signs to validate the spoken Word of His prophets. Signs were demonstrations to those who were unpersuaded to believe the Words, and many of them were recorded in the Scripture to give faith to those who read them. Jesus set His pattern which was carried on through the Words given to John in his gospel: "And many other signs truly did Jesus in the presence of his disciples, which are not written in this book: but these are written, that ye might believe that Jesus is the Christ, the Son of God; and that believing ye might have life through his name" (20:30-31).

Today no signs are given since there is no new revelation being written. The sign was evidence that the Words written were as authoritative as the spoken Words. The transition in Scripture is from the "sign" to the "written," and then to the "faith."[235] If one is faulted or faulty, so are the others and the result is equally deficient. If "signs" are bogus, so are the Words they substantiated. If the Words are fraudulent, then faith hangs on nothing.

Some today insist that "seeing is believing." In spiritual realms, this is not the case. It may have been so in the days when God was preparing His Word for the world, but not now. It is intended that man should "hear" and thereby believe. "So then faith cometh by hearing, and hearing by the word of God" (Rom. 10:17). The order in this day is to start with the already authenticated Word and then progress to faith by

---

[235] Hebrews 2:3,4; Mark 16:20; Romans 15:18,19; 2 Corinthians 12:12; Acts 14:3.

hearing. "These things have I written unto you that believe on the name of the Son of God; that ye may know that ye have eternal life, and that ye may believe on the name of the Son of God" (1 John 5:13). The written Words lead to belief resulting in absolute knowledge of eternal life.

The Sovereignty and Supremacy of God

In medicine, to take a drug without a bonafide prescription is not only illegal, but also dangerous. If a man drives on the wrong side of the highway because he does not accept the letter of the law, he is not only going to be arrested and possibly thrown into jail, but faces the possibility of injury or death. Playing games for entertainment or profit without following the rules is cheating, dishonest, and disrespectful of those with whom we play or compete. Society requires specific laws; otherwise, anarchy reigns, which is contrary to the will of God. Even in times of revolution or rebellion, God only allows it to go so far before He steps in to provide whatever and whomever it takes to curb the unruly. God, the Sovereign in all matters, does not limitlessly share His creation without the bounds of government, justice, penalty, and reconstruction. He maintains regulated order among heavenly beings, principalities, powers, men, animals, plants, and heavenly bodies. God's creation is a massive demonstration of His essential and absolute laws. Although some question His intervention, claiming the appearance of chaos, none should doubt the resolution of God's total ascendency over every atom, cell, thought, intention, and action in the universe.

The Dangerous Denial of the Word of God

It is disconcerting and dangerous to walk in the company of those who refuse to understand God's laws as set forth in His Word. God designed Israel as a Theocracy, but instead she chose a Monarchy. God had outlined exactly what He deemed necessary for the nation. He had chosen a certain people and place. The nation was His timing and His plan from the beginning. Israel was always in the mind of God, as is everything. There can be no "better" idea than what God could conceive and reveal through His Word. A journey from Genesis through Revelation exhibits God's fidelity, allegiance, and purity in print. Man, principality, or power can alter neither the Word nor the outcome of its eternal message. To deny that Word is to deny the mind and warrant of God, and even God Himself.

---

[236] *American Educators Encyclopedia* (Chicago, Ill.: The United Educators, Inc., Publ.), p. 927.

The Absence of a Standard without the Word of God

Men in society understand certain authoritative issues and legislated absolutes. The Legislative, Executive and Judicial branches of the national government have powers and restrictions defined in the Constitution of the United States. One branch does not create its own powers and restrictions, but the supreme fundamental law has been adopted, ratified and delivered to all the people equally. Men and women and children have lived in some variety of respectful harmony under this magnificent document for more than two hundred years. There are always scoffers who look for further changes by deletions and additions. Regardless of man's endeavors to make alterations, the framers were led in such a way that these highly regarded words and ideals have successfully taken our nation through thick and thin over the course of the past two hundred years. Still, the Constitution is not perfect, even though it sets a standard. The American Educator Encyclopedia makes an interesting comment about the deficiency of the Constitution:

> "Yet the Constitution has proved to have certain weaknesses. Its framers failed to make clear the division of authority between the national and the state governments . . . a failure which finally led to a bitter and costly civil war. Debate on this issue continues, with those in control of the government usually wanting it to be strong, while those not in power insist that the authority of the states be preserved and even increased."[236]

The same article states that "[s]ince it is man-made, the Constitution falls short of absolute perfection."[237] Any who lower the conception and continuation of the Scriptures to the level of the making of the Constitution are going to find that there will always be a search for perfection, without any satisfaction: thus a hundred more new translations of the Bible.

All man-made documents and efforts have and will fall short in the final analysis. This is a principle that appears in every attempt of man to produce something perfect. Church constitutions and bylaws have the same imperfections, even though Godly men try their best to put words together completely and sufficiently. Fallible men alone cannot construct infallible treatises. However, what about God? What about His revealed Words? What about these "works of men" and their eventual preservation through the millennia? Are the things of God equal to those of man, or absolutely distinct in origin and conclusion?

If our Bible is a man-made document or even a man-preserved document alone, Christianity is in a fallible position. The world is able to understand that man cannot produce a perfect volume in any order, especially something as complicated, ancient, and all-encompassing as the sixty-six books of Scripture written by more than forty

---

[237]Ibid.

individuals over a period of some sixteen hundred years. It must be recognized that man has not conceived, written or preserved the Scriptures. The Words of Scripture are not of man, nor does he preserve them. The giving and preserving of the Words of God are a supernatural event and process. Each book and each Word was the completed creation of God. There could be no improvement, revision, addition, or subtraction to perfect the Words breathed out by God.

Preservation is so important because it is through Scriptures, original and preserved, that "ye have eternal life." Jesus said, "Search the scriptures; for in them ye think ye have eternal life: and they are they which testify of me" (John 5:39).

The premise of a preserved, infallible Word incorporates the faith that the actual Words were conveyed by a miracle into books, and then collected by God into a unit by the overseeing of the Holy Spirit. The Spirit performed this by means of intervening upon men and attributing to them His perpetuation of the Scriptures for all eternity. It was not, and is not ever under the control of man without the direct supervision of God's eternal care. Anything else leads to the dilemma found in the Constitution of the United States: "Yet, the Constitution has proven to have weaknesses . . .."

Infallible doctrine is imperative to Christianity, but it exists only if infallible Words convey the absolute mind of God to man. Some assert that interpretations in the Constitution of the United States are endless. Special interest groups often try to determine and undermine what the designers originally intended. Everyone does not understand Scripture in every case, but it stands alone as perfect, unchangeable, definite, final, conclusive, and authoritative. God has His Words in His hands. No other document can compare with the Bible. It is the final, inexorable and uncompromising Word of God in all its parts.

All the rhetoric in the world will not suffice as a basis for an infallible Bible that pronounces infallible doctrine. The doctrine must, however, be founded squarely upon the sayings that God has given in those Scriptures. God is speaking. His mind is being transmitted to the world through the miracle of revelation, the method of His choice.

The Scriptural Standard of Purity versus "Evolution"

The Psalmist said, "Thy word is very pure: therefore thy servant loveth it" (Psalms 119:140). This purity is the heart of this matter. Does it mean that God has given us a "nice" Word, but no more? Perhaps it could mean that the Word was fresh, holy, honorable, moral, noble and virtuous. What more could we ask from God in a revelation He gave by his Holy Spirit as He carried men along in creating the original autographs? Could it be that the original creation, formulation, and presentation of the Words of God were intended to be like the rest of creation, as some skeptics contend? Is it a creation of the universe by the Word of God in the "original," and then left to abandonment so as to allow some form of evolution to take over? This false doctrine of "creation" has been termed "theistic evolution" by those who are so inclined to lean to the scholarship of "scientific investigation" apart from the unveiling of truth by the Holy Spirit in the Words of God. Although this terminology is meant to describe a theistic-evolution of the universe, it could be applied equally to the system that believes God has given His accurate Words in the "original" and subsequently abandoned them to ruination by men. This view persists as the antithesis to the truth.

If a student of the Scriptures can avoid what God has said exactly, and longs for some recognition in the theological circle of the "spiritual intelligentsia" by following the path of unbiblical higher criticism and lower criticism, a "theistic evolutionary" view may become a platform for acceptance both in secular and in certain Christian contexts. The question posed to those taking this course of freedom with the Scriptures would be, "Did God mean what He said in the creation accounts?" If certain manuscripts were found saying that God created everything in some primaeval condition, with the prospect of millions of years to complete the process, one could then conclude that His "original" in creation was just a beginning, now left to itself and the force of nature, taking whatever turn it may, evolving without constraints by the Creator. Of course, no such manuscripts exist, nor would any Bible believer expect them to have ever existed. In the same fashion, no manuscripts have or will reveal a process of inspiration or preservation. A process does not rule a perfect Bible any more than creation was subject to evolution. All of this contradicts the Scriptural standard of perfection.

The Words of God were, and are, "pure" from their eternal home in the mind of God, and remain so to this day. "Believest thou this?" One should allow the Scriptures to speak for themselves and let the very mind and intent of the Eternal and Almighty God settle the question once and for all.

"The words of the LORD are pure words: as silver tried in a furnace of earth, purified seven times" (Psalm 12:6). In the context of this absolute declaration, the ungodly are using words that contradict what are called, "pure words," those Words which are designated as "the Words of the LORD" (v. 6). In contrast to God's Word, the speech of the ungodly is described as "vanity" (v. 2), "flattering" (v. 2), and "double heart[ed]"(v. 2). This "vain" speech consists of a pronouncements that swell with emptiness, vanity, and falsehood. It employs the exposition of nothing and is full of worthlessness. The use of the description "vanity" implies that words of the ungodly will eventually bring about degeneration and death to the unwary listeners. "Flattering" words capture the hearts of saints. The addition of "proud things" indicates that this smoothness of mouth flows with eloquent and slippery verbiage which the clever spokesman intentionally sends forth upon his hearers.

In contrast to the wicked, who have an agenda to gain everyone by their tantalizing words, the Lord's Words are described as "pure." They contradict that which is worthless or vain. The "pure Words" are the powerful Words of God, Words of substance and value spoken by God with certainty. The wicked "flatter," while God always wills His Word to eternally work righteousness, conviction, and judgment.

Some have mistakenly said that the Bible has needed to be "tried" ("refined") seven times in order for it to be given as "pure." Actually, it was as "refined" silver from the beginning: it has never had any defects or foreign substances to make it less than perfect. God gave it that way, and it remains still in that same form. "*Are* pure"[238] attributes to "the Words of the Lord" a state of unbroken continuity. The thought is that they are just as pure today as at every earlier period in history.

The Call to Universal Submission to the Pure Words of God

The Old and New Testaments are the foundation of the faith. In the nature of its unbending proclamation, the Word of God is required to be pure, absolutely free from all corruption, so should be received by all true, Bible-believing Christians. Any position less than absolute, which allows a mixture or reduction to this purity, is considered grounds for God's judgment of "plagues" (Rev. 22:18) and taking away the corruptor's " . . . part out of the book of life, and out of the holy city, and from the things which are written in this book" (Rev. 22:19). God does not look lightly on those who would violate His pure, unadulterated Words.

Many critics of the Scriptures are guilty of doing exactly what God warned against. They have taken God's Words and permeated them with unforgivable contamination. Some of these so-called scholars have violated the sacred place of God's authority and, in their unbelief of His sovereign promise concerning His infallible Words, have attempted to adjust, arrange and coordinate the infallible through fallible, human manipulations of criticism, clarity, sophistication, and disobedience. Instead of the man humbly submitting to an absolute and inviolable formation of revelation by the provision of the Holy Spirit, he has, in many cases, taken it upon himself to attempt to improve upon what God has done in creating the Word, and has thereby brought the doctrines of inspiration and preservation to an alarming disgrace. When Christians should be trusting without any question the infallible Word of God, they are beginning to doubt that it even exists in one book. "Where has the Word of God gone?" "Who took it away?"

An argument that God gave man an infallible Word and subsequently left its preservation in his hands without the Holy Spirit's intervention, so that pastors, churches, scholars, scribes, colleges, and translators alone must keep it, does not fit with the sovereignty of God, Who promised that His Words would be kept pure for ever. Instead of looking at these promises from God, men have looked at the process of scholarship. Instead of believing God, men have bypassed Him and His truth; indeed, they have circumvented His testimony to His verbal, plenary inspiration and preservation of the Word. Scripture proclaims that God gave a pure Word, and God will keep and superintend that same pure Word from the first day to the last, and even forever.

---

[238]The Hebrew text here has no verb, so the King James translators supplied the word "are," since the

The Demand that God Speak for the Word

"Thy word is very pure: therefore thy servant loveth it" (Psalm 119:140). The Hebrew word translated "pure" comes from the verb *tsâraph* (צָרַף), speaking of a smelting or refining, with the express significance of separation from any dross. There can be no debris, impurity or contaminants in God's Word. This is nearly identical to the appellation that is imprinted on the cover of most Bibles, showing the very character of this Book as separate or holy. It is the "Holy Bible," a separated Book, distinct from all others in existence, past, present, and future.

The fact that it is "very pure" gives the Scripture the distinction that it excels above all else in purity. It is exceedingly pure from impurity. It is mighty in purity, having been tested and found without mixture. The second half of Psalm 119:140 gives the reason for the servant's love of this kind of Word; he understands "the word is very pure," and consequently loves it; without this Divine purity upon it, there cannot be that same desire, longing, confidence or hope. Believers love an uncontaminated Word today, just as in the days of the psalmist.

Some may ask if preservationists worship the Bible. The only answer the psalmist could find for his own heart was, "therefore thy servant loveth it." The Christian who has a trustworthy Bible is brought to that conclusion by the Holy Spirit, Who leads him into all truth. The Lord Jesus Christ, the Divine Word of God, is the Object of the adoration, and just as He is without corruption, so is His written Word. Just as the Christian hangs every hope upon the Saviour, so he hangs on every communication that comes from His heart in the written Word.

"Every word of God is pure: he is a shield unto them that put their trust in him" (Proverbs 30:5). In every passage cited, the present tense verb must be supplied, indicating that the Scriptures are qualitatively pure. It is not that they "were," but that they "are." They are absolutely pure forever. The Old Testament prophet had hope in an eternal and "pure Word:" "The grass withereth, the flower fadeth; but the word of our God shall stand for ever" (Isaiah 40:8). "For ever, O LORD, thy word is settled in heaven" (Psalm 119:89).

The New Testament proclaims the same. The Words are not mixed with any alloy or harmful material, and nothing can interfere with God's sovereignty in superintending and maintaining this purity. The Word speaks for itself: "Heaven and earth shall pass away, but my words shall not pass away" (Matthew 24:35). "Being born again, not of corruptible seed, but of incorruptible, by the word of God, which liveth and abideth for ever. For all flesh is as grass, and all the glory of man as the flower of grass. The grass withereth, and the flower thereof falleth away: but the word of the Lord endureth forever. And this is the word which by the gospel is preached unto you" (1 Peter 1:23-25).

---

absence of a verb communicates a state of being.

Proverbs 30:5 demands a high and narrow view of God's Word. It is not just to be admired for its overall existence, but to be placed under the microscope of the man of God for study in such detail that everyone in his congregation can see readily that not just the whole is pure, but each and "every word." This contrasts strongly with much of today's preaching, which often uses the expression, "a better rendering would be," followed by a corruption of the text.

Infallibility of the Bible in All Areas Addressed

All ought to recognize that the Bible claims to be infallible in all areas God chooses to address in the process of revealing truth in His Words. Any and every time the broad subjects of design, forms, spheres, cubes, cylinders, cones, or wedges are mentioned in Scripture, it is accurate. The Scripture teaches with accuracy in the arts although it is not a book of the arts. The same precision is found in its presentation of history, mathematics, natural science, physical education, economics, social science, law, health, homebuilding, psychology, political science, communications, government, and all other topics addressed in its infallible text. It is not a science book, nor a manual on economics, but is without any mixture of error in all subjects of which it speaks.

Since it is not a manual for every technical truth, God does not give every unnecessary detail. However, in any area He does purpose to reveal truths, such as the fact that planets and other heavenly bodies hang in space, He does not find it necessary to accommodate modern scientific terminology, nor does He expansively detail His knowledge of the subject. This does not mean the Scriptures are imprecise, and therefore to be shunned as antiquated and incorrect. The opposite is true: the Scriptures never fail in any of their revelations.

That is the breadth ("plenary") of it. The depth ("verbal") of it is found in that every Word is without error or mixture. Where plenary verbal inspiration is upheld, the totality of all Words is embraced as being given by the supernatural breathing of God through the prophets, so as to bring about these magnificent and pure Words. Conceptual revelation, which does not require accurate and preserved Words, is discarded by all serious Bible students; and verbal, plenary inspiration must take its place as paramount and final. The later is essential to every Word being pure.

Since "every word" is pure and refined by the hand of the Lord, there can be no dross in the revelation. John declares this truth, accompanied by two extreme warnings when he pens the final words to the deposit of the local churches in his Book of Revelation (22:18). This is no trifle. A scholar cannot ignore it. It is of a magnitude that requires us to reject perverted Bibles such as the NASV, NIV, NKJV, and others that take such liberties in changing the Words God has breathed. The text of the Revelation passage makes it clear that not only are concepts not to be added, but when a man deals with "the words of the prophecy of this book," he is not to "add" any other words that would swell the whole. The converse is also given in that no man must ever, "take away from the words of the book of this prophecy . . ." (Revelation 22:19). Each pure word is essential to the completion of God's whole revelation. Any "dross" or "mixture" added makes it an impure word, violating God's sacred, settled standard of perfection.

God manifests the true nature of this purity by saying: "For verily I say unto you, Till heaven and earth pass, one jot or one tittle shall in no wise pass from the law, till all be fulfilled" (Matthew 5:18). Technically, it is understood that this refers to the Old Testament law, but its principle certainly extends beyond this alone. A "jot" or "tittle" is smaller than any concept, individual commandment, or even one word, and refers to the minutia of the Hebrew text.[239] The Law does not exist without the Words. Neither the Words, nor the Law, can be infallible unless the very smallest detail contained and maintained in it is a supernatural work of the Holy Spirit of God, the Author and Guardian of the Scriptures. When God says in the passage, "in no wise," this is fact.

The Origination of Scripture as Pure Words

> 1 – To the chief Musician upon Sheminith, A Psalm of David. Help, LORD; for the godly man ceaseth; for the faithful fail from among the children of men.
> 2 – They speak vanity every one with his neighbour: with flattering lips and with a double heart do they speak.
> 3 – The LORD shall cut off all flattering lips, and the tongue that speaketh proud things:
> 4 – Who have said, With our tongue will we prevail; our lips are our own: who is lord over us?
> 5 – For the oppression of the poor, for the sighing of the needy, now will I arise, saith the LORD; I will set him in safety from him that puffeth at him.
> 6 – The words of the LORD are pure words: as silver tried in a furnace of earth, purified seven times.
> 7 – Thou shalt keep them, O LORD, thou shalt preserve them from this generation for ever.
> 8 – The wicked walk on every side, when the vilest men are exalted.
> Psalm 12:1-8.

In the context of this absolute guarantee from the Holy God of heaven and earth, the ungodly have corrupted and are corrupting words in contradiction to pure Words that constitute those that are characteristic of God (v. 6). Even as the psalmist delineates one category of Words as pure and the other as not, the believer cannot mutually embrace the words of the ungodly and the pure Words of God. The speech of the ungodly

---

[239] See chapter three by Gary Webb.

is described as vain (v. 2), flattering (v. 2), and double (v. 2), which means, by formal pronouncement, that their corrupt articulation swells with emptiness, vanity and fabrication. He characterizes this uninspired word as an exposition of nothing, declaring it vain. It is full of worthlessness, a verbal vanity that warrants this warning against fallible expressions that corrupt God's infallible inscriptions and eventually cause the spiritual demise of the listeners.

In addition, it is doubly sad that God sheds light on the hearts of the saints that have been captured, in some part, by the "flattering" words offered them by the ungodly man. These "proud things" are bestowed by means of alluring words and his smoothness of mouth is slippery ground, inviting others to "slip" with him. The device of carnal words will destroy him and then his listeners. Eventually, all that embrace these fallible words, choosing them instead of the pure Words of God, will slide into their unintelligible, quibbling morass.

The Motive for Violation of the Words of God

What is the motive? No doubt great swelling expressions, not unlike that of "sounding brass or a tinkling cymbal," are written to puff up the pride of the listener who will only accept something lofty. One example is instead of using the exact word, "hell," which is harsh and cruel, a teacher might appeal to the wicked with another term that is more palatable. In such cases there is no desire to hurt anyone's feelings. Some feel the Words of God are too provocative, strong, or caustic for a listener's pride. Not only do the unsaved cry for softer and smoother words, but professing saints do as well. As Drs. Sounding Brass and Tinkling Cymbal concoct their new "sounds" within the Scriptures, a new kind of spirituality, easier and not so abrupt, neutralizes the saints and non-saints alike, bringing a travesty of distortion in the communication of revelation. The sad effect from this fruit of corrupt motivation is that the wicked are coaxed into "Christianity" without the conviction that leads to repentance toward a Holy and Absolute God.

The infallible and pure Words of God are contrary to the most deceitful use of words among men. His Words are not worthless but quicken (Psalm 119:50,93), convert (Psalm 19:7), sanctify (John 17:17), conceive faith (John 20:31), cleanse (Ephesians 5:26), and protect (Psalm 17:4). There is no favorable comparison between men's words and those of God, but only hostile and unfortunate discrepancies. The words of those who pervert are weak at best, and treacherous in their fruit. The other, being the "pure Word(s)" of God, were given as refined silver, generated in their perfect form in the entire sixty-six books of the infallible Bible, God's Holy Word.

There needs to be some discernment about the refined Words of God. These Words were not refined by men after God gave them, but were the most refined they could be, that is, perfect, at their conception in the throne room of God long before this earth was spoken by His Pure Word into existence. Psalm 12:6 describes His

Words "as silver tried in a furnace of earth, purified seven times," but this does not occur through some process of higher or lower criticism; it is a punctiliar action on God's part that does not include any evolution or improvement over time. The Bible is not a pure Word because of any derivation, development, revision, recovery or improvement. The Words were pure in their transmission through the miracle of inspiration, and according to the passage "are pure" (qualitatively). It is an original condition that is maintained through God's preservation. The original readers of the Psalm found the Words to be so, and today we must accept them as being just as pristine because of God's promise in the passage. Our English Bible, demonstrating the intent that God's very Words are pure for all time and eternity, accurately communicates the state of being. The hope of the Godly "poor" and "needy" (v. 5) is the pure Words of God (Psalm 12:7).

The Keeping and Preservation in Psalm 12

Psalm 12:7 states, "Thou shalt keep them, O Lord, thou shalt preserve them from this generation for ever." The discussion is centered in what or to whom "them" is referring. If it refers to the Godly and faithful men of verse 1, it does not refer to the Words of God in verse 6.

A suffix in connection with a Hebrew verb can be used to indicate pronouns, e.g., "him" or "them." This cannot be seen in the English translation, but in the original languages, it is clear. For those who accept the original languages (not just the autographs) as authoritative, there are many advantages of considering the grammatical construction given by the Holy Spirit in the process of inspiration. Not only can those languages give helpful information on the gender of the verb, but they also can determine, in some regard, the antecedent. This would determine whether or not "preserve them" can possibly refer to "words," or if it goes back to refer to the people who are experiencing difficult times through the efforts of those who pervert God's words with their own.

In verses six and seven God is only addressing the subject of "Words." They are, "of the Lord," and are, "as silver tried in a furnace of earth, purified seven times." The contrast between that which is of the ungodly and that which is from God is unmistakable in this Psalm; God's "words are pure," and the words of the wicked are not. It is severely strained to suggest that in the immediate context, without skipping a beat, the Psalmist would plummet from one subject – "words of the Lord," to another – " . . . the poor . . . and . . . needy." God's Words are pure. Such is the absolute statement of God in this passage and many others.[240]

When the saints of the psalmist's day would sing Psalm 12, they were assured the promises of their continued protection and salvation would prevail by the continued preservation of the Words of God. Promises must be based on some agreement that

---

[240] A strong explanation for why the "them" of "keep them" in v. 7 is referring to "words" in v. 6 and not the "poor and needy" of v. 5 is found in chapter one on Psalm 12:6,7 by Thomas M. Strouse.

cannot be changed. If the promise is pure, lasting, absolute, flawless, genuine, holy, unaltered, undiluted, and virtuous, it can honestly be fulfilled through each generation. If the opposite is the case, the contract is worthless, like the "babbling" words of the wicked men of Psalm 12. The promise is only as good as the Words are. If the Words stand, so does the promise. If the Words fail, there can be no certification to the "poor" and "needy." All Christians must take hope in a preserved and infallible Word, or despair and doubt will fill their their hearts.

The Immutability of Purity by Time, Scribe, or Language Barrier

The final resolution on Psalm twelve rests upon God's superintending of His guarantee in a pure form, not only for that occasion, but also for all generations. God's Words are totally pure forever. All sixty-six books of God's revelation, "given by inspiration," come together to make the whole. All are given by the same Divine breath, and preserved by the same omnipotent hand: "For the prophecy came not in old time by the will of man: but holy men of God spake as they were moved by the Holy Ghost" (2 Peter 1:21). The Spirit brought together the canon of Scriptures, the perfect Books with the perfect Words. Over a period of 1500 years, using forty or so penmen in varied cultures, God gave man an infallible Book. Each section is made up of God's intended Words, which are equally pure, profitable, practical, and preserved.

Critical Biblical "scholars" are constantly jumping through academic, grammatical, and political hoops in trying to provide the world with an accurate Bible that they can never produce. They cannot really say that there are actually entirely pure Words that are wholly contained in one volume on the face of the earth. All kinds of material are produced that demonstrate their confusion on the subject. Their own misgivings and lack of a foundation sow doubt. If one begins with a false premise of a corruptible Bible, the conclusion will follow that no perfect revelation exists to which a man can refer.

Men who do not hold to the preservation of the "pure words" of God insist that we must go back to the "originals," which they know do not exist. At that point, there is a rush to the original languages that do exist, but they cannot confirm how "pure" these texts are. Since all believe that the only Scriptures we have are copies, it stands to reason that we might ask how carefully they were copied. Does a man actually have an accurate transmission of 1 John 5:7? Are there pure Hebrew and Greek texts? Where can one find them? What does one do without them? Can we trust God for other things if we can not trust His promise concerning the actual Words of revelation? Suffice it to say that without absolute preservation, there is not a lot to hope for Heaven. To embrace preservation provides a foundation on which to build, while to retreat from it annihilates the faith. It is a matter of the greatest importance for life and eternity, and certainly one too important to ignore. Since the passages of Scripture have been intentionally preserved by the sovereign God of truth, they remain as pure as when given by inspiration. Without the guarantee of the pure preservation of Scripture, the inspiration of the originals would be of little value. However, God promises an accurate, pure, unadulterated, preserved, available, and, therefore, derivatively, an inspired text for man on the earth.

Throwing out the false teaching of double-inspiration, that God inspired Scripture first in the original languages, and then re-inspired it in English through the King James translators, how does one ascertain a pure Bible in the original language, or in English, French, or any other tongue? There can be no other solution than to embrace God's guardianship over preservation of Holy Scripture, just as promised over and over in God's Word. "Impure Bible" is a contradiction of terms. God does not associate with anything impure. There are numerous volumes in existence today that valiantly defend a non-existing Bible and non-preserved originals, but if this premise is true, man's salvation, Saviour, sanctification, and sureness are all gone.

Commendations for Loyalty to Truth

The Apostle John repeatedly defended the truth and the pure Words of God in his gospel and epistles. In his last epistle, he commends those who are loyal to the truth. They esteem the truth (3 John 3-4) which is not merely words on paper, but a life-changing revelation. Others notice that the believers are actually experiencing the truths of Scripture. John delights in the fact that this truth dwells in the believers, and in addition, "shall be with us for ever" (2 John 2).

This truth cannot be separated from the pure Words of God. John quotes Jesus' prayer to the Father: "Sanctify them through thy truth: thy word is truth" (John 17:17). The very unmixed, refined, pure Word is that which John says, under inspiration, shall be with us forever. His commendation is that he finds God's "children walking in truth, as [they] have received a commandment from the Father" (2 John 4). It was commendable that the saints were walking or behaving in truth that was coming from the Words of God, which were not only accessible, available and applicable for Jesus' disciples of that day, but for John's disciples in his day and for God's disciples of any day. The saints always possess the very unmixed, refined, pure, incorruptible Words of God. It is a commendable thing to cling to those Words with tenacity, expecting to hear from God: " . . . well done thou good and faithful servant: thou hast been faithful over a few things, I will make thee ruler over many things: enter thou into the joy of thy lord" (Matthew 25:21).

Conclusion

God ordained purity for His Word. Anything of God, especially God's Word, should not be thought, believed, or taught to be anything but perfectly taintless. This fact parallels God's attributes of holiness and immutability. Purity assumes perfection. Purity requires every and all Words in the correct order. The passages on the purity of God's Word reveal a qualitative perfection that transcends any temporal boundary. To continue qualifying as God's Word, the Bible must remain pure, and it has. Since God characterized His Word as abidingly pure, all believers should expect that He would preserve it as such. This standard requires no doctrinal errors would reside within the Word of God at any time. None should be assumed. Anyone who teaches otherwise is in error. Instead, based on God's revealed truth in Scripture about His Word, believers can and should wholeheartedly contend for the verbal, plenary preservation of the Bible, resting with confidence that God has done what He promised.

CHAPTER SEVENTEEN

Old Testament Passages as Examples of Doctrines Changed by Textual Alterations

Thomas M. Strouse

Introduction

Textual Critics have attacked the OT just as they have the NT. These critics have applied the canons of textual criticism to the OT to question the veracity of the MT. These applied canons are: 1) the oldest reading is closest to the original and therefore must be the best;[241] 2) the more difficult reading is preferred over easier ones because scribes had the tendency to simplify; and 3) the shorter reading is preferred because scribes had the tendency to amplify.[242] The canons of textual criticism alter the OT text and affect doctrine. There are at least three significant Biblical reasons for rejecting this man-centered approach; it undermines the numerous Biblical promises of verbal plenary preservation (cf. Psm. 12:6-7; Mt. 4:4), contradicts the full approval the Lord Jesus Christ placed upon the received Hebrew text of the OT, and ministers questions (cf. 1Tim. 1:4) about the inspiration, preservation, inerrancy and infallibility of Scripture. Text critics promote the theory of scribal errors, which produce doctrinal errors in the text of the OT. This chapter will be an attempt to examine and refute representatives of the classic examples[243] of OT textual variants, of alleged scribal errors, and of doctrinal changes.[244]

---

[241]The initial attack upon the Words of God was very early (Gen. 3:1 ff.) and, consequently, antiquity cannot be the determining factor for the "best" reading. In spite of this Biblical evidence of early error, scholars accept the pre-Masoretic antiquity of the *LXX*, DSS, Syriac, Peshitta, Josephus, *et al*, for the supposed true readings against the MT. Furthermore, OT text critics do not consistently follow their canons since occasionally they reject the readings of the Dead Sea Scrolls (DSS) which predates the MT.

[242]Orthodox scribes would have been wary of the severe warnings in Rev. 22:18-19 (cf. Dt. 4:2; Prov. 30:5-6) and not tampered with Scripture. Variants came from apostates for doctrinal reasons.

[243]These are representative but not exhaustive examples.

[244]In light of the charge leveled by W. E. Glenny that "proponents of the doctrine of perfect, providential preservation . . . usually do not grapple with these kinds (OT) of textual issues. They seem to cover them up or avoid them . . ." (Beacham and Bauder, pp. 114-115), this chapter will respond to some of these alleged difficulties.

Textual Variants

Alleged Errors in the Masoretic Text

Genesis 10:4 vs. 1 Chronicles 1:7

Moses recorded that the descendants of Javan included the Dodanim. This same group of people is designated the Rodanim in the critical Masoretic Text of 1 Chronicles 1:7 and is supported by the *LXX* ῥοδίοι (*rhodioi*). Scholars are quick to point out that the latter spelling occurred because the scribe confused the first letter *daleth* ("ד") in *Dodanim* for the Hebrew letter *resh* ("ר") in *Rodanim*, since these Hebrew letters are distinguished only by the tittle or "horn" which is on the *daleth* and is missing on the *resh*. However, this charge of error runs counter to the Lord Jesus Christ's clear promise in Mt. 5:17-18 that the smallest letters (jot) and smallest parts of letters, vowels, or vowel points (tittle)[245] would remain intact until all Scripture is fulfilled. Actually, the Ben Chayyim Masoretic Text upon which the KJB was based reads "Dodanim" in both Genesis and 1 Chronicles. The Ben Chayyim text does not even allow the possibility of a spelling error at this juncture.[246] The fact that the Lord Jesus put His full approval upon the Hebrew text of jots and tittles should prevent the Christian from looking to inferior Hebrew texts and ancient translations to correct it. Occasionally an OT individual may have two different names or two different spellings for the same name such as Achan (Josh. 7:1), also called Achar (1 Chron. 2:7),[247] but the context often explains the differences. The text critic should repent of his skepticism concerning the Lord's authorized Hebrew text and heed Paul's advice: "yea, let God be true, but every man a liar" (Rom. 3:4).

Ruth 3:15

The MT of Ruth 3:15 reads "and he went וַיָּבֹא (*wâyyavō'*)[248] into the city," referring to Boaz, not Ruth, as the one who went into the city. The immediate context (v. 16) indicates that Ruth went, but the later context (4:1) indicates that Boaz went also. There is no reason to think that there is an error in the MT since both Ruth and Boaz did go to the city. The editors of the 1769 AV opted for giving the readers the sense of the context ("she went") rather than actually translating the Hebrew word in an effort to minimize questions about inerrancy of Scripture.[249] The Hebrew text must stand because it is not erroneous.

---

[245] The tittle can refer to the vowel points and accents that make consonants words. Cf. Walter Bauer, William Arndt, and F. W. Gingrich, *A Greek-English Lexicon of the New Testament and Other Early Christian Literature* (Chicago: The University of Chicago Press, 1952), p. 429.

[246] Cf. the Ben Chayyim rendering of Riphath/Riphath in Gen. 10:3/1 Chr. 1:6 and the critical MT rendering Riphath/Diphath in the same passages.

[247] This is an example of paronomasia or punning in the OT.

[248] The *qere* (the "called" marginal note in contradistinction to the *kethiv* or "written" text) reading is וּתָבוֹא (*watâbo*) "she went."

[249] The original KJB (1611) reads "he went." The NIV reads "he went," the ASV reads "he went," the

Alleged Errors in Masoretic Text "Corrected" by the LXX

Psalm 2:9

The KJB follows the MT, where Jehovah addressed His Messianic Son and promised "Thou shalt break them with a rod of iron: thou shalt dash them in pieces like a potter's vessel." This prophecy seems to be against the kings of the earth, concluding the battle of Armageddon (cf. Rev. 19:10 ff). The pointing on the verb "thou shalt break them" תְּרֹעֵם (*těrā`ěm*) is confirmed by the second verb "thou shalt dash them in pieces" תְּנַפְּצֵם (*těnăpptsām*) of the sentence. However, the *LXX* reads ποιμάνεις (*poimaneis*, "thou shalt rule") and the Greek back-translated into Hebrew, would point the first verb as תִּרְעֵם (*těrō'ām*). Although John cites Psm. 2:9 in Rev. 2:27, he was not necessarily quoting the *LXX*, since that presumption must be proved not assumed. There is no Biblical reason to challenge the pointing of the Hebrew verb in Psm. 2:9 since Christ promised perfect Words preservation, even to the extent of the jots and tittles of the Hebrew OT.[250]

Psalm 145

This Psalm has the appearance of being an acrostic. Each Hebrew verse begins with the succeeding and consecutive letter of the Hebrew alphabet in a fashion similar to Psalm 119. However, this Psalm only has 21 verses while the Hebrew alphabet has 22 letters, indicating a difference. The Psalmist, for whatever reasons, jumped from the letter *mem* (מ) in v. 13 to the letter *samech* (ס) in v. 14, omitting the intervening letter *nun* (נ). Critics are quick to allege out that the *nun* verse has been lost from the MT. Undaunted, they have discovered the "lost" verse in the *LXX*, which reads in this place "Jehovah is faithful נֶאֱמָן יְהֹוָה (*ně'ěmān Yěhōwâh*) in all his words and gracious in all his works." This addition to the Words of God to correct the Hebrew text is based on the penultimate authority of the *LXX*[251] and falls under the condemnation of Prov. 30:6, which states, "Add thou not unto his words, lest he reprove thee, and thou be found a liar" (cf. especially Rev. 22:18).

Amos 5:26

The MT spells the name for the pagan deity כִּיּוּן (*kēyyūn*)[252] ("*Chiun*" in KJB) in Amos 5:26, whereas Stephen referred to the deity as "*Remphan*" (Acts 7:43). It is often stated that Stephen quoted the *LXX* and corrected the MT Hebrew spelling

---

NASV reads "she went," the RSV reads "she went," and the NKJV reads "she went."

[250]Even the strange occurrences of vowel points with no consonants in, e.g., "unto me" in Ruth 3:5 (also "to me" in 3:17) and of the consonants and no vowels in the second "five" in Ezk. 48:16 must be acknowledged, whether the believer understands the phenomena or not. The believer must realize that not all things about God's Words can be readily explained, but "without faith it is impossible to please him" (Heb. 11:6).

[251]Is not this a form of "Ruckmanism," correcting the original language text with a translation?

[252]There is no Biblical warrant to suppose that the scribes mistook the consonants for *ripn* (*Remphan*) and *kiwn* (*Chiun*).

for this deity. However Stephen, under inspiration, gave the current name for the deity and did not quote the *LXX*, since his quotation differs from it. The "jots" and "tittles" of the MT should be left intact and the notion that the Biblical writers quoted the *LXX* rejected.

Alleged Scribal Errors

Numbers 25:9 vs. 1 Corinthians 10:8

The Apostle Paul alluded to the Jews' sin of fornication and God's judgment upon them as a warning to the Corinthians about immorality (1 Cor. 10:8). The passage to which Paul referred stated that "those that died in the plague were twenty and four thousand." However, the Apostle stated "neither let us commit fornication, as some of them committed, and fell in one day three and twenty thousand." Since Paul used the number 23,000 and Moses stated 24,000, some charge that an error occurred in either the OT or NT relative to the number killed. Some argue that Paul merely "rounded off" the OT figure for his purposes, but a difference of 1,000 remains. Instead of charging Moses with a scribal error or Paul with generalizing his reference, one should recognize that 24,000 Israelites were killed in the total judgment and that 23,000 of these were killed in *one* day.

1 Samuel 13:1

Allegedly, the numbers of Saul's age and length of reign have been lost in this verse. The KJB reads "Saul reigned one year; and when he had reigned two years over Israel." The Hebrew text reads literally "a son of one year Saul in his reign and two years he reigned over Israel."[253] There are no missing numbers in the MT, but critics assume that this passage must parallel other passages of royal ascension (e.g., 1 Kgs. 22:42[254]), and conclude it must read that Saul was a certain age when he began reigning and reigned so many years. The RSV and New Scofield Bible read "Saul was . . . years old," suggesting an omission. However the received OT text simply states that nothing happened in Saul's first year of reign but after two years he chose three thousand men. To charge that some of the Lord's Words have been lost when He stated He would preserve them all intact (Psm. 12:6-7; Mt. 4:4; 5:17-18; 24:35) attributes to God serious defects in His nature and character.

To compound this egregious sin is the effort by modern translators to add numbers they have guessed for the supposed missing numbers. For instance, the NASV reads "Saul was thirty years old when he began to reign and forty two" adding two numbers

---

[253]The 1611 KJB contained a marginal note that states "Hebr. The sonne of one yeere in his reigning."

[254]"Jehoshaphat was thirty and five years old when he began to reign; and he reigned twenty and five years in Jerusalem."

[255]Modern man should recognize that he is removed from the ancient idioms of the Bible, which were common place several thousand years ago in a different language and culture. The Bible scholar should admit his possible ignorance of idioms rather than cast doubt upon the Lord.

[256]Ahaziah was the son of a forty-two year old mother.

that have no manuscript or translational support. Likewise, the NIV reads thirty and forty-two, respectively, contradicting Acts 13:21, which states that Saul reigned 40 years. Such translations and lower criticism sin grievously when they show utter disdain for God's Divine approval of the Hebrew OT, add words to His Words, and contradict the NT Scriptures. Paul warned about the multitude who mishandles God's Words and separated himself from them, saying, "for we are not as many, which corrupt the word of God" (2 Cor. 2:17).

2 Kings 8:26 vs. 2 Chronicles 22:2

The author of 2 Kings recorded that Ahaziah was twenty-two years old when he began to reign (2 Kgs. 8:26). However, the chronicler stated that Ahaziah (Jehoahaz) was "forty and two years old" at the outset of his reign (2 Chron. 22:2). This difference in ages has prompted many scholars to level the charge of "scribal error" to the OT Masoretic Text. The MT states that Ahaziah was "the son of twenty two years" and "the son of forty two years" in the respective passages. This Hebrew idiom was the ancient way of expressing one's age to oneself or others.[255] The easiest explanation for this apparent error is to understand that Ahaziah's age was twenty-two (2 Kgs. 8:26) and his mother Athaliah's age was forty-two[256] at the time he began to reign. The evil queen Athaliah was certainly emphasized in both passages as the representative of the Omri dynasty. Since the Divinely approved Hebrew text reads forty-two, the efforts of the translators of the *LXX* to smooth out this apparent "error" must be rejected.[257]

Isaiah 9:3

The KJB follows the MT and reads "Thou hast multiplied the nation, and not increased the joy: they joy before thee according to the joy in harvest, and as men rejoice when they divide the spoil." The issue at hand is that the negative "not" לֹא (*lō*) seems out of place in the MT, since the Lord multiplied the nation of Israel. Although *lō* is the *kethiv*[258] reading in the MT, modern versions eliminate the negative,[259] believing that the context requires an increase in joy, not its negation. However, the joy of the nation of Israel was based on harvest time and spoils, not on a relationship with Jehovah. The Scriptures evince the truth that throughout the history of the Jewish nation the Israelites enjoyed carnal mirth, but not spiritual joy (Rom. 11:25-26).

---

[257]Students of the Bible should recognize apparent differences are for complementation and not for contradiction. For example, one may reconcile the apparent error of Judas' demise by realizing he hung himself (Mt. 27:5), and somehow his body fell and burst open (Acts 1:18).
[258]*Kethiv* refers to the word "written" in the MT and *qere* refers to the word "sounded" in its margin. In this case, another word לוֹ *lô* ("to him"), which sounds like the negative, is the marginal reading.
[259]Both the NKJV and NASV omit the negative.

Doctrinal Changes

Textual critics argue for variations which affect the doctrine of Scripture, the doctrine of God (Christology, Pneumatology), the doctrine of Salvation (hamartiology, anthropology), the doctrine of Worship, and the doctrine of Last Things. Representative verses are analyzed which demonstrate that OT textual criticism changes doctrine on the sifting sand of evidence from non-MT Hebrew texts, the *LXX*, the DSS, scribal emendations and even personal conjecture.

Changes in the Doctrine of Scripture

Joshua 8:3

Changes in numbers affect the doctrine of the verbal preservation of Scripture. Two examples illustrate changes. Some critics suggest that the number thirty thousand is too large for the ambush of the twelve thousand inhabitants of Ai (cf. 8:25). D. Howard suggests that an early copyist erroneously copied the number "thirty thousand" (v. 3) instead of the "five thousand" (v. 12). He has no manuscript for this supposed "copyist error," and states, "It is a drastic measure to postulate an emendation with no manuscript support, but it seems to be the best solution to a difficult problem."[260] A belief in the fallacious theory of scribal errors in the received Hebrew text ultimately prepares this OT scholar to suggest such blatant and arbitrary speculation. Man centered "wisdom" undermines the Bibliology of the OT and is worthless.

1 Samuel 6:19

The verse according to the MT indicates that fifty thousand and seventy שִׁבְעִים אִישׁ חֲמִשִּׁים אֶלֶף אִישׁ (*shiv'ēm 'ēsh chĕmishshēm 'eleph 'ēsh*, literally, "seventy men fifty thousand men") died at Bethshemesh because they committed sacrilege with regard to the Ark of the Lord. Many think this is an inordinately large number of men killed in such a small city, and suggest that a scribal error has occurred. The text does say that the Lord smote the people, presumably curious multitudes from surrounding areas, with "a great slaughter" מַכָּה גְדוֹלָה (*makkâh ghĕthōlâh*)[261] which would be far more than the mere seventy posited by Josephus and a few Hebrew manuscripts. Neither the context nor the external evidences warrants a departure from the received MT upon which the Lord put His full approval. Surely scholars who espouse the fallacious doctrine of "scribal errors" despise the doctrine of Scripture.

---

[260]David Howard, *Joshua: An Exegetical and Theological Exposition of Holy Scripture* (Nashville: Broadman Press, 1998), p. 203.
[261]Cf. the very great slaughter of 30,000 men in 1 Sam. 4:10.
[262]Cf. the "fiery flying serpent" (Isa. 14:29; 30:6).

Changes in the Doctrine of God

Numbers 21:8

When Israel sinned against the Lord, He sent fiery serpents הַנְּחָשִׁים הַשְּׂרָפִים (*hannĕchâshēm hassĕrâphēm*)[262] to bite them fatally (vv. 4-6). The Lord commanded Moses to make a "fiery serpent" שָׂרָף (*târâph*) to which Israel was to look for deliverance. The apostle John cited the Lord Jesus Who referred to this event when He illustrated His vicarious work on the cross and the need for sinners to look to the Lord for salvation, stating "And as Moses lifted up the serpent in the wilderness, even so must the Son of man be lifted up" (Jn. 3:14; cf. vv. 15-16). The *LXX* gives the word ὀφσίν (*ophsin*) for "serpent" but omits "fiery." Modern translations such as the NIV follow this omission and translate "snake," losing the typology of Christ's fiery nature.[263] John described the Lord Jesus Christ in Rev. 1:13-16 stating, "the Son of man . . . his eyes were as a flame of fire, and his feet like unto fine brass as if they burned in a furnace . . . and his countenance was as the sun shineth in his strength." Under the influence of the *LXX*, OT text scholars undermine Christology by their departure from the Divinely ordained Hebrew text.

1 Samuel 25:22

After having been ill-treated by Nabal, David prayed an imprecatory prayer upon all his enemies, stating, "So and more also do God unto the enemies of David . . . ." He apparently took Nabal's niggardliness as an offense against Jehovah and made an oath to the Lord to slay all enemies if David did not slay the males in Nabal's household. The *LXX* treats this oath as a self-imprecation, omitting "the enemies of." The NIV, following the *LXX*, reads "May God deal with David." The veracity of the Lord's Words, and ultimately of God Himself, is a stake here. Did David call down judgment upon himself, or upon his enemies? David had the precedent of Eli's praying an imprecation against Samuel in 1 Sam. 3:17. Nothing in the context or in a manuscript justify changing the recipients of God's judgment and consequently undermining His character.

Psalm 2:12

David the Psalmist (cf. Acts 4:25) enjoined the reader to "kiss the Son" נַשְּׁקוּ בַר (*nashshĕqū var*). David used the Aramaic word for son (*var*) rather than the Hebrew word בֵּן *bān* (cf. v. 7) to avoid the dissonance of בֵּן בֵּן *bān pen* ("son lest").[264] However, critics reject the Aramaic loan word in the MT because of fallacious dating schemes which do not allow for the early use of loan words, and opt for the Hebrew meanings of *var* such as "clean" or "purity." Therefore, critics take the Hebrew *var*

---

[263]"For our God is a consuming fire" (Heb. 12:29).
[264]Also, he may have used the Aramaic word בַר (*var*) as the object of faith for the foreign kings whose *lingua franca* was Aramaic.

adverbially and suggest "kiss purely or reverentially." This translation takes out of the passage the reference to the Son, eliminating the Christology of this passage. Strange translations occur when scholars question this text. The RSV and JB translate "kiss his feet" supposing that the Hebrew words for "rejoice" and "son" are fragmented pieces of the word "on his feet." The NEB puts in the margin "kiss the mighty one" on the assumption that רב *rav* ("mighty") was erroneously spelled backward for *var*.[265] Satan, using unbelieving scholarship, has attempted to remove from Psalm 2 the Messianic-King-Son as the requisite object of faith for the salvation of the heathen. The text critics' speculation and emendations eviscerate the person and work of Christ in the OT.

Psalm 24:6

Another passage in which the audience is questioned, and thus the veracity of God is at stake, is Psm. 24:6. The MT reads "your face, O Jacob" while the *LXX* reads "your face, O God of Jacob." Modern versions such as the NIV and RSV follow the *LXX*, assuming that the MT cannot be correct. However, this probably is a reference that harks back to Jacob (i.e., "as Jacob") when he saw the Lord face to face and named the place Peniel (Gen. 32:30). The passage is understandable without changes based on inferior authorities.

Psalm 72:5

This royal psalm gives David's prayer for the Messiah. David declares that the sons of the needy "shall fear thee" יִירָאוּךָ (*yērâ'ûkâ*) as long as the sun and moon endure. The *LXX* emends the verb and with a supposed Hebrew exemplar reads "and he will prolong" וְיַאֲרִךְ (*wĕyâ'arik*) referring to deity.[266] The variant reading alters God's promise, reflecting on the veracity of God. The *LXX* has no known Hebrew manuscript support to change God's Words, but the modern versions foolishly follow it.

Proverbs 8:22

This verse, which is couched in the great wisdom chapter of Proverbs 8, has been the source of theological battle since at least AD 325. Patristics such as Athanasius and Arius recognized that this passage referred to Christ as the Wisdom of God (1 Cor. 1:24, 30). The MT reads "The Lord possessed me קָנָנִי (*qananē*) in the beginning of his way . . . ." The verb *qanah* means "to beget," as in Gen. 4:1, and prepares for the "only begotten" Sonship teaching of the NT (Jn. 1:18; 3:16; cf. also Psm. 2:7). The *LXX*, however, uses the verb "created" ἔκτισε (*ektise*), teaching that God created the Wisdom (Jesus Christ) of God before the rest of His creation. The RSV and NEB read "created," clearly denying the deity of Christ and teaching Arianism. This example

---

[265] Derek Kidner, *Psalms 1-72, An Introduction and Commentary on Books I and 2 of the Psalms* (Downers Grove, IL: Inter-Varsity Press, 1973), pp. 52-53.

[266] The RSV reads "May he live . . ." and the NIV reads "he will endure" omitting the important teaching of the fear of the Lord (Prov. 1:7).

shows that ancient heresies are in early witnesses to the text and that the tenets of text criticism are in reality diabolical folly.

Isaiah 53:11

The influence of the DSS affects detrimentally the propitiatory nature of the death of Christ in this verse. The KJB translates the MT literally and reads "He shall see of the travail of his soul, and shall be satisfied." This is in harmony with other passages on the propitition[267] (satisfaction) of Christ, as John states: "and he is the propitiation for our sins: and not for ours only, but also for the sins of the whole world" (1 Jn. 2:2; cf. 4:10). The Hebrew of the DSS reads "he will see the light of life and be satisfied," replacing the aforementioned MT clause. The DSS rendering takes the propitition the Father requires for the sin that causes His righteous wrath from the Messiah and places it upon "the light of life." The expression "the light of life" has dualistic and gnostic overtones for the Qumran[268] Messiah and radically changes the doctrine of Christ's propitiation.

Changes in the Doctrine of Salvation

Job 7:20

The question as to whom was Job concerned about being a burden, "to myself" (MT) or "to you [God]" *(LXX)* is raised. The teaching of this verse affects anthropology. Supposedly, the Jewish scribes concluded that a scribe omitted the *kaph*, changing the word from עָלֶיךָ "upon you" (`âlekâ) to עָלַי "upon me" (`âlâ), and thus keeping Job from blaspheming God. There is no merit in holding that a Hebrew letter fell out of the text. The whole tenor of Job's confession was that he was a burden to himself; he recognized his human frailty.

Psalm 73:7

The reading of this verse affects the doctrine of sin. The MT reads "their eyes swell out from fatness" יָצָא מֵחֵלֶב עֵינֵמוֹ (yâtsâ' māchālev `ānāmō), whereas the NIV, based on the Syriac and *LXX,* reads "from their callous hearts comes iniquity." The Hebrew and the KJB give the manifestation of sin – materialistic covetousness. The *LXX* gives the reason for their sin – callous hearts. Which aspect of hamartiology was the Lord revealing – the root or manifestation of sin? The context argues for the latter, and the *LXX* is no authority to change the Biblical doctrine of sin.

---

[267]"Expiation" is a poor word historically and theologically and should be shunned. C. H. Dodd originated the word based on a faulty view of the nature of God in the OT.

[268]The Qumran sect represented a form of first century Gnosticism that embraced dualism and esoteric knowledge. This sect, which produced the DSS, should not be utilized as a source for Biblical truth. Cf. C. F. Pfeifer, *The Dead Sea Scrolls and the Bible* (NY: Weathervane Books, 1969), pp. 135-145.

Changes in the Doctrine of Worship

1 Samuel 1:24

After the Lord answered Hannah's prayer for a son, she brought Samuel to the house of the Lord in Shiloh for dedication. The Scripture states she took "three bullocks, and one ephah of flour, and a bottle of wine" to the Lord. However, the *LXX*, questioning the Hebrew consonants, reads a "bull of three years" μόσχω τριετίζοντι (*mosxō trietizonti*) and is now supported by the DSS.[269] The rationale for accepting the *LXX*/DSS reading is that these predate the current copies of the MT and must consequently be the better reading. However, the MT repudiates the erroneous reading. Hannah needed to make three offerings (with her three bullocks); her burnt offering, her purification offering after childbirth (Lev. 12; cf Lev. 3-4), and her peace offering in fulfillment of her vow (Lev. 7). Moreover, the quantity of flour was sufficient for three offerings. Using the principles of OT text criticism contradicts Scripture and undermines the doctrine of worship.

Ezekiel 45:5

Will the Levites receive everything the Lord wants them to have in connection with their service during the Millennium? They then will be re-instituted to serve as they did during the OT era. For their service, the Lord promised them twenty chambers עֶשְׂרִים לְשָׁכֹת (*'ĕsrēm lĕshâkōth*). However, the *LXX* omits the promise of these chambers, affecting the portion of God's promise to these servants of Jehovah.[270] During the Millennium, how will the Levites decide whether or not they will receive the 20 chambers for their service? Will they use a committee of textual critics to employ the latest in textual criticism to determine the correct reading?

Changes in the Doctrine of Eschatology

Jeremiah 27:1

The MT declares that Jeremiah received the command to make bonds and yokes in the beginning of Jehoiakim's reign (608 BC). Furthermore, Jeremiah was to send these symbols of Babylonian bondage, as an eschatological prediction, to Zedekiah who would not reign until 596 BC, or approximately twelve years later. Since a few Hebrew manuscripts[271] read "Zedekiah," critics suppose that an error occurred when the scribe transposed the name Jehoiakim in 26:1 to this passage. However, in fact the Lord commanded Jeremiah to make the tokens of bondage twelve years in advance of their being sent to the other kings and Zedekiah. The Lord by prophecy commanded Jeremiah to send them to Jehoiakim's successor, Zedekiah. The acceptance of a scribal error destroys the obvious prophecy that the MT demands.

---

[269] The NASV reads "a three-year-old bull" and does not footnote the change.

[270] Not only is the doctrine of worship affected but also the doctrines of Scripture (what God has said), of Theology Proper (the veracity of God), and of eschatology (prophetic fulfillment).

Ezekiel 40:49

The MT states that the Millennial Temple will have a vestibule twenty cubits by eleven cubits עַשְׁתֵּי עֶשְׂרֵה (`ashtā `esrāh. However, the *LXX* reads twenty cubits by twelve cubits, increasing the one dimension by almost one and a half feet (an increase of twenty square feet).[272] Will the builders of the Sanctuary have an altercation over whether to use the MT or *LXX* during the Millennium? Which Millennial carpenters will win out, the Judeans using the MT or the Hellenists using the *LXX*?

Numerous other passages could be cited to show that all of the major doctrines have erroneous and dangerous alterations. For instance, in the first nine verses of Joshua there are at least 13 differences between the MT and the *LXX*. In the books of 1 and 2 Samuel there are least 50 different readings between the *LXX* and the MT. Text differences cause doctrinal changes. Textual alterations based on non-approved penultimate authorities such as the *LXX*, DSS, Peshitta, etc. always give erroneous and therefore non-Biblical teaching.

Conclusion

The Lord promised to preserve all of His Words, including the jots and tittles of the Hebrew OT, and claimed that they were indeed preserved to His own day. Modern OT textual critics, using flawed logic and unbiblical textual principles, have rejected the Lord's decree of verbal plenary preservation, claiming errors exist in the Hebrew OT. They have denied that His Words have been preserved in the Hebrew Text. Critics must in turn allow penultimate authorities, such as the Greek translation, to correct the Hebrew text in which the Lord Jesus Christ placed full confidence. The approach of these OT text critics, who have produced the RSV, NEB, NIV, NASV, NKJV, etc., is minimalist as they constantly alter the Divinely approved Hebrew text and consequently change OT doctrine. OT doctrine based on the earlier testimonies, such as the *LXX*, the Peshitta, the Ugaritic, Josephus, *et al*, is always erroneous because none of these testimonies is a Divinely approved source for revelation. This kind of scholarship dishonors the Lord by denigrating His say in the matter of the OT text, and exalts man's vain attempts to correct Him. Paul admonished the Colossians to "beware lest any man spoil you through philosophy and vain deceit, after the tradition of men, after the rudiments of the world, and not after Christ" (Col. 2:8).

---

[271] The *LXX* omits verse one altogether.

[272] Even an amateur carpenter knows that a small miscalculation at the beginning of a project results in a catastrophe at the end.

CHAPTER EIGHTEEN

New Testament Passages as Examples of Doctrines Changed by Textual Alterations
Gary Webb and David Sutton[273]

INTRODUCTION

When Jesus preached to the Jews, He preached to people of some Biblical familiarity, but much apostasy. Their knowledge of religion did not come from personal investigation and firsthand experience of God in His Word, but from tradition passed down from respected people of earlier generations. This kind of knowledge was imperfect, deceptive, and often contrary to the Bible. For that reason, in the first major recorded sermon of Jesus, the Sermon on the Mount found in Matthew 5-7, the Lord repeatedly sought to correct this problem by saying, "Ye have heard that it was said by them of old time . . . but I say unto you . . .."[274] Each correction of this sort did not fix problems in the Old Testament itself, but righted Jewish misunderstandings. Their casual acceptance of tradition kept them from giving any real consideration to the teaching of the Bible itself.

A similar problem exists in regard to the affect of the textual issue on Bible doctrine. Many schools and the pastors who graduate from them continue to repeat the tradition that "the textual variants in the many manuscripts do not remove or significantly affect any doctrine taught in the New Testament." Support for this tradition even comes from well-respected defenders of the Received Text such as Robert L. Dabney (1820-1898):

---

[273]Gary Webb – Introduction, John 1:18, Matthew 5:22, John 7:8, Matthew 18:15, Index of Quotes (uses the Third Edition of the United Bible Society's *The Greek New Testament*, edited by Kurt Aland, Matthew Black, Carlo Martini, Bruce Metzger, and Allen Wikgren, published in 1975); Dave Sutton – John 3:13, Matthew 6:13, 1 John 5:7, Acts 9:31, Mark 1:2, John 14:15, Romans 5:1, Ephesians 4:6, Other Textual Variants (uses the Second and Fourth Editions of the same Greek New Testament, 4th Revised Edition, 2001, eds. Barbara Aland, Kurt Aland, Johannes Karavidopoulos, Carlo M. Martini, and Bruce Metzger, published in 1968).

[274]Matthew 5:21-22,27-28,31-32,33-34,38-39,43-44.

> This received text contains undoubtedly all the essential facts and doctrines intended to be set down by the inspired writers; for if it were corrected with the severest hand, by the light of the most divergent various readings found in any ancient MS or version, not a single doctrine of Christianity, nor a single cardinal fact would be thereby expunged . . . If all the debated readings were surrendered by us, no fact or doctrine of Christianity would thereby be invalidated, and least of all would the doctrine of Christ's proper divinity be deprived of adequate scriptural support. Hence the interests of orthodoxy are entirely secure from and above the reach of all movements of modern criticism of the text whether made in a correct or incorrect method, and all such discussions in future [sic] are to the church of insubordinate importance.[275]

One can hardly read any publication or article that deals with this issue without encountering a repetition of this tradition in one form or another.[276]

Although this notion of "no doctrines affected" has received widespread and largely unquestioned acceptance, it contradicts the indications of the Scriptures themselves that men would detrimentally alter the text of Scripture, and had in fact done so in the first century.[277] This tradition also does not stand up when one considers the doctrinal teaching of variants found in the Critical Text and in modern "conservative" versions like the New American Standard.[278] Indeed, the following examination of specific Biblical passages will demonstrate that textual variations followed by versions based upon the CT not only contradict established Bible teaching, but also undermine or pervert fundamental doctrines of the Christian faith.

THE DEITY OF CHRIST

John 1:18: "Begotten Son" or "Begotten God"

John 1:1-18 forms a single paragraph and constitutes perhaps the greatest Christological passage in the entire Bible. It begins with the Word Who is God, Who has been in fellowship with God from eternity past, and who is the Creator. He is the Light and has power to make men sons of God and give them life that is of God. This

---

[275] This quote appeared in the "Notable Quotes" section of Vol. 11, no. 5 of *Frontline Magazine*, ed. John C. Vaughn (Taylors, SC: Fundamental Baptist Fellowship, Sept/Oct 2001) 34.

[276] A list at the end of this chapter contains a sample of such quotes.

[277] Revelation 22:18-19: "For I testify unto every man that heareth the words of the prophecy of this book, If any man shall add unto these things, God shall add unto him the plagues that are written in this book: And if any man shall take away from the words of the book of this prophecy, God shall take away his part out of the book of life, and out of the holy city, and from the things which are written in this book." 2 Peter 3:16: "As also in all his epistles, speaking in them of these things; in which are some things hard to be understood, which they that are unlearned and unstable wrest, as they do also the other scriptures, unto their own destruction."

[278] The New American Standard Bible, La Habra, CA; The Lockman Foundation, 1975.

Word became flesh, dwelling among men and allowing them to behold God's glory. John the Baptist bore witness of Him. Every believer has received of the Word's Divine fullness of grace and truth. Although no man has seen the Father in all His glory, the incarnation of the Son, Who is with God, has declared the Father to man.

In this wonderfully weighty passage on the Person of Christ, John lays the foundation for the historical record of the life and teaching of Jesus that follows in the rest of his Gospel. He does this by setting forth the full Deity of the Second Person of the Godhead as the Word (God's unique revelation of Himself), declared not by means of pen and ink, but in human flesh.

Verse 18 in the *TR*/AV provides a vital portion of John's summary Christological statement that ties it with the rest of the revelation of Scripture. However, the reading of the CT/NASV introduces a concept foreign to Scripture but in agreement with heretical concepts of the Person of Christ. One can compare the English translations:

> No man hath seen God at any time; the only begotten Son, which is in the bosom of the Father, he hath declared him. (KJB)

> No man has seen God at any time; the only begotten God, who is in the bosom of the Father, He has explained *Him*. (NASV)

Some have stated that the CT makes a strong assertion of the Deity of Christ here because it has the word "God" rather than "Son,"[279] but they fail to fully consider the apostate and Satanic implications of the "only begotten God" reading.

Scripture reveals the Second Person of the Godhead is the eternal Son. Though He had no beginning, the Scripture also uses in connection with the word "Son" the concept of "begetting" to further stress this relationship.[280] David imparts this concept in Psalm 2:7: "I will declare the decree: the LORD hath said unto me, Thou art my Son; this day have I begotten[281] thee." The New Testament continues this theme as John speaks of Jesus as the "only begotten Son" (μονογενής,[282] *monogenās*), and other writers manifest Him as the "begotten" (perfect active indicative of γεννάω, *gennaō*) Son.[283] However, no passage written by John or anyone else in Scripture corresponds to the CT/NASV variant "only begotten God."[284]

---

[279] For an example, see the argument of Stewart Custer in *The Truth about the King James Version Controversy*, (Greenville, SC: Bob Jones University Press, 1981), p. 7.

[280] John uses γεννάω (translated "begotten" or "born") to indicate a communication of God's nature to man in salvation in I John 2:29, 3:9, 5:1.

[281] "Begotten" translates the Qal Perfect of יָלַד (*yâlad*).

[282] John 1:14; 3:16,18; and I John 4:9.

[283] Acts 13:33, Hebrews 1:5, 5:5.

[284] It is not surprising that the translation of the Jehovah's Witnesses, the *New World Translation*, follows the reading of the CT and even seeks to emphasize the heresy of this reading by translating "God" with a lower case *g*.

Not only does the CT/NASV introduce phraseology foreign to Scripture, but also that phraseology teaches errant theology. The word "God," as opposed to "Son," communicates nature or essence rather than position or relationship. Therefore, when μονογενής modifies "God" it introduces a Gnostic concept that Jesus is not fully God, but a begotten god, in essence a mere mighty being.[285] The theological language of Scripture uses descriptive words like holy, everlasting, Almighty, and merciful with the title "God" but does not permit "only begotten." The phrase "only begotten God" creates an unorthodox mixture,[286] as does the phrase "Mary, mother of God." Mary was the mother of Jesus, and Jesus was God, but "mother of God" expresses an erroneous concept. In the same way, Jesus is God and is the only begotten Son, but He is not the "only begotten God." This reading attacks Scriptural Christology and undermines and confuses the doctrine of the full deity of Jesus Christ.

John 3:13: Omission of "Which Is in Heaven"

Shortly after Jesus observed the first Passover of His earthly ministry, a Pharisee named Nicodemus came to Him by night, who recognized who Jesus was because of the miracles He performed. Piercing to the heart of the matter, Jesus told this ruler of the Jews that he must be born again if he was to enter the kingdom of God. Nicodemus, confused because of physical thinking, later asked how the things of the spiritual new birth could be. The Lord directly answered his question in John 3:13-18 by introducing Himself as the Son of man, the only One who had access to the Father in heaven, and by presenting Himself as the Son of God, whom God sent, and on whom every man must believe to have everlasting life. Believing that Jesus was the Divine Son and perfect Man was crucial for this religious leader, as for any other sinner, to receive the new birth. In the KJB the Lord declares:

> And no man hath ascended up to heaven, but he that came down from heaven, *even* the Son of man which is in heaven.

The NASV quotes Christ as saying,

> No one has ascended into heaven, but He who descended from heaven: the Son of Man.

---

[285]The Gnostics erroneously taught that Christ was only one of many "gods" that were mere "emanations" of the Almighty God. Such gnostic ideas were behind the fourth century false doctrine introduced by Arius. In response to his version of Gnosticism, the Nicene Council was called, and the Nicene Creed was developed to standardize teaching on the Trinity. The Arians were a pseudo-Christian group that sprang up in Alexandria, Egypt early in the fourth century, shortly before the Alexandrian manuscripts *Aleph* and *B* were made. According to Arius, Jesus Christ was not eternal, nor was He the God. He was instead a god created or begotten by God prior to creation. So, while the Father is "the God," Jesus was considered "a god" or a sub-deity, a created or generated god.

Jesus presented Himself to Nicodemus, in part, as the Son of man (3:13,14). This title is a phrase denoting humanity through being the offspring of man (cf. Num. 23:19; Ps. 8:4). However, the title is also Messianic. Jesus is the only One Who fulfills the prophecy of Daniel 7:13,14, and so He will rule in His everlasting dominion. The One on whom Nicodemus was to believe was the Son of man, who was in his presence, while He simultaneously existed in heaven. The CT, however, removes "which is in heaven."[287]

By calling Himself "the Son of man which is in heaven," Jesus testified to His dual natures, human and Divine.[288] As man, He was localized in the presence of Nicodemus; as God, He was simultaneously positioned in heaven in the bosom of the Father (cf. 1:18). The Lord knew that Nicodemus needed to understand His omnipresence, which included His humanity on earth and His deity in heaven. To omit the phrase "which is in heaven" is to attack the Divine Person of Jesus Christ. To omit this phrase also assaults the eternality of Christ. According to v. 14, the Son of man would be lifted up on the cross to be judged for man's sins. This judgment would result in the death of Christ's humanity; yet because the Son of man was in heaven, His full existence and essence would continue. Many purport that variants do not affect doctrine; yet this variant suggests that Christ, in His deity, could die. If so, then Christ would not be eternal; and if He is not eternal, then He is not God. Without this last clause of John 3:13, no other passage exists that clearly states the omnipresence of Christ (as God) while He was in unglorified flesh as man. This doctrine becomes entirely removed from the CT versions, despite CT advocates' claim that the CT removes no doctrine. This validates that claim as false. The CT, therefore, cannot be received because it rejects Christ's self-designation as "the Son of man which is in heaven."

THE SINLESSNESS OF CHRIST

Matthew 5:22: "Angry Without A Cause" or "Everyone Who Is Angry"

In the Sermon on the Mount (Matthew 5-7), Jesus sought to build upon the preaching of repentance of John the Baptist. Matthew states that repentance was the theme of Jesus' preaching (4:17). In Matthew 5 Jesus preached for repentance by giving

---

[286]The Arians, Sabellians, Judaizers, modalists, certain Pentecostals, the Restoration Fellowship, Jehovah's Witnesses, and Mormons have all appreciated the CT variant here. The Jehovah's Witnesses use John 1:1 to say that Jesus is "a god" and support this using John 1:18, saying that Christ is "an only begotten god," or a mighty being who is not Divine. Historical theology demonstrates that Arius was happy to call Christ θεός (*theos*, "god"), but he meant it in a CT variant of John 1:18 sense.

[287]"Which is in heaven" (ὁ ὢν ἐν τῷ οὐρανῷ, *ho ōn en tō ouranō*) is an attributive participle phrase functioning appositionally to the title "Son of man."

[288]Since Gnosticism teaches that all spirit is good and all flesh is evil, one can see how gnostic doctrine could influence the removal of this phrase that expounds Christ's full deity and humanity being in heaven.

the Beatitudes (5:3-12), which highlight the nature of true religion. The spirituality represented by this text would act as salt and light in the world (5:13-16). He upheld the perfect integrity of the Hebrew text and its teaching, and indicated that only a true Sciptural righteousness, which exceeded that of the scribes and the Pharisees, could obtain the kingdom of heaven (5:17-20). The Lord then endeavored to expose the Jews' need for repentance by contrasting their religious practice and understanding of righteousness with that of genuine, spiritual righteousness. He did this by means of a series of contrasts, saying, "Ye have heard that it was said by them of old time . . . but I say unto you . . . ."[289] The first of these points (Matthew 5:21-26) deals with anger.

The textual corruption of 5:22 in the CT appears through a comparison of the King James and the New American Standard translations:

> But I say unto you, That whosoever is angry with his brother without a cause shall be in danger of the judgment: and whosoever shall say to his brother, Raca, shall be in danger of the council: but whosoever shall say, Thou fool, shall be in danger of hell fire. (KJB)

> But I say to you that every one who is angry with his brother shall be guilty before the court; and whoever shall say to his brother, 'Raca,' shall be guilty before the supreme court; and whoever shall say, 'You fool,' shall be guilty *enough to go* into the hell of fire. (NASV)

In the *TR*/AV text Jesus condemns anger He describes as "without a cause."[290] However, in the CT/NASV, Jesus condemns "every one who is angry." The reading would condemn the Lord Jesus Himself, for He grew angry in Mark 3:5. Jesus sometimes uses hyperbole in the Sermon on the Mount to make His point,[291] so some might dismiss this seeming contradiction between Jesus' teaching and His behavior as hyperbolic language. However, this attempted solution fails in the face of the clear command found in Ephesians 4:26: "Be ye angry, and sin not: let not the sun do down upon your wrath." Here anger is permitted, but sinful expression of that anger is forbidden. The CT/NASV reading of Matthew 5:22 condemns the behavior of Jesus Himself and contradicts the teaching of Ephesians 4:26 on this same subject. In doing this the CT/NASV reading confuses the Scriptural understanding of righteousness in regard to anger.

---

[289] Matthew 5:21-22,27-28,31-32,33-34,38-39,43-44.

[290] "Without a cause" translates εἰκῆ (*eikā*), rendered "in vain" in five out of its seven appearances in the New Testament and meaning "without purpose" or "without just cause."

[291] Matthew 5:29-30 give two clear examples. Also, many see the complete prohibition of giving an

John 7:8: Not Going Up to the Feast At All?

John 7:1-13 records the opposition Jesus faced from His own half brothers, who did not at this time believe on Him as Messiah and Savior. Jesus had received opposition to His teaching in chapter 6, even having many of His disciples turn away from Him (6:66). Therefore, for a time, He avoided the region of Judea ("Jewry") because the Jews there sought to kill Him (7:1). In contempt of Jesus and His teaching, His half brothers urged Him to go up to observe the Feast of Tabernacles in Jerusalem where they knew that the religious authorities were against Him. Jesus refused to allow His half brothers to dictate to Him the course of His ministry. Later, though, He did indeed go up to attend the feast in Jerusalem.

A significant variant appears in the CT in 7:8 as a comparison of the King James Bible and the New American Standard Version indicates:

> Go ye up unto this feast: I go not up yet unto this feast; for my time is not yet full come. (KJB)

> Go up to the feast yourselves; I do not go up to this feast because My time has not yet fully come. (NASV)

Although the word order of the CT differs from the *TR*, the significant change occurs in the passage when the CT substitutes οὐκ (*ouk*, "not") for the *TR* reading οὔπω (*houpō*, "yet"). Therefore, while the *TR*/AV has Jesus saying that He would not go to the feast "at that time," the CT/NASV has Jesus saying that He would not go "at all."

A comparison with verse ten demonstrates the problem of the CT reading. Jesus did indeed later go up to the feast. The CT/NASV makes Jesus lie to His half brothers. Verse ten amplifies this attributed deception when it records that Jesus did not go openly but secretly.

This passage in the New American Standard Bible very clearly presents Christ as someone who lied to or deliberately deceived others. This contradicts the Bible's assertion of His sinlessness (1 Peter 2:22),[292] and would render Him unfit to serve as the Substitutionary Sacrifice for sinful man (1 Peter 3:18).

---

oath in 5:34 as tempered by examples of righteous swearing given in Scripture (Romans 9:1; 2 Corinthians 1:23; Hebrews 6:16-17).

[292]This verse explicitly reports that "neither was guile found in his mouth," so that the CT/NASV contradicts this portion of 1 Peter 2:22.

THE DOCTRINE OF GOD

Matthew 6:13: Omission of "For Thine is the Kingdom, and the Power, and the Glory, for ever. Amen."

Sitting on a mountain in Galilee, the Lord Jesus taught the multitudes who the possessors of the kingdom were, expounded the true interpretation of the Law, and condemned the hypocrisy, stubbornness, and corruption of the self-righteous. The Lord continued in Matthew 6 by exposing the phoniness of the hypocrite's prayer. As Christ gave instruction in both the manner and content of Biblical prayer, He taught His hearers that when they prayed, they were to follow His model.

The Lord began His model prayer by petitioning the Father and by expressing His desire for His name to be set apart. Then Christ prayed for God's promised kingdom and for His will to be accomplished upon the earth in the same way as it is in heaven, after which He spoke of praying for basic necessities and for forgiveness of one's sin debts in accordance with how one was willing to forgive those of others. The last entreaty was for God not to lead into temptation but to deliver from evil.

The reason to pray for these desires and the reason God will answer them in His will is "For thine is the kingdom, and the power, and the glory forever. Amen." Because the kingdom of heaven is the Father's, as King He is able to ensure that His will is obeyed and fulfilled. The Lord's followers were also to petition on the grounds of His possession of innate ability to provide for His own and to conquer all foes. The model prayer is to be followed because the glory belongs to God for Who He is, what He has done, is doing, and will do. The kingdom, power, and glory belong to God to such a degree as to extend to the eternities. The KJB reads:

> And lead us not into temptation, but deliver us from evil: For thine
> is the kingdom, and the power, and the glory for ever. Amen.

The NIV states:

> And lead us not into temptation, but deliver us from the evil one.

The CT omits the clause: "For thine is the kingdom, and the power, and the glory, for ever. Amen." "ὅτι σοῦ [293] ἔστιν[294] ἡ βασιλεία καὶ ἡ δύναμις καὶ ἡ δόξα εἰς τὸν αἰῶνας. ἀμήν"[295] The final statement in the Model Prayer provides the reasons why believers can pray for and expect answers to prayers and why the will of God will be accomplished despite the opposition of Satan and the world.

---

[293] Σοῦ (*Sou*) is a predicate genitive functioning as a possessive. Since the possessive comes early in the clause, the word order shows emphatically that the kingdom, the power, and the glory belong to the Father.

[294] The singular verb causes the three nominatives to be viewed as one unit.

The omission of the clause very likely occurred in the first or second centuries.[296] Since Satan is the mastermind behind the corruption of Scripture, one can apprehend why the doxological phrase is removed: Satan does not want God to be recognized or submitted to as Sovereign, as having all power, or as receiving all glory. Satan's kingdom is the world system (cf. Mt. 4:8,9; Eph. 2:2), which God will someday destroy (1 Cor. 15:24,25). Furthermore, God has the power to destroy it and Satan (cf. Rev. 20:10) as well as all who reject Him for salvation (cf. Rev. 21:8), and all glory belongs to the Lord forever (cf. Rev. 5:12,13). If the deceiver can eradicate "For thine is the kingdom, and the power, and the glory, for ever. Amen," then he has eliminated the clear statement that those three features belong solely to God, not to him. The CT must be rejected because it expunges this received testimony of the Lord's eternal kingdom.

I John 5:7: Omission of I John 5:7

1 John is written to believers to give them assurance of eternal life. In this general epistle, John gives several doctrinal and practical tests that identify true followers of Jesus Christ. Both kinds of tests are found in the first six verses of the fifth chapter; the doctrinal part is that in order to be saved one must believe that Jesus is the Messiah (5:1) and the Son of God (5:5). Both titles declare the deity of the Lord Jesus. John narrows his wording of the Lord's name to "Jesus," the name of His humanity. The Holy Spirit testifies to the human nature of Jesus Christ in that the Divine Son came to earth at the incarnation through means of both the water and the blood (5:6), as evidenced at the crucifixion (John 19:34). The Spirit bears witness of these two facets of Christ's perfect humanity, refuting the docetic doctrine that Jesus Christ only looked like a man.

Why is it that the Holy Spirit bears witness of the Divine and human nature of the Lord Jesus Christ, the Son of God? It is because there are three who are bearing record in heaven to this same fact. They are "the Father, the Word, and the Holy Ghost: and these three are one." The CT, however, removes from v. 7 and the beginning of v. 8 the words "in heaven, the Father, the Word, and the Holy Ghost: and these three are one. And there are three that bear witness in earth" ὅτι τρεῖς εἰσιν οἱ μαρτυροῦντες ἐν τῷ οὐρανῷ, ὁ πατήρ, ὁ λόγος, καὶ τὸ ἅγιον πνεῦμα καὶ οὗτοι οἱ τρεῖς ἕν εἰσιν. καὶ τρεῖς εἰσιν οἱ μαρτυροῦντες ἐν τῇ γῇ.[297] John wrote verses 7 and 8 as seen in the KJB:

> [7]For there are three that bear record in heaven, the Father, the Word, and the Holy Ghost: and these three are one. [8]And there are three that bear witness in earth, the Spirit, and the water, and the blood: and these three agree in one.

---

[295]One might argue the omission of the clause based on its absence in Lk. 11:2-4. Although this is a parallel passage to Mt. 6:13, the times, settings, and audiences clearly differ. Therefore, the argument is invalid.

[296]See chapter fifteen for a Scriptural explanation.

The NASV, on the other hand, reads John as saying:

> ⁷For there are three that testify: ⁸the Spirit and the water and the blood; and the three are in agreement.

By omitting the heart of v. 7, the CT removes the statement of the triune heavenly witness to Jesus Christ's natures. All three members of the Godhead are continuously testifying to of the Divine nature and Messianic authority of the perfect Man Jesus, but John's declaration of this fact is dissolved with the deletion of 1 John 5:7. Furthermore, removing the Johannine Comma cuts out the clearest single reference to the Trinity. Consequently, since some believers doubt the authenticity of 1 John 5:7, they will not quickly, if at all, use this verse to defend the deity of Jesus Christ. Some scholars will argue that there are other places to prove the doctrine of the Three-in-One; but is it not also the reality that by omitting 1 John 5:7, Satan functionally takes this Sword of the Spirit from the hands of Christian soldiers?

If the Comma were absent, the inspired Words of the apostle John would contain a grammatical error, gender discordance between the masculine participle "bear record" (v. 7) and the neuter appositives of v. 8 ("Spirit," "water," and "blood"). If the CT is correct, then there was a grammatical error in the originals. An error in the originals means that the Scriptures are not inerrant. Thus the doctrine of inerrancy would be meaningless with the Comma's absence, and the nature of God would be assaulted, for He would not have perfectly inspired His Word.

However, the Johannine Comma is inspired, and preserved in the *TR*. Consequently, there is gender agreement between that masculine participle "bear record" and the nouns "Father," "Word," and "Holy Ghost."[298] Since the Holy Spirit is a person, "Spirit" takes a masculine participle in v. 8 consistent with and built upon His taking the masculine participle in v. 7. Since the dominant gender prevails, "water" and "blood" in v. 8 also are modified by the masculine participle. However, when the third Member of the Godhead is spoken of independently in the NT, "Spirit" consistently takes the neuter participle, article, and pronoun (cf. Mt. 3:16; Jn. 14:17; Rom. 8:26; 1 Pet. 1:11). Because the CT removes the Johannine Comma, the masculine participle of v. 7a and the masculine anaphoric article of v. 8b become incongruous with the New Testament's customary gender usage for "Spirit." With the inclusion of v. 7, one can esteem and admire the doctrine and harmony of the Comma and one can understand the significance of v. 9 and the witness of God concerning His Son.

The CT claims 1 John 5:7 is counterfeit. This is not acceptable; therefore, the CT must be rejected. No doctrinal errors exist in v. 7, grammatical agreement is found in

---

[297]This portion of the two verses is known as the Johannine Comma.

[298]Although "Holy Ghost" is neuter, the third member of the Godhead is a "He," not an "it" (cf. John 14:16,17,26; Eph. 1:14; 2 Thess. 2:7). Thus, the masculine participle "bear record" correctly modifies the neuter noun "Holy Ghost."

One may attempt to find fault with the gender argument in the *TR* by arguing the gender

v. 7, and v. 7 rings true to God's sheep (cf. Jn. 10:27). The CT removes the Johannine Comma, but this verse was given by inspiration of God. Since it is part of the canon, God will continue to preserve it.

THE DOCTRINE OF THE CHURCH

Matthew 18:15: Omission of "Against Thee"

Matthew 18:15-20 records important instruction concerning the operation of the New Testament church. The word "church" (ἐκκλησία, *ekklāsia*) appears in the Gospels only here and in Matthew 16:18, where Jesus promised He would continue to build the church He had started and provide it continuous, victorious operation throughout the Church Age. In Matthew 18, He both taught essential principles of and provided Divine authority for church discipline. The passage, which provides a specific process of discipline to follow for a specifically defined conflict between church members, is unique. Its removal would entirely eliminate its teaching from Scripture.

A variant reading in verse 15 adopted by the CT and many modern versions removes the Lord's instruction here and contradicts teaching given in other passages:

> Moreover if thy brother shall trespass against thee, go and tell him his fault between thee and him alone: if he hear thee, thou hast gained thy brother. (KJB)

> And if your brother sins, go and reprove him in private; if he listens to you, you have won your brother. (NASV)

The *TR*/AV specifically defines the sin in question as an offence committed by one believer against another with the phrase "trespass against thee."[299] The Lord enjoins the offended Christian to go privately to the individual who sinned against him and seek to settle the matter before he includes others. If he cannot get the matter solved privately, he must then seek to do so with one or two more church members. If that does not work, the one or two provide sufficient testimony, and they bring the matter to the church body for discipline. When the church confronts the offending member, if he does not respond properly, it removes him from the membership, carrying out this action with the authority of Heaven, although the church may have only just

---

disagreement in v. 8 between the masculine participle "bear witness" and the neuter substantives "Spirit," "water," and "blood," but "Spirit" is already treated as masculine with the first participle.

[299]"Trespass" translates the Aorist Active Subjunctive of ἁμαρτάνω (*hamartanō*) indicating the possibility of such an event occurring. "Thee" accurately translates the singular σέ (*se*) and indicates an incident between two individuals.

a few people in its total membership. The Lord here provides a pattern for solving personal conflicts between members in a local church.

No other passage specifically deals with personal offences between church members, and none give the full process delineated here. In 1 Corinthians 5 Paul gives a different, shorter, and harsher disciplinary procedure for dealing with a church member who commits grievous and publicly known sins. 2 Thessalonians 3 gives instruction on how a church should handle members who continue to follow a pattern of disorderly behavior. Galatians 6 commands spiritual people to attempt to restore a believer whom they discover or catch in a lapse from Godly behavior.[300] None of these compare with the situation set forth in Matthew 18, and none of them require a private handling of the matter or detail the steps to church excommunication.

The variant reading of the CT/NASV destroys the specific context of the Lord's teaching, describing the situation by saying only, "if your brother sins." This reading makes private reproof necessary for sin, of all degrees and audiences; for example, if the newspapers exposed embezzling by a businessman who attends a New Testament church, the CT/NASV reading would require each member of the church to privately confront that man before speaking to anyone else about his sin. This contradicts the teaching of passages such as 1 Corinthians 5. Even worse, it condemns Jesus' public reproval of Peter in Matthew 16:22-24 and Paul's similar action in Galatians 2:11-14. This CT variant thus makes Christ a sinner and denigrates the One Who inspired the commendation of Paul's rebuke in Galatians.

Acts 9:31: "Churches" (ἐκκλησίαι, *ekklāsiai*) or "Church" (ἐκκλησία, *ekklāsia*)

After describing Stephen's death, Luke writes in the book of Acts that the local church at Jerusalem endured a great persecution, which scattered all but the apostles throughout the regions of Judaea and Samaria (Acts 8:1). Luke then reverts to the events of chapter 7 in order to relate the details of Stephen's burial, after which he informs the reader that Saul of Tarsus made havoc against the church at Jerusalem, contributing to the diaspora (8:2-4). Despite the persecution, believers continued to preach the gospel, and souls continued to be saved (8:5-40). By Acts 9 Saul had made preparations to travel north to Damascus to bring believing men and women back to the city of David, but on the road to Damascus he met the Lord Jesus Christ and received Him. Saul's new life in Christ was consumed with boldly preaching the Son of God, Jesus Christ. Following the conversion of Saul, the churches throughout all Judaea, Galilee, and Samaria had rest (9:31).

The KJB shows that Luke records,

---

[300]The phrase "overtaken in a fault" translates προληφθῇ... ἐν τινι παραπτώματι (*prolāphthā... en tini paraptōmati*).

[301]The lack of grammatical discord annuls the assumptions that variants are merely the result of sleepy scribes slipping with their pens and that variants are not the outcome of deliberate attempts to alter doctrine.

> Then had the churches rest throughout all Judaea and Galilee and Samaria, and were edified; and walking in the fear of the Lord, and in the comfort of the Holy Ghost, were multiplied.

The NIV records Luke as saying,

> Then the church throughout Judea, Galilee, and Samaria enjoyed a time of peace. It was strengthened; and encouraged by the Holy Spirit, it grew in numbers, living in the fear of the Lord.

The *TR* says that it was churches (ἐκκλησίαι, *ekklāsiai*–plural) that had rest, while the CT purports that it was the church (ἐκκλησία, *ekklāsia*–singular) that had rest. In the two texts, the article, participles, and verb all agree in number with their respective substantives; thus, there is no grammatical discord within the *TR* or the CT.[301] Simply put, either "churches" is correct and someone changed it and the other grammatical parts to the singular, or "church" is correct and someone altered it and the other parts to the plural. They cannot both be the pure Word of God.

If the singular "church" were the true reading, then the one church would be the Jerusalem assembly exercising its authority throughout Palestine. This idea of a single territorial church would indicate that all other assemblies in the region were still under the authority and part of the membership of the mother church. Hence, a universal (catholic), visible church arises. In concert with the territorial breadth of the assembly is the territorial authority of its leaders. If there were one church governing all other churches, then the leaders of the single church would be hierarchical leaders of the other assemblies.[302]

Stemming from the doctrine of the universal, visible church is the doctrine of the universal, invisible church, alleged to consist of all believers everywhere. Both teachings would be legitimate if "church" were the reading, and the doctrine that the church is "local only" would certainly be disabled if "church" were correct.

However, the singular "church" cannot be Scripture in this verse because the context of the chapter and the book as well as NT ecclesiology necessitate the plural "churches." First, the context of Acts 9 mentions only local congregations of believers. In 9:19 the assembly is called "the disciples which were at Damascus;" in 9:27,28 the church is the assembly at Jerusalem; in 9:32 the congregation is "the saints which dwelt at Lydda;" and in 9:36-43, the assembly is the believers at Joppa. In Acts 8:1 the disciples scattered abroad came from the single church at Jerusalem, and most of the groups mentioned in the chapter are within the tri-partite region spoken of in 9:31.

---

[302]Hierarchicalism was the doctrine of the Nicolaitans of Revelation 2:6,15. These people-conquerors used politics in the assembly to dominate their peers. God said He hated this practice.

Second, of the twenty-two times that the singular or plural word *ekklāsia* appears in Acts, all are clear references to a particular assembly or assemblies, including 2:47 and 20:28. When Luke speaks of the Lord adding to the church in 2:47, he is speaking of the local church at Jerusalem. In 20:28 where "church" may be a generic noun, Paul commands the Ephesian elders to feed the church of God, which would have been the church at Ephesus. The ecclesiology of Acts as well as the rest of the NT is that the church is only a local, visible body of believers.

Third, the pattern of Scripture is to identify congregations in a region as autonomous churches. When Paul wrote Galatians, he wrote to churches and addressed them as such (cf. Gal. 1:2). Paul said that the Thessalonians became followers of the churches of God in Judea (1 Thess. 2:14). Peter wrote to the strangers scattered throughout Pontus, Galatia, Cappadocia, Asia, and Bithynia (1 Pet. 1:1) and addressed the elders pastoring those churches (5:1,2). John wrote to seven independent, self-governing churches in Asia Minor (Rev. 2,3).

There is no basis in the context of Acts 9, nor of the entire book, nor of the entire Bible, to support the singular reading "church" as a universal, visible or invisible church. The CT reading is dangerous and must be rejected because the singular usage of *ekklāsia* in Acts 9:31 creates an unbiblical basis for a universal church made up of all believers or a catholic church hierarchy to govern the congregations of Scripturally independent churches.

THE INERRANCY OF THE SCRIPTURES

Mark 1:2: "In the Prophets" or "In Isaiah the Prophet"

Although in a more compact manner than the other three evangelists, Mark spends time at the beginning of his gospel introducing Jesus Christ to his audience. After naming Jesus as Messiah and Son of God, Mark presents the forerunner of the Mighty King by quoting two passages from the Old Testament. John the Baptist was that messenger (1:2) and that voice crying in the wilderness (1:3). The KJB says:

> As it is written in the prophets, Behold I send my messenger before thy face, which shall prepare thy way before thee.

In contrast the NASV reads:

> As it is written in Isaiah the prophet: 'Behold, I send you My messenger ahead of You, Who will prepare Your way.'

---

[303] The Prophets is the second of three divisions in the Hebrew OT: the Law (*Torah*), the Prophets (*Nebi'im*), and the Writings (*Kethubim*) (cf. Mt. 5:17; Lk. 11:50,51; 24:44).

In Mark 1:2 the *TR* reads "ἐν τοῖς προφήταις" (*en tois prophātais*, "in the prophets"), but the CT states "ἐν τῷ Ἡσαΐα τῷ προφήτῃ" (*en tō Āsaia tō prophātā*, "in Isaiah the prophet"). Since verses 2 and 3 are direct quotations from the OT, one can clearly and easily recognize that "Behold I send my messenger before thy face, which shall prepare thy way before thee" is from Malachi 3:1 and that "The voice of one crying in the wilderness, Prepare ye the way of the Lord, make his paths straight" is from Isaiah 40:3. Nevertheless, the CT credits both of these quotations to Isaiah, while the *TR* asserts they are from the prophets.

"In the prophets" perfectly identifies the quotations of Mk. 1:2,3 because Malachi and Isaiah are both in the second major division of the Hebrew OT.[303] However, the variant "in Isaiah the prophet" contradicts the context by attributing the verse from Malachi to Isaiah. Since copies of the autographs mirror the autographs, if "in Isaiah the prophet" is the true reading, one finds space to question the doctrine of inerrancy. Did John Mark make an error when writing the inspired message from the Holy Spirit?[304] Many variants of the CT are transpositions of words (e.g. "Jesus Christ" vs. "Christ Jesus" in 2 Cor. 1:1) and are considered by many to be insignificant differences from the *TR*. However, since God inspired individual words in a particular order (order affects emphasis), then to change the arrangement of those words would create errors in the copies. The variant "in Isaiah the prophet" bespeaks Satan's conspiracy to create doubt regarding the inerrancy of God's Word.

THE OBEDIENCE OF BELIEVERS

John 14:15: "Keep" (τηρήσατε, *tārāsate*)
or "Will Be Keeping" (τηρήσετε, *tārāsete*)

The Lord Jesus delivered the news of His departure to His disciples in John 13:33, news that left them troubled in heart. The Son of God would return, however, to receive them to Himself in heaven, having prepared mansions in His Father's house. In the mean time, they would be left on earth to do the Father's will and obey the Lord's commandments, being comforted by the indwelling Holy Spirit. Those who love the Lord would be those who keep His commandments. In fact, the mark of true disciples of the Lord Jesus was obedience to His commandments, words, and sayings (cf. 14:15,21,23,24). The KJB reads in John 14:15:

> If ye love me, keep my commandments.

---

[304] The doctrines of preservation and inerrancy are intertwined. Since God gave man His Word without error, then preservation of that Word would be inerrant, perfect preservation. If the copies man has today do not perfectly match the originals, then contemporary man does not have an inerrant Bible.

The NIV states:

> If you love me, you will obey what I command.

As the Lord spoke to His disciples, He used the third class condition with a subjunctive verb to show that the ones who meet the conditions for loving Him are those who keep His commandments. The textual variant relates to the word "keep." In the TR, "*keep*" (τηρήσατε, *tārāsate*) is a first aorist imperative from *tāreo*, which means "to keep, to guard, or to protect." In the CT, "keep" (τηρήσετε, *tārāsete*) is a future indicative from the same word and is translated "will keep." The former states the command to keep, while the latter presents the future act of keeping.[305]

The fundamental idea of the aorist tense is activity viewed as a whole without regard for the linear aspect of the activity.[306] The aorist imperative is a command that communicates the seriousness and thoroughness with which the commandments are to be guarded. At all times, Christ's disciples are to keep His commandments. This kind of obedience can only be practiced by a believer (cf. 1 John 5:18; 2 John 9).

The future indicative expresses that in the future one will be keeping His commands. But what about keeping the commands now?[307] The lost man trying to earn salvation through obedience realizes that he cannot and is not currently keeping Christ's commandments; but his hope, based on the CT reading, is someday to become obedient to the Scriptures. However, the aorist imperative of 14:15 would be a point of conviction to the unsaved religious man, for he would be exposed as not keeping the Lord's commands and therefore would be convinced by the Scriptures of not loving Christ. Furthermore, to alter the aorist imperative to the future indicative could make room for the believer to excuse present disobedience but speak of future victory.

One can easily see how the single letter would be changed to dull the prodding of the unbeliever's constant inability to keep the Lord's commandments. The CT is a corrupt manuscript because it does not expose in John 14:15 the religious lost man's inability to keep Christ's commands, nor does it convict the believer to always keep the Lord's commands.

---

[305]The different meanings of these words are formed by the change of only one letter (τηρήσατε to τηρήσετε). The doctrine of preservation is a teaching that includes the preservation of even the very letters.

[306]Cf. Wallace, *Greek Grammar beyond the Basics*, pp. 554-57.

[307]Verses 15 and 23 mirror one another in the protasis, but differ in the apodosis. In the latter verse, the volitive future is used to assert that a believer will be certain to keep the Lord's Words in the future. The former verse commands the believer is to keep the Lord's commandments even presently.

[308]The translations are identical concerning the point of discussion. However, the verb *echomen* in the UBS 1968 edition is given a "C" reading, which "means that there is considerable degree of doubt whether the text or the apparatus contains the superior reading." Kurt Aland et. al. eds., *The Greek New Testament*, (London: United Bible Societies, 2nd ed., 1968), p. xi. In other words, ἔχομεν *(echomen)* quite possibly

THE DOCTRINE OF SALVATION

Romans 5:1: ἔχομεν *(echomen)* **or** ἔχωμεν *(echōmen)*

In the book of Romans, the Apostle Paul wrote to believers in Rome an eleven-chapter treatise on salvation, followed by a five-chapter discourse on how to live out that salvation. In chapters 1-3, Paul settled that all are guilty before God: the heathen (1:18-32), the moralist (2:1-16), and the Jew (2:17-3:9). Man has fully failed to meet God's standard of righteousness; yet he can attain the righteousness of God, not by the law, but by faith (3:10-31). Paul then thoroughly refuted salvation through law keeping by proving that two of the most revered patriarchs, Abraham and David, were justified by faith alone (4:1-22). All of this establishes that anyone who believes on the crucified and resurrected Lord Jesus receives His imputed righteousness (4:23,24).

In light of the previous evidence that salvation is by faith and not by works, the conclusion follows that justification by faith alone causes man to have peace with God, and that peace comes "through our Lord Jesus Christ" (5:1). The phrase "being justified" represents a first aorist passive participle revealing that the believer is declared righteous as a point action in the past without any process. As a circumstantial participle of cause, it shows why one possesses peace with God: it is "because of having been justified [by God] out of faith." Paul states in the KJB:

> Therefore being justified by faith, we have peace with God through our Lord Jesus Christ.

If one follows the NIV footnote, the text states:

> Therefore, since we have been justified through faith, let us have peace with God through our Lord Jesus Christ."[308]

Herein lies the consideration: the words *we have* in the clause "we have peace with God" (KJB) translate the *TR* ἔχομεν *(echomen),* while the CT records the variant ἔχωμεν *(echōmen),* which translates as "we may have" peace with God. The *TR* ἔχομεν *(echomen)* is a present, indicative, active, first person, plural verb. The indicative mood

---

should be, ἔχωμεν *(echōmen),* as seen in the NIV's Rom. 5:1 footnote: "Some ancient manuscripts have 'Let us have peace.'"

The 1881 Westcott-Hort Greek Text reads ἔχωμεν *(echōmen).* Cf. B. F. Westcott and F.J.A. Hort, eds., *The New Testament in the Original Greek,* (New York: Macmillan, 1953), p. 358. While the UBS first, second, and third editions agree on the reading and on the "C" rating of ἔχομεν *(echomen),* the fourth edition changes the apparatus to an "A" rating, which "indicates that the text is certain." Barbara Aland et. al. eds., *The Greek New Testament* (Stuttgart: United Bible Societies, 4th revised ed., 2001), p. 3. The immoderate rating change is at least suspect.

Many commentators prefer the subjunctive reading over the indicative, influencing pastors and other Bible students to take the same position or the dual position of "we have peace" and "let us have peace."

is the mode of reality; thus, a literal translation is "we are having" peace with God. The CT ἔχωμεν *(echōmen)* is a present, active, subjunctive, first person, plural verb. The subjunctive mood is the mode of possibility, making this literally state "we may be having" peace with God. An alternative is to render this verb as a hortatory subjunctive: "Let us have" peace with God.

When Paul wrote ἔχομεν *(echomen)* under Divine inspiration, he declared that he and all those who were justified by faith at a set point in the past presently possess peace with God through the Lord Jesus Christ. Verse 2 shows that there has been and still is (εσχήκαμεν: *eschākamen*–perfect tense) the reality of access[309] as a result of coming to God through Christ by means of faith (cf. Jn. 1:51).

However, the subjunctive variant ἔχωμεν *(echōmen)* erases that certainty by communicating that justification merely offers the possibility of having peace with God. Paul stated in Romans 8:1-9 that there are only two categories of people: the carnally minded and the spiritually minded (unsaved and saved, respectively). Enmity with God is the result of the carnal mind (8:7), whereas the nature of the spiritually minded is life and peace (8:6). If a person is in the Spirit, he can please God and he has peace with God. The one justified by faith does not go on to obtain peace with God, but possesses peace with God, received at the moment of faith. If faith alone does not bring immediate and complete peace with God, then works must be required for salvation. The variant ἔχωμεν *(echōmen)* clearly intimates both a need for works to procure salvation and an uncertainty of its reception. ἔχωμεν *(echōmen)* supports the false doctrine of works salvation.

The best attempt to make this variant orthodox is to translate it as a hortatory subjunctive: "Let us have" peace with God.[310] However, even this falls short of the context, for the reality of justification is spiritual blessing (cf. 4:3-8,24; 5:2-5; Eph. 2:4-6), including peace with God (cf. Col. 1:21).[311] Although salvation does bring practical blessings, one cannot claim that ἔχωμεν *(echōmen)* teaches the need to have a practical peace with God, for Romans 1-11 discusses the position of salvation.[312]

Either ἔχομεν *(echomen)* is correct and ἔχωμεν *(echōmen)* is corrupt, or vice versa. The words differ by only one letter, but the one letter radically alters the message. The context of Romans 5:1 verifies ἔχομεν *(echomen)* is correct since having peace with God is a result of being justified by faith. To tamper with the text and transfer in the subjunctive ἔχωμεν *(echōmen)* is to deny the sufficiency of Christ's death, burial, and resurrection and to attack the doctrine of justification by faith alone. It is not true

---

[309]Ephesians 2:18 and 3:12 both use the present indicative ἔχομεν *(echomen)* to designate the reality of access. The context of the former verse teaches that both Jew and Gentile can draw near to God because the enmity against each other has been slain (2:16). The context of the latter verse indicates that Jew and Gentile alike, worshipping together in the local church, have boldness and access with confidence through faith in Christ.

[310]Murray weaves the subjunctive variant with the indicative in order to fit the context: "Paradoxically stated, it would mean: 'since we have it, let us have it.'" John Murray, *The Epistle to the Romans*, (Grand Rapids, MI: Wm. B. Eerdmans Publ. Co., 1968), pp. 158,9.

that the righteous only "may" have peace with God. Therefore, ἔχωμεν *(echōmen)* is errant and unreceivable.

Ephesians 4:6: "In You All" or "In All"

The book of Ephesians divides into two sections, which explain to believers how they fit into the local church for worship of the Lord. Based on the doctrinal provisions of chapters 1-3, all believers can fulfill the daily practices of NT worship through the assembly (ch. 4-6). Whether Jew or Gentile, all Christians are expected to walk in unity in their congregations; furthermore, there is no reason why they cannot walk in unity. In the first 16 verses of the fourth chapter, Paul exhorts believers in the church to walk worthy in unity (4:1-6); then he teaches of their enabling to walk worthy in unity (4:7-16).

Paul beseeches the Ephesian saints to walk worthily in unity, endeavoring to keep the unity that the Holy Spirit provides and works towards (4:1-3). The Apostle then gives reasons why a congregation should be unified (4:4-6): there is one body, the local church; there is one Spirit; believers are called to salvation in one confident hope of salvation; there is one Lord, Jesus Christ; there is one faith or body of beliefs; there is one water baptism through which Christians identify with Christ and are admitted into the fellowship of a local church (cf. 1 Cor. 12:13); and there is one God and Father of all, the Creator of all things, men, and angels. He is sovereignly and supremely above all and penetrates through all (cf. Ps. 139). Ephesians 4:6 in the KJB reads:

> One God and Father of all, who *is* above all, and through all, and in you all.

The NASV states:

> One God and Father of all who is over all and through all and in all.

The final aspect of God that Paul mentions in 4:6 is that He is "in you all." This statement is consistent with what other Scriptures teach about God's indwelling of believers (cf. Rom. 8:9,11). The CT removes the second person personal pronoun "you" (ὑμῖν, *humin*) and thus reads "in all" (ἐν πᾶσιν, *en pasin*). On the surface, it may seem

---

[311] One might argue that the hortatory subjunctives of Hebrews are a basis for understanding Romans 5:1 as one. Since Hebrews was written to saved and lost Jews, unbelievers are exhorted to join the author (v. 12, Paul) in partaking of salvation (cf. 4:1,11,16; 10:22-24), and believers are urged to apply the teachings to their Christianity. Romans was written to believers (cf. Rom. 1:6,7). The hortatory subjunctive argument, consequently, cannot extend from the one epistle to the other.

[312] "Peace" in chapters 1-11 is a positional peace associated with salvation (1:7; 2:10; 3:17; 5:1; 8:6; 10:15). In chapters 12-16 it is a practical peace associated with salvation (14:17,19; 15:13,33; 16:20).

like this would produce syntactical harmony in the last part of the verse: "above all and through all and in all."[313] However, the theological implications of this omission are insidious and incriminating.

In the last three prepositional phrases, the words rendered "all" (πάντων, πάντων, and πᾶσιν respectively) are adjectives, and the nouns used with the prepositions are elliptical. One could supply the word "things" or the word "men." It is true that God is above all things and above all men; it is true that God is through all things and through all men. But it is not true that God is in all things and in all men. To say that God is in all things is to teach pantheism. God's handiwork can be seen in the rocks and trees, but God is not in the rocks and trees. Hindus believe that He is, and so they worship many gods, for all is a god. To say that God is in all men is to teach universalism. This false doctrine deceives many (e.g. Unitarians) and parallels the attempt to develop one's fictitious innate goodness to earn salvation (e.g. theological liberalism). According to the Scriptures, God is only in those who receive His Son Jesus Christ by grace alone through repentant faith alone.

The CT is an insidious text because it supports the false doctrines of pantheism and universalism by saying in Ephesians 4:6 that God is "in all." The *TR* is doctrinally correct and consistent by saying only of believers that God is "in you all."

OTHER NEW TESTAMENT VARIANTS

The following list compiles other NT variants and explains their significance. There are far more variants than these,[314] and others could have been included in this list. The aim of this list is to show that the *Textus Receptus* (*TR*) and the Critical Text (CT) are different, and that the CT corrupts Scriptural doctrine and practice.

Matthew 1:7,8

These verses function to establish the genealogy of Christ through Joseph. The *TR* speaks of Asa while the CT inserts Asaph. Asa was the son of Abia (I Chron. 3:10), king of Judah and great grandson of Solomon. Asaph was a Psalmist of the tribe of Levi. Asa was in the line of Christ, Asaph was not. The "Asaph" reading undermines inerrancy.

Matthew 1:10

The *TR* states Amon, king of Judah, was son to Manasseh and the father of the boy king, Josiah. Amon lived in the middle 600's BC (c. 663-640). The CT says Amos was

---

[313]Colossians, the parallel epistle to Ephesians, states in 3:11: "Where there is neither Greek nor Jew, circumcision nor uncircumcision, Barbarian, Scythian, bond *nor* free: but Christ *is* all, and in all." One might argue from the last phrase that this verse is a basis for the Ephesians CT rendering. This line of thinking is errant because of the context of this verse.

First, Colossians is about the sufficiency of Christ, which is the meaning of the clause "Christ *is* all"; He is sufficient for the one who has put on the new man. Second, 3:10 teaches that the believer has put

in the line of Christ. This can only be Amos the prophet, who lived several generations earlier in the days of Uzziah king of Judah. The spurious "Amos" of verse 10 could not be the authentic Amos of Lk. 3:25 for at least two reasons: **1)** the two men lived in different eras. **2)** Matthew and Luke detail two different genealogies. Again, the doctrine of inerrancy is at stake.

Mark 16:9-20

Functionally, the CT omits this block of verses, removing the witness to the bodily resurrection of the Lord and leaving the disciples fearful. This omission also deletes the bodily ascension of the Lord Jesus Christ into heaven.

Luke 2:33

The *TR* explains the relationship between the Lord Jesus and Joseph and Mary: Joseph was His household authority, and Mary was His mother (cf. vv. 41,43,48,49). However, the CT reads "his father and his mother." This variant asserts that Jesus had Joseph, not God, as His father and, therefore, was not Divine.

Luke 22:43,44

The CT omits these two verses, and so removes both Christ's need for angelic strengthening because of the weakness of His humanity and eliminates His bloody sweat that fell to the ground in the Garden of Gethsemene. The *TR* text assaults gnostic Docetism, which alleges that Christ only seemed to have a real body.

John 3:25

The CT says that a singular Jew along with John's disciples came to the Baptist with a question about purifying as it pertained to Christ. To vary from the *TR* reading "Jews" is to understate the attention that the Lord Jesus Christ was receiving from the Jewish nation early in His public ministry.

John 7:53-8:11

Another difference between the *TR* and the CT is that the latter omits this entire block of verses. If the text is erased, then Jesus, in contradiction to the pretext, is in the private meeting of the officers, chief priests and Pharisees (7:45). With the removal of this section the rationalist is relieved of three supposed problems: that Jesus seemingly disobeyed the Law in not having the woman stoned, that the religious leaders were exposed as morally wicked, and that Jesus commanded the adulterous woman to sin no

---

on the new man, which is renewed in knowledge after the image of Him (Christ) that created him (the new man). So, Christ is in all that He created new at salvation. Colossians 3:11 supports the *TR*/AV reading in Ephesians 4:6.

[314]The *TR* contains 140,521 words, and the CT changes 9,970 of them, slightly more than 7%. D.A. Waite, *Defending the King James Bible* (Collingswood, NJ: The Bible for Today Press, 1996), p. xii. These changes are additions, subtractions, transpositions, repositions, and misspellings.

more. The twelve verses display Christ's grace to offer salvation, not condemnation (cf. 3:17). They also pull down the self-righteous facade of unsaved religious leaders and present the impossibility of ceasing from sin apart from receiving Christ.

Acts 8:37

The CT removes this verse. The only hindrance to the eunuch's being baptized would be lack of belief in Jesus Christ. The CT discards Philip's stating the condition to be met and the Ethiopian's confession of faith in Jesus Christ, the Son of God. The narrative thus communicates baptism apart from faith, supporting baptismal regeneration and infant baptism.

Romans 1:16

"The gospel of Christ" is the full association of the good news with Jesus Christ. Paul explained in verse 16 that he was ready to preach the gospel (1:15) because he was not ashamed of the gospel of Christ. The only gospel that saves is the gospel with reference to Christ, the gospel that belongs to Christ (cf. 2 Cor. 11:4). To remove the phrase "of Christ," as the CT does, is to detach the Messiah, Jesus Christ, from the good news of salvation. What Paul said he was not ashamed of, the CT is.

Romans 10:15

The Apostle quotes Isaiah 52:7 and Nahum 1:7 when he accentuates how beautiful the feet are that go to "preach the gospel of peace and bring glad tidings of good things." Both aspects are found in both OT references, but the CT omits the phrase translated "preach the gospel of peace." In so doing, the revised text misquotes the OT, withholds NT commentary, and muffles the peace that the gospel brings, something that the unsaved have never experienced.

1 Corinthians 5:7

Here the CT takes out the phrase "for us" (ὑπὲρ ἡμῶν, *huper hāmōn*), removing Christ's substitutionary death from this verse.

1 Corinthians 6:20

The CT omits "and in your spirit which are God's." The varied verse makes room for a man to think that he can glorify God externally in his body alone, as did the Pharisees, even though he is not glorifying God inwardly in his spirit. God receives glory when obedience is both outward and inward (cf. Mt. 5-7). Furthermore, the variant eliminates the truth that one's body and spirit belong to God.

2 Corinthians 1:6

The CT reverses the order of the last two parts of this verse: "which is effectual in the enduring of the same sufferings which we also suffer [1]: or whether we be comforted, *it is* for your consolation and salvation [2]" (AV). It then proceeds to remove "salvation" from the end of the second part. The Corinthians were to persist through sufferings. The *TR* interjects right away that salvation will work in them to endure amid sufferings. The CT's reversal not only de-emphasizes this, but it also mistakes the power of salvation in a believer's life amid affliction by saying the comfort is what aids.

Galatians 6:15

The CT removes the phrase "in Christ Jesus," and in essence removes the truth that salvific position in Christ is required for circumcision to be nothing.

Ephesians 3:9

The CT diverges from the truth in two places in this verse. First, it supplants the *TR*/AV reading "fellowship (κοινωνία, *koinōnia*) of the mystery" for the CT/NASV reading "administration (οἰκονομία, *oikonomia*) of the mystery." The former speaks of a the local church and the spiritual sharing between Jew and Gentile that takes place within the worship of the assembly. The latter speaks of the responsibility of household management with reference to the assembly (cf. οἰκονομία in Lk. 16:2; Eph. 1:10; 3:2; Col. 1:25). The CT contradicts context to make this verse about the management responsibility of the leaders of the assembly rather than the unity of the congregation.

Second, the CT removes the end phrase "by Jesus Christ." That God created all things through (διά, *dia*) Jesus Christ means that He was the intermediate agent of creation, creating even His church. To omit this phrase is to remove a statement of the Lord Jesus' deity and sovereignty and His consequent authority to head His assembly.

Philippians 3:16

Paul exhorts the Philippians to be like-minded in pressing toward the mark of the prize of the high calling of God in Christ Jesus (3:14,15). They were to walk by the same rule, being of the same mind. Only believers can follow the same standard and submit their thinking to the Scriptures. By removing the words "rule," "[being] of the same mind," the CT in this text allows for a church's internal disunity in practice and belief.

Colossians 1:2

The theme of Colossians is the sufficiency of Jesus Christ. The CT deletes "and the Lord Jesus Christ" from the second verse of the salutation. In so doing, the revision omits the teaching that grace and peace come from a dual yet singular source, God the Father and the Lord Jesus Christ. To disassociate grace and peace from Jesus Christ undermines His sufficiency and deity, since the singular article in Greek is used for both members of the Godhead.

Colossians 1:14

The shed blood of Jesus Christ is necessary for the remission of sins (cf. Rom. 5:9; Eph. 1:7), yet the CT erases "through His blood" from this verse, again attacking the sufficiency of Christ.

1 Thessalonians 5:27

The word "holy" is omitted in the CT. This depreciates the nature and essence of the brethren to whom this letter was to be read. Calling the brethren "holy" would be troubling to those who believe salvation comes through works.

2 Thessalonians 1:2; 3:12

The CT omits the possessive pronoun "our" (ἡμῶν, *hāmōn*) in both of these verses. As a result, the repeated point of personal relationship between the believer and God the Father and His Son is gone.

1 Timothy 3:3

The CT cuts out one of the qualifications of the bishop, "not greedy of filthy lucre." Thus, according to the "restored text," the pastor who gets gain shamefully is not disqualified.

1 Timothy 3:16

This is one of the great and clear verses on the deity and humanity of Christ: "God was manifest in the flesh." The verse teaches that Jesus Christ is God, and that God was made visible in a fully human body. This doctrine is highly offensive to most false religions. Furthermore, the Gnostic would have loathed this verse because he believed that all flesh is evil and all spirit is good. Consequently, if God became human flesh, then human flesh could be good.

The alleviation to the apostate's mind is to change *God* (Θεός, *Theos*) to *Who* (ὅς, *hos*), the reading of the CT. According to the alteration, God did not become flesh; Jesus, who to many is less than God, became flesh. Some would argue that doctrine is not affected because Christ's deity and humanity are found elsewhere. But doctrine is affected in this epistle and to this audience, dealing with this problem. Moreover, this difference in the CT voids one verse which profoundly states the deity and humanity of the Lord Jesus Christ.

1 Timothy 4:12

This great command to be an example is applied to every facet of life because the man of God might possibly be a wrong example in any of these areas. However, the CT omits "in spirit." This represents one of two possibilities: either to be an example in spirit is not a requirement, or to be a wrong example is not possible, since Gnostic doctrine taught that all spirit is good.

2 Timothy 4:1

By excluding the conjunction "therefore" (οὖν, *oun*) from vs. 1, the CT disconnects God's purpose in Scripture's inspiration (3:16,17) from the pastor's resultant command to "preach the Word" (4:2).

Titus 1:5

Although the KJB and both the NIV and the NASV translate the word "left" equally, the words behind the translation are different. In the *TR* Paul uses the aorist form of *kataleipō* while the CT uses the aorist form of *apoleipō*.

The *TR* verb suggests intensity and permanence (cf. Mt. 19:5) in Paul's leaving Titus in Crete in order to set things in order and ordain elders in every city. In contrast, the CT verb focuses on the act of being left behind (cf. 2 Tim. 4:13,20). The *TR* intimates Paul's motive and Titus' optimism and determination for ministering to Crete. There was to be no despair in being left on the island, as the CT might imply.

Titus 2:5

The translations of the AV and the NIV or NASV may seem synonymous with reference to the wives' work at home, but the words underlying the translations differ. The *TR* says that wives are to be "keepers at home" (οἰκουρούς, *oikourous*) while the CT says they are to be "workers at home" (οἰκουργούς, *oikourgous*). The former speaks of the wife's role as a watch over the home, while the latter speaks of the wife's activity as a worker at home. If the wife fulfills her role, the work will get accomplished, but getting work accomplished does not necessarily mean that the role is being fulfilled. The *TR* is stronger against women in the workplace than the CT.

Philemon 12

The CT omits Paul's command for Philemon to receive Onesimus. The master was to take the converted slave to himself in an act of forgiveness and brotherhood on Onesimus' own merit. The CT lifts such a mandate from Philemon and instead makes it optional (cf. v. 15).

Hebrews 3:1

The point of Hebrews is that Jesus Christ is superior and must be received as Lord and Savior. After two chapters establishing that the Son is superior, the CT fails to state the Man Jesus is Messiah by omitting "Christ" from His title.

Hebrews 12:20

The phrase "or thrust through with a dart" is removed in the CT, muting the NT commentary on Exodus 19:13.

James 2:10

The *TR* verbs "shall keep" (τηρήσει, *tārāsei*) and "[shall] offend" (πταίσει, *ptaisei*) are both future indicative, stating the hypothetical reality of a person keeping the entire Law and only offending it once. The CT changes both verbs to aorist subjunctives (τηρήσῃ, πταίσῃ, respectively), "might keep" and "might offend." The possibility of keeping and especially the possibility of only offending once fits with the common misinterpretation of 2:14 and 18 which creates a basis for works salvation and human perfection.

James 5:16

The *TR* translates "confess your faults one to another," while the CT translates "confess your sins one to another." "Faults" (παραπτώματα, *paraptōmata*) and "sins" (ἁμαρτίας, *hamartias*) can be used synonymously (cf. Mt. 6:14; Lk. 11:4), but the Scriptures never say to confess sins to anyone other than God (cf. I Jn. 1:9). Man's only responsibility is to forgive sin repented of (cf. Mt. 18:21). The teaching found in the *TR* is to make public one's misdeeds for the purpose of accountability. The CT, on the other hand, opens the door to the confessional.

1 Peter 1:16

Peter here states the basis for the command to become holy in every area of life (1:15), the commands of the OT (viz. Lev. 11:44). In the text under consideration, the *TR* commands the believer to continuously become holy (Ἅγιοι γένεσθε, *Hagioi genesthe*) while the CT reports the believer's future state of being holy (Ἅγιοι ἔσεσθε, *Hagioi esesthe*). Not only does the CT misinterpret the cited OT reference, but it also discards the Christian's foundational duty to become more and more "practically" set apart. It is true that the saint will be holy in the future, but God commands him to become holy now.

1 Peter 2:2

Here the CT says to desire the pure milk of the Word, so that one might grow up unto salvation. The *TR* never says to grow into salvation, for this is works salvation.

2 Peter 1:21

In this classic passage regarding inspiration, the CT removes the attributive adjective "holy" from its substantive "men." "Holy" is replaced with the preposition "from" (ἀπό, *apo*) and attached to God: they spoke "from God." Instead of commenting on the set-apart (righteous) nature of these human instruments, the CT merely calls them "men" and removes the Holy Spirit's role as Author of the Scripture by saying that the writer's source was God.

1 John 3:19

The CT changes the *TR*'s "we know" (γινώσκομεν, *ginōskomen*: present indicative active) to "we will know [for ourselves]" (γνωσόμεθα, *gnōsometha*: future indicative middle). In other words, a believer does not presently know whether he is of the truth, but will only know this in the future. This reading contradicts the theme of the book (cf. 5:13).

1 John 4:3

The deletion of "Christ is come in the flesh" in the CT is telltale of Gnostic tampering. In the *TR*, John teaches that the one who does not confess that Jesus Christ has come in human flesh is not of God. The Gnostic Docetist would allow someone else to believe that Jesus Christ is come in the flesh (cf. 4:2), although he would not hold to it himself. Therefore, to remain in spiritual standing, he must circumvent the negative confession. According to the CT, all that the Gnostic must confess is "Jesus"; he need not say anything about His coming in the flesh. The *TR* exposes the Gnostic as a false prophet and as unsaved; the CT does not.

2 John 9

The beloved apostle says that the one who has not God is the one transgressing and abiding not in the doctrine of Christ. Yet the CT removes "transgresseth" (KJB) (παραβαίνων, *parabainōn*) and replaces it with "runs ahead" (NIV) or "goes too far" (NASV) (both verbs are προάγων, *proagōn*). The *TR* speaks of this one as continuously overstepping the boundary. The CT word has the consistent understanding of a physically leading toward something. Hence, the revision either does not reveal the unbelieving habitual sinning, or it only speaks of going further in doctrine than one ought without including the activity of patterned sin.

3 John 8

The *TR* says, "to receive" journeying brethren, while the CT says, "to support" them. The infinitive of the CT (ὑπολαμβάνειν, *hupolambanein*) is almost exclusively associated with a mental activity (cf. Lk. 10:30; Acts 2:15), whereas the infinitive of the *TR* (ἀπολαμβάνειν, *apolambanein*) is almost exclusively associated with a physical activity (cf. Lk. 15:27; 23:41).

The *TR* teaches that believers are to physically receive other brethren, previously known or not. This hospitality is consistent with true faith (cf. James 2:14-17). The CT promotes a mental kind of support of the brethren that falls short of saving faith.

Jude 4

Part of earnestly contending for the faith is watching for ungodly men who creep into churches unawares and deny "the only Lord God, and our Lord Jesus Christ." These two sets of nouns are shown to refer to one person by the use of the single article, fully proclaiming the deity of Christ (cf. Titus 2:13). However, the CT removes the word "God" from the first phrase. The ensuing translation is "our Lord and Master, Jesus Christ." The text removes the explicit teaching that Jesus is God.

Revelation 1:5

The CT changes ἀγαπήσαντι (*agapāsanti*, "washed") in the TR to ἀγαπῶντι (*agapōnti*, "has freed"). This difference alters the work of the blood of Jesus Christ, allowing salvation without the washing action of His blood.

Revelation 5:14

In the CT v. 14 ends with "fell down and worshipped," omitting "that liveth for ever and ever." To strike the phrase out is to strike at the eternality of the Lamb, Jesus Christ.

Revelation 22:18,19

Despite the severe warning about adding to and taking away from the Words of this book, fifteen[315] changes have been made to these two verses. Two of the variants are the change of "book of life" to "tree of life" and changing "I testify" (v. 18) from the middle voice verb (συμμαρτυροῦμαι, *summarturoumai*) to an active voice verb with a personal pronoun (μαυτύρω ἐγὼ, *mauturō egō*). These verses illustrate the brazen work of apostates who change the Words of God at their own peril.

Revelation 22:21

Several variants are found in the last verse of the Bible. By removing the pronoun "our," the CT does not personalize the believer's relationship to and with Jesus Christ. Since the title "Christ" is deleted, the CT disassociates Jesus and the Messiah. Grace is not "with all" as the revision purports; it is "with you all," those who have believed on the Son, the Lord Jesus Christ. The curses of 22:18,19 are upon those who tamper with Scripture, for a believer does not change God's Words; he receives them.

SAMPLE OF QUOTES ON "NO DOCTRINE AFFECTED"

1. Sir Richard Bentley:

"The real text of the sacred writers does not now (since the originals have been so long lost) lie in any MS. or edition, but is dispersed in them all. 'Tis competently exact indeed in the worst MS. now extant; nor is one article of faith or moral precept either perverted or lost in them; choose as awkwardly as you will, choose the worst by design, out of the whole lump of readings . . . Make your 30,000 [variations] as many more, if numbers of copies can ever reach that sum: all the better to a knowing and serious reader, who is thereby more richly furnished to select what he sees genuine. But even put them into the hands of a knave or a fool, and yet with them the most sinister and absurd choice, he shall not extinguish the light of any one chapter, nor so disguise Christianity, but that every feature of it will still be the same." "Notable Quotes" in *Frontline Magazine*, John C. Vaughn, ed. vol. 11, no. 6 (Taylors, SC: Fundamental Baptist Fellowship) p. 34. Following the quote Bentley is identified as "universally acclaimed as one of the greatest classical scholars of all time and a defender of the Scriptures against the attacks of Deism."

2. Stewart Custer:

"The important thing to note is that *each of these four types of texts is theologically conservative.* . . . Not one of these texts can be called heretical or apostate . . . Every one

---

[315] The fourth edition has thirteen changes.

of the major doctrines of the faith is found in each kind of text. There is no attempt to twist or to disparage any of the great doctrines of the faith . . . . Most of the differences in modern Bibles are differences in translation rather than differences in text." Custer. *The Truth about the King James Version Controversy* (Greenville, SC: Bob Jones University Press, 1981), p. 6.

3. W. Edward Glenny:

"It is estimated that of these 400,000 variants, only 1-2% substantially affect the meaning of the text. About 98% are insignificant matters like spelling, word order, differences in style, or confusion concerning synonyms. Of those variants which significantly affect the meaning of the text, none of them affects the overall doctrinal content of Scripture or touches on any moral commandment or article of faith which is not clear elsewhere in Scripture. John Grassnick affirms this common belief. He states that 'the basic substance of Christian doctrine is not placed in jeopardy by a textual problem.' Even though differences of opinion on textual issues may lead to different interpretations of a few verses of Scripture, they will not affect the basic substance of Christian doctrine." *The Bible Version: The Perspective of Central Baptist Theological Seminary*, ed. Michael A. Grisanti (Minneapolis, MN: Central Baptist Theological Seminary, 1997), pp. 96-97.

4. Mark Minnick:

"And in the cases where we may not be sure which variant most accurately repeats the original wording, not one doctrine is affected. Not one truth is compromised. Every doctrine and truth of God's Word is taught in so many places, in synonymous or verbatim wording, that no variant obscures it." Minnick, "Let's Meet The Manuscripts" in *From the Mind of God to the Mind of Man*, ed. James B. Williams (Greenville, SC: Ambassador-Emerald International, 1999), p. 96.

SECTION SIX

Other Pertinent Exegesis for Every Word Preservation

CHAPTER NINETEEN

Test of Canonicity as Applied to Words
Kent Brandenburg

The contemporary question of textual critics is: which words did God inspire? This is an unanswered and ongoing question to the textual critics. Not only is it presently unanswerable to them, but in the view of the textual critics, it will never be answered.[316] This is, however, an answered and settled question for those who believe in perfect preservation, just as settled as the number of books in the Old and New Testaments is settled.

Whether whole books of the Bible were inspired is certainly more important than whether individual words were inspired. "Conservative scholars" believe that there are sixty-six inspired books of the Bible. They would say they are sure of this. When one begins a study on the epistle of James, for instance, he can be sure that James is God's Word. Has there been or are there criteria by which one judges which written material should be considered Scripture? How is it that one can be one hundred per cent certain that the twenty-seven books of the New Testament are actually all of what God wanted men to have? The criteria for and the certainty of the sixty-six books of the Bible are the same criteria and the same certainty for all of the Words of the Bible.

Canonicity

The answer to the above questions has been organized through the years since Scripture was delivered to mankind into what has been called the doctrine of can-

---

[316] The seminary professors of Central Baptist Theological Seminary in Minneapolis, MN compiled (and, therefore, endorsed) a group of essays to state their position on the preservation of Scripture in a volume entitled *The Bible Version Debate* (1997). Within this book, there are examples of the "non-perfect preservation of Scripture" position. "Still, only the original autographs of Scripture were directly inspired and wholly without error" (p. 21, by Roy E. Beacham). "The copyist made several errors in copying the text of Revelation which are still found in the *TR* text published today" (p. 49, by W. Edward Glenny). Glenny writes, " . . . it is easy to demonstrate 'that every manuscript has scribal errors in it'" (p. 77, Glenny), and " . . . the concept of the perfect preservation of Scripture does not work on the OT text" (p. 95, Glenny). Renee Pache is quoted from his *The Inspiration and Authority of Scripture*, in which he writes (p. 171), " . . . to reconstruct from all the witnesses available to us the text essentially preserved in all, but perfectly preserved in none" (p. 99, Glenny).

onicity. No specific passage lays out the doctrine of canonicity, but the teaching is gleaned from sorting through the whole Bible. For this reason, this chapter cannot be articulated through the exposition of one particular passage. The canon, by definition, is the inspired books of Scripture. *Canon* comes from the Greek *kanon* and probably the Hebrew *qaneh*, meaning "measuring rod." Therefore, *canon* and *canonical* came to represent the measurement by which books were determined to be in the Bible. When a book was canonical, it was recognized as having been inspired by God and as part of Scripture. These canonical books were received by God's Old Testament institution, Israel, and His New Testament institution, the church. Old Testament Israel and New Testament churches have recognized and received the thirty-nine books of the Old Testament. New Testament churches have recognized and received the twenty-seven books of the New Testament.

Canonicity of the Books of the Bible

The books that were recognized as canonical were received by God's institution as God's Word. There are three points to this recognition as it appears in the Old Testament. First, God's institution recognized that the book was authoritative. Old Testament texts verify the belief that its authors were writing under the authority of God. There are many passages that express this truth.[317] Exodus 34:27 says, "And the LORD said unto Moses, Write thou these words: for after the tenor of these words I have made a covenant with thee and with Israel." The people received the Words of the Pentateuch, which were written by Moses, as having been written under the authority of God. Second, the Pentateuch was authoritative because Moses wrote it, drawing from that the implication that it was under the inspiration of God because of his position as a prophet. Old Testament books were acknowledged as from God

---

[317]The Old Testament says "saith the Lord" to leaders of Israel eight hundred forty-one times. Two hundred forty-eight times "the word of the Lord" or "of God" came unto, was spoken unto, or commanded unto God's leadership or prophet in Israel or Judah. Twenty-eight times the Old Testament says "the Lord said unto me" to the Lord's prophets (mainly Moses). Ten times "God said unto" Abraham, Isaac, or Jacob. One hundred eight times "God said unto" Moses. Twelve times "God said unto" Joshua or Samuel. Three times "God said unto" David. Four times the "word of the Lord came to" the prophet.

[318]Compare, Exodus 34:27 and Joshua 23:6, among other places.

[319]Deuteronomy 18:20-22, "But the prophet, which shall presume to speak a word in my name, which I have not commanded him to speak, or that shall speak in the name of other gods, even that prophet shall die. And if thou say in thine heart, How shall we know the word which the LORD hath not spoken? When a prophet speaketh in the name of the LORD, if the thing follow not, nor come to pass, that *is* the thing which the LORD hath not spoken, *but* the prophet hath spoken it presumptuously: thou shalt not be afraid of him." Notice that the standard goes to "a word." Even if "a word" is spoken that God did not speak, the false prophet was to die.

[320]Deuteronomy 18:15-19, "The LORD thy God will raise up unto thee a Prophet from the midst of thee, of thy brethren, like unto me; unto him ye shall hearken; according to all that thou desiredst of the LORD thy God in Horeb in the day of the assembly, saying, Let me not hear again the voice of the

because they came from the Divinely designated man. Joshua 8:31 states, "As Moses the servant of the LORD commanded the children of Israel, as it is written in the book of the law of Moses . . . ."[318] God also revealed to Moses the criterion for the prophet, that is, perfect accuracy.[319] God raised up the office of the prophet to continue revealing His will, including His Words, to His people.[320] Books that were not spoken by God, and, therefore, were not written by His authoritative representatives, were rejected. Israel recognized that there were books that God was giving to His people.[321] Third, Israel received and kept the books that were given by God and written by His authoritative representative. This duty was required of Israel by God, even as recorded in Deuteronomy 4:40, "Thou shalt keep therefore his statutes, and his commandments, which I command thee this day, that it may go well with thee, and with thy children after thee, and that thou mayest prolong *thy* days upon the earth, which the LORD thy God giveth thee, for ever." The fulfillment of this duty is also witnessed in Nehemiah 8:3, which states, for example, "And he read therein before the street that *was* before the water gate from the morning until midday, before the men and the women, and those that could understand; and the ears of all the people *were attentive* unto the book of the law."[322] God's people, Israel, immediately and then continuously received the Divine, authoritative books of the Old Testament. Those that were not Scripture were not received and kept. The books that are not in God's Word are absent by the sheer power of God in His preservation.[323] He did not ensure the keeping of non-canonical Old Testament books. Only the ones that were received and kept progressively made it into the canon and then stayed there.

A further testimony to the canonicity of the Old Testament books comes from texts in the New Testament. The Lord Jesus Christ and the apostles freely quoted from the Old Testament as a source of authority. Early on there were examples of this reception of authority, such as Matthew 1:22, which says, "Now all this was done, that it might be fulfilled which was spoken of the Lord by the prophet." Another example is

---

LORD my God, neither let me see this great fire any more, that I die not. And the LORD said unto me, They have well *spoken that* which they have spoken. I will raise them up a Prophet from among their brethren, like unto thee, and will put my words in his mouth; and he shall speak unto them all that I shall command him. And it shall come to pass, *that* whosoever will not hearken unto my words which he shall speak in my name, I will require *it* of him." The ultimate fulfillment of this office, of course, is the Lord Jesus Christ.

[321]Deuteronomy 31:24-26, "And it came to pass, when Moses had made an end of writing the words of this law in a book, until they were finished, that Moses commanded the Levites, which bare the ark of the covenant of the LORD, saying, Take this book of the law, and put it in the side of the ark of the covenant of the LORD your God, that it may be there for a witness against thee." 1 Samuel 10:25, "Then Samuel told the people the manner of the kingdom, and wrote *it* in a book, and laid *it* up before the LORD. And Samuel sent all the people away, every man to his house."

[322]Another example of this occurring is Jeremiah 26:15,16, which says, "But know ye for certain, that if ye put me to death, ye shall surely bring innocent blood upon yourselves, and upon this city, and upon the inhabitants thereof: for of a truth the LORD hath sent me unto you to speak all these words in your ears. Then said the princes and all the people unto the priests and to the prophets; This man *is* not worthy to die: for he hath spoken to us in the name of the LORD our God."

[323]See previous chapters on Old Testament preservation – all Old Testament texts in each section.

Acts 28:25, which says, "And when they agreed not among themselves, they departed, after that Paul had spoken one word, Well spake the Holy Ghost by Esaias the prophet unto our fathers." Paul viewed Isaiah as one who spoke by inspiration.

The canonicity of the New Testament is very similar to that of the Old Testament. Often in explanations of New Testament canonicity, lists of tests or standards were applied to Scripture by means of "church councils," and from these councils came agreement on which books or epistles should be included in the canon. The New Testament gives no basis for relying on an essentially Roman Catholic "church council" to decide which books are Scripture and which ones are not. In many cases, the historical testimony of "church fathers" such as Clement of Rome, Ignatius of Antioch, Polycarp, and Athanasius is mentioned. Likely a tremendous amount of other historical evidence was destroyed during the many Roman persecutions of the first three centuries. The quotations of these first and second century historical figures are welcome witnesses, but not the essence of New Testament canonicity.

A first Scriptural test of New Testament canonicity is recognition of and reception as authority by God's institution in the New Testament, the church. The local church is "the pillar and ground of the truth" (1 Timothy 3:15), and it is the institution that received and kept God's Words.[324] Churches used, copied, passed along, believed, taught, and practiced the canonical books. The preponderance of the New Testament manuscripts gives thorough testimony of this. Churches read, copied and shared genuine epistles.[325] The apostles themselves received each other's books as the Word of God.[326] This first Scriptural criterion only comes because of a second -- the authority of the New Testament authors themselves. Just as Israel only received books from legitimate, true prophets, the local churches only received books that were inspired by God. The office of the apostle and first century signs and wonders were primarily a means of authentication of the Words of God and not the words of men (1 Thessalonians 2:13).[327] Books started in the manner of Colossians 1:1 ("Paul, an apostle of Jesus Christ by the will of God") because the churches were to and did understand that the writing was from God. There was certainty in the things wherein they were being instructed (Luke 1:4). The churches knew this, and the third criteria was that they received and kept the twenty-seven books of the New Testament. The non-canonical books or epistles were not received as inspired and kept by local churches (like a third letter to the Corinthians by Paul, cf. 2 Corinthians 13:1[328]). John 17:8 provides a good description of the process of canonicity when it states, "For I have given unto them the words which thou gavest me; and they have received *them*, and have known surely that I came out from thee, and

---

[324] See chapters twelve and thirteen.

[325] Colossians 4:16, "And when this epistle is read among you, cause that it be read also in the church of the Laodiceans; and that ye likewise read the *epistle* from Laodicea." 1 Thessalonians 5:27, "I charge you by the Lord that this epistle be read unto all the holy brethren."

[326] 2 Peter 3:15,16, "And account *that* the longsuffering of our Lord *is* salvation; even as our beloved brother Paul also according to the wisdom given unto him hath written unto you; as also in all *his* epistles, speaking in them of these things; in which are some things hard to be understood, which they that are unlearned and unstable wrest, as *they do* also the other scriptures, unto their own destruction."

they have believed that thou didst send me." The "I" is the Lord Jesus Christ, "them" is the church, and "thou" is God the Father. In the Lord's high priestly prayer to the Father, He outlines the future process of canonicity – the Lord giving the Words, and the church agreeing that the Words are from God.

There was a progression to the time period of canonicity. As an example, the New Testament advancement was penning, sending, receiving, using, sharing, copying, and delivering copies. This advance started with the authors writing the books and the churches getting their copies. Upon getting them, the churches acknowledged that the books or epistles were Scripture. Churches spread the recognition that the books or epistles were Scripture to other churches. Churches shared originals so that other churches could reproduce their own, or copied and sent these copies of the originals into other churches so that they could have their own edition from which to make copies.[329] Not all churches had their own manuscript to start, but there was general availability. Hand duplicating and travel were slow, but a copy would finally arrive. As a considerable number of churches received or reproduced their own manuscript, the churches were agreeing that this book or epistle was Scripture. For all the churches to finally amass manuscripts of every book, and then agree that all twenty-seven truly were Scripture, did take a significant amount of time. That agreement, however, signified canonicity. It is difficult to put an exact time of consummation on the period of canonicity, but it would be safe to say that the period, if beginning from the completion of the first book of the New Testament, was well over a century.

But who said that this was canonicity? Agreement of the churches is the New Testament stamp of authority. As already established Scripturally, God gave the church authority to receive, keep, and propagate His Word. That authority concerning His Word comes from His Word. The agreement of New Testament churches was the Holy Spirit's means of indicating what were the canonical books, since the Spirit of truth acknowledges truth (John 16:13). The Holy Spirit resided in New Testament churches.[330] When they agreed on the extent of the canon, the Holy Spirit, God Himself, was in essence designating the canon.

Israel and the churches received the thirty-nine Old Testament books. The churches received the twenty-seven New Testament books. Those believing in the canonicity of the sixty-six books consider this reception, due largely to recognition of the acknowledged roles of the prophet and the apostle, to be the essential criterion for canonicity. If any other books were supposed to have been a part of the canon, they would have been a part. The ones that are God's Word are included because this was God's will. These

---

[327]Hebrews 2:3,4; 2 Corinthians 12:12; Romans 15:19.
[328]Even though the Apostle Paul wrote this letter, the churches did not keep it because they did not recognize it as Scripture.
[329]Colossians 4:16, "And when this epistle is read among you, cause that it be read also in the church of the Laodiceans; and that ye likewise read the *epistle* from Laodicea."
[330]1 Corinthians 3:16, "Know ye not that ye are the temple of God, and *that* the Spirit of God dwelleth in you?" (cf. Ephesians 4:2-4, 1 John 4:6).

books fit the Divine prediction of what God was going to do. "Conservative scholars," essentially, are willing to acknowledge and receive the canonicity of all twenty-seven books of the New Testament based upon criteria similar to these, something that local churches themselves had long before already done.

Canonicity of the Words of the Bible[331]

There is essentially no difference in the Scriptural evidence for the canonicity of the books of the Bible and the canonicity of the Words of the Bible. Close examination of the aforementioned Scriptures employed as a basis for determining canonicity reveals little to no specific teaching for the canonicity of books per se. The appropriate passages use "Words" and not "books." The canonicity of books is actually more accurately a subset of the canonicity of Words, based on the Scriptural evidence. The "conservative scholars"[332] must depend on Scriptural principles to believe that the sixty-six books are the very books that were inspired originally. Historical figures and records are not dependable as a basis of belief. The orthodoxy of the councils and canons that are often trusted for the veracity of the twenty-seven book New Testament canon is questionable.[333] What are dependable are the Scriptures and the principles that they teach. Scriptural criteria settle the canonicity of the books of the New Testament. Likewise, Scriptural standards resolve the issue of the canonicity of the Words of the New Testament. Since God says what He is going to do and how He is going to do it, believers are to trust that it has occurred as He said.

There is general agreement among conservative Bible teachers that New Testament Christians have available to them the sixty-six books of the Bible. There is also general recognition that the Scriptural criteria have been met for inclusion of these books in the canon, and, therefore, these books have been accepted as genuine Bible. This is despite the existence of dubious church councils, disputable historical figures, witnesses in opposition to the councils and historical figures, and a lack of assurance that non-Scriptural material on canonicity has been preserved accurately. Some recognized scholars[334] get most of their authenticating material from older recognized scholars who received their information from generations of recognized scholars before them.

---

[331]The churches also agreed on the Words of the Old Testament. However, for the sake of brevity, this section will only discuss the canonicity of the New Testament. In both cases, Old and New Testaments, there was agreement from the churches about what were the Words.

[332]These would be (1) certain pastors recognized for scholarship, in certain cases "published," (2) teachers within local churches that have organized training at a more advanced level, (3) a classification of Christian worker not found in the New Testament – known as the seminary or Bible (or religious) college professor, and (4) the unattached author sometimes known as a free-lance writer. Many of these operate apart from the authority of the church (a local church).

[333]A perusal of the patristics clearly reveals unorthodoxy and apostasy with teachings of baptismal regeneration among other false doctrines. Believers should not rely on the testimony of unbelievers who espouse false doctrine as a basis for canonicity.

At best, such people can only hope that a patristic like Clement of Alexandria, among others, said what he said. Ultimately, however, for the saint of God, faith in God's sovereign power, based on the principles of the Scriptures themselves, form the bulwark for the perfect preservation of books.

Thinking from the preserved non-Scriptural historical data has formed many opinions about which words are a part of the canon. As with the canonicity of books, the Scriptural principles are reliable as a means of recognizing canonical Words. The deciding principle for the canonicity of Words is the agreement of the churches. The New Testament churches, local churches, agreed on the Words that were canonical. The Scriptures that teach the principles of canonicity formulate the belief that the churches were aware of and convinced of the responsibility of receiving and then keeping all the Words of the Bible. The reception of the books would be the reception of all the Words of each of the books, based on the applicable verses of Scripture. The manuscripts evidence a desire to keep all the Words.[335] This testifies to the belief that local churches have been used by God to keep His Words. Not to be forgotten is the Sovereign working of God regarding preservation. God said He would keep His Words, a truth which guides one to observe His providential hand in this crucial matter of canonicity as well.

The discernible period of time, during which this task of Word preservation proceeded to the printed edition, lasted from early sixteenth century to early seventeenth century.[336] This approximately 125 year period (c. 1516-1633) equals approximately the same or an even shorter length of time as the period of canonization of the books of the New Testament. During this time the churches incrementally progressed in their agreement over which Words were canonical. Men printed various editions of the Greek New Testament.[337] These editions rarely varied from each other. The text represented by this procession of printed editions was known as the *Textus Receptus*, the text that was received by the churches, using the Scriptural designation for what God told the churches to do with His Words, namely, receive them.

During the initial time in which the twenty-seven books were amalgamated and then canonized, the churches waited patiently for mutual agreement on the books. During this crucial time, churches patiently waited on the mutual agreement on the canonical Words. The churches agreed on the Words in the text behind the King James

---

[334]The recognition often does not come from a local church, but from a seminary, college, publishing house, or academic journal.

[335]The surviving manuscripts from the region of the Byzantine empire (the location where the New Testament records maximum church planting effort) evidence essentially 98% agreement on the Words.

[336]The invention of the printing press in 1440 by Gutenberg launched this period. Obedience to God's command to man to subdue and have dominion over the earth (Gen. 1:28) resulted in a machine that could amalgamate the Words of God into one printed edition.

[337]Erasmus (1516, 1519, 1527, 1535); Stephanus (1546, 1549, 1550, 1551); Beza (11 editions between 1565-1604); Elzevir (1633); and others.

Version of Scripture.[338] Although the words of the printed editions do vary, albeit seldom, there is as comprehensive testimony to the agreement among the churches over the canonicity of the Words as there was agreement over the canonicity of the books. At this time the English speaking churches became a large majority of New Testament churches, and they agreed on the King James Version and the text behind it. The obedient churches speaking the next most prominent languages also agreed on the *Textus Receptus* as the New Testament.

Scholars debate the orthodoxy of some of the men God used in the period of the printed edition. The exact belief and practice of historical figures is always up for question. However, no Scripture guarantees the preservation of facts concerning the life, beliefs, and practices of non-Scriptural historical figures. Opinions and explanations concerning these men are easily distorted. There is never valid reason to rely on extra-Scriptural human quotations either from the third or sixteenth centuries. Scripture, again, contains the standards for canonicity of God's Words.

There is ample explanation for why certain manuscripts[339] were not available or accepted during the era of the printed edition. The unavailable manuscripts in the printed edition period represent those that were refused or ignored by the local churches. Rather than a received text, these are a rejected text. If they did represent what God used churches to keep, they would have been available during at least the lengthy period of time between 1516 and 1881, and longer in actuality. A 375 year period of time during which churches did not have all of God's Words does not fit in with what the Scriptures teach about preservation. Once churches agreed on the Words, they rejected all differing texts as non-canonical.

The critic of the Scriptural position for canonicity might ask, "What about the time before 1516?" The Biblical teaching of perfect preservation says that all the Words were available. The early churches received all of God's Words, copied them, and passed them out and around. Historical evidence one way or the other is lacking as to exactly what words individual churches possessed, although documentation does exist that they used the TR text type. Variants obviously existed. However, during the first few centuries the churches rejected non-canonical books. The existent of variants does not stand as proof that churches did not have all the canonical Words available any more than the existence of non-canonical books proves that churches did not have all of the books of the New Testament. The books and Words were less available before the printed edition, but they were available.[340]

The local church is the temple of the Spirit of God (1 Corinthians 3:16), and the unity of the obedient local churches on the Words of Scripture represents the reception accepted as a test of canonicity. The affirmation of the local churches was also the affirmation of the Spirit of God on what He wrote. He accredited through His churches what God had preserved by means of local churches. To reject or spurn what

---

[338] Essentially Beza 1598, but in print today as *The New Testament in the Original Greek according to the Text followed in the Authorized Version* (1881, 1894, 1902, F.H.A. Scrivener).

[339] *Codex Sinaiticus, Codex Vaticanus*, etc.

the churches received is to insult the institution God ordained to keep His Words in the New Testament age, and, therefore, to affront God Himself. Churches have derived authority from God's Word itself to receive and keep God's Words. Later churches have used that authority to agree on what are God's Words, which God has used the earlier churches to preserve. The Words churches agreed were God's Words are God's Words.

To receive the Biblical principles of canonicity as applied to books, but reject those principles as they apply to Words, involves a contradiction. That contradiction undermines the Scriptural principles themselves. This provides a dangerous corollary to the rejection of preservation, namely, the rejection of the canonicity of Scripture.

Conclusion

The canonicity of books came by the agreement of God's institution, that is, Israel in the Old Testament, and the churches in the New Testament. The canonicity of books and the canonicity of Words do not differ. Israel and then churches agreed on the thirty-nine books of the Old Testament. They also affirmed the Hebrew Masoretic text of the Old Testament, the text behind the King James Version of the Bible. Churches agreed on the twenty-seven books of the New Testament. Churches also confirmed the *Textus Receptus* as the Words of God in the New Testament, the text behind the King James Version of the Bible. The Scriptural doctrine of canonicity says that the churches have all the Words, and, therefore, the canon as well.

---

[340]The Scriptural teaching on preservation, availability, and canonicity of Words guide the understanding of the availability of every Greek Word of the New Testament before 1881. Agreement on the translation assumes agreement on the Words behind the translation. Rejection of this ignores or perverts the Biblical teaching.

SECTION SEVEN

The Doctrine of Preservation as It Relates to the Doctrine of Separation

CHAPTER TWENTY

Separation Over the Veritable Words of God 1 and 2 Timothy

with Special Attention Given to 2 Timothy 2:11-26
Thomas Corkish

The War Is Declared

The war over the Words of the Bible is not over. It is an old engagement that has continued since the fall of Satan. It is still a satanic battle, and perhaps that is why it is so difficult–wrestling against principalities and powers.[341] Neither side is willing to capitulate, nor would be considered any less determined than the other. Millennia have passed without a truce. Some have vehemently defended the very Words, while others have depreciated them just as vehemently in conversation, writing, preaching, and teaching. Nevertheless, none of this has surprised God. He has known from eternity that the front line of rebellion would be an attack upon the very Words He had spoken. Lucifer has been the commander of this rebellion from the beginning. He not only led angels to renounce God's Words of truth, but then led a full scale warfare against God's people, which resulted in their defiance in the same arena: "Yea, hath God said . . . ?" (Genesis 3:1). Immediately, separation from God occurred, and during the few moments between the insolence of both Eve and Adam, horrible separation from each other came as quickly as had their blessed marriage. Then, when Adam obeyed Eve's words rather than God's, they threw the earth and all people into the blackness of separation from God's presence and light. Mankind declared war against God's truth and the veracity of His veritable Words. Man has proclaimed no "cease fire" to this very day.

All wars have casualties. This one is no different. Names, famous and infamous, have gone down in history, designated as victims of deception rather than defenders of the Truth. Some faithful saints have been willing to die for the very Words of God. They separated from the false teachings of friends and enemies, and denounced the errors of their day.

---

[341]Ephesians 6:12.

They will be God's special martyrs of the Word for all of eternity because of their willingness to suffer for truth. Adam and Eve failed because they succumbed to the treacherous snare of the serpent, which was subtle, clever, cunning, intelligent, and experienced in this business of deceit. Does it matter, this business of standing for the very Words of God? It does, especially if one understands that if the triumph had been won in Adam's warfare, it would have saved all mankind in its original state of created perfection. Treachery, separation from God, death that is both physical and spiritual, and the crucifixion of Jesus Christ would have been unnecessary. One should add to this the image that hell would be empty of men if Adam had not succumbed to that treacherous snare. If he had only understood the danger of standing with the enemy, the war would have ended right there -- but then, why speculate? No one can now prevent the beginning of the error in the garden, but a man can continue to make a line of defense during the sojourn God has given him.

In the garden, it was not a matter of a "King James Controversy." The very Words of God were at stake. No matter what the source of doubt, God's veritable Words have been the issue, not a mere preference for a differing version. It has always been a verbal, plenary issue. The King James Controversy is merely used to cloud the real debate as to what God means by preserving his very Words. It is true that He has not promised to preserve versions. Nevertheless, it is equally true that He has promised to preserve His veritable Words. That is why men have defended the inerrant Words of God, and will continue to do so until the return of the Lord Jesus in His kingdom.

When men can define the ground upon which they wage the war over the Scriptures, they can put away other items of personality, politics, preferences, and emotion. If the battle is raging in any of these forgoing arenas, the entire point has been missed. The battle is over the veritable Words themselves. That is the definitive struggle. Of course, any that enter the conflict are going to face some difficulty in making correct evaluations and practical application. The enemy uses this as part of his strategy against the truth. Just as Adam could not endure a departure from Eve because of her sin, men today cannot bear to think of the ultimate consequences of these enemies' defiance and error.

The debate about separating over preservation will not go away soon. Is a doubter who sows his doubt an enemy of the faith? Is he to be considered as such, or is he to be reckoned as an ally since he names, "Jesus?" How far does one go in separating from a brother who casts doubt upon the veritable Words of God? When he disallows a supernatural preservation after the process of inspiration, is he still a perfect preservationist? Is the struggle really as serious as some would make it? Should one attribute any consequences where deception is paramount concerning the Scriptures? Should application be made in the debate over the Holy Scriptures? Finally, upon coming to the impasse of fellow Christians who rebuff the veritable Words of God, can fellowship with them and their churches continue?

Since this issue will be discussed elsewhere, it will suffice to indicate here that the King James Bible is an accurate transmission of the very Words of God into English.[342] The method of that preservation will also be found in other references in this book. The concern here is separation, not the identity of the perfect text.

---

[342] See *Addendum* B by Thomas Strouse on how the KJB fits the Scriptural model of preservation.

When the nature of the argument over preservation does not proceed into a logical, rational, understandable, and defensible position, some on both sides will attack the person rather than to deal with the issue: what are the veritable Words of God? If so, the debate turns to personal battles and has not helped establish exactly what God has preserved for us. On the other hand, separation from those who reject perfect preservation will likely help the perfect preservationist to learn obedience to God and to realize that this is something that compromise will not solve.

So a sort of dilemma exists here. How does one discern properly what to do with the "opposition" in this regard? Some very "strong" believers have espoused the position that Bible preservation and translation are not issues to be concerned about. These are men who position themselves against any separation over the matter. They may easily sum it up in the expression, "Don't ask, don't tell." A position of neutrality seems logical to many, and those who support this pragmatic ideology have decided that God's intent of a defense of His veritable Words is inconsequential. This group sees capitulation to peers as the best way for Christians to get along with one another. They would argue that only some translations, like the Revised Standard Version, could cause any division in the ranks, and only because the National Council of Churches issues it, not because it is in error. The position of neutrality is not given Scriptural defense; neither does it have one.

What is the Answer Concerning Separation over the Very Words of God?

The veritable Words under discussion give notice of the necessity of separation from brethren and from church fellowship over false doctrine. The Words themselves have issued the command, rather than an individual preference of fellowship. Paul addressed these Words to the youthful pastor, Timothy, and gave profound insight for such an occasion. He apparently wrote 1 and 2 Timothy in quick succession. 1 Timothy 1 showed what a pastor should do with false teaching: " . . . that thou mightest charge some that they teach no other doctrine, neither give heed to fables and endless genealogies, which minister questions, rather than godly edifying which is in faith: . . . " (1:3). Some will say that this is only a concern over "doctrine," while the business of defending God's preserved Words is a lesser charge. It would be a strange thing if anyone could even have any "doctrine" without his study beginning with the genuine, perfect, total, preserved, and veritable Words of God. These are the Words given through men whom the Holy Ghost carried along.[343] That same Spirit also preserved the same Words for us, according to the promises of God. Can any other Words teach pure doctrine? No doctrine can stand without the accurate Words that God gave to actually teach it.

In Timothy's day, doubt about the resurrection and all its implications had crept into the local church. In that context, Paul committed a charge to this pastor which

---

[343] 2 Peter 1:20,21.

admonished him to war a "good warfare; holding faith, and a good conscience; which some having put away concerning faith have made shipwreck" (1 Tim. 1:19). Some would construe this to be not a specific mention of the Words of God. However, Timothy was charged to be exceedingly concerned about defending the very Words of God, which dictate all the doctrines of God. "If any man teach otherwise, and consent not to wholesome words, even the Words of our Lord Jesus Christ, and to the doctrine which is according to godliness; he is proud, knowing nothing, but doting about questions and strifes of words, whereof cometh envy, strife, railings, evil surmisings," and other corruptions (1 Tim. 6:3,4). The warfare concerning the very Words of God is not a trifle. The apostle tells young Timothy that all other words, except for the very Words given and preserved by the Spirit of God, are of "no profit," (2 Tim. 2:13), are "subverting" (v. 14), "profane" (v. 14), ungodly (v. 16), and bring shame (v. 15).[344]

All faithful pastors who dependably labor in the Word are to be honored in a very special way: "Let the elders that rule well be counted worthy of double honour, especially they who labour in the word and doctrine. For the scripture saith, Thou shalt not muzzle the ox that treadeth out the corn. And, the labourer is worthy of his reward" (1 Timothy 5:17-18). Timothy was apparently such a servant, with his special place in the battle, known from the day of his ordination. The charge he had received previously was to " . . . according to the prophecies which went before on [him] . . . to war a good warfare . . . ." He was to "fight the good fight of faith" (1 Timothy 6:12). No man of God has ever been exempted from this charge. It is a matter of course and obligation.

The pastor obviously cannot teach doctrine without the very Words of God – the doctrine and the Words go hand in hand. They are as inseparable as a newly married couple. God does not allow a divorce of His veritable Words from doctrine. His commandments forthrightly require Words, as does the gospel – "O Timothy, keep that which is committed to thy trust, avoiding profane and vain babblings, and oppositions of science falsely so called" (1 Timothy 6:20). The only way a pastor can do this is to have full possession of the very Words of God.

Pastors cannot wage warfare without shooting a volley or two at the foes of God's Word. Warfare addresses an enemy. Liberals and politicians can get by with firing shots, and those who stand unashamedly will not be neutral. God's Word is not a neutral issue. Men may need to expose others, even as the apostle exposed Hymenaeus and Alexander, stating: "I have delivered unto Satan that they may learn not to blaspheme." Godly pastors will allot time to expose false teachers in public preaching and teaching. Some, however, shun this course because many Christian "soldiers" are still in parade uniform, believing that a Christian is never to fire a shot. The faithful find they are in muddy foxholes with bombs going off on every hand. They are fired upon. They are weary and sad. Nevertheless, they still realize that they are in the right army and on the right side with the Lord. They defend His honor, glory, and Word.

---

[344]The Words were profitable, not ideas or concepts alone. Taking away or adding to the Words is not to "consent to" the Words, and, therefore, is not to consent to the doctrine. The questions

Nevertheless, how far should the warfare go, especially among brothers in the faith? Are churches to disfellowship over the doctrine of God's Word and its preservation? Chapters four through six of 1 Timothy tell the young pastor exactly what to do. Since it is a sin to corrupt the Words of God, he must, "rebuke before all, that others also may fear" (1 Timothy 5:20). Those who set an agenda to cause doubt or error concerning the very Words of God must be considered worthy of admonition rather than approbation. Error, left alone, will spread and destroy, and since that is not a satisfactory option, faithful saints must fight the erosion, and the necessity of division will follow. The Sword of the Spirit has always worked to cause division, as unpleasant as it may be.

Do other Scriptures support this thesis? Is it too severe to consider censorship, when commendation would better fit the political atmosphere of today's fundamental Christianity? Whatever the answer, the Word alone must dictate one's faith and practice. It is just as it was in the days of the Apostle Paul and the young pastor, Timothy. Standing too close with friendliness, out of fearfulness, or in fellowship can be a damaging thing for the pastor and his flock. If the young Timothys of this world do not make practical applications of Scriptural admonitions, the very Words of God will have no impact on either the soul or society. The Holy Spirit will put these Words to work in practical application. Believers must positively accept and obey everything God said in the Scriptures. Man must act upon the Words He has given in the process of inspiration and continual preservation by His Holy Spirit. The local church will only be effective if God's veritable Words are wielded powerfully and accurately before a needy world.

The Issue Is Defined

The Holy Spirit's admonition to Timothy and all pastors is that they must have some "faithful saying" (1 Tim. 1:15; cf. 2 Tim. 2:11) or "a trustworthy Word" that is "worthy of all acceptation" (1 Tim. 1:15). Without it, there is no direction, no proof, no absolute, and no help. Even if mankind were given this true Word in the originals, he would still require that the "trustworthy Word" be preserved for today and tomorrow, else the world would lose the absolutes which are anchored in those veritable Words.

The faithfulness that Paul expected of young Timothy must also be founded upon the "word of truth" which God pronounces trustworthy or faithful (2 Tim. 2:11). In this verse, "saying" is *logos,* or "word." Here, the Spirit is giving the criterion for His eternal "Word." Negatively, it cannot be inaccurate, dishonest, dishonorable, unreliable or failing in any regard. In contrast, it must be sure, reliable, precise, honorable, exact, dependable, correct and accurate, being the actual Word from the mouth and heart of God. It can be no less and be His Word.

---

of the textual critics which result in the subtraction of Words constitute the opposite of the consent as it is described in 1 Timothy 6:3,4.

The Servants Are Honored

If God was to approve of Timothy (2 Tim. 2:15), or any man of any time, reasonably, even essentially, the inerrant Word and Words must be established, preserved, and made available for his intensive study. God, being the honorable Author of this Word, would also be reliable to transmit and preserve the Words by His own ability and veracity. While some scholars believe He has done this, others do not. Some rely only on the proficiency of scholarship in the matter of textual criticism, others upon the superintendency and efficiency of God. As God demands a trustworthy or faithful standard for the man who is to be approved, He would not lessen the same criteria for Himself or His Word. He even claims that His Word "is a faithful saying" (v. 11).[345]

The standard for approval, spoken in verse fifteen, comes from a word (*dokimoi*) of which the meaning is taken from an ancient practice in the minting process of coins, some being found faithful to do an honest job in minting the coin and others not. In this illustration, the unapproved shaved the coins in the making, and through time, some craftsmen were taking an advantage that ended with the money in their own pockets. Eventually, the government in Athens saw that it needed to pass a law forbidding any shaving of coins, since even the best men took from the established standard. The result was that all had to meet stringent regulations for an accurate and consistent weight, consistent with authorized measurements. The men who were honorable and honest, and who gave full weight to the coin, rejected all counterfeits and allowed only the true value the law demanded into circulation. These men were called *dokimoi* or approved, and the authorities eventually dismissed those who cut corners for their own benefit.

Dokimos also indicates that the student who labors diligently, even to the point of exhaustion, in handling the Word of truth (2 Tim. 2:15b) is the one who meets the measure set forth by God Himself. He is not the "scholar" who will be found "shaving" that Word and by that doing injustice to the intent and weight God has placed upon it. Rather, he will be found among those who are faithful to his Sovereign's measure. He makes it a matter of intense effort to "rightly divide" it in his presentation of the King's riches to the world, setting it forth as that eternally established Word that contains all the jots and tittles just as God has set them forth. The result for the laborer is that he is found honorable. God values his intense efforts to be *dokimos* or "approved."

This standard, as set forth in the epistles to Timothy, was not a mere suggestion, but an imperative placed upon him. Timothy and others who were to read the epistle and handle the Word of truth were commanded never to alter the Words in any fashion, so as to make them counterfeit or of less weight than God sovereignly intended. A man would demonstrate God's approval by not violating this directive in any regard. Such a workman did not labor with absolute honesty in the word only to gain the acceptance of his peers, but he realized by the Spirit of God that in order to honor the Sovereign demands of a holy God, he must utilize every caution in handling the precious Word with full realization that he was that servant who was "approved unto God."

The faithful man divides or cuts the Word in such a way that it will always have the qualities of being straight or kept to the intended course. He will handle it rightly and teach it directly and correctly. He will realize that he has been given a powerful tool, even God's Words. Anything less then the perfection of that truth, and anything other than integrity in handling it, would constitute a sham unacceptable and dishonoring to the doctrine of inspiration. How could it possibly be that the God of perfection would allow His Word to be corrupted, yet still demand that it be the absolute standard for the man of God's consideration in every issue of life?

The Enemies Are Exposed

2 Timothy 2:17 indicates that there were and would be further attempts to erode and undermine the very Words of God by those of Hymenaeus' and Philetus' class. They presented a "word" that was undermining and erosive. This is a "word" that God describes as "their word." It was a *logos* that was uniquely and characteristically theirs, but not God's. "Hymenaeus," whose name indicates he was born of secular, unbelieving parents, was intentionally and without hesitation pointed out by the apostle as a traitor to God's Word. Because of the contact with the local church, it could be that Hymenaeus was considered a fellow "Christian," even though he was a leader who would pervert the Words, thus becoming a threat to the brethren. Philetus is listed along with him in second order, and it could be that he was a disciple of Hymenaeus, who was sanctioning his destructive ways of handling the Words of God.

This perversion was not something that had been completed sometime in the past, but was going on, even as the apostle was writing the epistle. The action of their teaching is shown by an active participle (continuous). They were known for their current teachings that were far from the very Words of God. They were in the process right at the moment (present active verb) of overthrowing "the faith of some." This was probably no news to Timothy and the Christians to whom he ministered. How long these men had been teaching is uncertain, but it is made known that their false doctrine was around long enough to have already done its destructive work.

The Invasion Is Uncovered

The context of 2 Timothy chapter two also presents this attack on God's Words. In contrast to those keeping the very Words of God, there is an abundance of evidence from the Scriptures to indicate that there will be others like these two men who will tamper with the very Words to supply substitute words described as "profane and vain

---

[345] "Saying" is the word *logos* that must meet the standard of excellence set by the eternal God: "Trustworthy (faithful) is the Word." God glorifies the Word, even as it glorifies Him.

babblings" (v. 16). These "profane" or base words are those that are common among men. They are not the "holy" Words of God set apart in sanctification by the Holy Spirit, but those that are "unhallowed," the carnal words of men. They can only attribute their source to the mind of man. A further description is given in that man's words, as a substitute for God's, are destitute of powerful content or "vain." The word is used to describe an empty vessel; it has no content. It is destitute of substance and purpose. It cannot compare with God's full, fruitful, lively and powerful Words.

"Vain babblings" represents one compound Greek word that means "empty noise." The "babbling" or "noise" has no meaning. The sound of it tells nothing. It directly counters God's Words, which give full meaning in their "unveiling" of God's mind. Though "babblings" are recognized as language or words, the King James Bible never translates it in that manner. Noise and the written unveiling of God greatly differ. They contrast in being understood and not being understood. The "vain babblings" are tampered with and God's veritable Words remain untampered.

The epistle warns Timothy and all Christians who will follow the Lord that the unprofitable words of these false teachers, who pervert God's veritable Words, are going to produce "more ungodliness" (v. 16), and "will eat as doth a canker" (v. 17).[346] This entire process is said to be growing or increasing. It will not end, but gain strength and influence in the world (v. 16). "Increasing" is stretching out longer than the original design. It is something that spreads and advances and has a culmination in even "more ungodliness," which is in distinction to God's holiness. Bibles that have more and more of man's unprofitable words are going to change the complexion of Christians and their churches. The standards are going to change. The emphasis will be altered. The power will be of men, but not of God. It will happen, and in fact is already in motion. As go the Words, so go the results.

God's Words were neutralized because men "erred" (v. 18), a word that means, "to stray from the mark." The Apostle Paul also notes other results. The disease of Bibliological errors spread to "canker" other areas, having grown like a cancer throughout a body. Man's corrupted words had now spread into a false doctrine concerning the resurrection. They spiritualized the true doctrine of the resurrection. Looking at it through their human words of error, some listeners concluded that the body would not go through a glorious transformation at some future event. Gnosticism set forth this error–the body could never have any relationship with that which was holy. It went so far as to teach that Jesus could not have been God due to Gnostic denial of the possibility of the union of flesh and God's Spirit.

The Gnostics taught an error that would further grow into the supposition that Christ could not have been literally resurrected, another result of the impossibility of spiritual contact with the physical. As this was compounded or "cankered" into still other doctrines, their word would automatically "eat" into essential doctrines of salva-

---

[346]*Gangraina* (γάγγραινα) or "canker" is the word "gangrene" now in English. It eats into the body that has been inflamed through disease. The infirmity has become so widespread that unless there is a cure, the decay will eventually attack the bones and finally death will set in. The heretics mentioned in the passage

tion, such as atonement by God's blood, and a host of other truths taught in Scripture. Timothy needed to remember and teach that when men twist the very Words of God, they do not fully appreciate how far the "canker" will "eat" until the whole body is destroyed. It is little wonder that Paul says this behavior will "overthrow the faith of some" (2:18). The error (v. 18) is more than a mistake, but is a deviation from the mark. God's standard is set. This class of heretics has intentionally deviated from that standard and set its own mark by which to judge, teach, and deceive.

The Purpose Is Positive

All is not lost, because however far the disease spreads, hope is still absolute. "Nevertheless the foundation of God standeth sure, having this seal, The Lord knoweth them that are his. And, Let every one that nameth the name of Christ depart from iniquity" (2 Timothy 2:19). This foundation is firm, it "standeth sure," and can be neither destroyed nor moved from its place, since God is the One who established it. It is His foundation. He has His seal on it. Neither spiritual disease nor error can penetrate it or wash it away, for, in reality, the foundation is Jesus Christ Himself. He is the rock, Mt 16:18, and the foundation: "For other foundation can no man lay than that is laid, which is Jesus Christ" (1 Cor. 3:11). He is the chief cornerstone (Eph 2:20). He is the very Word of God (John 1:1), and has a signet of ownership as Lord (2 Tim. 2:19).

Some might ask if God could have prevented the heresy. Of course He could have, and of course He did not. In fact, in the sovereignty of God's allowance, what transpires is not meant to be without benefit. The perversion is an evil, but God is still in control and assures every believer that even this tool of perversion by the adversary will result in a purposed kind of victory. In reality, and in the end, the erosion taking place then and now, the battle over the very Words of God, turns out to be a "tool" in His hand. He is not defeated, nor should His children be. Satan will not prevail in his attempts to destroy what the Lord God has promised to preserve, and God and His veritable Words will be triumphant in that which He has purposed from all of eternity.

Fruit is to be picked from the newly introduced words that will foster "foolish and unlearned questions" (v. 23). Though the entire process of spoiling God's Words is the untiring effort of the devil who sets the "snare" to lead the ignorant and unwary into his captivity, God is at work as well, and is using what takes place in this conflagration. Those who perpetrate this evil may not understand that God is manifesting them by this token, according to His perfect will (v. 26). It is not unlike what He unveils in 1

---

have already been eaten away with corrupted words and are now willing to share their horrible disease with others, if allowed to do so.

Corinthians 5:5. There He delivers a man " . . . unto Satan for the destruction of the flesh that the spirit may be saved in the day of the Lord Jesus." In Timothy, He delivers a man for subverting through his false teaching and preaching and for perverting the very Words of God (2 Timothy 2:14).

If God's deliverance of some people to Satan is to work, and if the one instance is parallel to the other, some interesting results should be carefully considered. The examples in 1 Corinthians and 2 Timothy show that God wills the ultimate gathering of His own. Both also show that God is not defeated in any event, but has in fact a calculated goal that can and will be achieved in each case.

In the Corinthian example, a man will be delivered to Satan because of immorality. God is seeking his repentance and the purity of the Corinthian local church. To accomplish this, the church must discern the corrupt member. Severance from him is not merely optional (1 Cor. 5:5-8). God knows the work that must be done in the individual man's heart, and in the hearts of all the believers who are bound together in the local church, but He also understands that men in the flesh baulk at discipline. Because of this, He reveals His warning and instruction: "Your glorying is not good. Know ye not that a little leaven leaveneth the whole lump? Purge out therefore the old leaven, that ye may be a new lump, as ye are unleavened . . . Therefore let us keep the feast, not with old leaven, neither with the leaven of malice and wickedness; but with the unleavened bread of sincerity and truth. I wrote unto you in an epistle not to company with fornicators . . . But now I have written unto you not to keep company, if any man that is called a brother be a fornicator . . . therefore put away from among yourselves that wicked person" (1 Cor. 5:6-13).

A similar instruction is found in what Paul tells Timothy. Separation between Christians over certain serious issues is extremely important for God to have His perfect work manifest. The believers of a local church must purge themselves of the saint who is conducting himself in an immoral manner, and must shun (2 Timothy 2:16) and depart from the iniquity or unrighteousness of those who turn the very Words of God into "profane and vain babblings" that will "overthrow the faith of some," gender strife, and produce novelties or "unlearned questions" among the saints (2 Tim. 2:16, 19, 22).

In both instructions God is looking for repentance and purity. The requirement of God for Timothy and his local church is not that they acquiesce to error for the sake of fellowship, but that there should be a Godly, firm and disciplined separation so that with "meekness" a correction will result in a God-given " . . . repentance to the acknowledging of the truth . . . that they may recover themselves out of the snare of the devil . . . " (2 Tim. 2:25-26).

The Issue Is Christian

Paul instructs Timothy in very certain terms. Timothy is to be the kind of pastor that will "put [the church] in remembrance, charging [her] before the Lord that [she] strive not about words to no profit, but to the subverting of the hearers" (2 Tim. 2:14). In preaching and teaching, notifying the hearers of the conflict over the very Words of God and what should be done about it was imperative. The apostle commanded Timothy to preach this practice actively and often. This common agenda was to regularly occupy his preaching. He could shun this responsibility by running away or by neglecting his charge. The same is true for any preacher today.

God does not, however, approve of a vindictive spirit. The apostle warns Timothy, and those that follow him, to maintain a Christian attitude in the battle. "And the servant of the Lord must not strive; but be gentle unto all men, apt to teach, patient, In meekness instruction those that oppose themselves; if God peradventure will give them repentance to the acknowledging of the truth; And that they may recover themselves out of the snare of the devil" (2 Timothy 2:24-26). Gentleness, teaching with tact, and a God honoring and patient spirit is always the mode for the Christian. Such a spirit exemplifies the attitude of the Lord Jesus. He raised His voice at times in His ministry, but never in ugliness, nor with vindictive venom. The Christian workman must manifest this kind of quality in the handling of the preservation issue. Still, he must separate from the error and instruct others to follow in that direction. As in all issues, servants are the "ministers of reconciliation." This does not mean sloppy sentimentalism or political motivation, but a glorifying of God's holiness in honor to His Holy Word.

The correct Godly spirit is essential, but it does not do away with this engagement in battle. Meekness and gentleness must not be looked upon as weakness, but as strength. Almighty God would only reveal to us the strongest position a believer might take. He provides the correct attitude of the Christian soldier who goes forth to war, and it is that spirit that is expressed by the Lord Jesus as He hung on the cross of Calvary to pay for the sins of the world. It is free from all malice and desire for revenge. The soldier of Christ should be looking for converts, not casualties. He seeks repentance, not retribution. In doing so, God reveals that He "give[s] them repentance." The one engaged by the believer might acknowledge the truth that is founded in God's veritable Words. He could recover or return to soberness. He could experience release from the captor's clutches. God would then have done His perfect will and work through his faithful servants who love the Words of God as He gave and preserved them.

Every church member should "depart from iniquity" (2 Timothy 2:19) and should pray that he would be obedient to God to "purge himself from these," so as to be "a vessel unto honour, sanctified, and meet for the master's use, and prepared unto every good work" (2 Timothy 2:21). Without diligence in this regard, and without separation, and without understanding what God is trying to accomplish, the effort will all end in frustration, fighting and fleeing. But with God's understanding, there will be repentance, recovery, reconciliation and revival. A living convert to the truth is better than a dead enemy without truth.

Conclusion

Since there is an actual spiritual war that is being waged over the veritable Words of God, all Christians must take a side. Neutrality is impossible. Pastors should obey Timothy's charge from the Apostle Paul and must separate themselves from those who are not "approved" because of their subversion. They must not approve of others who practice that which God considers profane. Godly and faithful men will praise that which God upholds and denounce that which He denounces.

God's churches must not fellowship with, but "shun" (2 Tim. 2:16), or "purge themselves from" (2 Tim. 2:21) assemblies and pastors that deny the perfect preservation of Scripture. When this error infests Bible colleges, relationships with the disobedient institutions must be severed. Pastors should not send their young people to sit with or under men who knowingly pervert the veritable Words of God. Men of God should scrutinize fellowship around camps, conferences, seminars, and other local churches. Preachers should faithfully follow God's admonition to put others in remembrance of these things. Teachers in the lowest grades in our church Sunday schools should take a firm stand for a sound Bibliology. From that point to the most advanced classes in our local church colleges, those who teach should have the same standard. Churches should instruct new members in this doctrine as well as others, and prospective members should not be admitted until the inspiration and preservation of God's veritable Words is understood on the level of the individual's ability. Churches should not support missionaries unless they understand the doctrine and accept it. Staff members without convictions in favor of God's preserved Words should not be hired. Churches should not hedge or dodge, and show no favoritism (1 Tim. 5:21) nor neutrality in the good fight for God.

The Apostle Paul gives his charge to young Timothy because there is more to being a spiritual pastor than preaching and praying. There must be separation from that which God disapproves.

CHAPTER TWENTY-ONE

Who Is a Heretic over the Preservation of Scripture?
Titus 3:10
Kent Brandenburg

At the height of papal power during medieval Roman Catholicism, Pope Innocent III led his apostate denomination to sanction the dogma of transubstantiation in 1215.[347] Innocent had declared that he would judge all and be judged by no one, so he took it upon himself to intervene in politics throughout Europe. Twice he excommunicated Holy Roman Emperor Frederick II. When King John of England displeased him, Innocent put that whole country under his interdict. He and his successors instituted and maintained the Holy Office of the Inquisition, a special court upon which the pope bestowed the power to investigate, try, and punish matters of "heresy." "Heresy" was any disagreement with the pope or a doctrine endorsed by the state religion of Roman Catholicism. In almost every case, the "heresy" being punished, often by death, was a truth clearly taught in the Bible. These corrupt religious leaders took a real Scriptural theme, heresy, and twisted it for their own devious purposes. In subsequent centuries, enforcement of this view of heresy[348] made this false teaching on the subject the most commonly held doctinal position.

This unorthodox view of heresy frequently resurfaces even among professing believers in contemporary sacerdotalist societies. Some have recently used the term in a very serious way aimed at those that are the strongest defenders of perfect preservation of Scripture.[349] The charge is that those advocating a perfectly preserved Bible are

---

[347]This is the perverted teaching that the bread and wine of the Roman Eucharist are miraculously transformed into the actual body and blood of Christ, teaching a continual sacrifice of Christ in the Mass, rather than the once-for-all sacrifice taught in Scripture. This was one teaching with which it was "heresy" to disagree.

[348]The Great Schism in 1459 was only a split in Roman Catholicism. Ferdinand and Isabella in Spain used their places of political power to destroy all non-Romanist belief in Spain shortly after 1492 when they came to power. The Counter-Reformation in the early to mid sixteenth century brought new life to the Romanist Inquisition with the pope giving authority to the Society of Jesus (the Jesuits) to carefully rid Europe of "heresy" wherever possible. Several reformers, themselves also the beneficiaries of state power, attempted to rid their territories of the "heresy" of believer's immersion by imprisoning and executing Anabaptists.

[349]"This gives us a criterion (one who is factious) for saying that large sections of the King James-Only Movement are very heretical." Beacham and Bauder, p. 183. To be completely fair, this is a common practice from many on the perfect preservation side as well.

responsible for creating a schism in modern fundamentalism. Those with this position on heresy imply and sometimes state that the "heretics" need to be excommunicated from the group.[350] Not out of the fear of excommunication, but out of the respect for the Bible, believers ought to review what Scripture says on the matter of heresy. The text is Titus 3:10. This passage should be examined first to determine what heresy is and how to eliminate it.

The Context of Titus 3:10

Titus is a New Testament epistle, a letter from the Apostle Paul to Titus, a pastor or protege that he had left in Crete. What Paul says to Titus in this epistle is Scripture. What one reads in Titus about anything is God's Word, coming from apostolic authority (Titus 1:1).

After Paul's first imprisonment, he took Titus with him to Crete for evangelism, discipleship, and church-planting work. When Paul departed, Titus stayed on to lead a particular church, but there were also other new congregations spread across this island; therefore, one of the first instructions that Paul gave Titus was to appoint and ordain other pastors in each assembly (1:5). Titus was to believe and practice the material written to him in the context of local churches.

God, through the Apostle Paul, wanted effective churches. Crete was a corrupt island that naturally influenced churches negatively, and problems resulted. Effective churches in difficult surroundings required sound leadership from the pastors. Titus and the pastors of these churches needed to fulfill the qualifications (1:6-9) without which they could not properly provide a pattern of good works (2:7,8), convince the gainsayers (1:9), rebuke with authority (2:15), and constantly affirm necessary truths (3:8). A church that would be effective with the Gospel (2:11-14) needed to behave in a particular fashion (2:2-3:3). Behavior was so inextricably connected with doctrine that right behavior needed to be enforced as a means of preserving right doctrine. Salvation of the lost through the ministry of the church was the overriding goal.

Some members of the churches would impede the sound doctrine and practice in their assemblies. Opposition to the Lord from within (1:9-16) would influence weak or even unconverted members. Enemies of the Lord would actually slip into the church (even as it says in Jude 4, "unawares"). God had an established means of dealing with those that would divert or hinder the God-ordained belief and practice of the local

---

[350]What is "the group?" It could be the mailing list of a university. It might be a fellowship of pastors. It is potentially an invitation roster for a well-known conference.

Excommunication could be the loss of special-speaker status. Money gets involved through speaking remuneration and love offerings. The major loss is one of prestige. There are many different ways to be excluded if one values the prominence that the smile of a college president might bring.

[351]"Heretick" is found only here in the New Testament. It is the transliteration of the Greek word

church (Matthew 18:15-17; Romans 16:17,18; 1 Corinthians 5; 2 Thessalonians 3:6-15). That means is recorded in Titus 3:10.

The Content of Titus 3:10

The subject of the action of this verse is "a man." "A man" is representative of any person, man or woman, who as a member of one of the local Cretian churches continues to be "an heretick"[351] after at least two admonitions from the church. From verse nine, the man is likely someone who is being admonished for foolish questions, genealogies, contentions, and strivings about the law.[352] The "heretick" was someone who caused divisions, who was factious or schismatic. The implication is that the heretic caused division when the church did not receive one of his unscriptural beliefs. The causes of division in verse nine were particular disputes that were prominent among false teachers on the isle of Crete. The words used, however, could easily take in any type of wrong belief and practice. In modern vernacular, the heretic is someone who will just not get along in a church.

The divisive activity was first to be avoided. These practices would only influence church members toward divisiveness. Unity is not only possible, but is to be maintained in a local church. Another way of keeping division out of the church is by disciplining out those members who refuse to get along with everyone else. Divisive people outside of the church were to be shunned. Inside the church, one was not to avoid another member who was involved in divisive activity, but rather to admonish him. If he continued in the divisiveness, then a second admonition was to occur. From Matthew 18:15-17, the assumption is that the second admonition was fulfilled in the presence of at least one or two others. After those two admonitions, if there was no repentance concerning the behavior, the heretic was to be rejected, that is, removed from the membership. After this removal, the membership was to avoid him just like they were to avoid the behavior recorded in verse nine.

The unity of a local church comes from agreement of the church on doctrine and practice (Matthew 18:19). The unity of a local church is akin to the unity of parts of a body (Romans 12; 1 Corinthians 12). The basis of that unity is one Spirit, one Lord, one faith, and one baptism (Ephesians 4:4-6). God did not command the church to avoid doctrine (3:9). Rather, doctrine and practice are fundamental to unity. Unity necessitates both the personal and mutual desire and endeavor within a church to stay

---

hairetikon (αἱρετικὸν). It essentially means to make one's personal opinions more important or authoritative than Scripture, or to antagonize God-ordained authority.

[352]"Foolish questions" were controversies over issues that were unscriptural. "Genealogies" were being understood figuratively as a means of receiving an unscriptural teaching. "Contentions" were any kind of self-serving strife. "Strivings" about the law come from those who would elevate rabbinical traditions to something equal to the Scripture itself.

unified (Ephesians 4:3). Titus 3:10 presents a final important means to maintain unity, namely, the removal from the church of those determined to cause schisms.

The Application to the Preservation Issue

When there is a church that believes and teaches the perfect preservation of every Word of Scripture in one edition, the heretic causes disunity in that local church through his contradictory belief and teaching. Perfect preservation and the availability of every Word are beliefs and teachings of Scripture. When a church has agreed on those positions, the heretic continues his contention with it.

On the other hand, a person is not a heretic who speaks out or writes against a teaching that conflicts with his local church. Heresy is a local church issue.[353] The only place for heresy in the New Testament is in a local church. The labeling of a belief or practice as heretical that disagrees with any other institution or movement other than a local church adds to the Word of God. God, of course, warned several times of the seriousness of adding to Scripture.[354]

New Testament churches are autonomous. Not denomination or religion, pope, university, or even council of churches, either state sponsored or not, has any authority over a local church.[355] Of course, the Lord Jesus Christ is the Head of His body, His body institutionally and particularly.[356] One church can refuse to fellowship with another church over a matter of conflicting doctrine or practice and will likely benefit from doing so. Separation is a means of protecting the doctrine and practice of a local church (preservation). The protection of doctrine in the New Testament is a local church issue (1 Timothy 3:15). God in His Word commissions no other institution to this task. Organizations (a university, etc.) or people (the pope, Catholic or Protestant) that would supplant or supercede a local church in the exposure or discipline of heresy are perverting Scriptural truth in the manner of Roman Catholicism from the dark ages to modern times, and as Protestantism during and after the Reformation.[357]

---

[353]Expanding the definition of heresy tends toward pride. Flesh has a tendency to crave recognition beyond the local church. This illegitimate elaboration also shifts truth to a container in which God has not promised to preserve it. Outside of its God-ordained container, truth is destined for corruption. Since truth is designed for local church practice, outside of it, truth is relegated to a kind of laboratory experiment, a sort of "truth in a test tube." Truth, alien of the proper setting, is like the manna that God gave in the wilderness – not used, it will spoil.

[354]Deuteronomy 12:32; Proverbs 30:6; Revelation 22:18.

[355]These institutions have no Scriptural authority even to exist.

Conclusion

To acquiesce to a parachurch charge of heresy is an admission that the one making the charge holds the correct doctrine. To be silenced by a charge of heresy from a faux authority is to concede authority to one not having any. Not only does concession illegitimately assign authority, but also it devalues the institution that does possess the authority, the local church. Done enough times with enough people, history tells and experience shows that non-Scriptural establishments become better respected than Scriptural ones.

Titus 3:10 reduces the teaching on heresy to the following formula. The heretic causes division in his church. If after being admonished twice, the heretic does not repent of his divisiveness, the church alleviates the heresy by removing the heretic from the membership. On the subject of heresy, everything else should be heresy.

---

[356] "Body" in "body of Christ," as all singular nouns, is used generically or particularly. The reality of the body exists in particular churches. The New Testament refers to the body of Christ generically when speaking of the church institutionally. All true churches are unified to the degree that the church or the body can refer to all local churches.

[357] Outside of a local church, who is responsible for rejecting heretics? If heretics are rejected outside of a local church, from what are they removed? Who determines the standards for heresy outside of the local church? Who decides who has violated those standards? Because there is no good answer to these questions, Scripturally or otherwise, Titus 3:10 is impossible to practice outside of its given context. The regular attempts to do so are the very reason why some believers see it as impossible to be consistent in matters of separation.

ADDENDA

ADDENDUM A

God's Providential Preservation of the Scriptures
Gary La More

God's providential preservation of the Scriptures cannot be separated from the doctrine of their verbal plenary inspiration.[358] The Holy Spirit persuades believers to adopt the same view of the Bible that Jesus believed and taught during the days of His earthly ministry. Jesus explicitly denied the theories of modern higher critics. He recognized Moses (Mark 12:26), David (Luke 20:42), and Daniel (Matt. 24:15) by name as the authors of their Old Testament books. Moreover, according to the Lord Jesus, all these individual Old Testament writings combined together formed one Divine and infallible Book which He called "the Scriptures." Jesus believed that these Scriptures were inspired by the Holy Spirit (Mark 12:36), that not one word of them could be denied (John 10:35), that not one particle of them could perish (Matt. 5:18), and that everything written in them was Divinely authoritative (Matt. 4:4,7,10).

This same high view of the Old Testament Scriptures was held and taught by Christ's Apostles. All Scripture, Paul declares, is given by inspiration of God (2 Tim. 3:16). Peter adds, "No prophecy of the scripture is of any private interpretation. For the prophecy came not in old time by the will of man: but holy men of God spake as they were moved by the Holy Ghost" (2 Peter 1:20-21). The Scriptures were the living Oracles through which God spoke (Acts 7:38), which had been committed to the Jews for safekeeping (Rom. 3:2), which contained the principles of Divine knowledge (Heb. 5:12), and according to which Christians were to pattern their own speech (1 Peter 4:11). To the Apostles, "It is written," was equivalent to, "God says."

Jesus promised that the New Testament would be infallibly inspired just as the Old had been (John 16:12-13). The Holy Spirit, Jesus pledged, would enable the Apostles to remember their Lord's teaching and understand its meaning (John 14:26). These promises began to be fulfilled on the day of Pentecost when Peter's Words were inspired to declare the meaning of Christ's death and resurrection (Acts 2:14-36). Paul

---

[358]Lloyd L. Streeter, *Seventy-five Problems with Central Baptist Seminary's Book 'The Bible Version Debate'* (LaSalle, IL: First Baptist Church of LaSalle, 2001), p. 126.

also was conscious of this same Divine inspiration (1 Cor. 14:37). In the last chapter of Revelation John the Apostle affirms the inspiration of that book in the strongest possible terms (Rev. 22:18-19).

Jesus and His Apostles regarded both the Old and New Testaments as the infallibly inspired Word of God, and the Holy Spirit, bearing witness in the believer's heart, assures him that this view is not mistaken.

The Eternal Origin of the Scriptures

While on earth, Jesus constantly affirmed that His message was eternal, since the very Words that He spoke had been given to Him by God the Father (John 12:49-50). The Lord also states emphatically in His "high-priestly" prayer that the Father gave Him the Words that He spoke to His Apostles. "For I have given unto them the Words which Thou gavest Me" (John 17:8). Since the Scriptures come from and reside with God, they are eternal. God gave to Jesus Christ His Son the Words of eternal life (John 6:68). These Words that Christ brought down from heaven for the salvation of His people now remain inscribed in Holy Writ. Words that bring eternal life must of necessity be eternal.

Jesus Christ, the Divine Word, worked providentially in history to develop the Hebrew and Greek tongues into fit vehicles to convey His eternal saving message. Hence in the writing of the Scriptures the Holy Spirit did not have to struggle, as modernists insist, with the limitations of human language; the chosen languages were perfectly adapted to the expression of His Divine thoughts.

"For ever, O LORD, Thy Word is settled in heaven" (Ps. 119:89). Although the Scriptures were written during a definite historical period, they are not the product of that period but of the eternal plan of God. "The grass withereth, the flower fadeth: but the Word of our God shall stand for ever" (Isa. 40:8). God speaks in them to every age, including the present. "For whatsoever things were written aforetime were written for our learning, that we through patience and comfort of the scriptures might have hope" (Rom. 15:4).

---

[359]The author of this brief chapter on the providential preservation of God's Word is highly indebted to Edward F. Hills and his *The King James Version Defended* (Des Moines, IA: The Christian Research Press, 1984). One should especially see pp. 110-114 of his book. Large portions of this section of Hills are liberally borrowed and extensively used for this chapter. Edward Hills contrasted providential preservation with miraculous preservation. While his recognition of the hand of God in the transmission of the Bible is praiseworthy, his view of providence is insufficient. The Bible promises a perfect and available Bible for every generation, and God worked providentially to insure this promised end. Although Hills,

Providential Preservation of the Scriptures[359]

Because the Scriptures are forever relevant, they have been preserved down through the ages by God's special providence. The Lord Himself proclaimed the reality of the providential preservation of the Scriptures of both Testaments during His life on earth: "Till heaven and earth pass, one jot or one tittle shall in no wise pass from the law, till all be fulfilled" (Matt. 5:18). "It is easier for heaven and earth to pass, than one tittle of the law to fail" (Luke 16:17). He declared that the Old Testament text in common use among the Jews during His earthly ministry was an absolutely trustworthy reproduction of the original text. Nothing had been lost from that text and nothing ever would be lost. It would be easier for heaven and earth to pass than for such a loss to take place.

Jesus taught that the same Divine providence which had preserved the Old Testament would preserve the New Testament. In the concluding verses of the Gospel of Matthew the believer finds His "Great Commission" to His assemblies throughout the ages. "Go ye therefore and teach all nations . . . ." This solemn charge implies the promise that, through the working of God's providence, His NT assemblies would always possess an infallible record of Jesus' Words and works.[360] Similarly, in His discourse on last things, the Lord assures His disciples that His promises would not only certainly be fulfilled but also remain available for the comfort of His people during that troubled period which shall precede His Second Coming. "Heaven and earth shall pass away, but my Words shall not pass away" (Matt. 24:35; Mark 13:31; Luke 21:33).

The Holy Spirit providentially guided churches to preserve His Words during the manuscript period. First, faithful scribes produced many trustworthy copies of the original New Testament manuscripts. Second, these trustworthy copies were read and recopied by true believers down through the centuries. Third, untrustworthy copies were not so generally read or so frequently recopied. Although they enjoyed some popularity for a time, yet in the long run they were laid aside and consigned to oblivion. Thus, as a result of this special providential guidance, the true text won out in the end, and today the believer may be sure that the text found in the vast majority of the Greek New Testament manuscripts, preserved by the God-guided usage of the Greek churches, is a trustworthy reproduction of the Divinely inspired original. Some have called it the Byzantine text, thereby acknowledging that it was the text in use in the Greek churches during the greater part of the Byzantine period (452-1453).[361] It is much better, however, to call this text the Traditional Text

---

a Presbyterian, accurately presents much truth in his useful book, references to him should in no way be construed as an endorsement of his covenant theology, infant sprinkling, or Calvinism.

[360] The Great Commission necessitates church perpetuity to the end of this age. All doctrine must be available to obey its command. Christ's commands are Scripture, and Scripture is perfect. To teach all things He commanded requires the preservation of every Word. The Words of Christ fit into the overall context of the Words of Scripture. That context must be perfect in order for His Words to be perfect and the inspired meaning certain. Therefore, the Great Commission implies perfect preservation of every Word of God.

because this text, which is found in the great majority of Greek New Testament manuscripts, has been handed down by the God-guided tradition of the Lord's *ekklāsiai* ("churches") from the time of the Apostles to the present day.[362]

God, by His special providence, has preserved the New Testament text in a threefold way through the priesthood of believers. In the first place, during the fourteen centuries in which the New Testament circulated in manuscript form, God worked providentially through the usage of the Greek-speaking churches to preserve the New Testament text in the majority of the Greek New Testament manuscripts.[363] In this way the true New Testament text became the prevailing Traditional Text. In the second place, during the 16th century when the New Testament text was being printed for the first time, God worked providentially to influence Erasmus, Beza, and others of that period to preserve the genuine reading.[364] Then in the third place, during the 450 years which have elapsed since the first printing of the New Testament, God has been working providentially through the usage and agreement of His churches to place and keep the stamp of His approval upon this God-guided printed text. It is upon this *Textus Receptus* that the King James Version is based.[365]

The Principles Involved

Richard Bentley, Theodor Zahn, B.B. Warfield,[366] and countless others have tried to devise a theory of the special providential preservation of the Scriptures which leaves room for naturalistic New Testament textual criticism. This, however, is impossible, for

---

[361] God also providentially used evil monks in the Eastern Orthodox denomination to preserve Greek MSS.
[362] Hills, p. 106.
[363] These churches of the early Byzantine area were Greek speaking. The churches did this early work in preservation. They did most of the early copying and spreading of the early copies. From those copies, much work was done providentially by Greeks of the Orthodox denomination. Churches in other languages also participated in preservation, including but not confined to Latin, French, and German speaking churches.
[364] Historic Baptists influenced this process. The KJV translators had Waldensian Bibles before them, Reformers had Waldensian relatives, and Anabaptists translated the Bible into German before Luther, etc.
[365] Hills, p. 107. Part of the miracle of providence is that God used some unbelievers to ensure the perfection and availability of Scripture for every generation. As God used the Babylonians in the Old Testament to chastise Israel, He employed apostate Greek Latin institutions to cooperate with New Testament churches in order to preserve all of His Words. God ensured that what was kept and agreed upon by the people of the churches would continue, sometimes in spite of the people participating. Some parts of the historical record are not humanly explainable outside of the providential preservation of God.
[366] B.B. Warfield (1893) wrote, "In the sense of the Westminster Confession, therefore, the multiplication of the copies of the Scriptures, the several early efforts towards the revision of the text, the raising up of scholars in our own day to collect and collate manuscripts, and to reform them on scientific principles – of our Tischendorfs and Tregelleses, and Westcotts and Horts – are all parts of God's singular care and providence in preserving His inspired Word pure." op. cit. Hills, p. 110.
Warfield was an outstanding defender of several doctrines of the orthodox Christian faith. Nevertheless, it is a fact that his thinking was not entirely unified. Through his mind ran two separate trains of thought that not even he could join together. The one train of thought was dogmatic, going back to the Protestant Reformation. When following this train of thought Warfield regarded Christianity as true. The other

the two concepts are mutually exclusive. Naturalistic New Testament textual criticism requires men to treat the text of the New Testament like the text of any other ancient book, and so ignore or denies the special providential preservation of the Scriptures. Hence, if one really believes in the special providential preservation of the Scriptures, he cannot follow the naturalistic method of New Testament textual criticism.[367]

For a believer, the only alternative is to follow a consistently Christian method in which all the principles are derived from the Bible itself; none must be borrowed from the textual criticism of other ancient books. The principles modified from what Edwards Hills wrote[368] are essentially:

Principle One: The Old Testament text was preserved by the Old Testament priesthood, the scribes, and Israel generally.[369]

Principle Two: When Christ died upon the cross, the Old Testament priesthood was abolished. In the New Testament dispensation every believer is a priest under Christ, the great High Priest. The New Testament text has been preserved through the Lord's true churches and the priesthood of believers in those churches.

Principle Three: The Traditional Text, found in the vast majority of the Greek New Testament manuscripts and employed in vernacular manuscripts by pre-Reformation Baptists, is the True Text because it represents the God-guided usage of His churches.

Principle Four: The first printed text of the Greek New Testament represents a forward step in the providential preservation of the New Testament. The editors and printers who produced this text were providentially guided.

Principle Five: Through the usage of Bible-believing Christians, God placed the

---

train of thought was apologetic, going back to the rationalistic era of the 18th century. When following this train of thought Warfield regarded Christianity as merely probable. This same divided outlook was shared by Warfield's colleagues at Princeton Seminary and by conservative theologians and scholars generally throughout the 19th and early 20th century. Even today this split-level thinking is still a factor to be reckoned with in conservative circles, although in far too many instances it has passed over into modernism. Hills, p. 110.

"Warfield's treatment of the New Testament text illustrates this cleavage in his thinking. In the realm of dogmatics he agreed with the Westminister Confession that the New Testament text had been "kept pure in all ages" by God's "singular care and providence," but in the realm of New Testament textual criticism he agreed with Westcott and Hort in ignoring God's providence, and even went so far as to assert that the same methods were to be applied to the text of the New Testament that would be applied to the text of a morning newspaper. It was to bridge the gap between his dogmatics and his New Testament textual criticism that he suggested that God had worked providentially through Tischendorf, Tregelles, and Westcott and Hort to preserve the New Testament text. But this suggestion leads to conclusions that are extremly bizarre and inconsistent. It would have one believe that during the manuscript period orthodox believers corrupted the New Testament text, that the text used by the Protestant Reformers was the worst of all, and that the True Text was not restored until the 19th century, when Tregelles brought it forth out of the Pope's library, when Tischendorf rescued it from a waste basket on Mt. Sinai, and when Westcott and Hort were providentially guided to construct a theory of it which ignores God's special providence and treats the text of the New Testament like the text of any other ancient book. But if the True New Testament Text was lost for 1500 years, how can one be sure that it has ever been found again?" Hills, p. 110 (*verbatim*).

[367]Hills, p. 111.
[368]Hills, pp. 111, 112.
[369]See chapter eleven on preservation in the Old Testament by Kent Brandenburg.

stamp of His approval on this printed text, and it became the *Textus Receptus* (Received Text). It is the printed form of the Traditional Text found in the vast majority of the Greek New Testament manuscripts and preserved among non-Greek speaking New Testament churches in translation.

Principle Six: The King James (Authorized) Version is an accurate translation of the *Textus Receptus*. God has placed the stamp of His approval on it through its long continued usage by English-speaking believers. God's churches have been led by the Spirit to defend its text as preserved and hence it should be used and defended today by Bible-believing Christians. God has not led His churches to declare the text underlying any other translation perfect. Spanish speaking Baptists, for example, do not claim the text underlying the Reina Valera is perfect. Since man is to live by every Word, saints can know where those Words are. They must be under the KJV, for only there has the Spirit led His churches to state they are perfectly preserved.

One knows that the *Textus Receptus* is the true New Testament text through the logic of faith.[370] Since faith comes from the hearing of the Word of God (Romans 10:17), the Word of God will be displayed by the Scriptural principles of preservation. Scripture says every Word of God would be preserved by God through His churches and available to every generation. Only the *Textus Receptus* was preserved by God through His churches and available to every generation. Therefore, only the *Textus Receptus* contains every Word of God.

One also knows that the King James Version is a faithful translation of the true New Testament text through the logic of faith. Since the formation of the *Textus Receptus* was God-guided, the translation of it was God-guided also. For, as the *Textus Receptus* was being formed, it was also being translated. The two processes were simultaneous. Hence the earlier versions, such as Luther's, Tyndale's, the Geneva, and the King James, were actually varieties of the *Textus Receptus*. And this was necessarily so according to the principles of God's preserving providence, for the *Textus Receptus* had to be

---

[370] As it relates to preservation, "logic of faith" is terminology coined by Hills (Hills, p. 113). For an excellent study on the logic of faith and the Bible, see Brother John M. Krinke's *Should Believers Accept the Preservation of God's Word(s) by Faith, or by History & Science?* (Greenwood, IN: John M. Krinke, 1997). Also on the issue of Bible preservation, the reader is directed to Kirk D. Divietro's study, *Preservation of God's Words* (Collingswood, NJ: The Bible for Today, 1997). These studies are excellent and should be read by all Bible-believing Christians.

[371] Hills, pp. 113, 114.

[372] Christianity has been plagued by accommodation time and again through the years, and in particularly this century. Harold J. Ockenga wrote about the liberalism at the turn of the 20th century:

> Destructive higher criticism of the Bible became the dominant approach among the theologians at the close of the nineteenth century and during the early twentieth century. When joined with naturalistic evolution, it produced liberalism . . . . It [liberalism] accommodated Christianity to modern scientific naturalism . . . whenever objections arose on the details of the Christian religion.

translated in order that the New Testament churches, the rank and file, might continue giving it their God-guided approval.[371]

Francis Schaeffer has a very interesting conclusion in his appendix to *What Difference Does Inerrancy Make?* He says:

> When [one] come[s] to the central things of doctrine, including maintaining the Bible's emphasis that it is without mistake, and the central things of life, then something must be considered. Truth carries with it confrontation. Truth demands confrontation; loving confrontation, but confrontation nevertheless. If [one's] reflex action is always accommodation regardless of the centrality of the truth involved, there's something wrong.[372]

God's Word will never pass away, but looking back through history, with tears the believer must say that because of lack of fortitude and faithfulness on the part of God's people, God's Word has often been bent and conformed to the surrounding, passing, changing culture of that moment, rather than as the inerrant Word of God judging the form of the world-spirit and the surrounding culture of the moment. The prayer of those in the Lord Jesus Christ is that succeeding generations will not have this sad tale told about them.[373]

It is interesting to note further that even some liberals have begun to recognize the devastating effect of theological accommodation and are beginning to grow weary of it and are wondering what to do. One such liberal, quoted by Francis Schaeffer, recently wrote:

The central theme of contemporary theology is *accommodation to modernity*. It is the underlying motif that unites the seemingly vast differences between existential theology, process theology, liberation theology, demythologization, and many varieties of liberal theology-all are searching for some more compatible adjustment to modernity. On the subject of modernity see Gary E. La More's *The Word of God and the Turning of the Tides: From Clothes to Fashions* (Scarborough, Ontario: Grace Missionary Baptist Church, 1996).

Yet accommodation has become fashionable among many evangelicals -- in spite of the devastating effect this has had theologically and culturally. (See Francis A. Schaeffer's *The Great Evangelical Disaster* (Westchester, IL: Crossway Books, 1984), pp. 99-100.) Francis Schaeffer did not espouse perfect preservation, nor did he defend the *TR*. However, if anyone, would apply his advice to perfect preservation, he would not give accommodation to anyone in the matter of a perfect Bible.

[373]Richard Teachout, *The Tidal Wave of Ecumenism and the Local Church, A Lesson from Promise Keepers* (Ste Foy, Québec: Études Bibliques pour AUJOURDOHUI!, 1997), pp. 28-29.

ADDENDUM B

The Translation Model Predicted by Scripture
Thomas M. Strouse

Introduction

The Lord Jesus Christ recognized that Scripture attested to its own Bibliology. When He was tempted by Satan He answered and said, "It is written, Man shall not live by bread alone, but by every word that proceedeth out of the mouth of God" (Mt. 4:4). The Lord affirmed several Bibliological truths self-attested by Scripture. He affirmed that Scripture was authoritative because God was its source ("proceedeth out of the mouth of God").[374] He affirmed that it was verbally and perfectly inspired because of its extent ("every word"). He affirmed that it was verbally and perfectly preserved because it was still extant ("it is written").[375] Following the Lord's example, the Bible believer must look to Scripture to develop a scriptural Bibliology. The Bible, as the ultimate Christian authority, self-attests to its doctrines of inspiration, of preservation, of translation practices, and of church responsibility in this process. This chapter is an effort to demonstrate what translation model the Scripture predicts relative to the aforementioned rubrics for Bibliological self-attestation. The models[376] tested are the *Textus Receptus*/King James Bible and the Critical Text/Modern Versions.[377] The Bible predicts that the best translation model will be the one that demonstrates the biblical view of perfect inspiration, perfect preservation, accurate translation, and local church responsibility.

---

[374]The Lord believed the written Scripture of the Old Testament was more authoritative than His own spoken word, harmonizing His belief and practice with Psm. 138:2, "I will worship toward thy holy temple, and praise thy name for thy lovingkindness and for thy truth: for thou hast magnified thy word above all thy name."

[375]The perfect tense of *gegraptai* could be rendered "it was written and still is written."

[376]"Model" includes the men and their principles relating to the respective Greek editions and resultant translations.

[377]Representatives of the CT/MV model are the ASV (American Standard Version, 1901), RSV (Revised Standard Version, 1952), BV (Berkeley Version, 1959), NWT (New World Translation, 1961), JB (Jerusalem Bible, 1966), NEB (New English Bible, 1970), LB (Living Bible, 1971), NASB (New American Standard Bible, 1971), TEV (Today's English Version: Good News for Modern Man, 1976), NIV (New International Version, 1978), and NRSV (New Revised Standard Version, 1989).

THE SCRIPTURAL REQUIREMENTS FOR INSPIRATION

Introduction

The Bible attests to its own inspiration. Inspiration is the process whereby the Holy Spirit led the writers of Scripture to record accurately His very Words; the product of this process was the inspired original. The Bible is permeated with the teaching of this inspiration in numerous passages. The most significant and specific passage is the *locus classicus* passage of inspiration – 2 Tim. 3:16.

The *Locus Classicus* – 2 Timothy 3:15-17

Paul gave these verses to Timothy in Ephesus so he would know the Lord's antidote for apostasy – His inspired *autographa* (cf. 2 Tim. 3:1-9). This classic and crucial passage is the clearest statement in the Bible declaring its own inspiration. Key to the exegesis of 2 Tim. 3:16 is several words and their respective syntax. The *Authorized Version (AV)* renders this verse, "All Scripture is given by inspiration of God, and is profitable for doctrine, for reproof, for correction, for instruction in righteousness." The key words for proper Bibliological understanding are "all" (πᾶσα, *pasa*), "Scripture" (γραφὴ, *graphā*), and "is given by inspiration of God" (θεόπνευστος, *theopneustos*).

Pasa

Although *pasa* as an adjective is used with an anarthrous noun, it should not be translated "every [scripture]." The focus of Paul does not seem to be on the individual words of the whole in a partitive sense, but on the whole of Scripture itself. *Pasa* may be translated as "all" when it used with technical nouns as in the case of Acts 2:36, which reads "all the house of Israel." Some other places in the Bible where *pasa* qualifies anarthrous nouns and should be translated "all" are Mt. 3:15 ("all righteousness," not "every righteousness"), Acts 7:22 ("all the wisdom," not "every wisdom"), and Col. 4:12 ("all the will of God," not "every will of God").[378] When *pasa* is used with an anarthrous noun that is technical, it should be translated as "all." The expression "all Scripture" declares the inspiration of all the Words of the

---

[378]Cf. also Acts 7:22; Rom. 11:26; Eph. 2:21, 3:15.

[379]The *New English Bible (NEB)* wrongly translates the verse "Every inspired scripture has its use for teaching the truth and refuting error, or for reformation of manners and discipline in right living" (2 Tim. 3:16).

[380]Cf. also Rom. 15:4, 16:26; Gal 3:8.

Bible, whereas the expression "every Scripture" inspired by God suggests that some Scripture may not be inspired.[379]

Graphā,

The word *graphā* is a technical noun in the Bible for "Scripture." Sometimes the biblical writers used *graphā* to refer to the whole collection of OT books. For instance, the Apostle John challenged the Jews concerning their OT to "search the Scriptures (*graphas*)" (Jn. 5:39). Luke recorded Paul's synagogue practice of expositing "out of the scriptures" at Thessalonica (Acts 17:2). Paul referred to the canonical OT in Rom. 1:2, stating "Which he had promised afore by his prophets in the holy scriptures (γραφαῖς ἁγίαις, *graphais hagiais*)," and Peter affirmed "that no prophecy of the scripture is of any private interpretation" (2 Pet. 1:20).[380]

The Biblical writers also used *graphā* to refer to individual portions of the Bible. Matthew recorded Christ's testimony that the verses of Psm. 118:22-23 were "the scriptures" (Mt. 21:42) and John revealed the Lord's citation of Psm. 41:9 as "scripture "(Jn. 13:18). Furthermore Paul cited the individual reference of Gen. 21:10 asking, "what saith the scripture?" (Gal. 4:30) and James referred to Gen. 15:6 as "scripture" (Jam. 2:23).[381] The Apostle Paul called Lk. 10:7 "scripture" along with Dt. 25:4 in 1 Tim. 5:18. All of the NT references to *graphā* refer either to part or the whole of the OT and/or the NT. The Bible writers treated *graphā* as a technical word for God's special revelation, either in part or whole.

Graphā is distinct from *gramma* (cf. "the holy scriptures" [τὰ ἱερα γράμματα, *ta hiera grammata*] in v. 15) in that the latter may refer to non-canonical literature. Although John used *grammata* to refer to Moses' pentateuchal writings (Jn. 5:47),[382] Luke used *gramma* to refer to a non-canonical collection bill (Lk. 16:6-7). *Graphā* always refers to the autographical scripture whereas *gramma* sometimes refers to non-canonical compositions. This distinction between these words might help one to recognize that Paul probably referred to the temple writings or scriptures (*apographa*) in v. 15 and the *autographa* in v. 16.

Theopneustos

The word *theopneustos* (θεόπνευστος) is translated with 6 words in the *KJB*, including the verb: "is given by inspiration of God." Since *theopneustos* is a verbal adjective (compare *pneustos* compound) and has a passive sense, grammatically it may be translated as the KJB rendering "is given by inspiration of God."[383]

Deciding where to place the "is" affects the meaning of the verse. If *theopneustos* is translated as an attributive adjective,[384] then the "is" would come after *theopneustos*

---

[381] *Vide* Jn. 7:38; Acts 1:16, 8:32, 35; Rom. 4:3, 9:17.
[382] Cf. also Lk. 23:38; Acts 26:24; Rom. 2:27; Gal. 6:11.
[383] Literally "is God-breathed."
[384] An attributive adjective modifies the noun with which it is associated, whereas a predicate adjective asserts something about its noun.

and the verse rendered "every God-inspired scripture is profitable," suggesting that some scripture might not be inspired. If *theopneustos* is translated as a predicate adjective then the "is" would be placed before *theopneustos* and rendered "all scripture is God-inspired and is profitable." Since *graphā* is a technical term and therefore treated as a definite noun, the Greek construction adjective (*pas*) + noun (*graphā*) + adjective (*theopneustos*) must be understood as predicate, placing the "is" prior to the second adjective. Paul's technical expression of inspiration demands a technical translation and application of *theopneustos*. All the original autographs (from Genesis to Revelation) were inspired, but only the original autographs were inspired. "Inspired" may not be applied to the original writers, the non-canonical Words of Christ or the apostles, to any Hebrew or Greek manuscripts, or to any Bible translations. The KJB rendering of this verse is both accurate and specific. The Bible self-attests to verbal, plenary (full) inspiration of the autographa.

Other Passages on Inspiration

Numerous other passages in the Bible self-attest to the inspiration of Scripture. For instance, Peter declared "For the prophecy came not in old time by the will of man: but holy men of God spake as they were moved by the Holy Ghost" (2 Pet. 1:21). The Holy Ghost came upon holy but fallible men so that they were Divinely moved (φερόμενοι, *pheromenoi*)[386] in the process of inspiration to produce the product of inspiration, namely the *autographa*. This verse teaches that the Holy Spirit led His human instruments to produce the perfect originals. Paul acknowledged that the words he wrote were the Holy Spirit's words, stating "Which things also we speak, not in the words which man's wisdom teacheth, but which the Holy Ghost teacheth; comparing spiritual things with spiritual" (1 Cor. 2:13). Peter confirmed Paul's evaluation, stating "As also in all his epistles, speaking in them of these things; in which are some things hard to be understood, which they that are unlearned and unstable wrest, as they do also the other scriptures, unto their own destruction" (2 Pet. 3:16).

Christ and the Biblical writers believed the very Words of Scripture would be fulfilled precisely. The Lord Jesus Christ said "Till heaven and earth pass, one jot or one tittle[387] shall in no wise pass from the law, till all be fulfilled" (Mt. 5:18). He believed the continuity of inspiration of the OT connected to that of the NT stating, "Is it not written in your law, I said, Ye are gods? If he called them gods, unto whom the word of God came, and the scripture cannot be broken . . . " (Jn. 10:35). The Apostle Paul

---

[386]The verbal root of this present passive participle is *pherō* (φερῶ), and Luke used this same root to demonstrate the influence of the wind on the ship upon which Paul was imprisoned ("And when the ship was caught, and could not bear up into the wind, we let her drive [ἐφερόμεθα, *epherometha*]") in Acts 27:15.

believed the very words he spoke and ultimately inscripturated were the Words of the Holy Ghost: "Which things also we speak, not in the words which man's wisdom teacheth, but which the Holy Ghost teacheth; comparing spiritual things with spiritual" (1 Cor. 2:13). Paul believed that nouns were inspired, stating "Now to Abraham and his seed were the promises made. He saith not, And to seeds, as of many, but as of one, And to thy seed, which is Christ." (Gal. 3:16). Christ believed that verbs were inspired, carefully choosing the verb "am" ([*egō*] *eimi,* εἰμι) in contrast to "was" in defending the doctrine of the resurrection against the Sadducees. He said, "I am the God of Abraham, and the God of Isaac, and the God of Jacob? God is not the God of the dead, but of the living" (Mt. 22:32; cf. Ex. 3:6).

The Lord God commanded the Biblical writers to write the Words of the Lord. The Lord commanded Moses to write, saying "Write this for a memorial in a book, and rehearse it in the ears of Joshua: for I will utterly put out the remembrance of Amalek from under heaven" (Ex. 17:14; cf. also Jer. 30:2). He commanded Habakkuk, saying "write the vision, and make it plain upon tables, that he may run that readeth it" (Hab. 2:2). He instructed the Apostle John to write his visions and send the book to the seven churches in Asia (Rev. 1:11)[388] and once not to write (Rev. 10:4).

The Biblical writers quoted other Scriptures. The Lord Jesus Christ cited Ex. 20:12 in Mt. 15:4 and Paul said that the Holy Spirit spoke through Isaiah citing Isa. 6:9-10 (Acts 28:26-27). Daniel claimed that the word of the Lord came to his contemporary Jeremiah who predicted the seventy year exile (Dan. 9:2; cf. Jer. 25:12). Paul held Luke's written word (Lk. 10:7) on the same level as Moses' Scripture (Dt. 25:4), stating "For the Scripture saith, Thou shalt not muzzle the ox that treadeth out the corn. And, The labourer is worthy of his reward" (1 Tim. 5:18).

The Biblical writers believed the precise predictions of the Scripture as "thus saith the Lord" and interpreted them literally. Matthew understood that the precise fulfillment of the virgin birth promise the Lord gave the house of David was in Jesus of Nazareth (Mt. 1:23; cf. Isa. 7:10-14). Peter believed that the prophecy found in Psm. 109:8 was fulfilled by Judas (Acts 1:20).[389]

The severe warnings in Scripture about tampering with the written word demand the view that the Lord did not want any of His inspired words changed. John's colophon predicted a terrible destiny for anyone tampering with the text, stating "For I testify unto every man that heareth the words of the prophecy of this book, If any man shall add unto these things, God shall add unto him the plagues that are written in this book: And if any man shall take away from the words of the book of this prophecy, God shall take away his part out of the book of life, and out of the holy city, and from the things which are written in this book" (Rev. 22:18-19).[390]

---

[387]The jot is the *yod* or smallest consonant of the Hebrew language and the *tittle* (literally "horn") is the vowel (point).
[388]Cf. Rev. 1:19; 2:1, 8 12, 18; 3:1, 7; 3:14; 14:13; 19:9; 21:5.
[389]Cf. Psm. 69:25.
[390]Cf. Dt. 4:2; 12:32.

The Model Example

The Lord revealed the model example of the process of inspiration in Jer. 36:1-32. In 605 BC, the year that Nebuchanezzar became ruler of Babylon, won the battle at Carchemesh, and deported Daniel, the Lord God spoke to Jeremiah. The Lord commanded Jeremiah to record his previous sermons (essentially chapters 1-35) in a book. The prophet obeyed and verse 4 records the inspiration process, stating "Then Jeremiah called Baruch the son of Neriah: and Baruch wrote from the mouth of Jeremiah all the words of the Lord which he had spoken unto him, upon a roll of a book." The scribe Baruch inscripturated each word accurately from the mouth of Jeremiah who received each Word from the Lord accurately.[391] God used fallible human instrumentality to record accurately all of Jeremiah's preached words up to that juncture. Later when Jehoiakim cut up and burned the scroll of Baruch (v. 23), the Lord instructed Jeremiah to write again the same words (vv. 27-28). Jeremiah gave the same words to Baruch who wrote them again and added the account of chapter 36 (v. 32) to the previous writing. The Lord inspired and preserved His very words.

Corollaries to Inspiration

Both infallibility and inerrancy are corollaries to the doctrine of inspiration. Infallibility refers to the belief that God was incapable of producing erroneous Scriptures. Inerrancy means that, in fact, the *autographa* do not contain any errors.[392] The aforementioned Scriptures teach the trustworthiness of God, the accuracy of Christ, and the Divine influence on the very Words of prophets and apostles. If the *autographa* are God-breathed as 2 Tim. 3:16 teaches, then they are infallible and inerrant. Although some passages may have apparent discrepancies suggesting textual errors (1 Sam. 13:1), historical errors (2 Chron. 22:2), scientific errors (2 Chron. 4:2), moral errors (Judges 11:29 ff.), or errors in prophecy (Isa. 7:14), there are satisfactory solutions to many. In the others, the believer must give the Lord the benefit of the doubt. Apparent errors and seeming inconsistencies are man's problems and not the Lord's.

---

[391]There is absolutely no warrant to suppose that Baruch edited Jeremiah's words, because the prophet received his words directly from the Lord.

[392]This definition includes the rejection of errors in grammar, history, morals, science, and prophecies, etc.

[393]Paraphrases such as the TEV, LB, and the Black Chronicles Bible (the Hip-Hop Bible) are really contemporary commentaries and will not be considered in this study.

The Models Tested

The OT and NT Scriptures self-attest to verbal plenary inspiration. The corollaries of the infallibility (the Divine author is incapable of error) and of the inerrancy (the Scriptures are in fact without error) of the *autographa* harmonize consistently with the teaching of the God-breathed originals. The *TR*/KJB model reflects the Biblical doctrines of inspiration, infallibility and inerrancy because the translators gave tacit affirmation to these doctrines, the underlying Hebrew, Aramaic and Greek texts declare these doctrines for the original language texts, and the words and phrases of the KJB teach inspiration, infallibility and inerrancy. The *TR*/KJB model fits the model predicted in Scripture.

The CT/MV model includes conservative and liberal translations and paraphrases.[393] The conservative translations (ASV, NASV, and NIV) reflect the Biblical doctrines of inspiration, infallibility and inerrancy[394] inasmuch as the translators tacitly affirm belief in these doctrines and the translations themselves have the wording and phraseology to fit this model. On the other hand, the liberal translations (BV, NWT, JB, RSV, NEB, and NRSV) utilized scholars with questionable orthodoxy, and their respective translations reflect this cacadoxy with suspect phraseology. The CT/MV model does not fit the model predicted in Scripture.

THE SCRIPTURAL REQUIREMENTS FOR PRESERVATION

Introduction

The Bible self-attests not only to perfect inspiration, infallibility and inerrancy but also to perfect preservation. The Scriptures teach both implicitly and explicitly the doctrine of verbal, plenary preservation as a fundamental truth.[395] For instance, the Lord promised the preservation of His Word for a thousand generations, stating, "He hath remembered his covenant for ever, the word which he commanded to a thousand generations" (Psm. 105:8). The following are some of the numerous passages which teach either directly or indirectly the doctrine of the perfect preservation of Scripture,

---

[394]Great concern is registered for those scholars of the CT/MV persuasion who favor an errant variant in manuscripts such as *aleph* or B instead of an inerrant reading of the original writer (cf. Mt. 1:7-8 and Mk. 1:2-3 in CT).

[395]Men, movements, and churches which are bereft of the fundamental doctrine of perfect preservation, can hardly be called "fundamentalist."

and the corollary truths of the necessity of receiving God's preserved Words and rejecting false readings.

The *Locus Classicus* Passages

Passages from both the OT and NT teach the nature and means of the preservation of Scripture. The *locus classicus* passages include Psm. 12:6-7, 119:111, 152, 160; Isa. 40:8; Mt. 5:17-18, and 24:35.[396]

Psalm 12:6-7[397]

The Psalmist bemoaned the impact of the ever-prevalent words of evil men. Of the seventy-nine Hebrew words in this Psalm, thirteen relate to the words of the wicked. The ungodly speak vanity (שָׁוְא, *shâwĕ'*, v. 2) and proud things (מְדַבֶּרֶת גְּדֹלוֹת, *mĕthabbereth gethōlōth*, v. 3) with their flattering lips (שְׂפַת חֲלָקוֹת, *sĕphach chĕlâhôth*, v. 2) and double heart (וְלֵב בְלֵב, *wâlāv bĕlāv*, v. 2) to puff (יָפִיחַ, *yâphēach*, v. 5) at the righteous. In sharp contrast, the Psalmist rejoiced in the purity and presence of the Words of the Lord (אִמְרוֹת יְהוָה, *'ĭmĕrōth Yĕhōwâh*). He likened God's pure Words (אֲמָרוֹת טְהֹרוֹת, *'ămârōth tĕhōrōth*) to precious silver which is purified through the seven-fold process of refining. The Psalmist declared that not only were God's Words pure but also that they were preserved from that generation forever (לְעוֹלָם, *lĕ'ōlâm*). He stated "thou shalt keep them" (תִּשְׁמְרֵם, *tishmĕrām*), referring back to the closest antecedent, the "words" (אִמְרוֹת, *'ĭmĕrōth*) of the Lord. Even though "words" is fp and the pronominal suffix on the verb "thou shalt keep them" is mp, this gender discordance is not uncommon, especially with reference to the writer's apparent effort to "masculinize" this extension of the patriarchal God – His Words (cf. Psm. 119:111, 129, 152, and 167 for the emphasis of this gender discordance). God's perfectly preserved Words are the only antidote to man's evil words.[398]

Psalm 119:111

The Psalmist rejoiced in the testimonies[399] of the Lord, and he took them as his everlasting heritage. He clearly declared the preservation of the Lord's testimonies (עֵדְוֹתֶיךָ, *'āthĕwōthechâ*, literally "thy testimonies") forever (לְעוֹלָם, *le`ōlâm*) since they (הֵמָּה, *hāmmâh*) were a joyous possession to him, as well as to future generations. Again the man of God referred to the fp noun ("testimonies") with the mp pronoun ("them") to masculinize this extension of God (cf. Psm. 12:6-7).

---

[396]Cf. also Psm. 78:1-8; 105:8; 119:89; Mt. 4:4; Jn. 10:35; and I Pet. 1:23-25.

[397]In the Hebrew Masoretic text the verses are 7 and 8 because the title is counted as verse one.

[398]Jeremiah's last message to Judah was the challenge that they "shall know whose words shall stand, mine, or theirs" (Jer. 44:28). This represents the perennial question of the ultimate authority, man's words or God's.

[399]The Psalmist used 10 different words as synonyms for the Word of God, including law, testimonies, ways, precepts, statutes, commandments, judgments, word, path, and word (utterance).

Psalm 119:152

The Psalmist had knowledge that God's testimonies were founded (יְסַדְתָּם, *yĕsathtâm*)[400] for preservation forever. The plural use of testimonies indicates that the very Words and not merely the concepts of God would be preserved. Again the Lord refers to the fp testimonies with a mp pronominal suffix on the verb to stress the importance of this grammatical anomaly for theological purposes.

Psalm 119:160

The same Psalmist connected the Lord's true (אֱמֶה, *'ĕmeth*)[401] Word and every one of His righteous judgments (מִשְׁפַּט, *mishpat*) with forever (לְעוֹלָם, *le`ōlâm*). The Lord declared through the Psalmist that all of His Words of truth and every one of His judgments would be preserved forever. One must conclude that the theological expression for these aforementioned promises is the perfect, verbal, plenary preservation of the *autographa*.

Isaiah 40:8

Isaiah contrasted the frailty of man with the permanence of God's Word when he uttered, "the grass withereth, the flower fadeth: but the word of our God shall stand for ever" (40:8; cf. v. 7).[402] Surely Isaiah alluded to the very words which he preached and ultimately inscripturated in his book. Isaiah could write (8:1), was commanded to write (30:8), and did write (34:16). Isaiah taught the perfect, verbal, plenary permanence of Scripture.

Matthew 5:17-18

The Lord Jesus Christ had just announced that He came not to destroy but to fulfill the law (v. 17). His fulfillment of the law would be so precise, He promised, that He would not just fulfill the thought of the law and the prophets (OT Scripture), but the very Words of the law, down to each letter or "jot" (*iota*; e.g., the smallest Hebrew letter, a consonant) and to the distinguishing marks above, beneath, and below the consonants or the "tittle" (*keraia*; e.g., "horns," vowels) of the law.[403] The very letters or the very Words of the very sentences of the very prophecies would be fulfilled, the Lord promised. Taken at face value, His promise was that He would fulfill the very Words of prophecy and not just general truths about prophecy, for how would one know if He had indeed fulfilled Scripture, if the very Words of prophecy were not fulfilled?[404]

---

[400]The root of this 2ms verb is *yâsad* meaning "to found, establish, fix."
[401]Truth can only be conveyed through words and not through concepts.
[402]Peter used Isa. 40:8 to affirm the perfect, verbal, plenary preservation of his words in sermons inscripturated in his epistles (1 Pet. 1:23-25).
[403]The Lord used the double negative *ou mā* (οὐ μὴ) for the emphatic negation of any loss of words.
[404]There is no warrant for assuming this promise applies only to the precise fulfillment of prophecy and not to the perfect preservation of all of the Scripture.

Matthew 24:35

The Lord Jesus Christ made the literal[405] promise about the permanency of His Words, stating "Heaven and earth shall pass away, but my words shall not pass away." He used the same root verb "shall pass away, perish, vanish" (παρελεύσονται, *pareleusontai*) for the subjects "generation," "heaven and earth," and "words." He specifically stated His Words (λόγοι, *logoi*), not merely His thoughts (cf. *noāma* [νόημα] in 2 Cor. 10:5 or *logismōn* [λογισμῶν] in Rom. 2:15), would be preserved forever. The Words to which He was referring must be His canonical Words since they will be the basis for judging mankind. After all, the Lord said "He that rejecteth me, and receiveth not my words, hath one that judgeth him: the word that I have spoken, the same shall judge him in the last day" (Jn. 12:48). His preserved Words are the standard for Christian living in every generation and will be the basis for His righteous judgment in the future. All of the Lord's spoken words[406] cannot be in view here since not all of His Words have been preserved and consequently His non-canonical words (*agrapha*) have no Biblical authority. There is one example of the Lord's supposed *agrapha* and God had it inscripturated in Acts 20:35, consequently making "it is more blessed to give than to receive" Biblically authoritative.

The Received Bible

Since the Bible teaches that God has preserved His OT and NT Scriptures both verbally and plenary, mankind has had the basic responsibility to receive God's permanent revelation. Beginning with God's oral revelation to Adam (Gen. 2:16 ff.) and ending with the inscripturation of Christ's Words (Heb. 1:1-2), man has had some or all of the Lord's progressive revelation up until and after the close of the Canon of Scripture. Man has been at the mercy of a gracious God, trusting that He will reveal all truth man needs for time and eternity. When God reveals His truth, man should receive this truth, and apply it accordingly. The Lord Jesus Christ taught and expected that man receive His revelatory truth. Indeed, first generation Christians, fulfilling their responsibility, received the oral revelation (apostolic preaching and teaching) as well as the inscripturated Words of the NT Scripture.

The Teaching of Christ

In the Lord's Prayer (Jn. 17:1-26), Christ revealed that God the Father gave Words (*rhāmata*, ῥήματα) to God the Son. Presumably these Words would be the "all scripture" of 2 Tim. 3:16. Certainly the process to which the Lord Jesus Christ alluded was

---

[405]Nothing in this verse is allegorical or hyperbolic since Scripture promises that heaven and earth will pass away (cf. 2 Pet. 3:10-13) and that God's Words will be preserved (cf. Psm. 12:6-7).

[406]Although not all of the Lord Jesus Christ's deeds and presumably Words were recorded (Jn. 21:25),

the process of inspiration, wherein the Father breathed out His Words to the Son, who in turn breathed out these inerrant and authoritative Words to His Biblical writers. The Lord's Biblical writers, in turn, received the Words and inscripturated them in the Canonical writings which were passed on to future generations, which would believe on the Savior through those writings (cf. v. 20).

This passage teaches several important Bibliological truths. First, the Lord inspired (v. 8) and preserved (v. 20) His Words. Second, man's responsibility was to receive God's inspired and preserved Words. Christ stated that believers "have received them." The word "received" translates *elabon* (ἔλαβον) which is a 3ʳᵈ person, plural, 2nd Aorist, indicative, active verb from *lambanō* (λαμβάνω) and it means "to take" or "to receive." The Lord has required and believers have expected to receive God's preserved Words. The received text mindset did not originate with Erasmus, but with God, Who does not allow the continuity of the preservation of His Words to be broken. The fact that believers in the first century, in the 17ᵗʰ century, and in the 21ˢᵗ century have had a received text mindset,[407] demands that this mindset is built upon Scriptural teaching, not historical necessity.

The Practice in the Churches

Jews who rejected Jesus as their Messiah heard the preaching of Peter about repentance and remission of sins, and received (ἀποδεξάμενοι, *apodexamenoi*) his authoritative words (Acts 2:41). They did not try to change or ignore Peter's preaching, but simply and gladly realized their responsibility before God and received the truth. Peter realized that the first response for these sinners was to receive the Divine revelation that they were sinners who needed the Savior. Christians begin the Christian life with the received text mindset, and must maintain this mindset their entire lives.

Philip preached the word of God in Samaria and Samaritans were saved. The apostles at Jerusalem sent Peter and John to help the church when they heard that Samaritans "had received the word of God" (Acts 8:14). The church in Samaria was established because Samaritans, or half-Jews, had received (δέδεκται, *dedektai*, perfect tense, continued receiving) the Word of God preached by a Jew. Again, sinners, in this case, Samaritans, realized their responsibility before God to receive His salvic revelation.

The Scripture states "that the Gentiles had also received the word of God" (Acts 11:1). They realized their responsibility before God was to receive His revelation, just as the Jews and Samaritans did. Likewise, the Bereans received the word of God and searched the Scriptures daily. Furthermore, the Thessalonians "received the word of God . . . as it is in truth, the word of God" (1 Thess. 2:13).

---

man is only responsible for the Lord's canonical Words found in the OT and NT Scripture.

[407]Believers in 1633 confirmed their belief in receiving the providentially preserved Scripture by naming the common Greek text the *textum . . . nunc ab omnibus receptum* ("the text now received by all").

The teaching of the Bible is clear that man has the responsibility to receive God's revelation. The Lord has revealed Himself through the media of oral and written communication. The Bible teaches that ancient man received the oral preaching and teaching of the prophets and apostles. Furthermore, the Bible teaches that man received the written inscripturation of the revelation of God in the form of the Old and New Testaments. The Bible teaches that the Lord condemns those who reject His revelation and blesses those who receive His revelation. Modern man must receive what God has preserved – the verbal, plenary, written revelation of God.

The Presence of Some False Readings

The early Christians knew from principle and fact that false readings would circulate in their midst. The OT predicted the occurence of such pseudo-revelation within the sovereign plan of God. Moses warned the Jews about false prophets who would prophesy and confirm their prophecy with signs and wonders, stating "If there arise among you a prophet, or a dreamer of dreams, and giveth thee a sign or a wonder, and the sign or the wonder come to pass, whereof he spake unto thee . . . " (Dt. 13:1-2). These false "revelations" would contradict the Lord's previous revelation and would prove if the Jews would hearken unto the false prophets or God. The Lord in His sovereign plan allowed false "revelation" to prove His people, "to know whether ye love the Lord your God with all your heart and with all your soul . . . and keep his commandments, and obey his voice . . . " (vv. 3-4). Rooting out "revelation" that contradicted the Lord's previously given revelation was an exercise in spiritual discernment.

Likewise, NT Christians recognized the fact of false readings that were foisted upon NT Scripture. Peter warned that the text of Pauline literature had been tampered with in the same way as other NT Scripture by pernicious heretics, stating "Paul…as also in all his epistles…which they that are unlearned and unstable wrest, as they do also the other scriptures, unto their own destruction" (2 Pet. 3:15-16). Since the first century local churches were the initial Divine guardians of the NT canon and text (Mt. 28:19-20; 1 Tim. 3:15), they had the responsibility to compare false readings with the *autographa* and reject heretical tampering (1 Thess. 5:21). Furthermore, the early churches had the responsibility to recognize pseudo-canonical literature and reject it, as Paul warned the Thessalonians: "That ye be not soon shaken in mind, or be troubled, neither by spirit, nor by word, nor by letter as from us, as that the day of Christ is at hand" (2 Thess. 2:2). The Lord requires believers to discern between the true and false canon and text of Scripture.[408]

---

[408]The Lord said, "My sheep hear my voice . . . " (Jn. 10:27).

[409]Although some may say preservation has not reached "the level of doctrine," one wonders how many

The Models Tested

The OT and NT Scriptures attest to the promise of verbal, plenary preservation of the Lord's Words. The Lord Jesus Christ not only promised to preserve His Words but also expected His churches to receive and guard His inscripturated Words. Furthermore, He has allowed attacks upon His Words through pseudo-canonical and textual assaults by heretics.

The *TR*/KJB model very clearly holds to the promises of verbal, plenary preservation and the responsibility to receive God's Words. The KJB is built upon the Received Text (*textus receptus*) and has been called "the received Bible." Biblically and historically the *TR*/KJB model has acknowledged and rejected false canonical and textual tampering. This model has rejected the apocryphal efforts of Romanism and the text critical efforts of liberalism. The *TR*/KJB model fits the model predicted in Scripture at these points.

Contrariwise, the CT/MV model rejects the doctrine[409] of verbal, plenary preservation and subsequent reception, and instead promulgates the denial of Biblically stated preservation and the necessity of restoration. Furthermore, this model rejects the Biblical teaching that canonical and textual tampering has occurred and advocates that all manuscripts[410] and all textual variants are part of Divine preservation with no Biblical discernment necessary. This model argues in favor of the imperfect preservation of the text because of the obvious differences in variants that must be sorted out through textual criticism to restore what God never preserved perfectly. The CT/MV model does not fit the model predicted in Scripture at these points.

THE SCRIPTURAL REQUIREMENTS FOR TRANSLATION PRACTICES

Introduction

Since there are over three thousand languages and dialects in the world today, Christians have attempted to translate part or all of God's Word into many of these languages. The Lord God confounded the languages at the Tower of Babel (Gen. 11:1-11) and necessitated the translation of His Word by believers into various languages, using certain translational techniques or practices.

---

times the Scriptures must state a truth before it becomes doctrine.
[410]The popular "totality of manuscripts" view is repudiated by the aforementioned Scriptures.

The Necessity of Translations

The Great Commission requires the translation of the Scriptures into various languages. The Lord commissioned NT immersionist assemblies to "teach all nations (*mathāteusatā panta ta ethnā*) . . . teaching them to observe all things whatsoever I have commanded you" (Mt. 28:19-20). The only way for this to have been accomplished was for the first local churches to translate the Scripture into the languages of the nations reached with the gospel. The Apostle Paul maintained the necessity for translations by stating that the NT revelatory mysteries as well as the OT Scriptures be "made known to all nations for the obedience of faith" (Rom. 16:25-26). The Scripture self-attests to the necessity of its translation.

The Translation Practices

The Bible self-attests to the practices required for translation work. Believers who took their responsibilities seriously no doubt carried out these practices. These responsibilities included a full Scriptural approach to Bibliology and the recognition that God's *autographa* were distinct from man's writing.

Bibliological Practices

The Christians of the first century recognized the necessity of translation work and applied their Bibliology to the practice of translating. For instance, they knew that the apostles wrote Scripture which was inspired by God (2 Tim. 3:16; 2 Pet. 3:16), that the very Words were inspired and preserved (1 Cor. 2:10-14, but especially v. 13), and were inerrant (Psm. 12:6-7; Jn. 10:35). The Apostle John concluded his Apocalypse with a warning in his colophon, stating: "For I testify unto every man that heareth the words of the prophecy of this book, If any man shall add unto these things, God shall add unto him the plagues that are written in this book: And if any man shall take away from the words of the book of this prophecy, God shall take away his part out of the book of life, and out of the holy city, and from the things which are written in this book" (Rev. 22:18-19). This caveat was not just for those copying the *autographa* but also for those handling God's Word in any way, including translating it.

Earlier believers passed on the practice of the careful handling of God's Words to them. For instance, Ezra and thirteen others helped the Jews understand the Law of Moses (Neh. 8:1-8). Whether the Scripture was translated from Hebrew to Aramaic or not, the preachers demonstrated the careful conveyance of God's Words to the people. "They read [aloud] in the book in the law of God distinctly (מְפֹרָשׁ, *mĕphōrâsh*),[411] and gave the sense (שֶׂכֶל, *sĕkĕl*),[412] and caused them to understand (וַיָּבִינוּ, *wayyâvēnū*)[413]

---

[411] This *Pual* participle comes from *pârash,* which means to "separate," "make distinct," or "give the exact sum [of silver]" (cf. Est. 4:7).

[412] This noun means good insight or understanding (cf. Prov. 3:4).

[413] This Qal imperfect verb comes from *bēn* and means to perceive or distinguish.

the reading" (v. 8). Ezra gave the audience the literal, word for word, static equivalency of God's Word. The people understood what the Lord had said to the original audience about the feast of Tabernacles (cf. Lev. 23:34-44).[414]

The Bible is Distinct Literature

The early Christians in the NT churches recognized that the Bible was distinct from man's writings. Paul asseverated this point, stating to the Thessalonians, "For this cause also thank we God without ceasing, because, when ye received the word of God which ye heard of us, ye received it not as the word of men, but as it is in truth, the word of God, which effectually worketh also in you that believe" (1 Thess. 2:13). The Thessalonians obviously had a high view of the *autographa* and were careful not to treat it as any other piece of literature. Paul's two epistles to them were the Word of God, and to be handled accordingly, the Thessalonians realized (cf. again 2 Thess. 2:2).

The Models Tested

The Scriptures attest to the necessity of Bible translations and the proper translational practice for these translations. Gentiles around the world have the need to know what God has said through His written Word. The Scripture self-attests to the proper Bibliological truths translators must hold and implement, including the belief in verbal, plenary inspiration, preservation and perfect inerrancy. They must translate with an effort to reveal distinctly, accurately, and verbally what the Lord said to the original audiences. Furthermore, translators must believe and handle Scripture as distinct from man's literature.

The *TR*/KJB model obviously believes in the necessity of translations since it is one. Furthermore, this model practices the self-attested Bibliological truths of Scripture, holding to inspiration, preservation, and inerrancy, while giving an accurate, word for word, static translation, and recognizing that the Bible is distinct from human literature. The *TR*/KJB model fits the model predicted in Scripture.

However, the CT/MV model rejects the Bibliological truths of preservation and inerrancy, producing a contemporary, culturally satisfying, dynamic equivalent translation,[415] based on textual and translational techniques used on secular literature. The CT/MV model does not fit the model of translation predicted in Scripture.

---

[414] Ezra did not give his audience a contemporary, cultural, dynamic equivalency for God's Word.

[415] Although the NASV and some other modern versions are not dynamic equivalent translations, they fails the Biblical model through their shortcomings relative to "thees and thous" and other translational infelicities.

THE SCRIPTURAL REQUIREMENTS FOR LOCAL CHURCH RESPONSIBILITY

Introduction

The Scripture self-attests to the agency responsible for handling the Bible. In the OT the agency was the Jewish Nation (Rom. 3:1-2)[416] and in the NT the local immersionist assemblies. These churches recognized and received the true revelation and rejected tampered "revelation." The local churches had the responsibility to make the Scriptures generally accessible to every generation and believers would universally recognize these local church-preserved Scriptures as the Words of God.

The Agency of the Local Church

Most of Christendom has acknowledged that the Great Commission (Mt. 28:19-20)[417] is for church age saints. Although definitions for "church" vary, this passage is the mandate for Christianity. An exegetical examination of this passage will reveal the nature and responsibility of churches.

Grammatically, and therefore contextually and Biblically, the Great Commission should be understood around three major parts of speech. The main verbal of Mt. 28:19-20 is the aorist imperative "teach' (μαθητεύσατε, *mathāteusate*) which could be rendered "make disciples" of all nations. The Lord addressed the eleven disciples (μαθηταί, *mathātai*)[418] and instructed them to make disciples as He had discipled them. Associated with this main verbal are the three participles "go" (πορευθέντες, *poreuthentes*), "baptizing" (βαπτίζοντες, *baptizontes*),[419] and "teaching" (διδάσκοντες, *didaskontes*). The first participle functions as a circumstantial participle that is dependent upon the imperative and maintains an imperatival thrust of "go." The remaining two present participles (baptizing, teaching) trailing the imperative are participles of manner, describing more the character of disciples than the means of discipleship. The third significant part of speech is the present

---

[416]Cf. Acts 7:38; Heb. 5:12; I Pet. 4:11.

[417]Other passages that embrace the teaching of the Great Commission include Mk. 16:15; Lk. 24:47; Jn. 22:21; and Acts 1:8.

[418]Although the eleven are the eleven apostles, they are addressed as disciples to represent all disciples who hear and obey (cf. Mt. 12:46-50; 27:57).

[419]The root verb *baptizō* means "to immerse, dip, plunge, dunk, put under" and is distinct from the words *rantizō* ("sprinkle") and *cheō* ("pour"). Scripture teaches the meaning (identification of believer with Christ [Mt. 3:6-8; Rom. 6:3-5]) and the mode (immersion [Mt. 3:16; Col. 2:12]), which mode

infinitive *tārein* (τηρεῖν), meaning "to observe, keep or guard."

The exegetical interpretation of the Great Commission declares that the apostles, representing disciples, were to go to the nations and make disciples of all men, Jew and Gentile, immerse them with reference to the Trinitarian formula for baptism, and instruct them regularly to guard all that the Lord Jesus Christ had commanded. In other words, the Lord commanded his assembly of immersed disciples (Mt. 3:5-11) to establish NT immersionist assemblies instructed in guarding His Words (OT and NT). He promised to be with this movement of immersionist assemblies "alway, even unto the end of the world" (*pasas tas hāmeras heōs tās suntelieias tou aiōnos*, literally "all the days until the completion of the age").

The apostles and early disciples corroborated this exegetical interpretation in the book of Acts.[420] On the day of Pentecost, Peter and the others discipled Jews by preaching the necessity of faith in Jesus of Nazareth the Christ and baptizing and instructing their converts (2:41 ff.). The Samaritans were made disciples, baptized and instructed regularly (8:12). Cornelius and his household were discipled, baptized and instructed (10: 45-48). During Paul's first missionary journey he discipled, baptized and organized churches (14:23). The Philippians (16:32-34), Thessalonians (17:2-4), and Corinthians (18:8) were organized into local churches as Paul carried out the Great Commission. By the end of the first century the Lord addressed seven churches (Rev. 2-3) which were still carrying out the Great Commission (because He was still in their midst [Rev. 1:13, 20]). In fact the church in Philadelphia was commended because she "kept (*etārāsas*) the word" of the Lord (3:10).

In harmony with this interpretation, the Scripture states that God's agency for preserving His truth is "the church of the living God, the pillar and ground of the truth" (1 Tim. 3:15). Contextually, this agency is the one that has bishops and deacons (vv. 1-13). The Scriptures do not countenance either a visible or invisible catholic (universal) church[421] notion involved in preserving truth. Instead, the Lord's local, visible, NT churches have been inextricably linked with His truth.[422]

---

secular literature and the Protestant reformers corroborated. The Lord Jesus Christ Himself, not Baptists, is the "sectarian" who requires believers' immersion only.

[420]The CT/MV model attempts to teach the doctrine of the territorial (visible, catholic) church by favoring variants in Acts 2:47, 8:37, and 9:31.

[421]Neither all Christendom, nor the Roman Catholic Church, nor Protestantism have the responsibility, privilege, or spiritual and theological wherewithal to be involved in the preservation of the Lord's truth.

[422]Based on Scriptural inference, local NT churches have influenced all legitimate manuscript readings and translations.

General Accessibility

Immersionist churches were given the Divine responsibility to guard God's Word.[423] His plan was and still is to preserve His Words through His churches. As churches evangelized the world, they made copies and produced translations. Since the NT church is God's only Scriptural place of special presence, service, and power, and since He gave the responsibility to guard His Word to the churches to whom He promised His permanent presence, it stands that the Lord's churches have indeed preserved His Words every day of the church age. Thus, Scripture attests to the general accessibility of the Words of God for every generation through the agency of the local church. The Lord promised mankind that His canonical Word would be accessible to all generations since it will eventually judge them, saying "He that rejecteth me, and receiveth not my words, hath one that judgeth him: the word that I have spoken, the same shall judge him in the last day" (Jn. 12:48). Historical evidence, which does not reveal all facts and therefore cannot either conclusively affirm or deny the Biblical prediction of general accessibility, should not preempt the promises of Biblical revelation. The OT and NT texts have been preserved perfectly and manifested in vernacular translations for every generation for the last 2,000 years.[424]

Universal Recognition

The first century churches recognized and received the apostolic writings that eventually became the NT canon. They believed the *autographa* were Divine Words for them, which they had the responsibility to receive, preserve, and distribute (cf. Col. 4:16; 2 Pet. 3:16; 2 Jn. 1:12, 2 Jn. 1:9-14; Rev. 2:1, 7 *et al*). The churches were filled with immersed believers who had the indwelling Holy Spirit to guide them into all truth (Jn. 14:26; 15:26; 16:13; I Jn. 2:20, 27). These same believers had the spiritual capacity to hear their Savior's voice and confirm His written Words with His spoken Words (Jn. 10:27). The Lord has guaranteed the universal recognition of His canonical Words through the agency of Spirit-indwelt believers in local assemblies, which in turn have received, preserved and distributed His Words to this very day.

The Models Tested

The Scriptures attest that the Lord planned to preserve His Words through Divinely given institutions, namely Judaism in the OT and the local church in the NT era. The immersionist assembly has had the responsibility throughout the church

---

[423]That the Lord Jesus Christ utilizes fallible mankind in the processes of His infallible Word is irrefutable. The Lord instructed Daniel to keep his writing (i.e. the Book of Daniel) until the end, but then asserted that Daniel's Book would be Divinely kept until the end (Dan. 12:4, 9).

age to guard the Lord's Words for His disciples. Because of the faithfulness of earlier churches, God's Words have been preserved and translated. His institution of the local church has guaranteed not only the general accessibility of all of Scripture but also the universal reception of the Word of God.

The *TR*/KJB model acknowledges what has been received by and preserved in local churches. Consequently, this model recognizes that Scripture has been accessible to every generation. Furthermore, the *TR*/KJB model obviously maintains the Scriptural teaching of the universal reception of the Word of God since it is called "the text received by all." The *TR*/KJB model fits the model predicted in Scripture.

The CT/MV model rejects the truth that the responsibility for maintaining God's Word is for the local church only. This model purports that this responsibility is for scholars within some alleged universal church, irrespective of their individual or collective relationships to Biblical immersionist assemblies. This model rejects the general accessibility of Scripture for every generation and denies the universal recognition of Divine Scripture, since scholars disagree over the variants. The CT/MV model does not fit the model predicted in Scripture.

Conclusion

The Lord Jesus Christ presented in Scripture the translation model He expected His disciples, in any generation and language, to embrace. The Scriptures demand that this model be based on relative Bibliological truths such as the doctrines of inspiration, preservation, translation practices, and local church responsibility. These four doctrines embrace a total of seven Scriptural sub-points, giving a total of eleven significant truths with which to measure translation models.

The Scriptures self-attest to verbal, plenary inspiration and perfect inerrancy, to verbal, plenary preservation, the received Bible, recognition of false readings, the necessity of translations which would be accurate and treated differently from all other literature, and the local church's responsibility to handle Scripture, maintain its general accessibility to mankind in every generation, and recognize canonical books and Words. The *TR*/KJB model fits all eleven Scriptural predictions for the Lord's approved model. The CT/MV does not fit unambiguously nine of the eleven Scriptural predictions for His model. The two truths the CT/MV model does perhaps fit are the predictions for inspiration and the necessity of translations. For a graphic summarization of the respective fitness of the *TR*/KJB and CT/MV models with the Scriptural predictions, see the successive chart.

The tragic failure of the CT/MV model is its man-centered approach to Bibliology. It is permeated with the promotion of human rationalism, the priority of historical

---

[424] Although many manuscripts and early translations were destroyed during the second and third centuries of Christianity, the Lord nevertheless preserved His Word in spite of man's neglect, ignorance or persecution.

evidence, a cavalier attitude towards translation practices, and erroneous agencies for handling the truth. Because this model rejects Scriptural teaching in its theological perspective, it fails to represent the truth in practice. Since it refuses the Lord's teaching on perfect preservation and the agency of the local church, it is unfaithful to God and cannot be trusted. Consequently, believers should reject this translation model that rejects the Lord's truth.

The Lord has predicted the translation model He wanted His people to embrace. The irrefragable conclusion is that the *TR*/KJB model fits the predicted Scriptural model and the CT/MV does not. If the *TR*/KJB model does not give God's people His Words, then Christians do not have them, and have no prospect of ever having them. However, Peter affirmed otherwise with encouraging and edifying words, saying "But the Word of the Lord endureth for ever" (1 Pet. 1:25).

CHART

Translation Model Predicted in Scripture

SCRIPTURAL REQUIREMENTS	TR/KJV	CT/MV
I. Inspiration (verbal, plenary) (II Tim. 3:16-17)	*Yes*	*Yes [?]*
Inerrancy (Psm. 12:6-7)	Yes	Yes [?]
II. Preservation (verbal, plenary) (Mt. 24:35)	*Yes*	*No [Concepts Only]*
Received Bible (Jn. 17:8)	Yes	No [Restored Bible]
Presence of False Readings (Dt. 13:1-5)	Yes	No [Total of MSS]
III. Translations (Rom. 16:25)	*Yes*	*Yes [Paraphrase]*
Accurate (Neh. 8:8)	Yes	No [Dynamic Equiv.]
Different from secular literature (I Thess. 2:13)	Yes	No [Same]
IV. Local Church Responsibility (Mt. 28:19-20)	*Yes*	*No [Univ. Church]*
General Accessibility (Jn. 12:48)	Yes	No [Limited]
Universal Recognition (Jn. 10:27)	Yes	No [Scholars Disagree]

ADDENDUM C

The Superiority of the Fideistic Approach to Preservation of Scripture
Kent Brandenburg

The Just Shall Live By Faith

God told Habakkuk, prophet to Judah, in Habakkuk 2:4, " . . . the just shall live by his faith." Faith in God is essential for pleasing Him (Heb. 11:6). The Scriptures are replete with this indispensable distinction in the lives of the just. Moses said, "The LORD *is* my strength and song, and he is become my salvation: he *is* my God, and I will prepare him an habitation; my father's God, and I will exalt him" (Ex. 15:2). David said, "I will love thee, O LORD, my strength. The LORD *is* my rock, and my fortress, and my deliverer; my God, my strength, in whom I will trust; my buckler, and the horn of my salvation, *and* my high tower. I will call upon the LORD, *who is worthy* to be praised: so shall I be saved from mine enemies" (Ps. 18:1-3). Jeremiah said, "The LORD *is* my portion, saith my soul; therefore will I hope in him" (Lam. 3:24). Paul said, "For therefore we both labour and suffer reproach, because we trust in the living God, who is the Saviour of all men, specially of those that believe" (1 Tim. 4:10). John said, "Whosoever shall confess that Jesus is the Son of God, God dwelleth in him, and he in God. And we have known and believed the love that God hath to us. God is love; and he that dwelleth in love dwelleth in God, and God in him" (1 John 4:15-16).

The prophet Habakkuk had been wondering why God did not intervene in the circumstances of Judah and set things straight (Hab. 1:2-4). He expected that the Lord would either bring spiritual revival to Judah or judge her for her wickedness. But God was doing neither, and this did not fit his own reasoning. The Lord answers Habakkuk's dilemma in the following verses (Hab. 1:5-11), but His answer also contradicted the prophet's own reasoning. The Chaldeans were a pagan people, and it did not make sense to him that God would use these pagans, a people far worse than even Judah, as a means of judgment. Habakkuk began examining his theology to get an understanding of these things (Hab. 1:12). In so doing, he recognized that God was eternal, omnipotent, sovereign, holy, and faithful. God explained to Habakkuk that the righteous live by faith (Hab. 2:4), that is, they just believe God based upon His Word. Later in this Old Testament prophecy, Habakkuk determined that even if the entirety of the normal circumstances of life were completely turned around, he would still rejoice in God (Hab. 3:17-19). God had given him the surefooted stability of the mountain goat. This is the confidence that believers have in the Lord, even before He clearly manifests His plan to them.

Living by faith is so integral to and synonymous with Biblical Christianity, and such a foundational truth in the New Testament, that this declaration of the Lord to Habakkuk is quoted in three New Testament passages (Rom. 1:17; Gal. 3:11; Heb. 10:38). The believer is a believer; he lives by faith because that is what it is to be a Christian. Faith is the basis of the righteousness from which someone lives (Rom. 1:17; Gal. 3:11). Those who do not live by faith are apostates and the Lord has no pleasure in them (Heb. 10:38). Faithlessness is a serious issue for serious people.

Mary, the mother of the Lord Jesus Christ, strived to believe in the miraculous conception and birth of Christ. Nothing in the context of Mary's reasoning and experience prepared her to believe this miracle was occurring. She expressed this in Luke 1:34 when she asked the angel Gabriel, who had announced Christ's birth to her, "How can this be, seeing I know not a man?" There is no certain record of an angel having talked to anyone on earth for over 400 years until Gabriel came to Zacharias and then came to Mary. Furthermore, no virgin birth had ever occurred, and Mary was and knew she was a virgin. God revealed through His holy angel that the Holy Ghost would come upon her. He also told her that her older relative Elizabeth was pregnant in another miraculous birth. The angel culminated this reassurance of Mary with the statement, "For with God nothing shall be impossible." The root of faith is the truth that nothing is impossible with God.

No man has witnessed creation, but by faith the Christian receives what God says about the origin of life (Heb. 11:3). Human reasoning does not fathom that tangible things were created from only words. Man cannot comprehend, except by faith, the instantaneous creation of something out of nothing. Similarly, Noah had not seen any rain or flood, but he trusted in the Lord and persisted in building the ark based, again, on what God had said (Heb. 11:7).

Based upon the cumulative faith passages in Scripture (especially Heb. 11:1-3; Rom. 10:17; cf. John 17:17), what is faith? Faith is a firm persuasion or conviction that everything that God says in His Word is true, that Scripture is authoritative when it speaks in every matter. Faith is the willing reception of Divine truth, the full assurance of the veracity of every teaching from God's Word. Faith is recognizing in mind and will that God and His Word, Which are real, are more real than even the personal

---

[425] See the previous chapters of this book (sections one through three).
[426] See *Addendum* B by Thomas Strouse entitled, "The Translation Model Predicted by Scripture."

experience of the believing individual. Faith is taking God at His Word. Faith is the relinquishing of the mind, emotions, and will to anything and everything that God said. Faith is the surrender of the soul to Who God says He is. It is possible for only that of faith to please God (Heb. 11:6).

Scripture promises the perfect preservation and availability of all the Words of God to every generation.[425] Since this is what God says, it is what faith expects. Based on these promises, one assumes that before the printing press all the Words were available in hand-made copies, and afterwards in the printed editions. Fulfillment of the Biblical teachings of perfect preservation and availability require the amalgamation of all the Words into one canonical, printed edition. The text behind the King James Version alone fulfills this Scriptural model.[426] The view of a perfect and available text fits with all the passages on preservation, and, therefore, this is the fideistic view of preservation of Scripture.

The Repudiation of Dependence upon Man's Thinking

On the other hand, God in His Word repeatedly repudiates reliance on human understanding and philosophy. While God is pleased by faith, He is not pleased when people choose their own thinking over His Words. Proverbs 3:5 clearly states this, saying, "Trust in the LORD with all thine heart; and lean not unto thine own understanding." God's Words should be trusted and followed because they are superior to man's. God pronounces this in Isaiah 55:8,9, declaring, "For my thoughts *are* not your thoughts, neither *are* your ways my ways, saith the LORD. For *as* the heavens are higher than the earth, so are my ways higher than your ways, and my thoughts than your thoughts." In the following two verses (Is. 55:10,11), God commends His Word as that upon which men can depend, saying, "For as the rain cometh down, and the snow from heaven, and returneth not thither, but watereth the earth, and maketh it bring forth and bud, that it may give seed to the sower, and bread to the eater: so shall my word be that goeth forth out of my mouth: it shall not return unto me void, but it shall accomplish that which I please, and it shall prosper *in the thing* whereto I sent it." The tendency of the thoughts of mankind is represented by man's condition before the flood, as described in Genesis 6:5, "And GOD saw that the wickedness of man *was* great in the earth, and *that* every imagination of the thoughts of his heart *was* only evil continually."[427] The Lord said in Mark 7:21, "For from within, out of the heart of men, proceed evil thoughts . . . .." Rather than the Bible being subjected to man's thoughts, man's thoughts ought to be subjected to the Bible (Hebrews 4:12).[428] Men are admonished to be very careful with

---

[427] Also Genesis 8:21, "And the LORD smelled a sweet savour; and the LORD said in his heart, I will not again curse the ground any more for man's sake; for the imagination of man's heart *is* evil from his youth; neither will I again smite any more every thing living, as I have done."

their "knowledge."[429] Instead of relying on human philosophy, God says to beware of it.[430] What seems right to man will often have tragic consequences.[431]

Men who question what God said, rather than believing it, insult the Lord. Scripture thoroughly dispels this human claim of Divine impotence. God does not want His ability questioned[432] or His way (timing or manner) disputed;[433] since He has proven Himself totally and sufficiently, He simply wants to be believed.[434] The hypothesis that God did not preserve His Words, so man needs to restore them, lies at the root of textual criticism. This line of thinking rejects what Scripture states about preservation, depending instead on the uninspired words of men, both contemporary and historical.[435] On the basis of their futile, temporal thoughts, men argue that it is unreasonable to accept that somehow every Word has remained available for every generation. In so doing, these men have wrested from their particular circle of influence the assurance of a perfect Bible. The responsibility exhorted and the example patterned in the New Testament is the reception, not restoration, of God's Words.[436] The willingness to receive them and the assurance that they are all perfectly available is based upon God's promises to preserve every Word. Faith and doubt are mutually exclusive (Rom. 14:23). Any application of the pertinent passages on preservation that does not leave one with the assurance that he has a Bible with all the Words of God cannot be accepted from a position of faith. The position that all the Words exist somewhere, but are still yet to be found, does not fit into the teaching of Scripture, and, therefore, must be rejected.

Great Faith Versus Little Faith

The Lord Jesus Christ, impressed with the faith of a centurion in Matthew 8:10, said concerning him, "Verily I say unto you, I have not found so great faith, no, not in Israel." The understanding of "great faith" is qualitative, not quantitative; it is not

---

[428]"For the word of God *is* quick, and powerful, and sharper than any twoedged sword, piercing even to the dividing asunder of soul and spirit, and of the joints and marrow, and *is* a discerner of the thoughts and intents of the heart."

[429]1 Corinthians 8:2, "And if any man think that he knoweth any thing, he knoweth nothing yet as he ought to know."

[430]Colossians 2:8, "Beware lest any man spoil you through philosophy and vain deceit, after the tradition of men, after the rudiments of the world, and not after Christ."

[431]Proverbs 14:12, "There is a way which seemeth right unto a man, but the end thereof *are* the ways of death."

[432]Isaiah 59:1, "Behold, the LORD'S hand is not shortened, that it cannot save; neither his ear heavy, that it cannot hear."

[433]2 Peter 3:9,10, "The Lord is not slack concerning his promise, as some men count slackness . . . But the day of the Lord will come . . . "

[434]Isaiah 45:6-10, " That they may know from the rising of the sun, and from the west, that *there is* none beside me. I *am* the LORD, and *there is* none else. I form the light, and create darkness: I make peace, and create evil: I the LORD do all these *things*. Drop down, ye heavens, from above, and let the skies pour

an amount of faith, but a kind of faith. That great faith is not quantitative is seen in the Lord's expression, "faith as a grain of mustard seed" (Matthew 17:20). The term "great" carries with it a temporal aspect. "Great faith" is "long-termed faith." Such faith persists through the kinds of opposition that normally hinder people from believing. When the Lord said someone has "little faith" (Mt. 6:30, 8:26, 14:31, 16:8), He meant he had faith that would not endure opposition. An understanding of the kinds of dissension that stop one little in faith can manifest whether one today had "little faith." In Matthew 6:30 the "little faith" is manifested by worry over whether God will take care of his needs. The fear of a storm impels the Lord to confront the disciples in a boat on the Sea of Galilee over their "little faith" (Matthew 8:26, and again in 14:31). In Matthew 16:8, when the Lord warns the disciples of the leaven of the Pharisees, instead of attending to the Lord's warning, they thought about not having any bread. He called that "little faith." They should have persisted in their belief that God could provide their needs, especially in light of His feeding of the five thousand, but they did not.

The "little faith" of some manifests itself by their denial of the Second Coming, since it has been so long since the Lord ascended into heaven (2 Peter 3:3,4). The "little faith" of others is revealed by their unwillingness to continue believing that God can keep them saved (1 Peter 1:5). The refutation from "textual scholars" is most often enough to expose the "little faith" of these who do not believe in the perfect preservation of Scripture. The "little faith" of these wavers under mounds of published writings of men. Perfect preservation requires a miracle. The absence of sufficient human explanation and "adequate" historical documentation is enough of a hindrance to the "little faith" of many on the issue of preservation. The need for a miracle from God in the consolidation of all the Words into one available edition of Scripture is enough to stop the belief of some. To many, there is no reasonable justification to depend on Divine providence, so alternative views are concocted and the numbers of "doctrines of Scripture" that have been preserved are emphasized.[437]

The basis for perfect preservation is faith; other views are built on human rational-

---

down righteousness: let the earth open, and let them bring forth salvation, and let righteousness spring up together; I the LORD have created it. Woe unto him that striveth with his Maker! *Let* the potsherd *strive* with the potsherds of the earth. Shall the clay say to him that fashioneth it, What makest thou? or thy work, He hath no hands? Woe unto him that saith unto *his* father, What begettest thou? or to the woman, What hast thou brought forth?"

[435]There are many examples of this reliance on contemporary or historical "scholarship." For example, Glenny on p. 81, declares: "Kurt Aland recently found 52 variants in the Majority text-type in two verses (2 Cor. 1:6,7)." Glenny also quotes R. W. Klein on p. 84, saying, "Samuel's MT is a poor text, marked by extensive haplography and corruption – only the MT of Hosea and Ezekiel is in worse condition." In light of what the Bible says on preservation, the answer to Glenny, or anyone like him, is: "Who cares what Aland or Klein thought or said?"

[436]See chapter four on John 17:8 by Thomas Strouse.

[437]Douglas Kutilek, in his *Westcott and Hort vs. Textus Receptus: Which Is Superior?* Research Report Number 45 (Hatfield, PA: Interdisciplinary Biblical Research Institute, 1996), on p. 12 says, "No fundamental point of doctrine rests upon a disputed reading: and the truths of Christianity are expressed in the text of Westcott and

ism, "the doctrine that human reason, unaided by Divine revelation, is an adequate or the sole guide to attainable religious truth."[438] People who take a view that is "unaided by Divine revelation" are not normally known as Bible-believers, therefore, most people that profess to be Bible-believers do not usually want to consider their positions rationalistic.

Those who espouse the "majority" text view claim to simply determine what words are found in the majority of the manuscripts, and the words that survive that test are essentially deemed to be the text of Scripture. Counting is the sole criterion. This is rationalistic.[439] The proponents of the minority text view use the humanly devised laws of textual criticism, which treat the Bible like uninspired books, in an attempt to ascertain the readings most likely found in the original manuscripts. This view also applies human reason as the sole guide. Neither of these could be considering the God of the Bible, for neither of them provides perfection, and God is perfect. He is perfect, and He is powerful enough to keep something perfect, from the soul of a man to every Word of Scripture. In contrast, the received text position receives what God has supernaturally preserved by faith. Some advocates of the received text do not believe in perfect preservation, basing their position upon Divine providence alone.[440] However, received text people at least depend on Scriptural principles to defend their position. In many cases, the other points of view do their best to argue away as many texts on preservation as possible,[441] and contend that faith is an invalid criterion for receiving the perfect text of Scripture.[442] This is in line with centuries of satanic rationalism.

Becoming Like a Little Child

On more than one occasion, the Lord Jesus Christ asserts a prerequisite for kingdom citizenship is becoming "like a little child" (Matthew 18:2-5; Mark 10:15; Luke 18:17). Little children are simple, dependent, helpless, unaffected, unpretentious, and unambitious. A little child is sinful, but he is naive and unassuming, trusting of others.

Hort as in that of Stephanus." There are many of these kinds of statements that attempt to shift the focus of preservation to "doctrines" rather than "words," even though there is nowhere in the Bible that God said that He would preserve "the doctrines" (this is not to say that He would not preserve the doctrines, since they are found in and built upon the Words). This shift in emphasis is the same shift that was made to produce the neo-orthodox view of inspiration. They fit the same pattern, so this shift in emphasis is telltale. Both the neo-orthodox view of inspiration and this rationalistic view of preservation leave one with a Bible that contains errors.

[438] *Websters New Universal Unabridged Dictionary* (New York: Random House, 1996), p. 1602.

[439] This author calls this the "math view." Thousands more copies of the *TR* exist today than those of the Hodges-Farstad text (called the "majority" text). The *TR* text printed by the Trinitarian Bible Society and Bible For Today (Scrivener's 1881) remains the true majority text. Jack Moorman deals excellently with this issue in his book, *Hodges/Farstad 'Majority' Text Refuted By Evidence* (Collingswood, NJ: Bible For Today, [N.d.]).

[440] Based on Scripture, they are in error.

[441] There are many contemporary examples of this, such as Combs' "The Preservation of Scripture, pp. 3-44.

[442] Normally, the attack on faith looks something like this: "Because the Bible makes no explicit promise that God would preserve every word in one printed edition, there is no basis for believing that God did this; therefore, one should conclude that there is either no Scriptural basis for preservation of Scripture, that God has preserved

These are the applicable qualities of the one who will enter the kingdom of God. So much in the plan of salvation is unbelievable to the intellectual, from the virgin birth, to the incarnation itself, to the blood atonement. The simplicity of God's plan results in Him receiving the praise and glory. This is His stated purpose for choosing the weak and foolish things of the world -- that no flesh should glory in His presence (1 Corinthians 1:21-29). The rationalist considers the doctrine of one perfect, available edition of the complete Bible untenable because of rationalistic concerns. The one with the faith of a little child can suspend those concerns and receive by faith that God did just what He said He would do.

Faith is often ridiculed as unintelligent or unreasonable, almost naive (a "leap in the dark"). The rationalist will attack inspiration with apostate source criticism, to give a humanistic explanation for the origin of Scripture. Such theological liberals say that their approach is the intelligent alternative to the doctrine of inspiration. The attack on perfect preservation is founded upon the same premise. Instead of just believing God, men speculate on the percentage of error assumed to exist. The wobbly foundation upon which the rationalist-preservationist stands is the assertion that "all of the doctrines alone have been preserved," which effectually leaves the believer with a conceptual preservation. This is not acceptable to the "little child" type of faith. The "little child" is "naive" enough to believe that no matter how complex the rationalistic argument is against one perfect edition of the Bible, it must be rejected.

The wisdom of God is faith while the wisdom of this world, which is earthly, sensual, and devilish, is rationalism (James 3:15). As persuasive as it may be, external evidence is only authoritative insofar as it lines up with what God has said. If it does not, then it can only fit into the "wisdom of this world" category. The preservation debate is a trying of faith (James 1:3). The faith that passes the test is one that rejects this wisdom of the world and receives with meekness the Word, which, unlike mere concepts, is able to save men's souls (James 1:21). That is what childlike faith will do.

---

every word only somewhere on planet earth, found or not, or that God has every word in safe-keeping next to Him in heaven." The words "trinity" and "rapture" do not appear in the Bible, but this does not demonstrate these doctrines do not reside in God's Word. The words "one printed edition" also do not appear in Scripture, but this does not mean that the Bible does not teach "one printed edition." Larry D. Pettegrew argues in this manner in *The Bible Version Debate*, pp. 31-33, saying, "It is *not* (emphasis his) biblical faith to trust in human assumptions which are only peripherally associated with the explicit revelation from God. For example, it is biblical faith to believe that Noah built an ark that safely housed his family and numerous animals during a universal deluge. The Scriptures explicitly say it was so. However, it is not biblical faith to believe that Noah's ark has been perfectly preserved in the ice on top of Mount Ararat . . . it is not Biblical faith to believe that God, through providence or direct superintendence, oversaw the production of on particular copy, edition, or translation of Scripture in order to perfectly replicate the autographs. The Bible nowhere teaches the notion. Extending the concept of faith to include secondary, non-biblical assertions is both cultic and unscriptural." Preservation of Noah's ark obviously does not parallel preservation of Scripture because God did not promise to preserve the ark. Pettegrew calls men "cultic" who believe in the perfect preservation of the Bible in one printed edition (classic *ad hominem* argument, logical fallacy). By explaining away or ignoring the Bible, he concludes that "the Bible nowhere teaches the notion," just like Jehovah's Witnesses argue away the doctrine of the Trinity.

Conclusion

A common critique by theological liberalism of Biblical fundamentalism is that it is "anti-intellectual and otherworldly."[443] Professing fundamentalists levy this same critique against New Testament churches that believe God has perfectly preserved His Words in one printed edition. What is called "anti-intellectual" is actually faith. New Testament churches have always believed the Bible to be their only authority for faith and practice, knowing that the "just shall live by faith." God is pleased by faith, not by man's reasoning. The only Scriptural approach to the doctrine of the preservation of Scripture is the fideistic approach. The only view based on a response of faith in God's Word is the view that God has perfectly preserved His Words and that they are and have been available to every generation.

---

[443] *The Testimony* of Central Baptist Theological Seminary (Fall, 2001, Vol. 43, No. 1), on the back side, says, "Richard Mouw's address critiqued fundamentalism for its supposed anti-intellectualism, its otherworldliness, and its separatism."

SELECT BIBLIOGRAPHY

Critical Text

Books

Aland, Kurt and Barbara. *The Text of the New Testament.* Grand Rapids, MI: Wm. B. Eerdmans Publishing Co., 1987.

Aland, Kurt. et. al. eds. *The Greek New Testament.* London: United Bible Societies, 1968. 2nd Revised Edition.

_____. *The Greek New Testament.* New York: United Bible Societies, 1975. Third Revised Edition.

Aland, Barbara. et. al. eds. *The Greek New Testament.* Stuttgart: United Bible Societies, 2001. Fourth Revised Edition.

Baigent, Michael and Richard Leigh. *The Dead Sea Scrolls Deception.* New York: Summit Books, 1991.

Beacham, Roy E. and Bauder, Kevin T. (eds.) *One Bible Only?* Grand Rapids, MI: Kregel Publications, 2001.

Brotzman, Ellis R. *Old Testament Textual Criticism: A Practical Introduction.* Grand Rapids, MI: Baker Books, 1994.

Bruce, F. F. *Are the New Testament Documents Reliable?* Grand Rapids, MI: Wm. B. Eerdmans Publishing Co., 1954.

Bruce, F. F. *Second Thoughts on the Dead Sea Scrolls.* Grand Rapids, MI: Wm. B. Eerdmans Publishing Co., 1956.

Carson, D. A. *The King James Version Debate: A Plea for Realism.* Grand Rapids, MI: Baker Book House, 1979.

Colwell, Ernest C. *Studies in Methodology in Textual Criticism of the New Testament.* Leiden: E. J. Brill, 1969.

_____. *What is the Best New Testament?* Chicago: The University of Chicago Press, 1952.

Comfort, Philip W. and Barrett, David P. (eds.). *The Complete Text of the Earliest New Testament Manuscripts.* Grand Rapids, MI: Baker Books, 1999.

Custer, Stewart. *Does Inspiration Demand Inerrancy?* Nutley, NJ: Craige Press, 1968.

_____. *The Truth about the King James Controversy.* Greenville, SC: Bob JonesUniversity Press, 1981.

Ellicott, C. J., J. B. Lightfoot, and Richard Chenevix Trench. *The Revision of the English Version of the New Testament.* New York: Harper & Brothers, 1873. 3 Volumes.

Elliott, J. K. *Essays and Studies in New Testament Textual Criticism.* Cordoba: Ediciones El Almendro, 1992.

Epp, Eldon Jay and Gordon D. Fee. *Studies in the Theory and Method of New Testament Textual Criticism.* Grand Rapids, MI: Wm. B. Eerdmans Publishing Co., 1993.

Farmer, W. R. *The Last Twelve Verses of Mark.* Cambridge: Cambridge University Press, 1974.

Finegan, Jack. *Encountering New Testament Manuscripts: A Working Introduction to Textual Criticism.* Grand Rapids, MI: Wm. B. Eerdmans Publishing Co., 1974.

Greenlee, J. H. *Introduction to New Testament Textual Criticism.* Grand Rapids: Wm. B. Eerdmans Publishing Co., 1964.

Grisanti, Michael (ed.). *The Bible Version Debate*. Minneapolis, MN: Central Baptist Theological Seminary, 1997.

Hammond, C. E. *Outlines of Textual Criticism Applied to the New Testament*. Oxford: The Clarendon Press, 1880.

Kenyon, Frederick G. *Handbook to the Textual Criticism of the New Testament*. Grand Rapids: Wm. B. Eerdmans Publishing Co., 1951.

Klein, Ralph W. *Textual Criticism of the Old Testament: The Septuagint after Qumran*. Philadelphia: Fortress Press, 1974.

Lake, Kirsopp. *The Text of the New Testament*. 6th ed. Revised by Silva New. London: Rivingtons, 1959.

McCarter, P. Kyle. *Textual Criticism: Recovering the Text of the Hebrew Bible*. Philadelphia: Fortress Press, 1986.

Metzger, Bruce M. *A Textual Commentary on the Greek New Testament*. London: United Bible Societies, 1975.

_____. *The Text of the New Testament*. London: Oxford University Press, 1964.

Nestle, Erwin and Aland, Kurt. *Novum Testamentum Graece*. 24th ed. Stuttgart: Privilegierte Wurttembergische Bibelanstalt, 1960.

Nestle, Eberhard. *Introduction to the Textual Criticism of the Greek New Testament*, translated from the 2nd edition, with corrections and additions by the author, by William Edie, and edited with a preface by Allan Menzies. New York: G. P. Putnam's Sons, 1901.

Parvis, Merrill M. and Wikgren, A. P. (eds.). *New Testament Manuscript Studies*. Chicago: The University of Chicago Press, 1950.

Robertson, A. T. *An Introduction to the Textual Criticism of the New Testament*. Garden City, NY: Doubleday, Doran & Company, 1928.

Salmon, George. *Some Thoughts on the Textual Criticism of the New Testament*. London, 1897.

Soden, Hermann F. von. *Die Schriften des Neuen Testaments*. 2 vols. Goettingen: Vandenhoeck und Ruprecht, 1911.

Souter, Alexander. *The Text and Canon of the New Testament*. London: Gerald Duckworth and Co., Ltd., 1965.

Streeter, Burnett H. *The Four Gospels: A Study of Origins*. London: Macmillan and Co., 1930.

Tasker, R. V. G. (ed.). *The Greek New Testament*. Oxford: Oxford University Press, 1964.

Taylor, Vincent. *The Text of the New Testament*. NY: St. Martin's Press Inc., 1961.

Tischendorf, Constantinus. *Novum Testamentum Graece*. 8th ed. 2 vols. Lipsiae: Giesecke and Devrient, 1869-72.

Thuesen, Peter J. *In Discordance with the Scriptures*. Oxford: Oxford University Press, 1999.

Tov, Emanuel. *Textual Criticism of the Hebrew Bible*. Minneapolis: Fortress Press, 1992.

Vaganay, Leo. *An Introduction to the Textual Criticism of the New Testament*. Transl. by B. V. Miller. London: Sands and Co., Ltd., 1937.

Voobus, Arthur. *Early Versions of the New Testament*. Stockholm: Estonian Theological Society in Exile, 1954.

Westcott, Brooke Foss and Hort, Fenton John Anthony. *The New Testament in the Original Greek*. 2 vols. London: Macmillan and Co., 1881.

White, James R. *The King James Only Controversy*. Minneapolis, MN: Bethany House Publishers, 1995.

Whitney, S. W. *A Critical Examination of Certain Readings, Textual and Marginal, in the Original Greek of the New Testament*. Boston, 1892. 2 Volumes.

Williams, James B. (ed.). *From the Mind of God to the Mind of Man*. Greenville, SC: Ambassador-Emerald International, 1999.

Wurthwein, Ernst. *The Text of the Old Testament.* Translated by Erroll F. Rhodes. Grand Rapids, MI: Wm. B. Eerdmans Publishing Co., 1979.

Articles

Aland, Kurt. "The Greek New Testament: Its Present and Future Editions," *Journal of Biblical Literature,* 87 (June, 1968), 179-86.

Birdsall, J. Neville. "Current Trends and Present Tasks in New Testament Textual Criticism." *Baptist Quarterly,* 17 (July, 1957), 109-14.

Black, Matthew. "The United Bible Societies' Greek New Testament Evaluation Reply, *The Bible Translator,* 28 (1977), 116-120.

Bruce, F. F. "The End of the Second Gospel," *Evangelical Quarterly,* (July, 1935), 169-81.

Clark, Kenneth W. "The Theological Relevance of Textual Variation in Current Criticism of the Greek New Testament," *Journal of Biblical Literature,* 85:1 (March, 1966), 1-16.

Colwell, Ernest Cadman. "Genealogical Method: Its Achievements and Its Limitations," *Journal of Biblical Literature,* 66 (1947), 109-33.

Combs, William. "Erasmus and the *Textus Receptus.*" *Detroit Baptist Seminary Journal* 1:1 (Spring, 1996): 35-53.

_____. "The Preface to the King James Version and the King James-Only Position." *Detroit Baptist Seminary Journal* (Fall, 1996): 253-67.

Fee, Gordon D. "Modern Textual Criticism and the Revival of the *Textus Receptus.*" *Journal of the Evangelical Theological Society* 21 (1978): 19-33.

Kutilek, Douglas. *Westcott and Hort vs. Textus Receptus: Which Is Superior?* Research Report Number 45. Hatfield, PA: Interdisciplinary Biblical Research Institute, 1996.

Schnaiter, Samuel E. "Textual Criticism and the Modern English Version Controversy." In Focus on Revelation. XVI no. 1 of *Biblical Viewpoint.* Edited by Stewart Custer. Greenville, S.C.: Bob Jones University Press, 1982.

Wallace, Daniel B. "Some Second Thoughts on the Majority Text." *Bibliotheca Sacra* 146:583 (July-September, 1989): 270-90.

_____. "Inspiration, Preservation, and New Testament Textual Criticism." *Grace Theological Journal* 12:1 (Spring 1992): 21-50.

_____. "The Majority Text and the Original Text: Are They Identical?" *Bibliotheca Sacra* 148:590 (April-June 1991): 158-66.

_____. "Mark 1:2 and New Testament Textual Criticism." *Biblical Studies Press,* available at http://www.bibl.org, 1997.

"Majority" Text

Books

Hodges, Zane C. *A Defense of the Majority Text.* Dallas, TX: Dallas Theological, N.d.
_____, and Arthur Farstad, eds. *The Greek New Testament According to the Majority Text.* 2nd edition. Nashville, TN: Thomas Nelson Publishers, 1985.
Letis, Theodore P. (ed.) *The Majority Text: Essays and Reviews in the Continuing Debate.* Grand Rapids, MI: Institute for Biblical Textual Studies, 1987.
Pickering, Wilbur N. *The Identity of the New Testament Text.* Nashville, TN: Thomas Nelson Publishers, 1977.
Sturz, Harry A. *The Byzantine Text-Type and New Testament Textual Criticism.* New York: Thomas Nelson Publishers, 1984.

Articles

Borland, James A. "The Preservation of the New Testament Text," *The Master's Seminary Journal* (Spring 1999), 41-51.
Hodges, Zane C. "Modern Textual Criticism and the Majority Text: A Response," Journal *of the Evangelical Theological Society,* 21:2 (June, 1978), 143-145.
_____. "Modern Textual Criticism and the Majority Text: A Surrenjoinder," Journal *of the Evangelical Theological Society,* 21:2 (June, 1978), 161-164.

Textus Receptus

Books

Abbot, Ezra. *A Defense of the Reading "Only Begotten Son" in John 1:18.* 1856, 1861, 1875. Reprinted by Pensacola, FL: Vance Publications.
Birks, T. R. *Essay on the Right Estimation of Manuscript Evidence in the Text of the New Testament.* London: Macmillan, 1878.
Burgon, John W. *The Last Twelve Verses of the Gospel According to S. Mark Vindicated Against Recent Critical Objectors and Established.* London: James Parker and Co., 1871.
_____. *The Revision Revised.* Fort Worth: A. G. Hobbs Publications, 1983 Reprint.
_____, and Miller, Edward. *The Causes of the Corruption of the Traditional Text of the Holy Gospels.* London: George Bell and Sons, 1896.
_____, and Miller, Edward. *The Traditional Text of the Holy Gospels Vindicated and Established.* London: George Bell and Sons, 1896
Clark, Gordon H. *Logical Criticisms of Textual Criticism.* Jefferson, MD: The Trinity Foundation, 1986.
Clarke, Kent D. *Textual Optimism: A Critique of the United Bible Societies' Greek New Testament.* Sheffield, England: Sheffield Academic Press, 1997.
Cloud, David. *Dynamic Equivalency: Death Knell of Pure Scripture.* Oak Harbor, WA: Way of Life Literature, 1990.
_____. *For the Love of the Bible.* Oak Harbor, WA: Way of Life Literature, 1999.

_____. *Myths about the King James Bible.* 5 Vol. Oak Harbor, WA: Way of Life Literature, 1999.

_____. *Way of Life Encyclopedia of the Bible and Christianity.* Oak Harbor, WA: Way of Life Literature, 1994.

Coy, George H. *The Inside Story of the Anglo American Revised New Testament.* Dallas, OR: Itemizer-Observer, 1973.

Fowler, E. W. *Evaluating Versions of the New Testament.* Watertown, WI: Maranatha Baptist Press, 1981.

Fuller, David Otis. *Counterfeit or Genuine?* Grand Rapids: Kregel, 1975.

_____. *True or False?* Grand Rapids: Kregel, 1973.

_____. *Which Bible?* Grand Rapids: Kregel, 1970.

Green, Jay P. *The Gnostics, The New Versions, and The Deity of Christ.* Lafayette, IN: Sovereign Grace Publishers, N. d.

Green Jay P. *The New Versions and the Doctrines of Grace.* Lafayette, IN: Sovereign Grace Publishers, N. d.

Henderson, Ebenezer, and Moses Stuart. *A Defense of the Reading "God Was Manifest in the Flesh" in 1 Timothy 3:16.* 1832. Reprinted by Pensacola, FL: Vance Publications.

Hills, Edward. *The King James Version Defended!* Des Moines, IA: The Christian Research Press, 1973.

Hoskier, H. C. *Codex B and Its Allies: A Study and an Indictment.* London: Bernard Quaritch, 1914.

_____. *Manuscripts of the Apocalypse: Recent Investigations.* Aberdeen, NY: The University Press, 1922.

Hymers, R. L. *Ruckmanism Exposed.* Collingswood, NJ: The Bible For Today, 1987.

Letis, Theodore P. *The Ecclesiastical Text.* Philadelphia, PA: Institute for Renaissance and Reformation Biblical Studies, 2000 (2nd ed).

_____. *Edward Freer Hills's Contribution to the Revival of the Ecclesiastical Text.* Thesis for the Master of Theological Studies, Candler School of Theology, 1987.

Malan, Solomon Caesar. *A Plea for the Received Greek Text and for the Authorised Version of the New Testament.* London: Hatchards, 1869.

_____. *A Vindication of the Authorized Version of the English Bible from Charges Brought Against It by Recent Writers.* London: Bell and Daldy, 1856.

Mauro, Philip. *Which Version? Authorized or Revised?* Boston: Scripture Truth Depot, 1924.

Maynard, Michael. *A History of the Debate over 1 John 5:7-8: A Tracing of the Longevity of the Comma Johanneum.* Tempe, AZ: Comma Publications, 1995.

McClure, Alexander. *The Translators Revived.* Litchfield, MI: Maranatha Bible Society, n.d., reprint of 1858 ed.

Miller, Edward. *A Guide to the Textual Criticism of the New Testament.* Collingswood, NJ: Dean Burgon Society, Inc., 1979.

Moorman, Jack. *Hodges/Farstad 'Majority' Text Refuted By Evidence.* Collingswood, NJ: The Bible for Today Press, N. d.

Nolan, Frederick. *An Inquiry into the Integrity of the Greek Vulgate or Received Text of the New Testament.* N.p., 1815.

Paisley, Ian R. *My Plea for the Old Sword: The English Authorised Version (KJB).* Belfast, Ireland: Ambassador Productions, 1997.

Sargent, Robert J. *Landmarks of English Bible: Manuscript Evidence.* Oak Harbor, WA: Bible Baptist Church Pub., 1989.

Scrivener, F. H. A. *A Plain Introduction to the Criticism of the New Testament.* 4th ed. Edited by E. Miller. 2 vols. London: George Bell and Sons, 1894.

Sorenson, David H. *Touch Not the Unclean Thing: The Text Issue and Separation.* Duluth, MN: Northstar Baptist Ministries, 2001.
Streeter, Lloyd L. *Seventy-five Problems with Central Baptist Seminary's Book, The Bible Version Debate.* LaSalle, IL: First Baptist Church of LaSalle, 2001.
Strouse, Thomas. *The Lord God Hath Spoken: A Guide to Bibliology.* Newington, CT: Emmanuel Baptist Theological Press, 2000.
Surrett, Charles L. *Which Greek Text? The Debate among Fundamentalists.* Kings Mountain, NC: Surrett Family Publications, 1999.
Trench, Richard Chenevix. *On the Authorized Version of the New Testament: In Connection with Some Recent Proposals for its Revision.* London: J. W. Parker and Son, l858.
Van Bruggen, Jakob. *The Ancient Text of the New Testament.* Winnipeg, Canada: Premier, 1976.
Waite, D. A. *Defending the King James Bible, A Four-fold Superiority: Texts, Translators, Technique, Theology.* Collingswood, NJ: Bible for Today Press, 1992.
_____. *Dean Burgon's Warnings on Revision of the Textus Receptus and the King James Bible.* Collingwood, NJ: Bible for Today, 1998.
_____. *Fundamentalist Mis-Information on Bible Versions.* Collingswood, NJ: The Bible for Today Press, 2000.

Articles

DiVietro, Kirk D. *Preservation of God's Words.* Collingswood, NJ: The Bible for Today, 1997.
Krinke, John M. *Should Believers Accept the Preservation of God's Word(s) by Faith, or by History & Science?* Greenwood, IN: John M. Krinke, 1997
Strouse, Thomas. "Should Fundamentalists Use the NASV?" *Sound Words from New England,* 2:1 (July-August), 2001.

Books and Articles on the Inspired and Preserved Hebrew Vowel Points

Bishop, George Sayles. *The Doctrines of Grace and Kindred Themes.* New York: Gospel Publishing House, 1919.
Burnett, Stephen G. *From Christian Hebraism to Jewish Studies: Johaness Buxtorf (1564-1629) and Hebrew Learning in the Seventeenth Century.* Leiden, the Netherlands: E. J. Brill, 1996.
Buxtorf I, Johannis. *Tractatus de punctorum vocalium, et accentuum, in libris Veteris Testamenti Hebraicis, origine, antiquitate, & authoritateoppositus Arcano punctationis revelato, Ludovici Cappelli.* Basileae : Sumptibus Haeredum Ludovici König: Typis Martini Wagneri, 1648.
Buxtorf II, Johannis. *Tiberiassive Commentarius masorethicus quo primùm explicatur, quid Masora sit: tum historia Masoretharum ex Hebræorum annalibus excutitur. Secundò clavis Masoræ traditur. Denique.* Basileæ Rauracorum: Sumptibus & Typis Ludovici König, 1620
Gill, John. *John Gill's Expositor.* In Online Bible Millennium Editon. Version 1.03.02. Winterbourne, Ontario, Canada: Timnathserah, Inc, Sept. 2001.
_____. *A Dissertation concerning the Antiquity of the Hebrew Language, Letters, Vowel Points, and Accents.* Originally published in 1767, available at http://www.onlinebible.net/topics6.html.
Moncrieff, John. *An Essay on the Antiquity and Utility of the Hebrew Vowel-Points.* London, England: Whittaker, Treacher, and Arnot, 1833.
Orlinsky, Harry M. Ed. *The Library of Biblical Studies, Jacob Ben Chajim Ibn Adonijah's Introduction to the Rabbinic Bible and The Massoreth Ha-Massoreth of Elias Levita.* Trans. and notes by C. D.

Ginsburg. 2nd ed. New York: KTAV, 1968.

Owen, John. *Biblical Theology: The History of Theology from Adam to Christ.* Morgan, PA: Soli Deo Gloria, 1994.

_____. *Of the Divine Original, Authority, Self-Evidencing Light, and Power of the Scriptures; with an Answer to that Inquiry, How We Know the Scriptures to be the Word of God,* in vol. IX, *The Works of John Owen.* ed. William H. Gould and Charles W. Quick. Philadelphia, PA: Leighton Publications, 1865.

_____. *Of the Integrity and Purity of the Hebrew and Greek Text of the Scripture; with Considerations on the Prolegomena and Appendix to the Late "Biblia Polyglotta,"* in vol. IX, *The Works of John Owen.* Ed. William H. Gould and Charles W. Quick. Philadelphia, PA: Leighton Publications, 1865.

Turretin, Francis. *Institutes of Elentic Theology.* Vol. 1. Trans. George M. Giger. Ed. James T. Dennison, Jr. Phillipsburg, NJ: P & R Publishing, 1992.

Commentaries, Grammars, and Other Resources

Adams, Jay E. *The Christian Counselor's Commentary, 1 Corinthians, 2 Corinthians.* Hackettstown, NJ: Timeless Texts, 1994.

Alford, Henry. *Alford's Greek Testament.* Vol. 1. 1844; reprinted. Grand Rapids, MI: Baker Book House, 1980.

Arndt, William F., and F. Wilbur Gingrich. *A Greek-English Lexicon of the New Testament and Other Early Christian Literature.* Chicago: University of Chicago Press, 1958.

Barnes, Albert. *Barnes Notes on the New Testament.* The Gospels. Edited by Robert Frew. 1884-85; reprint ed., Grand Rapids, MI: Baker Book House, N.d.

Bauer, Walter, William Arndt, and F. W. Gingrich. *A Greek-English Lexicon of the New Testament and Other Early Christian Literature.* Chicago: The University of Chicago Press, 1952.

Bell, Rod. "A Note from the President: Charting the Course: The Fellowship Principle," *Frontline.* Sept.-Oct. 2002, Vol 12, No. 5.

Broadus, John A. *Commentary on the Gospel of Matthew.* Vol.1 of *An American Commentary on the New Testament.* Edited by Alvah Hovey. Valley Forge: Judson Press, 1886.

Brown, Francis. *The Brown-Driver-Briggs Hebrew and English Lexicon.* Based on the Lexicon of William Gesenius[1] as Translated by Edward Robinson; edited by Francis Brown with the co-operation of S. R. Driver and Charles A. Briggs. Lafayette, IN: Associated Publishers and Authors, 1981.

Bullinger, E. W. *Figures of Speech Used in the Bible.* 1898; reprinted, Grand Rapids: Baker Book House, 1968.

Campbell, Ernest R. *First Corinthians.* Silverton, OR: Canyonview Press, 1989.

Dana, H. E. and Julius R. Mantey. *A Manual Grammar of the Greek New Testament.* Toronto: The Macmillan Company, 1957.

Danker, Frederick William. ed. *A Greek-English Lexicon of the New Testament and other Early Christian Literature.* 3rd ed. BDAG. Chicago, IL: University of Chicago Press, 2000.

Gaebelein, Arno C. *The Gospel of Matthew.* 1910; reprint ed., New York: Loizeaux Brothers, 1961.

Garner, Albert. *1 Peter, 2 Peter.* New Testament Commentary. Lakeland, FL: The Blessed Hope Foundation, 1975.

Gesenius, William. *Hebrew-Chaldee Lexicon to the Old Testament.* Translated into English by Samuel P. Tregelles. Grand Rapids, MI: Wm. B. Eerdmans Publishing Co., 1980.

Gromacki, Robert G. *Called To Be Saints, An Exposition of 1 Corinthians*. Grand Rapids, MI: Baker Book House, 1977.
Grudem, Wayne A. *The First Epistle of Peter*. Grand Rapids, MI: Wm. B. Eerdmans Publishing Co., 1988.
Hiebert, D. Edmond. *Second Peter and Jude*. Greenville, SC: Unusual Publications, 1989.
Hogarth, D. G. *The Biblical World, A Dictionary of Biblical Archeology*. Grand Rapids, MI: Baker Book House, 1966.
Howard, David. *Joshua: An Exegetical and Theological Exposition of Scripture*. Nashville: Broadman Press, 1998.
Kantzer, Kenneth S. ed. *Evangelical Roots: A Tribute to Wilbur Smith*. Nashville: Thomas Nelson Inc., Publishers, 1978.
Kidner, Derek. *Psalm 1-72, An Introduction and Commentary on Books I and II of the Psalms*. Downers Grove, IL: Inter-Varsity Press, 1973.
King James Bible Commentary. Nashville, TN: Thomas Nelson Publishers, 1999.
Kittel, Gerhard, ed. Translated by Geoffrey W. Bromiley. *Theological Dictionary of the New Testament*. Grand Rapids, MI: Wm. B. Eerdmans Publishing Co., 1977.
La More, Gary E. *The Word of God and Turning of the Tides: From Clothes to Fashions*. Toronto, ON: Grace Missionary Baptist Church, 1996.
Laurin, Roy L. *First Corinthians: Where Life Matures*. Grand Rapids, MI: Kregel Publications, 1987.
Liddell, H. G. and R. Scott. *A Greek-English Lexicon*. Oxford, England: Clarendon Press. 1968.
Lloyd-Jones, D. Martin. *Studies in the Sermon on the Mount*. Grand Rapids: Wm. B. Eerdmans Publishing Co., 1959.
Manton, M.E. *A Dictionary of Theological Terms*. London: Grace Publications Trust, 1996.
Morgan, G. Campbell. *The Gospel According To Matthew*. Old Tappan, NJ: Fleming H. Revell Company, 1929.
Oats, Larry. Syllabus for Workshop IV, "KJV Controversy: Let's Talk Portion Presentations and Responses," *National Leadership Conference*, Calvary Baptist Church, Lansdale, PA, Feb. 27-Mar. 1, 1996.
Pershbacher, Wesley J. *Refresh Your Greek*. Chicago: Moody Press, 1989.
Pfeifer, C. F. *The Dead Sea Scrolls and the Bible*. New York: Weathervane Books, 1969.
Plummer, Alfred. *An Exegetical Commentary on the Gospel According to St. Matthew*. 1915; reprint ed., Grand Rapids: Baker Book House, 1982.
Rienecker, Fritz. *A Linguistic Key to the Greek New Testament*. Translated and edited by Cleon L. Rogers, Jr. Grand Rapids, MI: Zondervan Publishing House, 1976.
Robertson, A. T. *A Grammar of the Greek New Testament in the Light of Historical Research*. Nashville, TN: Broadman Press, 1934.
Schaeffer, Francis A. *The Great Evangelical Disaster*. Westchester, IL: Crossway Books, 1984.
Smith, Jacob Brubaker. *Greek English Concordance*. Scottdale: Herald Press, 1975.
Strouse, Thomas M. *Biblical, Theological, and Religious Glossary*. Virginia Beach, VA: Tabernacle Baptist Theological Press, 1992.
Teachout, Richard. *The Tidal Wave of Ecumenism and the Local Church, A Lesson from Promise Keepers*. Ste Foy, Québec: Études Bibliques pour AUJOURDUHUI!, 1997.
Vincent, Marvin R. *Word Studies in the New Testament*. Peabody, MA: Hendrickson Publishers, N.d.
Vine, W. E. *Expository Dictionary of New Testament Words*. Old Tappan, NJ: Fleming H. Revell Company, 1966.
Waite, D. A. *First Peter Preaching Verse by Verse*. Collingswood, NJ: The Bible for Today Press,

2001.

Wallace, Daniel B. *Greek Grammar beyond the Basics*. Grand Rapids, MI: Zondervan Publishing House, 1996.

_____. *The John Ankerberg Show Transcript*. "Which English Translation of the Bible is Best for the Christian to Use Today." Chattanooga, TN: The Ankerberg Theological Research Institute, 1995.

Wenham, G. J. ed. *New Bible Commentary, 21st Century Edition*. Leicester, England: Inter-Varsity Press, 1994.

Westcott, Brooke Foss, and Fenton John Anthony Hort. *The New Testament in the Original Greek*. 1882; reprinted., Collinswood, NJ: The Bible For Today, 1985.

Whitcomb, J., and H. Morris. *The Genesis Flood: The Biblical Record and Its Scientific Implications*. Philadelphia: The Presbyterian and Reformed Publ. Co., 1961.

Wigram, George V. *The Englishman's Greek Concordance of the New Testament; Being an Attempt at a Verbal Connexion Between the Greek and the English Texts: Including a Concordance to the Proper Names; with Indexes, Greek-English and English-Greek; and A Concordance of Various Readings*. 1839; reprinted. Grand Rapids, MI: Zondervan Publishing House, 1970.

Willmington, Harold L. *The Outline Bible*. Wheaton, IL: Tyndale House Publishers, Inc. 1999.

Yates, Kyle M. *The Essentials of Biblical Hebrew*. New York: Harper & Row Publishers, 1954.

Yeager, Randolph O. *The Renaissance New Testament*. Gretna, Louisiana: Pelican Publishing Company, Inc., 1985.

Scripture and Topical Index

Genesis 1:3, 36

Genesis 1:28, 203

Genesis 2:7, 79

Genesis 2:15, 98

Genesis 2:16ff, 246

Genesis 3:1, 53, 106, 153, 209

Genesis 3:1-6, 131

Genesis 3:1-8, 87

Genesis 3:4, 106

Genesis 3:24, 98

Genesis 4:1, 160

Genesis 4:9, 99

Genesis 6:5, 261

Genesis 8:21, 261

Genesis 11:1-11, 249

Genesis 11:7, 36

Genesis 12:1-3, 30, 110

Genesis 15:2; 43:19; 44:4, 123

Genesis 15:6, 239

Genesis 21:10, 239

Genesis 30:31, 99

Genesis 32:30, 160

Exodus 3:6, 241

Exodus 12:43-45, 110

Scripture Index

Exodus 15:2, 259

Exodus 15:26, 100

Exodus 17:14, 241

Exodus 19:13, 189

Exodus 20:1, 36

Exodus 20:5,6, 100, 104

Exodus 20:12, 241

Exodus 33:20, 77

Exodus 34:27, 198

Leviticus 3-4, 162

Leviticus 7, 162

Leviticus 11:44, 80, 190

Leviticus 18:4,5, 100

Leviticus 23:34-44, 251

Leviticus 25:18, 103

Leviticus 26:3, 102

Numbers 23:19, 169

Numbers 25:9, 156

Numbers 27:18-19, 110

Deuteronomy 1:1, 36

Deuteronomy 4:2, 88, 100, 115, 153, 241

Deuteronomy 4:2 and 12:32. 105, 110

Deuteronomy 4:40, 199

Deuteronomy 5:5, 88

Deuteronomy 5:29; 6:4,5; 30:1-14, 86

Deuteronomy 5:29; 7:9; 12:28; 19:9; 23:3; 19:29, 90

Deuteronomy 6:1-10, 89

Deuteronomy 6:6-9, 106

Deuteronomy 8:1-3, 36

Deuteronomy 8:3, 35, 38–39, 79, 118

Deuteronomy 11:18-21, 106

Deuteronomy 11:22, 100

Deuteronomy 11:27, 102

Deuteronomy 12:32, 224

Deuteronomy 13:1-2, 248

Deuteronomy 13:4, 103

Deuteronomy 18:15-19, 198

Deuteronomy 18:20-22, 198

Deuteronomy 21:22-23, 110

Deuteronomy 25:4, 239, 241

Deuteronomy 27:8, 36

Deuteronomy 28:29, 105

Deuteronomy 29:9, 87, 100

Deuteronomy 30:11-14, **85,** 44, 87–88, 90

Deuteronomy 30:15-20, 90

Deuteronomy 31:24-26, 199

Deuteronomy 31:24-30, 36

Joshua 1:7-8, 110

Joshua 5:2-5; 7-12, 110

Joshua 7:1, 154

Joshua 8:29, 110

Joshua 8:30-35, 37

Joshua 8:31, 199

Joshua 22:5, 100

Joshua 23:6, 198

Judges 11:29ff, 242

Ruth 3:5, 155

Ruth 3:15, 154

Ruth 3:17, 155

1 Samuel 1:24, 162

1 Samuel 3:17, 159

1 Samuel 6:19, 158

1 Samuel 13:1, 156

1 Samuel 25:22, 159

2 Samuel 15:16, 99

1 Kings 2:3, 101

1 Kings 8:46, 89

1 Kings 22:42, 156

2 Kings 8:26, 157

2 Kings 17:9; 18:8, 98

2 Kings 17:13, 101

2 Kings 22:8-20, 105

1 Chronicles 2:7, 154

1 Chronicles 29:19, 101

1 Chronicles 28:1, 123

2 Chronicles 4:2, 242

2 Chronicles 22:2, 157, 242

2 Chronicles 34:21, 105

2 Chronicles 34:31, 101

Ezra 7:10,11, 106

Nehemiah 1:9, 101

Nehemiah 8:1-8, 250

Nehemiah 8:1-9, 36

Nehemiah 8:3, 199

Nehemiah 8:8, 36, 257

Job 7:20, 161

Job 27:18, 98

Psalm 2, 160

Psalm 2:7, 160, 167

Psalm 2:9, 155

Psalm 2:12, 159

Psalm 5:12, 33

Psalm 6:1, 29

Psalm 8:4, 33

Psalm 12:1-8, 147

Psalm 12:6,7, 29, 110, 153, 156, 244, 246, 250, 257

Psalm 12:6-7, 119:111, 152 160, 244

Psalm 12:7, 99, 149

Psalm 14:1, 30

Psalm 14:1-3 and 53:1-3, 80

Psalm 17:4, 148

Psalm 18:1-3, 259

Psalm 19:7, 148

Psalm 21:3, 33

Psalm 24:6, 160

Psalm 28:7, 33

Psalm 34:14, 98

Psalm 34:19, 33

Psalm 41:9, 239

Psalm 43:5, 33

Psalm 69:9, 80

Psalm 69:25, 241

Psalm 72:5, 160

Psalm 73:7, 161

Psalm 78:1-8; 105:8; 119:89, 244

Psalm 78:7, 101

Psalm 105:8, 243–244

Psalm 109:8, 241

Psalm 118:22-23, 239

Psalm 119, 32–33, 99, 102, 155

Psalm 119:1, 99

Psalm 119:2, 99, 102

Psalm 119:4, 99

Psalm 119:5, 99

Psalm 119:7, 99

Psalm 119:9, 99

Psalm 119:11, 99, 244

Psalm 119:17, 102

Psalm 119:33, 102

Psalm 119:34, 102

Psalm 119:50,93, 148

Psalm 119:55,56, 102

Psalm 119:56,60,63,67,69, 102

Psalm 119:88,100, 102

Psalm 119:89, 22, 54, 112, 145, 230, 244

Psalm 119:89,152, 80

Psalm 119:101,106,115, 102

Psalm 119:129, 32

Psalm 119:129, 152, 169, 99

Psalm 119:134,136,145, 102

Psalm 119:140, 142, 145

Psalm 119:146,158,167,168, 102

Psalm 119:152, 32, 245

Psalm 119:160, 245

Psalm 138:2, 35, 237

Psalm 141:3, 98

Psalm 145, 155

Proverbs 3:5, 261

Proverbs 4:23, 98

Proverbs 6:24, 99

Proverbs 8:22, 160

Proverbs 13:3, 98

Proverbs 14:12, 262

Proverbs 16:17, 98

Proverbs 27:18, 98

Proverbs 30:5, 145–146

Proverbs 30:5-6, 153

Ecclesiastes 12:13, 101

Song of Solomon 5:7, 98

Isaiah 6:9-10, 241

Isaiah 7:10-14, 241

Isaiah 7:14, 242

Isaiah 9:3, 157

Isaiah 21:11, 98

Isaiah 33:13, 89

Isaiah 40:8, 62, 145, 230, 244–245

Isaiah 42:9, 59

Isaiah 45:6-10, 262

Isaiah 52:7, 186

Isaiah 55:8,9, 261

Isaiah 55:10,11, 261

Isaiah 59:1, 262

Jeremiah 25:12, 241

Jeremiah 26:15,16, 199

Jeremiah 27:1, 162

Jeremiah 30:2, 241

Jeremiah 31:6, 98

Jeremiah 36:1-32, 242

Jeremiah 36:4, 36, 114

Jeremiah 44:28, 31, 244

Lamentations 3:24, 259

Ezekiel 11:20, 101

Ezekiel 22:5, 89

Ezekiel 36:27, 103

Ezekiel 40:49, 163

Ezekiel 45:5, 162

Ezekiel 48:16, 155

Daniel 7:13,14, 169

Daniel 9:2, 241

Daniel 9:4, 101

Daniel 10:21-11:45, 54

Daniel 12:4, 102

Daniel 12:9, 102

Amos 2:4, 105

Amos 5:26, 155

Nahum 1:7, 186

Nahum 2:2, 98

Habakkuk 1:2-4, 259

Habakkuk 1:5-11, 259

Habakkuk 1:12, 259

Habakkuk 2:2, 241

Habakkuk 2:4, 260

Habakkuk 3:17-19, 260

Habakkuk 3:19, 29

Zechariah 13:7, 79

Malachi 3:1, 79, 179

Malachi 3:7a, 105

Matthew 1:7,8, 184, 243

Matthew 1:10, 184

Matthew 1:22, 199

Matthew 1:23, 241

Matthew 2:5, 78

Matthew 3:5-11, 253

Matthew 3:6-8, 252

Matthew 3:6-17 21:25-27, 56

Matthew 3:12; 9:37,38, 60

Matthew 3:16, 56, 174, 252

Matthew 3:16,17, 47

Matthew 4:4, **35,** 25, 38, 66, 79–80, 111, 118–119, 153, 237, 244

Matthew 4:1-11, 35, 131

Matthew 4:4; 5:17-18; 24:35, 156

Matthew 4:7,10, 79

Matthew 4:8,9, 173

Matthew 4:23, 42

Matthew 5:3-12, 42, 170

Matthew 5:13-16, 42, 170

Matthew 5:17,18, **41, 245,** 38, 62, 88, 154, 244–245

Matthew 5:17-20, **43**

Matthew 5:18, 44, 46, 49, 53, 88, 111, 147, 240

Matthew 5:18-19, 47–50

Matthew 5:21,27,31,33,38,43, 42

Matthew 5:21-22,27-28,31-32,33-34,38-39,43-44, 165, 170

Matthew 5:22,28,32,34,39,44, 42

Matthew 5:29-30, 170

Matthew 6:13, 172

Matthew 6:13, 165, 173

Matthew 6:14, 190

Matthew 6:30, 8:26, 14:31, 16:8, 263

Matthew 7:29, 21

Matthew 8:10, 262

Matthew 8:26; 14:31, 263

Matthew 12:3,5, 21

Matthew 12:46-50; 27:57, 252

Matthew 13:10,11,13,16, 60

Matthew 13:13,15, 60

Matthew 15:4, 241

Matthew 16:8, 263

Matthew 16:18, 67, 111, 175

Matthew 16:22-23, 52, 176

Matthew 17:5, 39

Matthew 17:20, 263

Matthew 18:2-5, 264

Matthew 18:15, 165, 175

Matthew 18:15-17, 223

Matthew 18:19, 223

Matthew 18:20, 121

Matthew 18:21, 190

Matthew 19:4, 21

Matthew 19:5, 189

Matthew 19:17, 112

Matthew 20:8, 123

Matthew 21:42, 239

Matthew 22:31, 21

Matthew 22:32, 241

Matthew 23:23, 45

Matthew 24:3, 60

Matthew 24:4-31, 60

Matthew 24:15, 229

Matthew 24:35, 59, 246, 53, 60–61, 64, 97, 145, 257

Matthew 25:21, 124, 151

Matthew 26:24; 26:31, 79

Matthew 27:5, 157

Matthew 28:19-20, 37, 54, 56, 67, 111, 113, 115, 248, 250, 252, 257

Mark 1:2, 178, 79, 132, 165, 178–179

Mark 1:2,3, 179, 243

Mark 7:21, 261

Mark 9:2-12, 91

Mark 10:15, 264

Mark 12:26, 21, 229

Mark 13:31, 71, 231

Mark 16:9-20, 185

Mark 16:15, 252

Mark 16:20, 139

Luke 1:2, 124

Luke 1:4, 200

Luke 1:34, 260

Luke 1:63, 79

Luke 2:33, **185**

Luke 4:4, 79

Luke 4:10, 79

Luke 4:20, 124

Luke 6:3, 21

Luke 10:7, 67, 239, 241

Luke 10:30, 191

Luke 11:2-4, 173

Luke 11:50-51, 38, 49, 111, 178

Luke 12:48, 125

Luke 12:42; 16:1-8, 123

Luke 15:27; 23:41, 191

Luke 16:2, 187

Luke 16:6-7, 239

Luke 16:10, 45

Luke 16:17, 231

Luke 18:17, 264

Luke 20:42, 30, 229

Luke 21:33, 231

Luke 22:43,44, **185**

Luke 23:38, 239

Luke 24:27, 21, 11

Luke 24:44, 38, 49, 111, 178

Luke 24:46, 79

Luke 24:47, 252

Scripture Index

John 1:1, 169, 217

John 1:12, 54, 56

John 1:14, 3:16,18, 167

John 1:1-18, 166

John 1:18, 166, 169

John 1:18; 3:16, 160

John 1:45, 105

John 2:4; 7:6,8, 30; 8:20 12:23; 27-28; 31-32; 13:1,31, 52

John 2:22, 52

John 3:11, 54

John 3:13, 168, 165, 168–169

John 3:13-18, 168

John 3:14, 159

John 3:25, 185

John 3:15-16; 6:37,44; 10:28-30, 52

John 4:34, 37

John 5:30, 53

John 5:36-37, 54

John 5:39, 142, 239

John 5:46, 78

John 5:47, 239

John 6:68, 72, 230

John 7:8, 171, 165

John 7:38, 239

John 7:53-8:11, 185

John 8:28, 54

John 8:51-55, 112

John 10:27, 22, 112, 115, 175, 248, 254, 257

John 10:30, 52, 56

John 10:35, 229, 240, 244, 250

John 12:14, 79

John 12:49; 14:10, 53

John 12:48, 33, 53, 67, 112, 246, 254, 257

John 12:49-50, 72, 230

John 13:16, 52

John 13:18, 239

John 13:34-35, 111

John 14:15, **179,** 112, 165, 179–180

John 14:21, 112

John 14:23,21,24, 56, 112

John 14:26; 16:13, 112

John 15:4-7, 72

John 15:10, 112

John 15:20, 113

John 16:12-13, 229

John 17:1-26, 246

John 17:8, **51,** 38, 51–54, 67, 72, 90, 112, 132, 200, 230, 257, 263

John 17:11, 56

John 17:17, 36, 119, 148, 151, 260

John 17:20, 54, 56

John 19:21,22, 79

John 19:30, 52, 77

John 20:29, 139

John 20:31, 38, 148

John 21:25, 246

John 22:21, 252

Acts 1:8, 252

Acts 1:16, 8:23,35, 239

Acts 1:18, 157

Acts 1:20, 241

Acts 2:1ff, 111

Acts 2:14-36, 229

Acts 2:15, 191

Acts 2:36, 67, 238

Acts 2:41, 55, 247

Acts 2:41-47; 8:12; 9:18; 10:24-48; 16:33; 18:8, 56

Acts 2:47; 8:37; and 9:31, 253

Acts 4:25, 159

Acts 6:2-8, 111

Acts 7:22, 238

Acts 7:38, 104, 229, 252

Acts 7:43, 155

Acts 8:1, 176–177

Acts 8:14, 55, 247

Acts 8:37, 186

Acts 8:37-39, 56

Acts 9:6, 77

Acts 9:31, 176, 165, 178

Acts 11:1, 55, 247

Acts 13:5, 124

Acts 13:33, 167

Acts 14:3, 139

Acts 15:21, 37, 110

Acts 15:23, 78

Acts 18:5, 133

Acts 18:12ff, 133

Acts 19:32-41, 111

Acts 20:27, 72

Acts 20:35, 246

Acts 26:16, 124

Acts 26:24, 239

Acts 28:25, 200

Acts 28:26-27, 241

Romans 1:2, 239

Romans 1:6,7, 183

Romans 1:16, 186

Romans 1:17, 80, 260

Romans 1:18-21, 87

Romans 1:21, 89

Romans 1:23, 71

Romans 2:2, 53

Romans 2:15, 246

Romans 2:27, 239

Romans 3:1,2, 37, 104, 110, 252

Romans 3:2, 117, 229

Romans 3:4, 154

Romans 3:10-12, 80

Romans 3:23-25, 37

Romans 4:3, 9:17, 239

Romans 4:21, 62

Romans 5:1, 181, 36, 114, 165, 181–183

Romans 5:9-10, 37

Romans 6:3-5, 252

Romans 8:1-9, 182

Romans 8:9,11, 183

Romans 8:16, 115

Romans 8:26, 174

Romans 9:1, 171

Romans 9:3-5, 104

Romans 9:4, 62

Romans 10:1-10, 86

Romans 10:6-8, 89–90

Romans 10:9; 14:9, 77

Romans 10:15, 186

Romans 10:17, 70, 88, 139, 234, 260

Romans 11:25-26, 157

Romans 14:23, 262

Romans 15:3,4, 80

Romans 15:4, 230, 238

Romans 15:18,19, 139

Romans 16:17,18, 223

Romans 16:25,26, 124, 250

1 Corinthians 1:18, 126

1 Corinthians 1:21-29, 265

1 Corinthians 1:24,30, 160

1 Corinthians 2:10, 124, 250

1 Corinthians 2:10-14, 250

1 Corinthians 2:13, 44, 51, 240–241

1 Corinthians 2:14, 124

1 Corinthians 3:11, 217

1 Corinthians 3:5-17, 125

1 Corinthians 3:16, 201, 204

1 Corinthians 4:1-5, 123, 126

1 Corinthians 5:5, 218

1 Corinthians 5:5-8, 218

1 Corinthians 5:6-13, 218

1 Corinthians 5:7, 186

1 Corinthians 6:20, 186

1 Corinthians 7:19, 113

1 Corinthians 7:31, 61

1 Corinthians 8:2, 262

1 Corinthians 9:25; 15:53,54, 71

1 Corinthians 10:8, 156

1 Corinthians 11:2, 93

1 Corinthians 12:13, 183

1 Corinthians 13:1, 22

1 Corinthians 14:37, 230

1 Corinthians 15:3,4, 77, 80

1 Corinthians 15:45, 79

2 Corinthians 1:1, 179

2 Corinthians 1:6, 186, 263

2 Corinthians 1:20, 31, 62

2 Corinthians 1:23, 171

2 Corinthians 2:17, 135, 157

2 Corinthians 5:17, 63

2 Corinthians 10:5, 246

2 Corinthians 11:4, 186

2 Corinthians 12:12, 139, 201

2 Corinthians 13:1, 200

Galatians 1:2, 56, 178

Galatians 1:9, 57

Galatians 1:20, 79

Galatians 2:5, 114

Galatians 2:11-14, 176

Galatians 3:8, 238

Galatians 3:11, 260

Galatians 3:16, 46, 62, 241

Galatians 3:27-28, 57

Galatians 4:30, 239

Galatians 6:11, 239

Galatians 6:15, 187

Ephesians 1:3, 66

Ephesians 1:10; 3:2, 187

Ephesians 1:14, 174

Ephesians 1:9; 3:3,5,8; 6:19, 124

Ephesians 2:18 and 3:12, 182

Ephesians 2:20, 217

Ephesians 2:21, 66, 238

Ephesians 3:9, **187**, 125

Ephesians 3:15, 238

Ephesians 2:8, 77

Ephesians 3:3, 78, 124–125

Ephesians 3:9, **187**, 125

Ephesians 4:2-4, 201

Ephesians 4:3, 224

Ephesians 4:4-6, 223

Ephesians 4:6, **183**, 165, 183–185

Ephesians 4:11-16, 37

Ephesians 5:26, 148

Ephesians 6:10-19, 125

Ephesians 6:12, 209

Philippians 2:5-11, 52

Philippians 3:16, **187**

Colossians 1:1, 200

Colossians 1:2, **187**

Colossians 1:14, **187**

Colossians 1:21, 182

Colossians 1:25, **187**

Colossians 1:26,27; 4:4, 124

Colossians 2:8, 163, 262

Colossians 2:12, 56, 252

Colossians 4:3, 125

Colossians 4:12, 238

Colossians 4:16, 114, 132, 200–201, 254

Colossians 4:17, 114

Colossians 3:15-16, 115

1 Thessalonians 1:6; 2:13, 55

1 Thessalonians 2:13, 200, 247, 251, 257

1 Thessalonians 5:27, 188, 200

2 Thessalonians 1:2; 3:12, 188

2 Thessalonians 2:2, 131–133, 114–115, 135, 251

2 Thessalonians 2:7, 174

2 Thessalonians 2:15; 3:6, 93

2 Thessalonians 3:6-15, 223

1 Timothy 1:4, 53, 153

1 Timothy 1:11, 18-20; 4:6-16, 125

1 Timothy 1:12, 125

1 Timothy 1:15, 213

1 Timothy 1:19, 212

1 Timothy 1:20, 23

1 Timothy 3:1,8, 112

1 Timothy 3:2, 120

1 Timothy 3:3, 188

1 Timothy 3:9, 125

1 Timothy 3:14, 67

1 Timothy 3:15, **117**, 24, 37, 54, 57, 67, 70, 112, 116–120, 125, 200, 224, 248, 253

1 Timothy 3:16, **188**

1 Timothy 4:10, 259

1 Timothy 4:12, **188**

1 Timothy 4:13, 114

1 Timothy 5:17-18, 212

1 Timothy 5:18, 67, 239, 241

1 Timothy 5:20, 213

1 Timothy 5:21, 220

1 Timothy 6:3,4, 212–213

1 Timothy 6:12, 212

1 Timothy 6:20, 212

2 Timothy 1:7, 23

2 Timothy 1:12, 77

2 Timothy 2:2, 132

2 Timothy 2:11, 213

2 Timothy 2:11-26, **209**

2 Timothy 2:13, 212

2 Timothy 2:14, 218–219

2 Timothy 2:15, 22, 45, 93, 132, 214

2 Timothy 2:16, 218, 220

2 Timothy 2:16,19,22, 218, 220

2 Timothy 2:17, 215

2 Timothy 2:19, 217, 219

Scripture Index **299**

2 Timothy 2:19-21, 125, 219–220

2 Timothy 2:24-26, 114, 219

2 Timothy 2:25-26, 218

2 Timothy 3:1-9, 238

2 Timothy 3:15-17, 65, 238, 68

2 Timothy 3:16, 23, 31, 36, 53, 67, 93, 97–98, 224, 238, 242, 246, 250

2 Timothy 3:16,17, 22, 36, 67, 257

2 Timothy 4:1, 188

2 Timothy 4:10, 23

2 Timothy 4:13,20, 189

Titus 1:1, 222

Titus 1:2, 59, 62

Titus 1:5, 189

Titus 2:5, 189

Titus 2:13, 191

Titus 3:10, 221, 114, 221–225

Philemon 1-2, 114

Philemon 12, 189

Philemon 21, 78

Hebrews 1:1-2, 246

Hebrews 1:5; 5:5, 167

Hebrews 2:3,4, 134, 201

Hebrews 3:1, 189

Hebrews 4:12, 70, 262

Hebrews 5:12, 229, 252

Hebrews 6:13; 10:23; 11:11; 12:26, 62

Hebrews 6:16-17, 171

Hebrews 9:17, 77

Hebrews 11:33, 62

Hebrews 2:16 and 10:12, 77

Hebrews 10:7, 79

Hebrews 10:38, 260

Hebrews 11:1, 139, 260

Hebrews 11:1-3, 260

Hebrews 11:3, 260

Hebrews 11:6, 155, 259, 261

Hebrews 11:7, 260

Hebrews 12:20, 189

James 1:10, 63

James 1:18, 70

James 1:19-21, 24

James 1:21, 265

James 2:10, 189, 113

James 2:14-17, 191

James 2:23, 239

James 3:15, 53, 265

James 5:16, 190

1 Peter 1:4, 72–73, 133

1 Peter 1:5, 105, 263

1 Peter 1:1-9, 69

1 Peter 1:11, 174

1 Peter 1:12-2:3, 70

1 Peter 1:15,16, 80

1 Peter 1:16, **190**

1 Peter 1:18, 71

1 Peter 1:23, 70, 72

1 Peter 1:23b-25, **69–70,** 72–73, 88, 145, 244–245

1 Peter 1:25, 72, 256

1 Peter 2:2, **190**

1 Peter 2:2, 69, 71, 73

1 Peter 2:22, 171

1 Peter 3:18, 77, 171

1 Peter 4:3, 63

1 Peter 4:10, 124

1 Peter 4:11, 21, 229, 252

2 Peter 1:2,3, 88

2 Peter 1:4; 3:13, 62

2 Peter 1:1-15, 134

2 Peter 1:12-21, 86

2 Peter 1:14, 62

2 Peter 1:16, 91

2 Peter 1:16-21, 134

2 Peter 1:16-21; 3:1-10, 64

2 Peter 1:17-21, 92

2 Peter 1:19, 134

2 Peter 1:20,21, 36, 97, 211, 229, 234

2 Peter 1:21, **190,** 76, 93, 240

2 Peter 3:1, 133

2 Peter 3:2, 91–92

2 Peter 3:3,4, 134–135, 263

2 Peter 3:9,10, 262

2 Peter 3:10, 61, 63

2 Peter 3:10-13, 62, 246

2 Peter 3:16, 51, 166, 229, 240, 250, 254

2 Peter 3:15-16, 114, 200, 248

2 Peter 3:15-17, 131–135, 115

1 John 1:9, 190

1 John 2:2, 161

1 John 2:3-5, 113

1 John 2:14,24,27; and 3:15,17,24, 72

1 John 2:15, 61

1 John 2:20,27, 254

1 John 2:27, 115

1 John 2:29, 3:9, 5:1, 167

1 John 3:19, 190

1 John 3:22,24, 113

1 John 4:3, 190

1 John 4:6, 201

1 John 4:9, 167

1 John 4:15-16, 259

1 John 5:2-3, 56

1 John 5:7, 173, 47, 150, 165, 173–174

1 John 5:7,8, 135

1 John 5:13, 140

1 John 5:18, 180

2 John 1:9-14, 254

2 John 1:12, 254

2 John 2, 151

2 John 9, 191, 180

3 John 3-4, 151

3 John 8, 191

Jude 4, 191, 222

Revelation 1:3, 113, 115

Revelation 1:3, 11; 14:13, 79

Revelation 1:3; 22:7, 9, 115

Revelation 1:4, 120

Revelation 1:5, 191

Revelation 1:11; 2:1, 115

Revelation 1:13,20, 253

Revelation 1:13-16, 159

Revelation 1:19; 2:1, 8:12; 3:1, 7; 3:14; 14:13; 19:9; 21:5, 241

Revelation 2:1,7, 254

Revelation 2-3, 115, 120–121, 178, 253

Revelation 2:6,15, 177

Revelation 2:27, 155

Revelation 3:10, 113, 119

Revelation 3:8,10, 55, 119

Revelation 3:14, 241

Revelation 4:8, 66, 92

Revelation 5:12,13, 173

Revelation 5:14, 191

Revelation 6:14, 61

Revelation 7, 61

Revelation 10:4, 241

Revelation 12:17, 113

Revelation 14:12, 113

Revelation 19:10ff, 155

Revelation 19:16, 79

Revelation 20:10, 173

Revelation 21:1, 63

Revelation 21:8, 173

Revelation 22:7,9, 113

Revelation 22:18-19, **192,** 51, 54, 115, 134, 144, 146–147, 153, 155, 166, 230, 241, 250

Revelation 22:21, 192

Accessibility, 254, 13, 39, 87–90, 254–255, 257

Alexandrian Text, 9, 168

Apographa, 9, 239

Apologetic, 43, 233

Apostate, 12, 52, 55, 91–92, 94, 121, 153, 167, 188, 192, 221, 232, 260, 265

Attack, 129, 131, 23–24, 42, 64, 70, 87, 91, 94, 114, 116, 131–135, 153, 168–169, 182, 187, 192, 209, 211, 215–217, 249, 264–265

Authority, 11–12, 19, 21–23, 35–36, 39, 41, 43–50, 52, 59, 62, 66, 79–80, 87, 89, 93, 99, 115, 118–119, 124–125, 131, 141, 144, 155, 160–161, 174–175, 177, 185, 187, 197–202, 205, 220, 222–225, 237, 244, 246, 266

Autographa, 9, 13, 29, 35–36, 46, 51, 63, 81, 238–240, 242–243, 245, 248, 250–251, 254

Available, 23–24, 35, 53, 62–64, 66–68, 72, 80, 85–94, 109–110, 117–118, 131–132, 134, 151, 197, 202, 204, 214. 230–231, 234, 261–263, 265–266

Availability, 23, 35–37, 39, 63, 66–67, 85, 87–90, 93–94, 201, 205, 224, 232, 261

Baptized, 55, 57, 186, 253

Bauder, 153, 221

Bell, 97

Bentley, 192, 232

Bible, 51, 146, 198, 202, 9–15, 19–24, 36–38, 43–59, 63, 65–66, 68, 70–72, 76, 78, 86–89, 94, 97, 109, 112–113, 116–117, 119, 121, 126, 131–132, 134, 136, 139, 141, 143–146, 148–152, 156–157, 165–166, 171, 178–179, 181, 192–193, 197–198, 205, 209, 211, 216, 221–222, 230, 232–235, 237, 238–240, 245–246, 248–252, 255, 261–266

Bibliological, 250, 52, 114, 216, 237–238, 247, 250–251, 255

Brandenburg, 21, 59, 85, 97, 197, 221, 259, 44, 110, 114, 131, 233

Biblical Criticism, 9, 9–10, 13, 55

Byzantine Text, 9, 231

Canonical, 10, 14, 33, 36, 51, 53–54, 56, 111–112, 114, 116, 133, 198, 200–201, 203–204, 239, 246–247, 249, 254–255, 261

Canonicity, 197–198, 202, 197–205

Case Study, 110, 114–115

CHRIST, 51, 166, 10–11, 21, 24, 33, 35–39, 41, 45–48, 51–57, 59–64, 66–67, 69, 71–72, 75–80, 86, 90–93, 104–105, 111–113, 115–116, 118, 120–121, 123–126, 132, 134–135, 139, 145, 153–155, 159–161, 163, 166–169, 171–174, 176, 178–192, 199–201, 210, 212, 216–217, 219, 221, 224–225, 230–231, 233, 235, 237, 240–242, 245–249, 252–255, 260, 262, 264

Church, 10, 117, 120, 175, 252, 12–13, 24, 37–38, 49, 51, 55–57, 65, 85, 104, 107, 109, 111–127, 132–135, 141, 144, 166, 175–178, 182–183, 187, 191, 198, 200–204, 211, 213, 215, 218–220, 222–225, 231, 237, 247, 252–257

Churches, 120, 176, 9–11, 13–14, 37–38, 51, 54, 556–57, 70, 94, 111–116, 118–122, 125, 127, 131–132, 134, 136, 144, 146, 176–178, 191, 198, 200–205, 210–211, 213, 216, 220, 222–225, 231–235, 241, 243, 247–255, 266

Cloud, David 136

Codex, 10, 9–10, 14, 115, 136, 204

Consonants, 13, 17, 30–31, 36, 38, 43–44, 88, 154–155, 162, 245

Corkish, 139, 209

Critical Text, 10, 9–11, 14, 46–49, 135, 166, 184, 237

***CT*, 14, 257,** 66, 68, 70–71, 109, 122, 133, 135, 166–192, 237, 243, 249, 251, 253, 255–257

Cult, 37, 111, 265

Custer, 192, 47, 167, 192–193

Deity, 166, 52, 135, 155–156, 160, 166–169, 173–174, 187–188, 191

Discipline, 9, 111, 175, 218, 224, 238

Doctrinal, 158, 21, 46, 78, 152–153, 163, 166, 173–174, 183–184, 193

Doctrine, 158–159, 161–162, 172, 175, 181, 192, 207, 10–12, 19–24, 35–36, 41, 45–50, 56–57, 62, 64–65, 67–68, 70, 75–76, 80–81, 85, 97–99, 131, 134–135, 142, 153, 161–163, 165–166, 168–169, 172–177, 179–182, 184–185, 188, 191–193, 197–198, 202, 205, 211–213, 215–216, 220–225, 229, 231, 235, 238, 241–243, 248–249, 253, 263–266

Doctrines, 137, 153, 165, 12, 19, 23, 52, 87, 98, 103, 144, 162–163, 166, 179,

184, 193, 202, 212, 216, 232, 237, 243, 255, 263-265

Dynamic Equivalence, 10

DSS, 14, 110–111, 153, 158, 161–163

Edition, 10–11, 13, 127, 192, 201, 203–204, 224, 261, 263-266

Ekklāsia, 176, 72, 109, 111, 121, 175–178, 232

Eternality, 72–73, 169, 191

Evolution, 142, 10, 47, 143, 149, 234

False Teachers, 42, 48, 65, 91–94, 133–136, 212, 216, 223

Faith, 10, 19, 22, 24, 36, 38, 42, 45, 47–48, 50, 55, 63, 65, 69, 77, 80, 49, 53, 71, 85–86, 88, 92, 93, 113, 116, 118–119, 125–127, 139, 142, 144, 148, 150, 155, 159–160, 166, 181–184, 186, 191–193, 203, 210–215, 217–218, 223, 232, 234, 250, 253, 259–266

Fideistic, 259

Fundamentalism, 10, 19, 121, 222, 266

Fundamentalist, 19, 20, 51, 55, 243, 266

Gender, 22, 32, 99, 149, 174, 218, 244

Glenny, 20, 46, 48, 97, 153, 193, 197, 263

GOD, 9, 11–13, 19–25, 29–33, 35–39, 41–42, 44–48, 50, 52–56, 59, 61–73, 75–80, 85–90, 97–107, 109–110, 113–127, 131–132, 134–136, 139–162, 165–169, 172–179, 181–188, 190–193, 197–205, 209–220, 222–224, 229–235, 237–256, 259–266

Greek, 16, 9–14, 19, 23, 38, 42–43, 45–46, 48–49, 57, 62–63, 65, 70, 75, 77, 88, 114, 116, 119–120, 150, 155, 163, 165, 181, 184, 187, 198, 203, 205, 216, 222, 230–234, 137, 240, 243, 247

Hebrew, 16, 17, 9–17, 19, 23, 29, 32–33, 35–35, 38–39, 41, 43–49, 66, 85, 88–89, 98–99, 102, 110–111, 116–118, 144–145, 147, 149–150, 153–163, 170, 178–179, 198, 205, 230, 240–241, 243–245, 250

Heretic, 221, 114–115, 216–217–221–225, 248–249

Higher Criticism, 10, 48, 143, 234

History, 10–11, 13, 19, 22–23, 37–38, 48, 50, 52, 54, 97, 102, 104–105, 132–133, 144, 146, 157, 209, 225, 230, 235, 242

HOLY SPIRIT, 11, 55, 66, 71, 75, 80, 111, 132, 142–145, 147, 149, 173–174, 177, 179, 183, 190, 201, 213, 216, 229–231, 238, 240–241, 254

Hort, 9–10, 48–49, 51, 181, 232–233, 264

Immersed, 10, 56–57, 115, 253–254

Infallibility, 11, 146, 19, 35, 43, 153, 242–243

Inerrancy, 11, 178, 257, 19, 35, 48, 153–154, 174, 178–179, 184–185, 242–243, 251, 255

Inspiration, 11, 36, 65, 238, 257, 9, 35–36, 44, 46–47, 49, 51–52, 54, 56, 65–68, 81, 85, 88–90, 97–98, 103, 114, 118, 134, 143–144, 146, 149–151, 153, 156, 175, 182, 188, 190, 198, 200, 210, 213, 215, 220, 229–230, 237–240, 242–243, 247, 251, 255, 264–265

Institution, 104, 11, 23–24, 37–38, 57, 66, 85, 106–107, 111, 114, 116, 120, 131, 198, 200, 205, 220, 224–255, 232, 254–255

Ipsissima Verba, 11

Ipsissima Vox, 11

Israel, 97, 10–11, 13–14, 36, 41–43, 60, 79, 54, 85–87, 89–90, 101–102, 104–107

JESUS, 51, 10, 21, 24, 30, 33, 35–39, 41–54, 56–57, 59–63, 67, 69, 72, 75–77, 79–80, 86, 91–92, 105, 111–113, 115–116, 118, 120–121, 123, 125, 127, 134, 139, 142, 145, 151, 153–154, 159–160, 163, 165, 167–176, 178–179, 181–192, 199–201, 210, 212, 216–219, 224, 229–231, 235, 240–241, 245–247, 249, 253–255, 259–260, 262, 264

Jot, 41, 38, 42– 47, 49–50, 62, 111, 147, 154–156, 163, 214, 231, 240–241, 245

King James Version, 11, 13, 15, 23, 48, 50, 66, 120, 127, 204–205, 232, 261

La More, 69, 91, 123, 229, 127, 235

Letters, 11–14, 41, 43–46, 66, 68, 78–79, 88, 114, 118–119, 132–133, 154–155, 180, 245

Liberal, 52, 212, 235, 243, 265

Locus Classicus, **11, 238, 244,** 33

LXX, **11,** 10, 15, 38, 49, 33, 39, 111, 152, 154–163

Manuscripts, 11, 9–14, 23, 38, 48–49, 62, 66–67, 117, 131–133, 135–136, 143, 158, 162, 165, 168, 181, 200–201, 203–204, 231–234, 240, 243, 249, 255, 264

Masoretic Text, 11, 15, 32, 48–49, 29, 89, 154–155, 157, 205, 244

Miller, 117, 119

Minnick, 21, 109, 193

Models, 243, 249, 251, 254, 237, 255

MT, 15, 11, 14, 110, 153–163, 263

NASV, 15, 46, 118, 146, 155–157, 162–163, 167–168, 170–171, 174–176, 178, 183, 187, 189, 191, 243, 251

Neo-evangelicalism, 12

Neo-orthodoxy, 97

Neutrality, 211, 220

New Testament, 165, 9–15, 23–24, 37, 48–50, 59, 75, 46–47, 62, 67, 85–86, 89–94, 105, 109, 114, 118–122, 12–125, 131–132, 135, 144–145, 167, 170, 174–176, 184, 197–205, 222, 224–225, 229–235, 248, 260, 262, 266

Nichols, 65, 117, 70

Oats, 22–23

Obedience, 36, 43, 71, 86, 110, 113–114, 179–180, 186, 203, 211, 250

Obey, 47, 56–57, 76, 86–87, 90, 92, 98, 102–103, 110–111, 113–114, 126, 179–180, 213, 220, 231, 248, 252

Old Testament, 153, 10–13, 15, 21, 23, 35, 42,–46, 49–50, 66–67, 72, 75, 85, 88, 90–94, 97–99, 102, 104–105, 107, 111, 117–119, 211, 131, 134, 144–145, 147, 165, 178, 197–202, 205, 229–233, 237, 248, 260

Omission, 45, 70, 118, 156, 159, 168, 172–173, 175, 184–185

Omniscience, 89

Original Languages, 12, 149–151

Original Manuscripts, 12, 24, 37, 57, 115

Para-church, 12, 24, 37, 57, 115

Pastor, 10, 24, 39, 57, 65, 106, 111–112, 119–121, 144, 165, 181, 188, 202, 211–213, 219–220, 222

Paul, 9, 31, 36,–37, 46, 51, 54–56, 65, 77, 79–81 88, 90–91, 110, 112–114, 116–117, 119, 123–127, 132–135, 154, 156–157, 163, 176, 178, 181–183,

186–187, 189, 200–201, 211, 213, 216–220, 222, 229, 238–241, 248, 250–251, 253, 259

Perfect Passive, 75, 35, 76–79, 81, 93

Perfect Preservation, 20, 23–24, 52, 62, 64–65, 68, 70, 80–81, 98, 126, 131–132, 179, 197, 203–204, 210–211, 220–221, 224, 231, 235, 237, 243, 245, 256, 261, 263–265

Perpetuity, 70–71, 231

Plenary, 13, 23, 35, 39, 41, 43–45, 50, 68, 144, 146, 152–153, 163, 210, 229, 240, 243, 245–256, 248–249, 251, 255, 257

Preservation, 13, 29, 38, 11, 20–25, 27, 30, 33, 35, 39, 41, 45–50, 52–53, 56–57, 62–71, 73, 75–76, 78–81, 88, 90, 95, 97–100, 102–106, 109–110, 114–118, 122, 126–127, 131–132, 142–144, 149–153, 155, 158, 163, 179–180, 195, 197, 199, 203–205, 207, 210–211, 213, 219–221, 224, 229–234, 237, 243–245, 247–249, 251, 253–257, 259, 261–266

Preserve, 20, 23, 29, 32–33, 37, 47, 57, 70, 97–99, 102, 107, 109–117, 119, 131–132, 142, 147, 149, 152, 156, 163, 175, 205, 210, 214, 217, 224, 231–233, 249, 254, 262, 264

Prophecy, 53, 59, 62–63, 69, 78–80, 104, 113, 134, 146–147, 150, 155, 162, 166, 169, 229, 239–242, 245, 248, 250, 260

Providence, 94, 230–233, 235, 263–265

Providential, 153, 203, 229–233, 247

Rapture, 41, 64, 114, 132, 265

Received Text, 11, 13–14, 38, 48, 54–55, 57, 153, 165–166, 204, 234, 247, 249, 264

Repentance, 42–43, 45, 55, 86–87, 148, 169–170, 218–220, 223, 247

Ruckmanism, 155

Roman Catholic, 11, 37, 51, 56, 221, 224, 253

Salvation, 10, 36, 42, 54, 56–57, 66–67, 69–73, 77–78, 80, 85–87, 89–90, 124, 149, 151, 158–160, 167, 173, 180–191, 200, 216–217, 222, 230, 259, 263, 265

Satan, 21, 23, 35, 38, 75, 79, 94, 87, 106, 127, 131–134, 136, 160, 172–174, 179, 209, 217–218, 237

Topical Index **311**

Scripture, 10–14, 19–25, 31–32, 35–39, 41, 43–48, 50–55, 57, 59, 62–68, 70–73, 76–81, 85, 89–91, 94, 97–100, 102–103, 109–112, 114, 117–120, 125–126, 131–136, 139, 141–148, 150–154, 157–158, 162, 166–168, 171, 173–175, 177–178, 180, 183–184, 187–188, 190, 192–193, 197–205, 210, 212–213, 215, 220–224, 229–234, 237–255, 257, 259–266

Second Coming, 59–64, 93, 134–135, 231, 263

Security, 49, 77

Seminaries, 19, 49, 57

Separation, 209, 10, 12, 24, 133, 145, 210–211, 218–220, 224–225

Sin, 42, 45, 80, 156–157, 161, 170, 172, 175–176, 185–186, 190–191, 210, 213

Sinaiticus, 9, 13, 14, 115, 135, 204

Sinlessness, 169, 46, 171

Sovereignty, 98, 102, 140, 144–145, 187, 217

Strouse, 29, 35, 51, 109, 153, 237, 46, 99, 111, 119, 127, 132, 149, 210, 260, 263

Sutton, 75, 165, 35, 46, 93, 110

Textual Criticism, 13, 9–10, 19–20, 47–50, 131, 153, 158, 162, 214, 233, 249, 262, 264

Textus Receptus, **13,** 9, 11, 15, 55, 89, 184, 203–205, 232, 234–235, 237, 249

Tittle, 41, 38, 43–44, 45–47, 49–50, 62, 111, 147, 154–156, 163, 214, 231, 240–241, 245

TR, 15, 9, 11–14, 46, 71, 111, 122, 167, 170–171, 174–175, 177, 179–181, 184–185, 187, 189–191, 197, 204, 235, 243, 249, 251, 255–257, 264

Transfiguration, 91

Translation, 10–11, 13–14, 33, 49, 51, 57, 78, 116, 102, 122, 180, 182, 179–182, 184–186, 189, 192–193, 204, 243, 249, 253, 255, 263

TRINITY, 47–48, 89, 112, 135, 168, 174, 265

Variant, 14, 47–49, 122, 133, 135, 136, 153–154, 160, 165–167, 169, 171, 175–176, 179–182, 184–186, 192–193, 204, 243, 249, 253, 255, 263

Verbal, 14, 12, 19–23, 35, 39, 45–48, 50, 65–66, 68, 85, 118, 144, 146, 148, 152–153, 158, 163, 210, 229, 239–240, 243, 245, 248–249, 2551-252, 255, 257

Vowels, 13, 17, 38, 44, 36, 66, 88, 154–155, 245

Waite, 23, 70, 117, 185

Westcott, 9–10, 48–49, 51, 88, 181, 232–233, 263

Williams, 131, 193

Words of men, 29, 71, 200, 216, 262

Words of God, 139, 209, 30, 31, 35, 52, 54–55, 62–63, 65–66, 71, 79, 85–86, 88–89, 99, 106, 115, 118, 121, 134, 142–144, 147, 149, 151, 153, 155, 192, 200, 203, 205, 210–213, 215–220, 252, 254, 261–262

Wallace, 51, 53, 75 114, 132, 135, 180

Webb, 19, 41, 165, 46, 66, 88, 147

The Authors

Kent Brandenburg, *editor-in-chief*

Dr. Kent Brandenburg (BA, MA, MDiv, DD) is the pastor/planter of Bethel Baptist Church, an independent Baptist church in El Sobrante, California, established in 1987. Growing up in Indiana and Wisconsin, he received Christ as a child and surrendered to preach as a teenager. As a pastor, his preaching and teaching are characterized by careful exegesis using the original languages and then practical application of the text in its context, already doing such through most of the Old and New Testament books. Pastor Brandenburg has authored *Sound Music or Sounding Brass: The Issue of Biblically Godly Music*, among other booklets, papers, pamphlets, studies, and materials, plays, and tracts. Another book, *Fashion Statement: The Issue of Biblically Godly Dress* is near completion. He serves the Lord with his wife Bridget and their four children.

Thomas Corkish

Dr. Thomas Corkish (BA, MA, DD, and PhD) was born again by God's grace in 1949. He made a series of changes in his Christian growth that moved him from the University of Miami to the United States army, jazz entertainment, new evangelicalism, and finally since 1963 pastoring independent Baptist churches. In his leadership of the Anchor Baptist Church in Salt Lake City, Utah since 1976, Dr. Corkish has founded and operates a church school and college, hosts an annual Bible conference attended by many across the Western U.S., produces the monthly *Lifeline*, read by many, and has published a book helping to evangelize Mormons. He is an expository preacher, a strong separatist, and Baptist by conviction. For years he has been a regular counselor to pastors and missionaries and church conference speaker. He has been married to his wife Eberle since 1956 and has two grown children.

Gary E. La More

Dr. La More (AA, BA, MA (Hons.), MDiv, PhD, and DD) received Christ in 1959. In addition to having been a Christian school principal, he has served on the faculty of Maranatha Baptist Bible College (1976-1980) and was Vice President and Academic Dean of Baptist Bible College Canada (1980-1985). He is now in his seventeenth year as pastor of Grace Missionary Baptist Church, Scarborough, Ontario, Canada, his fourth church in 30 years of pastoring. He is also president of the Historic Baptist Bible Institute and Seminary, and he teaches in Spanish regularly in a Spanish-speaking church based Baptist college in the U.S., having taught or teaching courses in Baptist History, U.S. History, World History, and N.T. Greek. Dr. La More has had two books published in Spanish: *Materiales Sobre Historia Bautista Y Otros Temas Afines* and *Una Breve Introducción A La Hermenéutica Biblica*, and is close to publishing up to five others. He and his wife Georgel were married in 1967 and have three grown children.

Charles Nichols

Born and raised in Eastern South Dakota, Charles Nichols came home from college, when his father became ill, to run the family farm and began faithfully attending the church of which his mother had become a part. He heard the testimony of converted gangster George Mensik and was gloriously saved. A year later his pastor's daughter became his wife. After serving two years in the Army during the Korean War, he surrendered to pastor, and in 1961 sold the livestock and farm machinery to head to Bible College. Since receiving a MDiv in 1969, Pastor Nicols has pastored two independent Baptist churches, the first for 20 years in Cody, WY and the second for 15 years in Ramsey, MN. A strong separatist by conviction, he preaches the Bible expositionally and maintains a balanced ministry of edifying the saved and evangelizing the lost. He has operated a Christian school and out of many young people from their various churches who have surrendered for full time service is their son, a pastor in California. His wife and he have raised two sons and three daughters, now with 15 grandchildren.

Thomas Strouse

Dr. Thomas M. Strouse was saved in 1969 and surrendered his life to the Lord Jesus Christ in 1970. He, his wife Jan, and their fourteen children have been members of and served in independent Baptist churches in Wisconsin, South Carolina, Virginia, and Connecticut. Dr. Strouse has headed up several different seminaries for 25 years and has been on several pastoral staffs for 15 years. He has been intensely involved in training ministerial students in seminaries in the United States, Puerto Rico, Indonesia, and Korea. He received his formal education from *Purdue University* (BS), *Maranatha Baptist Graduate School of Theology* (M.Div), and *Bob Jones University* (PhD). He is a member of 10 Who's Whos and has written eight books. He is currently the Dean and Professor Emeritus of *Emmanuel Baptist Theological Seminary* in Newington, CT.

David Sutton

David A. Sutton is assistant pastor of Bethel Baptist Church in El Sobrante, CA, and principal of the church school, Bethel Christian Academy. Having been saved growing up in Washington State, he graduated from Maranatha Baptist Bible College in Watertown, WI in 1992 with a degree in secondary education. He and his wife Cathy joined the ministry of Bethel that year, first teaching and then also becoming principal in 1996. In the year 2000 Pastor Sutton was awarded the Master of Religious Education degree from Tabernacle Baptist Theological Seminary in Virginia Beach, VA. For several years as a deacon in the church, he has carefully prepared and taught adult Sunday school curricula through diligent exegesis of the text of Scripture. He is involved in teaching Greek grammar and syntax to students, members, and area pastors. He is the father of two daughters.

Gary Webb

Gary Webb trusted Jesus Christ as his Savior when 15 years old and had his first introduction to fundamental Christianity when he joined an independent Baptist church after his junior year in college. He attended Clemson University on a football scholarship and graduated *cum laude* with a B.S. in Administrative Management. He then attended Bob Jones University, received a Master of Divinity degree in 1983 and a Doctor of Ministry degree in 1992. Dr. Webb has pastored Calvary Baptist Church in Carrboro, NC since 1983. He has served in advisory capacities with a mission board and a Bible college, preaches in revival meetings and Bible conferences, and has a regular radio broadcast. He is married to the former Kathie Mosier, and they have three children.